CREATING A GLOBAL AGENDA

Assessments, Solutions, and Action Plans

Edited by
Howard F. Didsbury, Jr.

WORLD FUTURE SOCIETY
Bethesda, MD • U.S.A.

Editor: Howard F. Didsbury, Jr.

Editorial Review Board: Deirdre H. Banks, David G. Cox, James
J. Crider, Howard F. Didsbury, Jr. (Chairman),
Charles H. Little, Theodore J. Maziarski,
Andrew A. Spekke, Stephen H. Van Dyke

Staff Editors: Edward Cornish, Jerry Richardson

Production Manager: Jefferson Cornish

Editorial Coordinator: Sarah Warner

Editorial Consultants: Jennifer Furness, Connie Jalette, Cissie Kelly,
Judith Lun, Patty McNally, Laurie Packard

Layout and Production Assistant: R. Lynn Barnes

Cover Photo: NASA

Published by:
World Future Society
4916 St. Elmo Avenue
Bethesda, Maryland 20814-5089 ● U.S.A.

Library of Congress Catalog Number: 84-050980

International Standard Book Number: 0-930242-25-4

Printed in the United States of America

Contents

Note

This volume was prepared in conjunction with the World Future Society's Fifth General Assembly and Exposition, "WorldView '84," held in Washington, D.C., June 10-14, 1984. Kenneth W. Hunter served as general chairman of the conference. He was assisted by David Smith, staff coordinator.

The papers presented here were selected from the very large number submitted to the Editorial Review Committee. The emphasis in this volume, *Creating a Global Agenda: Assessments, Solutions, and Action Plans,* precluded the inclusion of a number of distinguished papers whose subject matter did not fall within the general theme of the volume. The committee regrets that space limitations permitted only a small number of papers to be published in this volume. In addition, many papers had to be cut substantially. Footnotes and other scholarly paraphernalia were minimized so that as wide a selection of thoughts as possible could be presented.

Preface

The main emphasis of the vast majority of papers that comprise this volume is placed on *solutions* to significant problems. One suspects people have grown weary of merely hearing about problems. Also, they are beginning to suspect that the proliferation of studies and research commissions may be a conscious or unconscious means of avoiding the necessity of decision-making. In this connection, one cannot help but recall the old saying, "When the devil doesn't want something done, he appoints a committee."

Like all such collections of insights of a number of writers, there is a certain arbitrariness about the organization of the papers in this volume. It is hoped that the present arrangement assists the reader in getting the greatest value from this collection.

First and foremost, it is felt that the paramount problem confronting humanity is the threat of nuclear conflict. Hence the first section of the volume is concerned with "Reducing the Nuclear Peril." This section begins with a brief documentary survey and then presents practical suggestions and action plans to reduce the peril.

Still focusing on the global scene, section two, "Elements of a Peaceful World," offers a number of suggestions for creating a more promising and stable international order. This section includes one of the last papers of the late Aurelio Peccei, the distinguished founder and guiding spirit of The Club of Rome and a concerned citizen of the world.

"Responses to Technological Change," the third section, presents a wide range of papers concerned in one way or another with the impact of continuing technological innovations. The main focus is on the United States, though the insights and solutions, in many instances, have much wider applications.

The fourth section, "Early Warning Signals," may seem at first to violate our general emphasis on solutions in that the two authors represented in this section outline some clear and present dangers to the viability of democratic society. However, they make their presentations so cogently that practical actions necessary to lessen, if not eliminate, the dangers appear self-evident.

The final section, "A Common Global Project," presents the essence of S.J. Res. 236, a joint resolution of the U.S. Senate relating to cooperative East-West ventures in space as an alternative to a space arms race. The resolution was offered by Senators Spark M. Matsunaga, Claiborne Pell, and Charles McC. Mathias, Jr., on February 9, 1984. Such a joint project could also include the rest of the members of the human family in common space adventures.

Reducing the
Nuclear Peril

To Make the World Safe for Humanity

by

Howard F. Didsbury, Jr.

In 1963, Pope John XXIII in his encyclical *Pacem in Terris* declared "Justice, . . . right reason and humanity urgently demand that the arms race should cease; that the stockpiles which exist in various countries should be reduced equally and simultaneously by the parties concerned; that nuclear weapons should be banned; and that a general agreement should eventually be reached about progressive disarmament and an effective method of control." But the nuclear arms race has accelerated and the number of nuclear powers continues to grow. Humanity's peril becomes graver as catastrophe looms ever more likely. To recite the catalog of horrors awaiting humanity in such an event would be repetitive. The fundamental, vital question today is, What can be done to prevent such an eventuality?

As this peril is the result of human thought and action, it seems reasonable to believe that human ingenuity and determination can, if timely and sensibly applied, greatly reduce this global threat. Given sufficient time, this threat may be virtually eliminated. However, before such a happy day dawns, it is absolutely necessary to recognize a wide range of impediments that must be understood.

First of all, there is the problem of the immense complexity of the issues to be considered. How can we convey these issues in all of their complexity and ramifications in such a way as to make them understandable to the average citizen? How can we comprehend the dynamism of the "scientific-technological syndrome," which operates as follows: Is it scientifically possible? If so, is it technologically feasible? If so, we must assume the worst-case scenario (the potential enemy will develop it, so we must develop whatever it is before he does), and the cycle goes on and on. As John Paul II observed, "a purely functional science . . . can be completely enslaved by one or other ideology."

In many instances, humanity labors under the burden of history. We have a world of nation-states in which competition and

Howard F. Didsbury, Jr., is professor of history and executive director, Program for the Study of the Future, Kean College of New Jersey, Union, New Jersey. He is also director of media projects for the World Future Society.

rivalries seem unavoidable. In many cases, historical antecedents foster mutual distrust and mutual paranoia. National rivalries over access to increasingly scarce resources should not be overlooked, though they are frequently masked by ideological pronouncements. On a larger scale, there are tensions and antagonisms between and among different cultures and civilizations, each of which is convinced of its different but equally valid solutions to human problems. These cultural and civilizational differences are products of historical developments and differing traditions and historical experiences. They must be taken into consideration.

"Psychic numbness" may also be an impediment. The massive destructiveness and the astronomical casualties inherent in nuclear war are so frightening that many people "block out" the prospect in order to be able to function in the face of such a potential peril. They think and act as if the peril did not exist—as if by ignoring it the potential disaster is denied.

In this much-lauded age of remarkable instanteous telecommunications media, diplomacy and especially negotiation become increasingly difficult. Negotiation with "the whole world watching" inhibits frankness and serious contacts. How do negotiations avoid having "compromise" misconstrued with "appeasement"? Moreover, the structure of mass telecommunications media makes it easy to turn on or turn off national propaganda campaigns. In an increasingly politically polarized world, the absence of those who are "neutral" or "uncommitted" poses a serious problem, as there are few to serve as brokers between the nuclear superpowers.

These are but a few of the genuine impediments we face. Our task is further complicated by the prevalence of a number of unhelpful ideas or attitudes. The source of their appeal is easy to understand, as they are in themselves simplicity personified. They are straightforward, simple summary statements of the world problematique. One such idea views the nuclear challenge before the world as a contest between "good" and "evil" somewhat akin to the Zoroastrian theological description of the struggle between Ahura-Mazda, the God of Good, and his adversary, Ahriman, the Power of Evil. Such an orientation is not particularly congenial to either diplomacy or negotiation. Another unhelpful idea is the one that assumes a miraculous transformation of human values and attitudes, which will then usher in a universal sense of global good will. Still others are enthralled with the quest for the "absolute weapon" and/or the "absolute defense." The attainment of absolute, general military superiority over the potential enemy is pursued with enthusiasm by others with the correlative assumption of then negotiating from a position of superiority. This seems to suggest a peculiar, if not unique, meaning of negotiation. When one encounters these and similar prescriptions to the peril we face, one cannot help but respect the wisdom of the philosopher Alfred North Whitehead, who cautioned long ago, "Seek simplicity but distrust it."

In approaching our perilous global situation, we should avoid reliance on a sudden transformation of values and outlook among peoples of the nation-state system as the sole means of creating a more stable and more peaceful international order. Equally, we should guard against a conviction of inevitable nuclear catastrophe as a result of actions of the superpowers. Instead, we need to develop innovative plans and take practical first steps that are designed to reduce immediately the likelihood of nuclear conflict—or conflict resulting from error or technological malfunctioning or the actions of nuclear terrorists.

Let us rely on "self-interest," not on "good will." A series of arrangements meeting the demands of national self-interest may, in time, create conditions encouraging the growth of confidence—and ultimately result in good will. Only the passage of time will tell. In the meantime, certain reasonable, verifiable first steps can be taken that are to the advantage of each superpower.

Forthwith a joint moratorium should be declared on vitriolic rhetoric. Such a move will tend to create a more congenial environment to pursue negotiations leading to mutual security, global nuclear stability, and control. As has been noted, first, practical measures of advantage to each superpower will tend to build confidence, making further practical steps more attractive.

The main aim of this paper is to present a survey of a number of concrete proposals for reducing the nuclear threat. Instead of merely referring to a specific proposal, we have included the precise wording of the proposal in most instances in order to clarify what is proposed exactly and to prevent ambiguity or misinterpretations.

There are a number of innovative ideas and practical steps that can be taken now to lessen global tensions and reduce the nuclear peril. Let us consider a few:

I. The "Nuclear Weapons Freeze and Reductions" resolutions as proposed by U.S. Senators Mark O. Hatfield and Edward M. Kennedy on October 31, 1983. In the words of the latter, "The fundamental rationale for the freeze is the self-evident proposition that the best way to stop the nuclear arms race is to stop it." The resolution states:

(a) The Congress finds that —

(1) the greatest challenge facing the Earth is to prevent the occurrence of nuclear war by accident or design;

(2) the nuclear arms race is dangerously increasing the risk of a holocaust that would be humanity's final war; and

(3) a mutual and verifiable freeze followed by reductions in nuclear warheads, missiles, and other delivery systems is needed to halt the nuclear arms race and to reduce the risk of nuclear war.

(b) As an immediate arms control objective, the United States and the Soviet Union should—

(1) pursue an immediate and complete halt to the nuclear arms race;

(2) decide when and how to achieve a mutual verifiable freeze on the testing, production, and further deployment of nuclear warheads, missiles, and other delivery systems; and

(3) give special attention to destabilizing weapons whose deployment would make such a freeze more difficult to achieve.

(c) Proceeding from the freeze, the United States and the Soviet Union should pursue major, mutual, and verifiable reductions in nuclear warheads, missiles, and other delivery system [sic], through annual percentages or equally effective means, in a manner that enhances stability.

It is important to note that "anything which cannot be verified will not be frozen," as Senator Kennedy stressed.

II. Concomitant with, or independent of, a nuclear weapons freeze could go an immediate comprehensive test ban (CTB) as proposed by Nobel Laureate Glenn T. Seaborg. In his open letter to the June 13, 1983, issue of *Chemical & Engineering News,* Seaborg makes the following major points:

A CTB would have great benefits to the U.S. in slowing and reversing the nuclear arms race, in strengthening international efforts to prevent further proliferation of nuclear weapons, and in providing new momentum in arms control negotiations.

A CTB would halt that aspect of the arms race that is most threatening, the qualitative improvements in nuclear weapons. Such improvements in offensive weapons continue to make them ever more dangerous. Improvements in defensive weapons might tempt either side to launch a first strike on the assumption that this can be done with relative impunity or needs to be done before the other side achieves an effective defense.

A CTB is absolutely essential if the tenuous nonproliferation regime now in effect is not to unravel.

With each passing year . . . the ability to monitor compliance with a CTB has become more assured.

III. An additional device designed to reduce the risk of a nuclear exchange between the superpowers is proposed by U.S. Senators Sam Nunn and John Warner. This is a "nuclear risk reduction system," outlined in the report of the Nunn/Warner Working Group on Nuclear Risk Reduction issued in November 1983.

Nuclear Risk Reduction Centers would be established in Moscow and Washington, D.C., and staffed by nationals of the other nation. Russians would man the center in Washington, D.C., and Americans the one in Moscow. "These centers would maintain a 24-hour watch on any events with the potential to lead to nuclear incidents." They would be linked directly to their respective relevant political and military authorities both by means of communication channels and organizational relationships.

There are at least five possible functions for these Risk Reduction Centers, according to the report.

First, to discuss and outline the procedures to be followed in the event of possible incidents involving the use of nuclear weapons.

Second, to maintain close contact during incidents precipitated by nuclear terrorists.

Third, to exchange information on a voluntary basis concerning events that might lead to nuclear proliferation or to the acquisition of nuclear weapons, or the materials and equipment necessary to build weapons, by sub-national groups.

Fourth, to exchange information about military activities which might be misunderstood by the other party during periods of mounting tensions.

Fifth, to establish a dialogue about nuclear doctrines, forces, and activities.

IV. Additional dramatic steps toward reducing the nuclear peril were recently set forth by former U.S. defense secretary Robert S. McNamara in an article in the December 5, 1983, *Newsweek* entitled "What the U.S. Can Do." Before he presents his 18 steps, he insists that two paramount principles must be accepted: "First, we must recognize that each side must maintain a stable deterrent—a nuclear arsenal powerful enough to discourage anyone else from using nuclear weapons." And, "Second, we must recognize that nuclear weapons have no military value whatsoever other than to deter one's opponent from their use."

Secretary McNamara observes that, of his 18 steps, "Some of these steps would require agreement with the Soviet Union, but many could be taken unilaterally." This is evident as we list the whole range of proposals. In essence, the 18 points are:

1. Negotiate a reduction in the ratio of nuclear warheads to missile launchers, ultimately moving to single-warhead missiles.

2. Renounce the strategy of launch-on-warning.

3. Announce that we would not retaliate against a nuclear strike until we had ascertained the source of the attack, the size of the attack, and the intentions of the attacker.

4. Strengthen command-and-control systems.

5. Renounce the strategy of "decapitation" strikes. ["Decapitation" is designed to destroy the political structure of the enemy and thereby prevent command and control decisions from being made.]

6. Strengthen our conventional forces.

7. Announce immediately a policy of no-early-first-use of nuclear weapons.

8. Propose that NATO heads of government announce that, within five years, NATO's conventional forces will have been strengthened to the point where NATO will adopt a policy of "no-

first-use" of nuclear weapons.

9. After consultation with our allies, withdraw half of our 6,000 nuclear warheads now stockpiled in Western Europe.

10. Redeploy to rear areas the remaining nuclear warheads deployed along West Germany's eastern border.

11. Negotiate with the Soviets to establish a nuclear-free zone—perhaps 60 miles wide—on both sides of West Germany's eastern border.

12. Unilaterally halt development of destabilizing weapons systems and those that have no deterrent value.

13. Negotiate a ban on weapons in space.

14. Introduce "permissive action links" into every NATO warhead. These devices—known as "PAL's"—would make it impossible for anyone to detonate the warhead without a specific electronic or mechanical input from the president. . . . We should endeavor to obtain the agreement of the Soviets to apply similar devices to their warheads.

15. Negotiate a comprehensive test ban with the Soviets.

16. Strengthen nuclear nonproliferation programs.

17. Negotiate the establishment of a joint U.S.-Soviet information and crisis-control center.

18. Announce a strategy of lesser retaliation. If a nuclear war starts, one must try to stop it; this lesser-response strategy would lead to a de-escalation rather than an escalation of any nuclear conflict.

Many of these measures duplicate or complement proposals we have already considered. Others advance the level and range of negotiations as the momentum of the negotiating spirit gains impetus. If the whole process of negotiation is correctly perceived, it becomes clear that agreements that are, on balance, in the self-interest of all concerned, and are seen to be such, are agreements that will be respected. Any expectation of "dictating" a viable agreement is an exercise in fantasy and encourages the pursuit of an unattainable goal.

V. In the reduction of global nuclear hazards and the lowering of tensions between the United States and the Soviet Union, smaller nations have a vital role to play. Canadian Prime Minister Pierre Trudeau stated the objective succinctly: "Our central purpose must be to create a stable environment of increased security for both East and West. We must aim at suppressing those nearly instinctive fears, frustrations, or ambitions which have so often been the reason for resorting to the use of force." There is hope that this objective can be achieved. As a result of his contacts in Eastern and Western capitals, he found "ten principles of a common bond between East and West:

1. Both sides agree that a nuclear war cannot be won.
2. Both sides agree that a nuclear war must never be fought.

3. Both sides wish to be free of the risk of accidental war or of surprise attack.

4. Both sides recognize the dangers inherent in destabilizing weapons.

5. Both sides understand the need for improved techniques of crisis management.

6. Both sides are conscious of the awesome consequences of being the first to use force against the other.

7. Both sides have an interest in increasing security while reducing cost.

8. Both sides have an interest in avoiding the spread of nuclear weapons to other countries.

9. Both sides have come to a guarded recognition of each other's legitimate security interests.

10. Both sides realize that their security strategies cannot be based on the assumed political or economic collapse of the other side.

Based upon this commonality of interests, Prime Minister Trudeau urges the need for "a forum in which global limits might be negotiated for all five nuclear-weapons states" (U.S., USSR, Britain, France, and China). The Non-Proliferation Treaty, up for renewal in 1985, could be an occasion for the nuclear-weapons powers to exercise a positive influence on nations that have not yet signed the treaty by reaching their own agreement on dramatic limitations or reductions in nuclear arms. Later, initial steps could be explored to reduce conventional as well as nuclear forces in Europe. And, in addition, arms-control strategies to limit new weapons technology could be explored by all parties. "We must work," the Prime Minister counsels, "with due respect for the fragility of political trust, for the importance of building carefully, for the need to search for common ground." He concludes: "The choice we face is clear and present. We can without effort abandon our fate to the mindless drift toward nuclear war. Or we can gather our strength, working in good company to turn aside the forces bearing down on us, on our children, on this earth."

In this brief survey of practical steps to reduce the threat of universal destruction, a number of measures have been considered—ranging from a nuclear-weapons freeze and a comprehensive test ban to the creation of a forum of nuclear-weapons powers to initiate limitations and reductions leading ultimately to dramatic reductions in both nuclear and conventional arms. The fear of annihilation can be removed; the scandal of extravagant armaments expenditures can be stopped. Though in the context of present harsh language between the superpowers it may seem odd to suggest a brighter human future, we need to do so. In place of the suspicion and animosity currently in vogue, the United States and the Soviet Union could utilize their joint talents and resources in a common project to explore space. This suggestion was recently proposed by Senator Spark Matsunaga.

The fear of enemies being removed (as a Catholic prayer intones), humanity can utilize its genius, planetary resources, and

determination to come to grips with common challenges confronting all of humanity on this tiny island in space we call our earth.
   Now is the time to begin to make the world safe for humanity!

The Comprehensive Test Ban

by

Glenn T. Seaborg

I urge all who wish early progress in nuclear arms control to throw their support behind a comprehensive test ban (CTB) as the simplest and quickest way of moving forward.

A CTB would have great benefits to the U.S. in slowing and reversing the nuclear arms race, in strengthening international efforts to prevent further proliferation of nuclear weapons, and in providing new momentum in arms control negotiations.

A CTB would halt that aspect of the arms race that is most threatening: the qualitative improvements in nuclear weapons. Such improvements in offensive weapons continue to make them ever more dangerous. Improvements in defensive weapons might tempt either side to launch a first strike on the assumption that this can be done with relative impunity or needs to be done before the other side achieves an effective defense.

A CTB is absolutely essential if the tenuous nonproliferation regime now in effect is not to unravel. At the insistence of non-nuclear weapon states, the superpowers pledged in both the Limited Test Ban Treaty of 1963 and the Nonproliferation Treaty (NPT) of 1970 that they would move earnestly and quickly to the negotiation of a treaty to end all nuclear testing. The fact that they have not followed through on these pledges is repeatedly called to their attention, as for example, when they try to enlist new adherents to the NPT. More frightening is the rising tide of revolt on this issue among those who have signed. At the last (1980) NPT Review Conference, dissension was so rife that it proved impossible to issue the customary communique at the end of the meeting. A clear warning was issued that if, by the time of the next Review Conference in 1985, there has not been very substantial progress toward a CTB, withdrawals from the NPT could be expected.

Glenn T. Seaborg is professor of chemistry, Lawrence Berkeley Laboratory, University of California, Berkeley, California.

11

A great virtue of a CTB would be its simplicity. The two sides would simply agree to stop testing! Negotiators for the U.S., U.K., and U.S.S.R. reported to the UN Committee on Disarmament in July 1980 that they had agreed on the main outlines of a CTB. It would rely on automatic seismic detection stations on the territories of the three powers, supplemented by a system of voluntary onsite inspections designed to ensure that any claim of a possible violation, or any rejection of such a claim, was based on serious information. Ultimate recourse to the UN Security Council was provided for in case disagreement persisted. What was lacking in 1980 was the political will to approve what the negotiators had agreed to. It is still lacking, and therein lies a task for those who would influence events.

As I have described in my book *Kennedy, Khrushchev, and the Test Ban,* negotiations for a CTB in the early 1960s broke down over U.S. insistence that obligatory onsite inspection was needed in order to be sure that the Soviets would not cheat. I think now, in retrospect, that even at that time we were wrong. The likelihood that the Soviets would have risked international censure by trying to cheat was very small when they could not have been sure of what we would detect. What they could have gained from the very small tests they might have sneaked by could not have affected the military balance. With each passing year since then, the ability to monitor compliance with a CTB has become more assured. At this time, tests above one kiloton have a high probability of being detected and identified, whether through seismic or satellite means, or through intelligence sources (see, e.g., Lynn R. Sykes and Jack F. Evernden, "The Verification of a Comprehensive Test Ban," *Scientific American,* October 1982. Even more than in the 1960s, it seems unlikely today that the Soviets would take large political risks for the chance of making the insignificant military gains they could achieve through clandestine tests under a CTB.

By contrast with the simplicity of a CTB, modalities being negotiated for actual arms reduction are immensely complex. Even if an agreement were possible, it is likely to require years of negotiation—years during which new and more dangerous weapons could be fashioned to increase the planet's peril. The issues involved—whether to count missiles or warheads; whether to count British and French weapons on our side and weapons deployed in Asia on the other side; definitions of which weapons are to be considered strategic, intermediate, or tactical; how to deal with bombers and submarines; how to count the various categories and how to define equality; how to define a new, versus an improved, weapon—are brainbusting, approaching the metaphysical, requiring extended argument just to define the questions. Obviously, these obstacles must ultimately be overcome and nuclear arms reduction must be achieved if the preservation of human life is to be assured. In the meantime, let's proceed with the easily understood and quickly attainable goal of CTB. It can prevent the current situation from becoming much worse.

The concept of a mutual nuclear freeze seems simple enough, but the requirement that there be verification procedures inside the other country poses great difficulties. Like arms reduction, a comprehensive freeze would require extensive and elaborate negotiations involving several teams of negotiators over a period of years. It seems unlikely that it can be negotiated if one side considers itself inferior and, in the crazy mathematics of the arms race, it is highly likely that one side or the other will consider itself inferior.

As an objection to the CTB, it has been argued that "prooftesting" of weapons in the stockpile is needed from time to time to assure that they remain operable. Those who offer objections of this sort ignore the fact that any inconvenience we suffer under a CTB would be visited also on our adversaries. In contradiction to this objection, moreover, Norris Bradburg, former director of the Los Alamos Laboratory, has stated: "The assurance of continued operability of stock-piled nuclear weapons has in the past been achieved almost exclusively by nonnuclear testing—by meticulous inspection and disassembly of the components." One should be quite clear about this: It is improvements in nuclear weapons that require testing; the aim of a comprehensive test ban is specifically to prevent or impede such improvements.

The benefits of a CTB far outweigh the risks. If we had been able to negotiate a CTB with the U.S.S.R. in 1963, when it was necessary to settle for a Limited Test Ban, we and the rest of the world would be much better off. We are negotiating today at a higher and more dangerous level. It would be to our great advantage to achieve a CTB now before we proceed to an even higher and still more dangerous level.

The Military Role of Nuclear Weapons: Perceptions and Misperceptions

by

Robert S. McNamara

The public, on both sides of the Atlantic, is engaged in debate on controversial questions relating to nuclear weapons: the desirability of a nuclear freeze; the deployment of Pershing II and cruise missiles to Western Europe; the production of the MX missile and the B-1 bomber; the development of the neutron bomb; and proposals to reduce the risk of nuclear war by such measures as the withdrawal of tactical nuclear weapons from forward areas and the declaration of a strategy of "no launch on warning."

These questions, however, cannot be thoughtfully discussed, and certainly not adequately answered, until there has been general agreement on the military role of nuclear weapons. If there is confusion in the public mind on this matter, it only mirrors the disagreement among those most familiar with such weapons and their implications.

I would ask the reader momentarily to guess whether the following statements come from leaders in peace movements:

> At the theatre or tactical level any nuclear exchange, however limited it might be, is bound to leave NATO worse off in comparison to the Warsaw Pact, in terms both of military and civilian casualties and destruction. . . .To initiate use of nuclear weapons . . . seems to me to be criminally irresponsible.

> I am in favor of retaining nuclear weapons as potential tools, but not permitting them to become battlefield weapons. I am not opposed to the strategic employment of these weapons; however, I am firmly opposed to their tactical use on our soil.

Robert S. McNamara was U.S. secretary of defense from 1961 to 1968 and president of the World Bank from 1968 to 1981. Copyright © 1983 by Robert S. McNamara.

The European allies should not keep asking us to multiply strategic assurances that we cannot possibly mean, or if we do mean, we should not want to execute because if we execute, we risk the destruction of civilization.

The answer is that none do. The first is by Field Marshall Lord Carver, chief of the British Defence Staff from 1973 to 1976; the second by General Johannes Steinhoff, former chief of staff of the Federal German Air Force; and the third by former secretary of state Henry A. Kissinger.[1]

And, if one were to accept all three propositions, there follows logically the statement of Admiral Noel A. Gayler, former commander in chief of U.S. forces in the Pacific: "There is no sensible military use of any of our nuclear forces. Their only reasonable use is to deter our opponent from using his nuclear forces."[2]

On the other hand, a number of statements by senior officials in the Reagan administration have suggested that a nuclear war could be limited. Secretary of Defense Caspar Weinberger contends that: "The nuclear option [i.e., early first use of nuclear weapons] remains an important element in deterring Soviet [conventional] attack." And in the same vein,[3] former secretary of state Alexander Haig, also a former NATO supreme commander, concedes that it is unlikely nuclear war could be limited, but argues that "adoption of a policy of no first use would remove a threat which deters Soviet aggression and, therefore, would increase the danger of war." [4]

More broadly, President Reagan—in proposing a program to develop an anti-ballistic missile defense in March 1983—said that "our objective should be to move to an impenetrable defense against Soviet nuclear strikes, thereby totally neutralizing their offensive nuclear forces." He added that it would be in our interest for the Soviets to possess a similar defense, thus stating in effect that the Soviet Union and the United States should both be better off if nuclear weapons were totally eliminated. (Under such circumstances, NATO would depend, of course, solely on conventional forces for deterrence of Soviet aggression.) And on June 16, 1983, the President made an even more categorical statement in favor of a non-nuclear world: "I pray for the day when nuclear weapons will no longer exist anywhere on earth."[5]

A similar thought has been expressed by Melvin Laird, secretary of defense in the Nixon administration: "A worldwide zero nuclear option with adequate verification should now be our goal. . . . These weapons . . . are useless for military purposes."[6]

These quotations from European and American political and military leaders show the depth of doubt and division that exist today. It is clear that there are three quite contradictory and mutually exclusive views of the military role of nuclear weapons:

• Such weapons can be used in a controlled or selective way, i.e., they have a war-fighting role in defense of the NATO nations.

15

Therefore, a strategy of "flexible response," which has been the foundation of NATO's war plans since 1967, including possible "early first use of nuclear weapons," should be continued. Underlying this policy is the belief that NATO can achieve "escalation dominance"—i.e., NATO can prevent the Warsaw Pact from extending the use of nuclear weapons beyond the level NATO chooses, with the implication that a nuclear war, once started, can remain limited.

• Any use of nuclear weapons by the United States or the Soviet Union is likely to lead to uncontrolled escalation with unacceptable damage to both sides. Therefore, nuclear weapons have no military use other than to deter first use of such weapons by one's adversary.

• Although initiating the use of nuclear weapons is likely to lead to uncontrolled escalation, with devastation of both societies, the threat of such use by NATO acts as a deterrent to both Soviet conventional and nuclear aggression. It is not practical to build up an equivalent deterrent in the form of conventional forces; therefore, the threat of early use of nuclear weapons should never be withdrawn.

I propose to examine these views by exploring four questions:

• What is NATO's present nuclear strategy and how did it evolve?

• Can NATO initiate the use of nuclear weapons, in response to a Soviet attack, with benefit to the Alliance?

• Even if the "first use" of nuclear weapons is not to NATO's advantage, does not the threat of such use add to the deterrent and would not the removal of the threat increase the risk of war?

• If it is not to NATO's advantage to respond to a Soviet conventional attack by the use of nuclear weapons, can NATO's conventional forces, within realistic political and financial constraints, be strengthened sufficiently to substitute for the nuclear threat as a deterrent to Soviet aggression?

II

Questions of the military utility of nuclear weapons are addressed most realistically in the context of the possibility of warfare in Europe. Throughout the postwar period, the security of Europe has been the centerpiece of U.S. foreign policy; it is likely to remain so indefinitely. In no other region have the two great powers deployed so many nuclear weapons. In no other part of the world are military doctrines that specify the use of nuclear weapons granted such wide-ranging credibility.

The use of nuclear weapons has been an integral part of NATO's military strategy virtually since the inception of the Alliance.[7]

Shortly after the North Atlantic Treaty was ratified in 1949, estimates were made of the size of the Soviet military threat as a basis for developing NATO's military strategy and force structure. Believing that the U.S.S.R. could muster as many as 175 divisions against Western Europe, NATO military planners concluded that the Alliance would require 96 of its own divisions—which were larger than those of the Soviet Union—in order to mount an adequate defense. This estimate was accepted by the NATO ministers in February 1952 at their annual meeting in Lisbon.

It soon became clear, however, that the member nations were not willing to meet these so-called Lisbon force goals. Instead, the Alliance turned consciously to nuclear weapons as a substitute for the financial and manpower sacrifices that would have been necessary to mount an adequate conventional defense.

That budgetary considerations were a key factor in NATO's decision to rely on nuclear weapons is evident from the following statement by then Secretary of State John Foster Dulles:

> The total cost of our security efforts (and those of our Allies) . . . could not be continued long without grave budgetary, economic, and social consequences. But before military planning could be changed the President and his advisers . . . had to make some basic policy decisions. This has been done. The basic decision was to depend primarily upon a greater [nuclear] capacity to retaliate instantly by means and at places of our own choosing. As a result it is now possible to get and to share more basic security at less cost.[8]

Nor was this new emphasis only rhetorical. A Presidential Directive (NSC-162/2) ordered the Joint Chiefs of Staff to plan on using nuclear armaments whenever it would be to the U.S. advantage to do so. Changes were made in the organization and plans of the U.S. Army so that it would be better able to fight on nuclear battlefields. By late 1953, substantial numbers of tactical nuclear weapons—artillery shells, bombs, short-range missiles, nuclear mines, and others—were beginning to be deployed in Europe. The buildup of NATO tactical nuclear weapons continued steadily, peaking in the mid-1960s at around 7,000. Although large numbers of conventional forces were retained on the continent, until the early 1960s their only purpose was seen to be to contain an attack long enough for nuclear strikes to defeat the aggressor.

If there were any doubts about the seriousness of NATO's nuclear threats in the 1950s, they should have been dispelled by the following statement by General Bernard Montgomery, the Deputy Supreme Allied Commander in Europe, who said in late 1954:

> I want to make it absolutely clear that we at SHAPE are basing all our operational planning on using atomic and thermonuclear weapons in our own defense. With us it is no longer: "They may possibly be used." It is very definitely: "They will be used, if we are attacked."[9]

By December 1954, the NATO ministers felt comfortable enough with the nuclear strategy to reduce the force-level objective from 96 to 30 active divisions. Two years later, the Alliance formally adopted the policy of "massive retaliation" in a document known as MC 14/2.

Whether the balance of nuclear forces between the Warsaw Pact and NATO, as it was developing during the mid-1950s, justified adoption of NATO's nuclear strategy is arguable. But its merit had become questionable to many by the early 1960s. Soon after taking office in January 1961, the Kennedy administration began a detailed analysis of the policy's strengths and weaknesses.

These studies revealed two major deficiencies in the reasoning that had led to the adoption of MC 14/2: first, the relative balance of NATO and Warsaw Pact conventional forces was far less unfavorable from a Western perspective than had been assumed (the power of Soviet forces had been overestimated and that of NATO forces underestimated); and second, there was great uncertainty as to whether and, if so, how nuclear weapons could be used to NATO's advantage.

President Kennedy, therefore, authorized me as Secretary of Defense to propose, at a meeting of the NATO ministers in Athens in May 1962, to substitute a strategy of "flexible response" for the existing doctrine of "massive retaliation."

The new strategy required a buildup of NATO's conventional forces, but on a scale that we believed to be practical on both the financial and political grounds. Instead of the early massive use of nuclear weapons, it permitted a substantial raising of the nuclear threshold by planning for the critical initial responses to Soviet aggression to be made by conventional forces alone. The strategy was based on the expectation that NATO's conventional capabilities could be improved sufficiently so that the use of nuclear weapons would be unnecessary. But, under the new doctrine, even if this expectation turned out to be false, any use of nuclear weapons would be "late and limited."

Our proposal of the new strategy was the result of the recognition by U.S. civilian and military officials that NATO's vastly superior nuclear capabilities, measured in terms of numbers of weapons, did not translate into usable military power. Moreover, we understood that the initial use of even a small number of strategic or tactical nuclear weapons implied risks that could threaten the very survival of the nation. Consequently, we, in effect, proposed confining nuclear weapons to only two roles in the NATO context:

• Deterring the Soviets' initiation of nuclear war.

• As a weapon of last resort, if conventional defense failed, to persuade the aggressor to terminate the conflict on acceptable terms.

The proposed change in NATO's strategy met with strong opposition. Some opponents argued that the United States was seeking to "decouple" itself from the defense of Europe. These critics shared our view that a "tactical" nuclear war in Europe would quickly escalate to a strategic exchange involving the U.S. and Soviet homelands, but they saw this danger as the primary factor that deterred Soviet aggression. Any reduction in this prospect, they argued, might cause the Soviets to believe that hostilities could be confined to Central Europe, and thus tempt them into adventures.

Other critics maintained that the proposed buildup of NATO's conventional forces was totally beyond what the Alliance would be willing to support. Still others argued that we had greatly exaggerated the dangers of limited uses of nuclear weapons.

The argument raged for five years. It was not until 1967 that NATO adopted the strategy of "flexible response," inscribing it in a document known as MC 14/3.

The revised strategy proposed to deter aggression by maintaining forces adequate to counter an attack at whatever level the aggressor chose to fight. Should such a direct confrontation not prove successful, the strategy proposed to escalate as necessary, including the initial use of nuclear weapons, forcing the aggressor to confront costs and risks disproportionate to his initial objectives. At all times, however, the flexible-response strategy specified that efforts should be made to control the scope and intensity of combat. Thus, for example, initial nuclear attacks presumably would be made by short-range tactical systems in an attempt to confine the effects of nuclear warfare to the battlefield. Even so, the strategy retained the ultimate escalatory threat of a strategic exchange between U.S. and Soviet homelands to make clear the final magnitude of the dangers being contemplated.

"Flexible response" has remained NATO's official doctrine for more than 15 years. Its essential element, however—building sufficient conventional capabilities to offset those of the Warsaw Pact—has never been achieved. Indeed, during the late 1960s and early 1970s, the Alliance may have fallen farther behind its opponent. Although NATO has made considerable strides in improving its conventional posture in more recent years, most military experts believe that the conventional balance continues to favor the Warsaw Pact; they thus conclude that an attack by Soviet conventional forces would require the use of nuclear weapons, most likely within a matter of hours. NATO's operational war plans reflect this belief. The substantial raising of the "nuclear threshold," as was envisioned when "flexible response" was first conceived, has not become a reality.

Before turning to the question of whether NATO can initiate the use of nuclear weapons—in response to a Soviet attack—with benefit to the Alliance, I should perhaps comment on the evolution of Soviet nuclear strategy over the past three decades.[10]

For much of the postwar period, Soviet military doctrine appears to have assumed that war between the great powers would include the use of nuclear weapons. Soviet publications stressed the use of both long- and intermediate-range nuclear weapons in the initial hours of conflict, to destroy concentrations of enemy forces and the ports, airfields, and other facilities necessary to support military operations. And these publications emphasized as well the use of tactical nuclear weapons on the battlefield.

The way that Soviet soldiers trained, the protective clothing and decontamination equipment with which they were equipped, and the nature of their military exercises—which for years always included a nuclear phase—suggested that the written expressions of Soviet military doctrine constituted deadly serious descriptions of the way the U.S.S.R. planned to fight the next war.

In fact, until the mid-1960s, writings of Soviet military officials consistently maintained that the only conflict possible between the great powers was an all-out nuclear war. They asserted, moreover, that it was possible to prevail in such a conflict, and they urged the military and social preparations necessary to ensure that the U.S.S.R. emerged triumphant from any nuclear conflict. It was these writings that, in the late 1970s, were used so devastatingly by opponents of nuclear arms control in the debate on the SALT II Treaty.[11]

By that time, however, this portrayal of Soviet military doctrine was becoming badly out of date.

Official Soviet doctrine changed slightly in the mid-1960s as Soviet writers began to admit the possibility of a "war by stages" in Europe, in which the first phase would be a conventional one. Although they asserted that this initial stage would be very short, and further noted that the conflict "inevitably" would escalate to all-out nuclear war, the previous doctrinal rigidity had been broken.

Soviet experts and military officials debated the inevitability of nuclear escalation throughout the 1960s and much of the 1970s. By the time of a famous speech of Leonid Brezhnev at Tula in 1977, the question seems to have been settled: Soviet theorists then admitted the possibility of a major protracted war between East and West in which nuclear weapons would not be used.

Indeed, the Soviets now officially maintain that they would not be the first to make use of nuclear weapons. As stated by Defense Minister Ustinov in 1982: "Only extraordinary circumstances—a direct nuclear aggression against the Soviet state or its allies—can compel us to resort to a retaliatory nuclear strike as a last means of self-defense."[12]

This is a new position for the U.S.S.R. It was first articulated by Brezhnev at the U.N. Special Session on Disarmament in June 1982. Previously, Soviet spokesmen had only been willing to say that they would not use nuclear weapons against non-nuclear powers.

Along with this shift has come the explicit and repeated renunciation of what Soviet spokesmen had declared for more than two decades: that it was possible to fight and win a nuclear war. All Soviet writers and political leaders addressing this question now solemnly declare that "there will be no victors in a nuclear war."

Does this doctrinal shift suggest that the U.S.S.R. is no longer prepared for nuclear war with Europe? Certainly not. In addition to the deployment of intermediate-range SS-20 missiles, the Soviets are busily modernizing their shorter-range nuclear-armed missiles in Europe (SS-21s, SS-22s, and SS-23s). Two types of artillery tubes capable of firing nuclear charges have been seen with Soviet units in Eastern Europe in larger numbers in recent years. And there are now many more aircraft capable of delivering nuclear bombs deployed with Soviet forces in Europe than was the case not many years ago.

The U.S.S.R. is obviously prepared to respond if NATO chooses to initiate nuclear war. I turn, then, to the question of whether NATO can initiate the use of nuclear weapons, in response to a Soviet conventional attack, with benefit to the Alliance.

III

Doubts about the wisdom of NATO's strategy of flexible response, never far from the surface, emerged as a major issue in the late 1970s; debate has intensified in the ensuing years. The debate hinges on assessments of the military value of nuclear weapons.[13]

The nuclear balance has changed substantially since the Kennedy administration first proposed a strategy of flexible response. Both sides have virtually completely refurbished their inventories, increasing the number of weapons of all three different types—battlefield, intermediate-range, and strategic—and vastly improving the performance characteristics of both the weapons themselves and their delivery systems. Because the Soviet Union was so far behind the United States in the early 1960s, the quantitative changes, at least, appear to have been more favorable for the U.S.S.R. The ratio of warheads on strategic and intermediate-range launchers, for example, has shifted from a very great U.S. advantage in 1962 to a far more modest advantage at present.

As the Soviet Union moved toward and then achieved rough parity in strategic and intermediate-range forces, a crucial element of the flexible-response strategy became less and less credible.

It will be recalled that this strategy calls for the Alliance to initiate nuclear war with battlefield weapons if conventional defenses fail, and to escalate the type of nuclear weapons used (and therefore the targets of those weapons), as necessary, up to and including the use of strategic forces against targets in the U.S.S.R. itself. Given the tremendous devastation that those Soviet strategic forces that survived a U.S. first strike would now be able to inflict on this country, it is difficult to imagine any U.S. president, under any circumstances, initiating a strategic strike except in retaliation against a Soviet nuclear strike. It is this reasoning that led to the much criticized statement by Henry

Kissinger in Brussels in 1979, quoted earlier. Kissinger's speech was criticized not for its logic, however, only for its frankness.

In short, a key element of the flexible-response strategy has been overtaken by a change in the physical realities of the nuclear balance. With huge survivable arsenals on both sides, strategic nuclear weapons have lost whatever military utility may once have been attributed to them. Their sole purpose, at present, is to deter the other side's first use of its strategic forces.

Thus, given that NATO would not be the first to use strategic nuclear weapons, is it conceivable that the first use of tactical weapons would be to its military advantage?

The roughly 6,000 NATO nuclear weapons now deployed in Europe consist of warheads for air-defense missiles, nuclear mines (known as atomic demolition munitions), warheads for shorter-range missiles, nuclear bombs, and nuclear-armed artillery shells. The North Atlantic Assembly recently published a rough estimate of the distribution of these weapons.[14] It is shown in the table below.

U.S. Nuclear Warheads Located in Europe in 1981

Bombs to be delivered by aircraft	1069
Artillery shells (203mm and 155mm)	2000
Missiles: Pershing IA	270
Lance and Honest John	910
Air defense and atomic demolition charges	1750
Total	5999

According to these figures, nuclear artillery shells comprise the largest portion of the stockpile, about one-third of the total. They are also the weapons that cause the greatest worry.

There are two types of nuclear artillery shells in the NATO inventory: those for 155mm howitzers and those for 203mm cannons. Both the howitzers and the cannons are dual-capable: they can be used to fire shells containing conventional explosives as well as nuclear weapons. The precise ranges of these systems are classified, but most accounts put them at around 10 miles. Because of the short range of nuclear artillery, the guns and their nuclear shells tend to be deployed close to the potential front lines of any conflict in Europe—there are, in effect, approximately 2,000 short-range nuclear warheads concentrated at a few sites close to the German border.

Atomic demolition munitions (ADMs) also raise particular concerns. These weapons are about 25 years old and probably no longer reliable. Intended to block mountain passes and other "choke points" on potential Soviet invasion routes, their effects would be felt on NATO territory. Moreover, to be effective they would have to be emplaced before a war actually began. Such an action could aggravate a crisis and would probably contribute to the likelihood of the war starting. At the same time, because ADMs would have to be used at the very onset of the conflict, their use would mean that NATO had not tested the ability of its conventional forces to contain a Warsaw Pact invasion.

Similar problems beset nuclear-armed air defense systems. They are old and probably unreliable. And they are intended for use at the onset of a conflict—to disrupt the large-scale air attacks that would accompany a Warsaw Pact invasion—thus negating the strategy of "flexible response."

In an acute crisis in which the risk of war seemed to be rising, these characteristics of nuclear artillery, mines, and air defense systems would be likely to lead to pressures on NATO's political leaders, particularly the U.S. president, to delegate the authority to release these weapons to the military commanders on the scene. Whether such authority were delegated or not, it is these characteristics—most importantly the vulnerability of NATO's nuclear artillery—that lead many observers to predict that the Alliance would use tactical nuclear weapons within hours of the start of a war in Europe. In effect, whether its military or civilian leaders retained decision authority, NATO would be likely to face the choice of either using its battlefield nuclear weapons or seeing them overrun or destroyed by the enemy.

In terms of their military utility, NATO has not found it possible to develop plans for the use of nuclear artillery that would both assure a clear advantage to the Alliance and at the same time avoid the very high risk of escalating to all-out nuclear war.

Current guidelines on the initial use of nuclear weapons date from the early 1970s.[15] A former member of the High Level Group, a special official committee established by NATO in 1978 to examine the Alliance's nuclear posture, stated recently that despite discussions lasting for years, "NATO has not yet managed to agree on guidelines for the follow-on use of nuclear weapons if a first attempt to communicate NATO's intentions through a controlled demonstrative use did not succeed in pers··.·ding the adversary to halt hostilities."[16]

Two problems stand in the way.

First, since the assumption is made that NATO will be responding to a Warsaw Pact invasion of Western Europe, and since the artillery has short range, the nuclear explosion would occur on NATO's own territory. If a substantial portion of the 2,000 nuclear artillery shells were fired, not only would the Warsaw Pact likely suffer heavy casualties among its military personnel, but large numbers of NATO's civilian and military personnel also would likely be killed and injured. There also would be considerable damage to property, farmland, and urbanized areas.[17]

Moreover, there is no reason to believe that the Warsaw Pact, now possessing tactical and intermediate-range nuclear forces at least comparable to those of NATO, would not respond to NATO's initiation of nuclear war with major nuclear attacks of its own.

These attacks would probably seek most importantly to reduce NATO's ability to fight a nuclear war by destroying command and control facilities, nuclear weapon storage sites, and the aircraft, missiles, and artillery that would deliver NATO's nuclear weapons. Direct support facilities like ports and airfields would likely also be attacked in the initial Warsaw Pact nuclear offensive. Thus the war would escalate from the battlefield to the rest of Western Europe (and probably to Eastern Europe as well, as NATO retaliated).

What would be the consequences of such a conflict? In 1955, an exercise called "Carte Blanche" simulated the use of 335 nuclear weapons, 80% of which were assumed to detonate on German territory. In terms of immediate casualties (ignoring the victims of radiation, disease, and so forth), it was estimated that between 1.5 and 1.7 million people would die and another 3.5 million would be wounded—more than five times the German civilian casualties in World War II—in the first two days. This exercise prompted Helmut Schmidt to remark that the use of tactical nuclear weapons "will not defend Europe, but destroy it."[18]

Additional studies throughout the 1960s confirmed these results. They prompted two of my former aides in the Pentagon to write in 1971:

> Even under the most favorable assumptions, it appeared that between 2 and 20 million Europeans would be killed, with widespread damage to the economy of the affected area and a high risk of 100 million dead if the war escalated to attacks on cities.[19]

Have the more modern weapons deployed on both sides in the 1970s changed the likely results of nuclear war in Europe? Not at all! A group of experts was assembled recently by the U.N. Secretary General to study nuclear war. They simulated a conflict in which 1,500 nuclear artillery shells and 200 nuclear bombs were used by the two sides against each other's military targets. The experts concluded that as a result of such a conflict there would be a minimum of five to six million immediate civilian casualties and 400,000 military casualties, and that at least an additional 1.1 million civilians would suffer from radiation disease.[20]

It should be remembered that all these scenarios, as horrible as they would be, involve the use of only a small portion of the tactical nuclear weapons deployed in Europe, and assume further that none of the roughly 20,000 nuclear warheads in the U.S. and U.S.S.R.'s central strategic arsenals would be used. Yet portions of those central forces are intended for European contingencies: the United States has allocated 400 of its submarine-based Poseidon warheads for use by NATO; the Soviet Union, it is believed, envisions as many as several hundred of its ICBMs being used against targets in Europe.

Is it realistic to expect that a nuclear war could be limited to the detonation of tens or even hundreds of nuclear weapons, even though each side would have tens of thousands of weapons remaining available for use?

The answer is clearly no. Such an expectation requires the assumption that even though the initial strikes would have inflicted large-scale casualties and damage to both sides, one or the other—feeling disadvantaged—would give in. But under such circumstances, leaders on both sides would be under unimaginable pressure to avenge their losses and secure the interests being challenged. And each would fear that the opponent might launch a larger attack at any moment. Moreover, they would both be operating with only partial information because of the disruption to communications caused by the chaos on the battlefield (to say nothing of possible strikes against communications facilities). Under such conditions, it is highly likely that rather than surrender, each side would launch a larger attack, hoping that this step would bring the action to a halt by causing the opponent to capitulate.[21]

It was assessments like these that led not only Field Marshall Lord Carver, but Lord Louis Mountbatten and several other of the eight retired chiefs of the British Defence Staff as well, to indicate that under no circumstances would they have recommended that NATO initiate the use of nuclear weapons.

And it was similar considerations that led me to the same conclusions in 1961 and 1962.

It is inconceivable to me, as it has been to others who have studied the matter, that "limited" nuclear wars would remain limited—any decision to use nuclear weapons would imply a high probability of the same cataclysmic consequences as a total nuclear exchange. In sum, I know of no plan that gives reasonable assurance that nuclear weapons can be used beneficially in NATO's defense.

I do not believe that the Soviet Union wishes war with the West. And certainly the West will not attack the U.S.S.R. or its allies. But dangerous frictions between the Warsaw Pact and NATO have developed in the past and are likely to do so in the future. If deterrence fails and conflict develops, the present NATO strategy carries with it a high risk that Western civilization, as we know it, will be destroyed.

If there is a case for NATO retaining its present strategy, that case must rest on the strategy's contribution to the deterrence of Soviet aggression being worth the risk of nuclear war in the event deterrence fails.

IV

The question of what deters Soviet aggression is an extremely difficult one. To answer it, we must put ourselves in the minds of several individuals who would make the decision to initiate war. We must ask what their objectives are for themselves and their nation, what they value, and what they fear. We must assess their proclivity to take risks, to bluff, or to be bluffed. We must guess at how they see us—our will and our capabilities—and determine what we can do to strengthen their belief in the sincerity of our threats and our promises.

But most difficult of all, we must evaluate all these factors in the context of an acute international crisis. Our problem is not to persuade the Soviets not to initiate war today. It is to cause them to reach the same decision at some future time when, for whatever reason—for example, an uprising in Eastern Europe that is getting out of control, or a U.S.-Soviet clash in Iran, or conflict in the Middle East—they may be tempted to gamble and try to end what they see as a great threat to their own security.

In such a crisis, perceptions of risks and stakes may change substantially. What may look like a reckless gamble in more tranquil times might then be seen merely as a reasonable risk. This will be the case particularly if the crisis deteriorates so that war begins to appear more and more likely. In such a situation, the advantages of achieving tactical surprise by going first can appear to be more and more important.

As I have indicated, the launch of strategic nuclear weapons against the Soviet homeland would lead almost certainly to a response in kind that would inflict unacceptable damage on Europe and the United States—it would be an act of suicide. The threat of such an action, therefore, has lost all credibility as a deterrent to Soviet conventional aggression. The ultimate sanction in the flexible-response strategy is thus no longer operative. One cannot build a credible deterrent on an incredible action.

Many sophisticated observers in both the United States and Europe, however, believe that the threat to use tactical nuclear weapons in response to Warsaw Pact aggression increases the perceived likelihood of such an action, despite its absolute irrationality. They believe that by maintaining battlefield weapons near the front lines, along with the requisite plans and doctrines to implement the strategy that calls for their use, NATO confronts the Warsaw Pact with a dangerous possibility that cannot be ignored.

In contemplating the prospect of war, they argue, Soviet leaders must perceive a risk that NATO would implement its doctrine and use nuclear weapons on the battlefield, thus initiating an escalatory process that could easily get out of control, leading ultimately to a devastating strategic exchange between the two homelands. It is not that NATO would coolly and deliberately calculate that a strategic exchange made sense, they explain, but rather that the dynamics of the crisis would literally force such an action—or so Soviet leaders would have to fear.

Each step of the escalation would create a new reality, altering each side's calculation of the risks and benefits of alternative courses of action. Once U.S. and Soviet military units clashed, perceptions of the likelihood of more intense conflicts would be changed radically. Once any nuclear weapons had been used operationally, assessments of other potential nuclear attacks would be radically altered.

In short, those who assert that the nuclear first-use threat serves to strengthen NATO's deterrent believe that, regardless of objective assessments of the irrationality of any such action, Soviet decision-makers must pay attention to the realities of the battlefield and the dangers of the escalatory process. And, in so doing, they maintain, the Soviets will perceive a considerable risk that conventional conflict will lead to the use of battlefield weapons, which will lead in turn to theater-wide nuclear conflict, which will inevitably spread to the homelands of the superpowers.

In fact, it was a desire to strengthen the perception of such a likely escalation that led NATO to its December 1979 decision to deploy the new intermediate-range Pershing II and the nuclear-armed cruise missiles in Europe. The key element in that decision was that the new missiles would be capable of striking Soviet territory, thus presumably precipitating a Soviet attack on U.S. territory and a U.S. retaliation against the whole of the Soviet homeland. The new weapons thus "couple" U.S. strategic forces with the forces deployed in Europe, easing concerns that the Soviets might perceive a firebreak in the escalatory process. So long as the escalation is perceived to be likely to proceed smoothly, the logic continues, then the Warsaw Pact will be deterred from taking the first step—the conventional aggression—that might start the process.

But for the same reason that led Henry Kissinger to recognize that a U.S. president is unlikely to initiate the use of U.S.- based strategic nuclear weapons against the U.S.S.R., so a president would be unlikely to launch missiles from European soil against Soviet territory.

And, as I have indicated, more and more Western political and military leaders are coming to recognize, and publicly avowing, that even the use of battlefield nuclear weapons in Europe would bring greater destruction to NATO than any conceivable contribution they might make to NATO's defense.

There is less and less likelihood, therefore, that NATO would authorize the use of any nuclear weapons except in response to a Soviet nuclear attack. As this diminishing prospect becomes more and more widely perceived—and it will—whatever deterrent value still resides in NATO's nuclear strategy will diminish still further.

There are additional factors to be considered. Whether it contributes to deterrence or not, NATO's threat of "first use" is not without its costs: it is a most contentious policy, leading to divisive debates both within individual nations and between the members of the Alliance; it reduces NATO's preparedness for conventional war; and, as I have indicated, it increases the risk of nuclear war.

Preparing for tactical nuclear war limits NATO's ability to defend itself conventionally in several ways. Nuclear weapons are indeed "special" munitions. They require special command, control, and communications arrangements. They require special security precautions. They limit the flexibility with which units can be deployed and military plans altered. Operations on a nuclear battlefield would be very different from those in a conventional conflict; NATO planning must take these differences into account.

Moreover, since most of the systems that would deliver NATO's nuclear munitions are dual-purpose, some number of aircraft and artillery must be reserved to be available for nuclear attacks early in a battle, if that became necessary, and are thus not available for delivering conventional munitions.

Most important, though, the reliance on NATO's nuclear threats for deterrence makes it more difficult to muster the political and financial support necessary to sustain an adequate conventional military force. Both publics and governments point to the nuclear force as the "real deterrent," thus explaining their reluctance to allocate even modest sums for greater conventional capabilities.

To the extent that the nuclear threat has deterrent value, it is because it in fact increases the risk of nuclear war. The location of nuclear weapons in what would be forward parts of the battlefield; the associated development of operational plans assuming the early use of nuclear weapons; the possibility that release authority would be delegated to field commanders prior to the outset of war—these factors and many others would lead to a higher probability that, if war actually began in Europe, it would soon turn into a nuclear conflagration.

Soviet predictions of such a risk, in fact, could lead them to initiate nuclear war themselves. For one thing, preparing themselves for the possibility of NATO nuclear attacks means that they must avoid massing their offensive units. This would make it more difficult to mount a successful conventional attack, raising the incentives to initiate the war with a nuclear offensive. Moreover, if the Soviets believe that NATO would indeed carry out its nuclear threat once they decided to go to war—whether as a matter of deliberate choice or because the realities of the battlefield would give the Alliance no choice—the Soviets would have virtually no incentive not to initiate nuclear war themselves.

I repeat, this would only be the case if they had decided that war was imminent and believed there would be high risk that NATO's threats would be fulfilled. But if those two conditions were valid, the military advantages to the Warsaw Pact of preemptive nuclear strikes on NATO's nuclear storage sites, delivery systems, and support facilities could be compelling.

The costs of whatever deterrent value remains in NATO's nuclear strategy are, therefore, substantial. Could not equivalent deterrence be achieved at lesser "cost"? I believe the answer is yes. Compared to the huge risks that the Alliance now runs by relying on increasingly less credible nuclear threats, recent studies have pointed to ways by which the conventional forces may be strengthened at modest cost.

V

In 1982, General Bernard Rogers, the present Supreme Allied Commander in Europe, stated that major improvements in NATO's conventional forces were feasible at a modest price.[22] These improvements, he said, would permit a shift from the present strategy requiring the early use of nuclear weapons to a strategy of "no early use of nuclear weapons." General Rogers estimated the cost to be approximately 1% per year greater than the 3% annual increase (in real terms) that the members of NATO, meeting in Washington, had agreed to in 1978.

An experienced Pentagon consultant, MIT Professor William W. Kaufmann, has taken General Rogers's suggestions of 4% annual increases in NATO defense budgets and analyzed how those funds could best be allocated to improve the Alliance's conventional defenses. After an exhaustive analysis, he concluded that a conventional force could be acquired that would be sufficiently strong to give a high probability of deterring Soviet aggression without threatening the use of nuclear weapons.[23]

Recently, an international study group also analyzed the possibilities for moving away from NATO's present nuclear reliance.[24] The steering committee of this "European Security Study" included among its members General Andrew Goodpaster, who once served as the Supreme Allied Commander in Europe; General Franz-Josef Schulze, a German officer, formerly commander in chief of Allied forces in Central Europe; and Air Marshall Sir Alasdair Steedman, formerly the United Kingdom's military representative to NATO.

Their report concludes that NATO's conventional forces could be strengthened substantially at very modest cost—a total of approximately $20 billion, which would be spent over a period of five or six years. For comparative purposes, note that the MX missile program is expected to cost $18 billion over the next five years.

The European Security Study stated that, to constitute an effective deterrent, NATO's conventional forces did not have to match specific Soviet capabilities. Rather, these forces need only be strong enough to create serious concerns for Warsaw Pact planners whether or not their attack could succeed.

To accomplish this, the study concluded, NATO's conventional forces would have to be able to:

- Stop the initial Warsaw Pact attack.
- Erode the enemy's air power.

- Interdict the follow-on and reinforcing armored formations that the Pact would attempt to bring up to the front lines.
- Disrupt the Pact's command, control, and communications network.
- Ensure its own secure, reliable, and effective communications.

The report outlines in detail how NATO could achieve these five objectives utilizing newly available technologies, and accomplishing with conventional weapons what previously had required nuclear munitions. These technological advances would permit the very accurate delivery of large numbers of conventional weapons, along with dramatic improvements in the ability to handle massive quantities of military information.

The effectiveness of the new technologies was testified to most recently by Senator Sam Nunn, a leading congressional expert on European defense issues:

> We now have at hand new conventional technologies capable of destroying the momentum of a Soviet invasion by means of isolating the first echelon of attacking forces from reinforcing follow-on echelons. These technologies . . . capitalize on three major advances. The first is the substantially improved lethality of improved conventional munitions. . . . The second is the. . . . growing capability of microelectronics to enhance the rapid collection, processing, distribution, and ability to act upon information about the size, character, location, and movement of enemy units. . . The third is improved ability to move and target quickly large quantities of improved conventional firepower against enemy force concentrations.[25]

The potential of these new conventional technologies is great. Unfortunately, they have not yet been accepted by any NATO nation for incorporation in its force structure and defense budget.

Moving from the present situation to revised strategic doctrines, war plans, and force structures to implement a conventional deterrent strategy could not be accomplished overnight. Still, over time, NATO's basic strategy could be modified within realistic political and financial constraints.

The process should probably begin with a statement by the Alliance, at a summit meeting of its heads of government, of its intention to move to a policy of deterrence of Soviet conventional-force aggression solely through the use of non-nuclear forces.

This statement of intention could then be followed by the drafting of detailed plans and programs. Conventional defense improvements would be set in motion; new doctrines would be debated and approved; parliaments would be tested as to their willingness to support the modestly larger expenditures necessary for strengthening the conventional forces.

In the meantime, immediate steps could be taken to reduce the risk of nuclear war. For example:
- Weapons-modernization programs designed to support a strategy of early use of nuclear weapons—such as those to produce

and deploy new generations of nuclear artillery shells—could be halted.

The Alliance's tactical nuclear posture could be thoroughly overhauled, with an eye toward shifting to a posture intended solely to deter the first use of nuclear weapons by the Warsaw Pact. Such a shift would permit major reductions in the number of nuclear weapons now deployed with NATO's forces in Europe; no more, and probably less, than 3,000 weapons would be sufficient. Those weapons which raise the most serious problems of release authority and pressures for early use—atomic demolition munitions and nuclear air defense systems—could be withdrawn immediately. Nuclear artillery could be withdrawn as the program to improve the conventional posture was implemented.

• The creation of a zone on both sides of the border in Europe, beginning in the Central Region, within which no nuclear munitions could be deployed, could be proposed to the Soviets.[26] The agreement to create such a zone could be verified by on-site inspections on a challenge basis. The Soviet Union has stated officially that it supports a nuclear-free zone, although it proposed that the width of the zone be far greater than is likely to be acceptable to NATO. If agreement could be reached on the size of the zone and adequate methods established to verify compliance with the agreement, such an agreement could build confidence on both sides that pressures for early use of nuclear weapons could be controlled.

VI

I now want to conclude this article by stating unequivocally my own views on the military role of nuclear weapons.

Having spent seven years as secretary of defense dealing with the problems unleashed by the initial nuclear chain reaction 40 years ago, I do not believe we can avoid serious and unacceptable risk of nuclear war until we recognize—and until we base all our military plans, defense budgets, weapon deployments, and arms negotiations on the recognition—that *nuclear weapons serve no military purpose whatsoever. They are totally useless—except only to deter one's opponent from using them.*

This is my view today. It was my view in the early 1960s.

At that time, in long private conversations with successive presidents—Kennedy and Johnson—I recommended, without qualification, that they never initiate, under any circumstances, the use of nuclear weapons. I believe they accepted my recommendation.

I am not suggesting that all U.S. presidents would behave as I believe Presidents Kennedy and Johnson would have, although I hope they would. But I do wish to suggest that if we are to reach a consensus within the Alliance on the military role of nuclear weapons—an issue that is fundamental to the peace and security of both the West and the East—we must face squarely and answer the following questions.

● Can we conceive of ways to utilize nuclear weapons, in response to Soviet aggression with conventional forces, that would be beneficial to NATO?

● Would any U.S. president be likely to authorize such use of nuclear weapons?

● If we cannot conceive of a beneficial use of nuclear weapons, and if we believe it unlikely that a U.S. president would authorize their use in such a situation, should we continue to accept the risks associated with basing NATO's strategy, war plans, and nuclear-warhead deployment on the assumption that the weapons would be used in the early hours of an East-West conflict?

● Would the types of conventional forces recommended by General Rogers, Professor William Kaufmann, and the European Security Study serve as an adequate deterrent to non-nuclear aggression by the U.S.S.R.? If so, are we not acting irresponsibly by continuing to accept the increased risks of nuclear war associated with present NATO strategy in place of the modest expenditures necessary to acquire and sustain such forces?

● Do we favor a world free of nuclear weapons? If so, should we not recognize that such a world would not provide a "nuclear deterrent" to Soviet conventional aggression? If we could live without such a deterrent then, why can't we do so now—thereby moving a step toward a non-nuclear world?

Notes

1. Lord Carver's statement is in *The Sunday Times* (London), February 21, 1982; General Steinhoff's is quoted in Hans Gunther Brauch, "The Enhanced Radiation Warhead: A West German Perspective," *Arms Control Today,* June 1978, p.3; and Mr. Kissinger's in Henry A. Kissinger, "NATO Defense and the Soviet Threat," *Survival,* Nov./Dec. 1979, p. 266 (address in Brussels).

2. *Congressional Record,* 97th Cong., 1st sess., July 17, 1981, Washington: GPO, 1981, p. S 7835.

3. Secretary of Defense, *Annual Report to the Congress, FY 1984,* U.S. Department of Defense, February 1, 1983, Washington: GPO, 1983.

4. Speech in Washington, April 6, 1982.

5. *The New York Times,* June 17, 1983.

6. *The Washington Post,* April 12, 1982.

7. An excellent brief history of NATO's conception of the role of nuclear weapons is presented in J. Michael Legge, "Theater Nuclear Weapons and the NATO Strategy of Flexible Response," Santa Monica (Calif.): RAND Corporation, R-2964-FF, April 1983. For this section, I have also drawn on unpublished writings of David A. Rosenberg and David Schwartz.

8. John Foster Dulles, "The Evolution of Foreign Policy," Department of State Bulletin 30, No. 761, January 25, 1954, p. 108.

9. Address to the Royal United Services Institute, London; cited in Robert E. Osgood, *NATO: The Entangling Alliance,* Chicago: University of Chicago Press, 1962, p. 110.

10. Much of the following discussion is based on James M. McConnell, "The Shift in Soviet Military Development from Nuclear to Conventional," manuscript to be published in *International Security*.

11. See, for example, Richard H. Pipes, "Why the Soviet Union Thinks It Could Fight and Win a Nuclear War," *Commentary*, July 1977, p. 21.

12. D.F. Ustinov, "We Serve the Homeland and the Cause of Communism," *Izvestia*, May 27, 1982.

13. For this section, I have drawn on *Arms Control and National Security*, Washington: Arms Control Association, 1983; the unpublished writing of William W. Kaufmann and Leon V. Segal; and recent discussions with military and civilian experts, not all of whom agree with one another.

14. North Atlantic Assembly's Special Committee on Nuclear Weapons in Europe, *Second Interim Report on Nuclear Weapons in Europe*, Report to the Committee on Foreign Relations, U.S. Senate, 98th Cong., 1st sess., Washington: GPO, 1983, p. 59.

15. *NATO Facts and Figures*, 10th edition, Brussels: NATO Information Service, 1981, pp. 152-54.

16. *Second Interim Report on Nuclear Weapons in Europe*, op. cit., p. 7.

17. A 100-kiloton tactical nuclear weapon would be needed to destroy approximately 50 to 100 armored fighting vehicles (e.g., tanks) in dispersed formation, the equivalent of a regiment. Such a weapon would create general destruction (of structures and people) in a circle with a diameter of 4.5 miles (an area of 15 square miles). A blast circle of this size, in typical Western European countries, would be likely to include two or three villages or towns of several thousand persons. In addition, depending on the nature of the weapon and height of burst, a much larger area could be affected by fallout. Several hundred of such tactical nuclear weapons would be required to counter an armored development in Europe. See Seymour J. Deitchman, *New Technology and Military Power*, Boulder (Colo.): Westview Press, 1979, p. 12.

18. Helmut Schmidt, *Defense or Retaliation?* New York: Praeger, 1962, p. 101; Schmidt's comment and the exercise result are cited in Jeffrey Record, *U.S. Nuclear Weapons in Europe*, Washington: Brookings, 1974.

19. Alain C. Enthoven and K. Wayne Smith, *How Much Is Enough?* New York: Harper & Row, 1971, p. 128.

20. *General and Complete Disarmament: A Comprehensive Study on Nuclear Weapons: Report of the Secretary General, Fall 1980*, New York: United Nations, 1981.

21. This discussion is based on a presentation by Vice Admiral John M. Lee (Ret.) in St. Petersburg, Florida, December 17, 1981.

22. General Bernard W. Rogers, "The Atlantic Alliance: Prescriptions for a Difficult Decade," *Foreign Affairs*, Summer 1982, pp. 1145-56.

23. Unpublished writings of Professor Kaufmann.

24. *Strengthening Conventional Deterrence in Europe*, Report of the European Security Study, New York: St. Martin's Press, 1983.

25. *Congressional Record*, 98th Cong., 1st sess., July 13, 1983, Washington: GPO, 1983, p. S 9853.

26. Such a proposal was made in the Report of the International Commission on Disarmament and Security Issues, *Common Security: A Program for Disarmament*, London: Pan Books, 1982.

Now Is the Time

by

John Platt

The development of a global peace-keeping system is now urgent and may be easier than we think.

The Certainty of Change

In the next few years, we will probably make an evolutionary jump to a new global management system. Our great technological developments of the last 40 years, especially in biology, weapons, and communications, are transforming the world and are leaving us with no alternative. They are squeezing us into the future like a melon-seed squeezed between the fingers. We are like people on a raft being swept onward through a turbulent rapids, with problems coming at us from every direction. We cannot fight the river but we must paddle furiously and together as new dangers or new opportunities appear.

Many of the new problems are very serious indeed, but the greatest danger of all, the hard rock just ahead, is the danger of the escalating nuclear arms race between the United States and the Soviet Union. Neither fear nor elaborate arms-control efforts nor improved weapons nor peace movements have slowed it down. There seems no way now to avoid nuclear catastrophe unless we can develop very quickly a larger framework, some kind of worldwide system for nuclear management and peace-keeping We need some new arrangement that all the major powers would be willing to adopt simply because it would be so much safer for them than the present arrangements.

The time we may have for doing this is not very long. At the rate things are going, we may pass a point of no return within something like five years, by 1989 or so, with breakdown becoming inevitable if we do not make a major reconstruction by that time. Today we may be in a pre-Revolution or pre-Constitution era, somewhat like 1784 or 1914. If we do slide into a nuclear

---

John Platt is a consultant, lecturer, and author on science and society. The author of The Step to Man, *he currently resides in Cambridge, Massachusetts.*

holocaust, it would still mean a global restructuring; any peoples who are left afterwards will still know how to make nuclear weapons and will still have to create a peace-keeping system in their devastated world. It would be infinitely simpler to do it ahead of time.

After examining the long record of power struggles, the historian William H. McNeill puts it this way:

> To halt the arms race, political change appears to be necessary. A global sovereign power willing and able to enforce a monopoly of atomic weaponry could afford to disband research teams and dismantle all but a token number of warheads. Nothing less radical than this seems in the least likely to suffice.
>
> [*The Pursuit of Power,* 1982]

It is curious how many of our best social thinkers and futurists avoid dealing with this catastrophe-or-change turnaround that is so close at hand. They pass on to other problems, or to "surprise-free" projections of 20-year development, or ultimate global reforms, or hoped-for changes in morality or the psyche. But most of these analyses and predictions would be totally upset either by catastrophes or by a revolutionary step-up in global organization. It is the conventional wisdom of 1784 or 1914.

The Nation-State Barrier

There are others who do deal with the catastrophe problem but who speak and act as though our framework of nation-states will remain uncoordinated indefinitely. This includes not only hawks but doves. Any yielding of sovereignty to a larger management structure is said to be "out of reach" at present. Whether they urge increased strength, or arms-control treaties, or disarmament, there is no explicit vision of a new global system. No one would deny that the building of any new system will be immensely difficult, but so are the present fragmentary arms-control efforts.

What frustrates these efforts, the hard core of the catastrophe problem, is the nation-state framework itself. To go back to the raft analogy, we are behaving like paddlers on opposite sides paddling harder and harder against each other instead of having a plan to steer together. The truth is that no arrangement with independent national control of nuclear weapons can be stable or can be steered. As *The Federalist Papers* said 200 years ago:

> A man must be far gone in Utopian speculations who can seriously doubt, that if these States should either be wholly disunited, or only united in partial confederacies, the subdivisions into which they might be thrown would have frequent and violent contests with each other. . . .
> To look for a continuation of harmony between a number of independent unconnected sovereignties, situated in the same neighborhood, would be to disregard the uniform course of human events, and to set at defiance the accumulated experience of ages. . . . The causes of hostility among nations are innumerable.

35

Recently this kind of instability in competitive interactions has been studied in the laboratory, in the new social-science field of "non-zero-sum games." These simulate situations in real life in which both parties may win or lose together, and the arms race is a particular kind of non-zero-sum dilemma of this sort. The instability in such a game has now been demonstrated by thousands of experimental and theoretical studies of conflict and cooperation between individuals and groups who win or lose different amounts with each other. In this kind of game, no matter what either player does, locked-in confrontations become permanent, and escalations will continue indefinitely to a breakdown. It is like children trying to build a tower of blocks indefinitely high, which will eventually collapse no matter how careful they are. These are social-interaction laws as inevitable as gravity, unless the game is by-passed by fitting it into some larger framework of communications and cooperative advantage. It is wishful thinking by hawks as well as doves—whether we start with the armed hostility of balanced forces or with mutual good-will—to suppose that *any* arrangements between independent nations can get past these theorems so as to remain stable for long.

If we are to move forward, would it not be worth starting a discussion of some larger workable alternative so as to see whether any other arrangement is possible and to make vivid how easy or difficult it might be? There are ways out, as we know from these social-science studies, as well as from many cases of successful peace-making in the real world. Locked-in game-theory confrontations can finally be changed if a larger view is imposed, for example by third-party pressure, re-negotiating the payoffs, or moving to a new system. If we had leadership to begin to think about this question and to debate some possible plans and develop a larger view, it might change our whole framework of discussion; and a step-up to some minimum global nuclear-management system in the immediate future might not be nearly as difficult as we suppose.

Sudden and astonishing step-ups to new levels of organization have happened repeatedly at crisis times in history. Sometimes they are created by empire-builders, sometimes by small alliances. But sometimes they are created by agreement in peacetime, under the leadership of a dedicated group, as in the case of the U.S. Constitution or the partial economic integration of the European Common Market.

With strong leaders and a sound design, a movement toward a better world system today could also take off, because it would be supported by many factors. The U.S. and the U.S.S.R. have many mutual interests besides arms-control. And the worldwide problems of food, health, energy, the monetary system, aviation, communications, environmental protection, the oceans, and space are too large for even these nations to deal with by themselves.

A global technology, with the global problems it creates, both makes possible and demands a step up to a global level of human organization.

The Need for Design

But the military nation-state will not disappear by wishing it. Arms and sovereignty have a purpose: to protect people from coercion by others and to strengthen them in pursuing their own interests. In a state of anarchy between nations, they perform the function that government would perform better, trying to protect life, liberty, and the pursuit of happiness. No group or nation would even conceivably be willing to give up its arms and troops unless some minimum system was already in place that would keep the peace and guarantee these objectives.

The design of such peace-keeping systems is not impossible. In civil life they are all around us. It took thousands of years, but we have social and political structures today that keep the peace over enormous areas of the world, larger than ever before. Most of them grew very gradually, of course, and it is a very different thing to have to plan a total peace-keeping system that can move into full operation almost immediately. This is why the examples of the U.S. Constitution and the European Common Market are so important, because they show that it can be done.

Nevertheless, any design of a global peace-keeping system that would be adoptable and generally workable from the beginning will require far more than a copy of some older system. It will also need major inputs of what can be called social technical knowledge. There are technical requirements for a self-stabilizing social structural design with democratic or mutual self-management by the parties, just as there are technical requirements for designing the supports of a table or a bridge so that it will be stable under gravity and varying loads.

It is not generally realized how much we have learned in the last few years about social and political feedback and stabilization mechanisms. Great advances have come not only from studies of game-theory, but from experimental and theoretical studies of cybernetics, psychological reinforcements, management theory, theories of democracy, micromotives and macrobehavior ("social traps"), and the art and science of negotiation. Our knowledge of social structure and stability goes far beyond what the Federalists knew. The knowledge will be essential in the design of any acceptable and stable peace-keeping system.

There is a widespread ignorance of these stabilization principles that is a defect in many global proposals. A self-governing structure that takes care of the interests of its participants is not a hierarchical pyramid of command, but a complex of interacting feedback loops, like the interacting blood loops and nerve networks of our bodies. It does not necessarily require either a world parliament to debate, or a nuclear autocrat to decide and act, as many writers suppose. Yet at the same time, goodwill and ingenuity are not enough; and strengthening the United Nations is not enough. [The Charter of the U.N. violates rules of stability that were known to the Federalists.]

What is needed at this point is to bring together multinational social and technical study groups to analyze and make proposals for the stabilization and design problem. The aim would be to apply sound feedback and control principles to outline a minimum global nuclear management system, one that would offer equal security to the participating states, protection against terrorists and mad nuclear dictators, and stabilizing feedbacks—"checks and balances"—with fail-safe mechanisms that could make patriots and conservatives on both sides feel more secure with the system than without it. We need, so to speak, a new Hamilton, Jay, and Madison to come together to write the new Federalist Papers on which a new working Constitution can be securely built.

The Four Requirements

A design-study group will have to work on hundreds of questions, but underlying them are four general requirements that any peace-keeping management system will need to satisfy if it is to be persuasive to the world. They are principles of stability and acceptability that in fact were emphasized so long ago by the Federalists, but that have been neglected or violated in many discussions of how to keep the peace. [See "The Federalists and the Design of Stabilization," in John Platt, *The Step to Man*.]

The first of these requirements for a peace-keeping system is, of course, that it be workable and effective. Its structure must be designed so that the roles and rewards of administrators and personnel lead to almost automatic feedback responses adequate against a host of dangers: coups d'etat, the rise of Hitlers, or renewed confrontations and escalations, as well as financial crises and bureaucratic rigidity. The system should have a range of time-constants for different needs, from rapid emergency action to long-run deliberation.

An effective feedback system must also be tough-minded, prepared to assume the worst, because as Hamilton said, men are "ambitious, vindictive, and rapacious." "If men were angels, no government would be necessary." The checks and balances should be operating to avert problems long before they become serious. Only if it is "realist" in this sense can such a system convince intelligent conservatives in every country to adopt it. This does not mean that it will operate primarily by last-ditch punishment or retaliation, because this would produce hostilities and dissipate the feelings of security and goodwill that are essential. It must create instead a thousand little continuous pressures and rewards for cooperative behavior, both of men and nations, of the kind that make any good organization satisfying and effective.

The second requirement of a good design is that it be modifiable. The structure should not be trivially changeable, veering with every wind, but it needs to be open to criticism and adjustment with reasonable speed to revealed imperfections or changed circumstances, if it is not to break down under growing stresses. No system is perfect or can stay perfect for long. And when governments or leaders have initial objections to a particular design, as they always will, it is much easier for them to adopt if it offers a clear mechanism for amendment later.

The third requirement is that any new system for global nuclear management, requiring political acceptance by numerous parties, must be an absolute minimum system. There should be nothing in it that is not essential for its effectiveness. Adoption of any workable system is going to be almost, if not quite, impossible, and every requirement that encroaches unnecessarily on the present interests of the participants should be eliminated.

This also means that individual countries will have to give up, at least within this system, those demands on other countries that have nothing directly to do with the peace-keeping mechanism. This will be one of the hardest concessions for countries to make, and there will have to be other channels through which these important interests can be pursued. But no ideological objections, no refusal to communicate with de facto governments, and no righteous indignation over their past actions or their present corruption or oppression should be allowed to increase by a single degree the enormous difficulty of adopting any real peace-keeping system.

The fourth requirement is that an adoptable design needs to offer its participants not only a minimum of negatives, but a maximum of positive advantages of personal and national self-interest, both for the present and the future. For the nuclear powers, each side will take immediate delight, of course, in a visible nuclear build-down on the other side; and the world will rejoice with both of them. With a peace-keeping system that we can begin to trust, there will also be new opportunities for unhampered development in every country, and a worldwide surge of hope and economic improvement. The conversion of the giant defense industries and their scientists and engineers into a peace-keeping system and then into new enterprises would have to be supported, but it would cost no more than they cost now; and it could be as dramatic as the surge of growth after World War II and the injection of the Marshall plan.

For a peace-keeping system to be adopted and successful, it must be effective, modifiable, minimal, and rewarding. As with building a successful commercial enterprise, we do not need a system that punishes and postures and fantasizes, but a working system that bargains and compromises, that manages and watches and responds.

Within these general guidelines, there are many alternative

self-stabilizing arrangements that would be stable—just as with living systems, where there are many different kinds of self-stabilizing biological creatures that have learned how to survive. This again helps to make the initial negotiations easier, because many of the specific demands and preferences of different countries can be accommodated in a complex system, as long as the crucial stability rules are not broken.

Stages in the Process

The process of analyzing possible designs and then going on to a working peace-keeping system could be done in three stages, although they might overlap.

The first stage will be the assembly of one or more technical-analysis and design groups, who would work full time for many months on general stability principles and applications and alternative proposals. Such groups might be organized under European or other auspices, or in any of several centers of advanced study. They would need to include practical politicians and diplomats and experts in law and economics and science and arms, as well as experienced negotiators and social analysts. Qualified people from both East and West should be in every such group, to avert the danger the Federalists warned against when they said, "Men often oppose a thing, merely because they have had no agency in planning it, or because it may have been planned by those whom they dislike." The long-run peace-keeping process, like government itself, is a political process involving informed participation by all parties, bargaining, compromise, and wary trust, and it will not work unless it has these characteristics from the beginning.

This stage can make use of the many years of hard work and ideas that have already gone into arms-control negotiations and treaties between East and West. Questions of multinational administrative structure, of financing, of what laboratories and plants and bases are to be monitored and controlled, of access and adequate guards, of fail-safe mechanisms, and so on and on, are discussed in hundreds of documents going back to 1945. The difference here is that the analyses are directed toward creating a business organization, not a double-spy system. Some large multinational corporations might even serve as models. It could be a refreshing change. No arms discussions afterwards would be the same.

The second stage of the process of adoption will be the effort to explain to a worldwide public how such a system would work to increase everyone's security. This means making converts; and energetic political leadership will be important. Yet the worldwide peace movement and nuclear-freeze movement today show that, in these matters, millions of people are already ahead of their governments. There is now both a political and economic constituency for the world as a whole, just waiting to be tapped.

Any group of leaders with a well-designed plan that offers some immediate hope to everyone could sweep the planet almost overnight.

The third stage of the process will be the actual convening of a top-level design-negotiation conference between East and West to decide on a system and adopt it and begin the steps of implementation. It would have to work out hundreds of details to meet the needs of all the participant countries as well as possible, and it would need technical advisers who have taken part in the original design-study groups, to make sure that stability requirements are not compromised. The recent Law of the Sea Conference was remarkably successful negotiation of this kind, with agreement worked out by a hundred nations on a hundred points over a 7-year period. At the end it was marred by the withdrawal of the U.S. after a change of administrations—which shows the danger of excessively long negotiations—but the general success and the negotiating mechanisms developed there may provide useful lessons for the nuclear peace-keeping design negotiations that lie ahead.

Easier Than We Think

The whole process might go faster than anyone supposes. Things are far more complex now, but it is worth remembering that the U.S. Constitution was hammered out in four months by less than 40 delegates. The stabilization-design problem is no longer a question of confrontation and counting; it focuses on fresh and larger arrangements. Lesser details might not be such sticking-points as they usually are, because there would be good adjustment mechanisms for working them out later in an ongoing system. And public enthusiasm and mass pressure, along with the nuclear urgency, might make the delegates surprisingly eager to finish their task and move into the new world.

If experienced and influential representatives of the great powers agree on and endorse the main features of a peace-keeping system, they might be able to convince every country that it would be a hard-headed improvement in security. All around the world, it could give such an increased sense of plan, of security, and of hope, that people across the political spectrum would rally to it, allies would press and bargain for its adoption, and the move to a new system and the reduction of nuclear armaments might suddenly become psychologically and politically easier than anyone believed. After these turbulent rapids, if we survive, there is a boundless ocean of new potentialities opening out before us.

What is important is to get the first step started now. When people need to build a new building, they call in architects. Calling together a conference of architects who can design a safer structure for the world must be done eventually. Now is the time.

Elements of a Peaceful World

Population, Environment, and Human Needs

by

Frances Breed

Although the global rate of population growth has moderated somewhat over the last decade, the revised United Nations projections provide no cause for complacency. Together with the impacts of rising consumption and increase in per capita resource use, the rise in human numbers from the current 4.6 billion to 6 billion in the year 2000—and more than 10 billion in the decades beyond—will lead to widespread degradation of natural resources and the environment. The struggle to meet basic human needs will in turn be undermined.

Although population pressure is seldom the sole cause of natural-resource damage, it is often a major contributor. Conversely, stabilization of human numbers at levels lower than projected will not insure the wise stewardship of resources—but continuation along the current demographic path will all but preclude significant improvements in environmental management and human conditions in many of the world's poorer countries. The ultimate consequences, such as reduced biological diversity, impairment of natural goods and services on which economic activities are based, and social disruptions and human misery, will affect people everywhere.

According to the medium U.N. projections, the population of Africa—where per capita food production is declining and large areas of fertile land are being turned to waste by overcropping, overgrazing, and deforestation—is expected to quadruple before stabilizing. The population of Latin America—where urban shantytowns are mushrooming—will triple, Asia's numbers are projected to rise from 2.5 billion to 6 billion. Obviously, social and technological changes of unprecedented scope will be required if anything near these totals is to be reached without widespread hunger and social breakdowns. Even these projections assume a progressive spread of birth control that is by no means assured.

Frances Breed is manager, population program, National Audubon Society, New York, New York.

Because of the tremendous demographic momentum arising from the Third World's youthful age structure, a rapid shift to small families is essential in many cases just to prevent a rise in the rate of increase.

To the extent that the demographic pressures can be eased in a humane way—by simultaneously attaining low birthrates and low death rates—the formidable tasks of adjustment will be eased. In any case, adapting to massive population increases will almost certainly entail heavy environmental costs that will make our planet a less hospitable place.

Population-related social and ecological problems are already unfolding in the regions where future demographic growth will be the highest. The surge in human numbers, together with economic inequality, sluggish economic growth, and the scarcity of unexploited arable lands, results in increases in the number of "marginal" people—those who lack access either to good farmland or to a productive job. Despite migration to cities, rural populations are still growing at close to 2% a year in much of Africa and Asia, and land-settlement or colonization schemes cannot absorb more than a small fraction of the tide of potential farmers. The resulting rise in the number of landless people contributes to many other severe social and ecological problems— among them runaway urbanization, mass underemployment, and the destruction of soils, forests, and wildlife.

Landless laborers, sharecroppers, and marginal farmers together constitute the majority of rural residents in most countries of Asia and Latin America, and they are rising in number in Africa, where land inadequacy has only recently emerged as a serious problem. In noncommunist Asia, reports the FAO, some 30% of the rural labor force is now completely landless. Perhaps as many more are farming marginal plots or renting under oppressive conditions. The concentration of larger holdings in a few hands joins population growth as an explanation for widespread landlessness. In Latin America, according to the FAO, 7% of the landowners possessed 93% of the arable land as of 1975, illustrating the need for attention to land tenure as well as to demographic patterns.[1]

Throughout much of Sub-Saharan Africa, traditional tenure systems, in which land is owned by the tribe and allocated to individuals for use but not for sale, have historically predominated. The apparent availability of large "unused" areas has further fed the notion that landlessness is not a threat in Sub-Saharan Africa. This relatively benign image of African tenure problems is increasingly misleading. The empty spaces create a mistaken impression. In vast areas of Africa the climate, soils, or other ecological factors make farming or even sustained grazing impossible. Elsewhere the soils and meager rainfall necessitate lengthy fallow periods if soil productivity is to be maintained— and economically feasible technologies for more intensive agriculture are often not available.

Land scarcity is emerging as a problem in more and more parts of Africa. Where populations are pressing against the arable land base, a common result has been a transition from tribal to individual land rights— accompanied by land accumulation by some and landlessness for others. The trends have progressed furthest in areas growing commercial export crops, such as West Africa's cocoa regions and East Africa's coffee lands. But they are fast appearing in peasant food-crop areas as well.[2]

The problem of landlessness in Sub-Saharan Africa may be most advanced in Kenya. By the early 1970s, nearly one-fifth of rural households were landless.[3] Kenya provides an ominous portent for the rest of black Africa. Doubling every 24 years or so, Africa's population is outpacing the expansion of cropped areas, which, according to FAO data, increased by only 12% between the early 1960s and 1975. Increasing land scarcity and competition are inevitable in much of the continent.

Throughout the Third World, people who lack opportunities in the countryside often migrate to cities (or to other countries) in search of employment. Because of the combined effects of rural-urban migration and natural increases among urban residents, developing-country cities grew by an average of 4% annually in the 1970s—overwhelming social capacities to provide adequate housing and services. Slums and squatter settlements are the fastest-growing sectors of most Third World cities. According to U.N. projections, cities will have to absorb even greater increases in population in the next two decades.[4] Exactly how the mushrooming shantytowns will be supplied with adequate food, fresh water, fuel, and housing is unclear.

In their desperate effort to meet current survival needs, marginal people are often forced to spread over the landscape—with disastrous effects on natural resources and wildlife.[5] Due to circumstances beyond their control, the poor must take actions that undermine long-term development prospects for themselves and their countries.

The spread of agriculture outside of traditional farming zones is the largest single cause of deforestation in the developing countries today. Where lands are suitable and proper technologies are available, forest clearance for farming is often desirable—so long as it is accompanied by watershed protection, preservation of natural areas, and enforcement of sustainable land uses. But much of today's deforestation is on lands that are not suited for agriculture; valuable species, other resources. and ecological functions can be destroyed without commensurate social benefits.

Tropical rain forests have already been reduced from their natural domain by about 40%, and, according to the recent FAO/UNEP assessment, are shrinking at a rate of 7.5 million hectares a year. The spread of peasant farming, shifting cultivation, commercial farming (especially the creation of pasturelands in Latin

America to produce beef for export), and unregulated logging are the principal causes of rain-forest clearance. But these figures, which describe the permanent decline of closed forests, understate the magnitude of the Third World's deforestation problem. Another 4.4 million hectares per year of tropical closed forest are partially logged. In Africa and Latin America an additional 3.8 million hectares of "open woodlands" are cleared, mainly for farming, each year. Throughout Africa, Asia, and Latin America, the vegetative cover of huge areas is being severely degraded through overgrazing, fuelwood collection, and a decline in crop fallow cycles.[6]

The thoughtless clearance of tropical rain forests is of special concern to ecologists because unique biological riches are being lost even before scientists have had a chance to examine them. Thousands, possibly millions of plant and animal species, most of them still unnamed, will become extinct over the next two decades if current trends in forest conversion continue.[7] The costs—in terms of the loss of potential industrial and agricultural products, of genes useful in crop breeding, of new medical substances, of genetic materials for use in genetic engineering—will be sustantial. The ecological impacts of such large-scale extinctions cannot be foreseen, but must be cause for concern. Tropical forest disruption also threatens the wintering grounds of migratory birds that are ecologically and aesthetically important in countries of the temperate zone.

In hilly and mountainous regions, such as the Himalayan hills, the Andes, Central America, and East Africa, farmers increasingly clear steep slopes that should be kept in forest or perhaps tree crops. Often the topsoil washes away within a few years, destroying the productive potential of the hills and causing serious problems downstream as reservoirs, canals, and harbors fill with silt. Hillside deforestation, especially of smaller watersheds, also disrupts the hydrological cycle, resulting in increased flooding in rainy periods and desiccation of springs and streams in dry periods.

In semiarid zones of Africa and Asia, farmers are forced to move into low-rainfall fringes that, when the inevitable drought comes, turn into dust bowls. Meanwhile, the spread of cultivation squeezes herders into ever more restricted areas and the problem of overgrazing is intensified. Often the emerging inadequacy of the land base in relation to population and available technology is partially concealed by a decline in the soil-preserving fallow period, a process that is turning huge fertile areas of semiarid Africa and Asia into wasteland.[8]

The loss of biological diversity and wildlife habitat that is occurring as the world's remaining natural areas are cleared for agriculture, logged, inundated by reservoirs, or otherwise disrupted is of special concern. It is an unfortunate irony that many of the countries richest in biological resources are among the poorest economically. No system of parks and reserves is likely to withstand the demands for land and resources that will be posed by burgeoning numbers of destitute people, whatever the long-term costs to humanity of biological depletion.

The setting aside of a representative array of ecosystems, as is being promoted by UNESCO's Biosphere Reserves program, should be an essential element in developing planning. But the underlying threats to the integrity of such reserves must also be addressed. Direct financial assistance from richer countries for reserve establishment and maintenance is one need; if parks are set aside for the benefit of all humanity, then all humanity should help bear the costs. More basically, however, economic reforms that provide people with alternatives to invading protected areas are required. And even this will be insufficient if high rates of population growth continue.

Providing people with the opportunity to meet their basic needs and the encouragement of family planning can be mutually supportive. Both are required if the earth's biological diversity—so important for economic, ecological, and spiritual reasons—is to be protected from massive assaults. And progress in both areas, experience shows, is feasible—most commonly where local people, especially women, participate in the planning of development and population programs and are given adequate support.

In an effort to deny the importance of the population side of the population/resource balance, some have argued that each child is born not only with a mouth to feed but also with two hands for producing; that humans in effect "create" usable resources and that the growth rates or absolute size of populations do not warrant concern. But the relevance of this statement to the conditions prevailing in much of the world is dubious. Too many of today's infants will never go to school, will have no land to farm, will have no access to a job productive enough to provide a decent income. Hundreds of millions will be inadequately nourished during childhood—some to the point of brain damage— and will lack ready access to safe water supplies; currently, according to WHO statistics, some 40,000 infants and small children die each day, mainly because of the combined effects of undernutrition and poor sanitation.[9]

Arguments based on the roles of human effort and ingenuity in creating usable resources tend to ignore the extent to which human economic activities rely on natural systems, which in turn can be damaged by human misuse. Frequently, what is recorded in economic statistics as "growth" entails damage to biological capital such as fertile soils, forests, productive estuaries, and natural ecosystems that provide checks against pests and disease. As a result, the long-term benefits to society are undercut.

Ever wider and more intensive exploitation of renewable resources can have heavy short-term costs as well, especially when poorer, politically marginal groups lose the resources on which their livelihoods are based. As a recent comprehensive report on environment and development in India concluded:

> A significant section of India's population exists beyond the pale of the mainstream Indian society. Each time a major development project goes up, or there is a fresh inroad into the remote areas for untapped natural resources, a new ecological niche is destroyed and another lot of these marginal people are uprooted and pauperized.[10]

Calculations of future carrying capacity also frequently fail to take full account of the costly trade-offs involved, the negative feedbacks, and the broader environmental consequences of achieving a certain goal. For example, calculations of ultimate food-producing potential often do not reflect the impacts of required reductions of forest area (and the resultant economic and ecological costs), or do not take full account of alternate demands on water supplies assumed to be available for irrigation. Calculations of potential economic output may ignore the impacts of increased atmospheric carbon dioxide and of increased pollution and acid rain, and may involve untested assumptions about the availability and costs of obtaining raw materials.

The point is not that economic development—and especially efforts to ensure that the basic needs of the world's poor are met—should not be pursued with urgency. But calculations of global and regional production possibilities often fail to take account of the hidden ecological and human costs of producing a given level of goods. They also tend to include totally unrealistic assumptions about the ability of societies to reorganize and plan activities and to redistribute goods.

We cannot dismiss the very real current challenges posed by rapid population growth simply because calculations can demonstrate the theoretical potential of a region to support some huge number of people. In many of the poorest countries. unchecked population growth will in all likelihood mean the continued razing of forests, the impoverishment of topsoils, the destruction of natural areas, the spread of urban shantytowns, food shortages, and minimal economic progress at best. National and international economic reforms, improved land management strategies, and many other measures are obviously called for in addition to family planning services and population education. Reductions in those demands of the affluent that put stress on resources and the environment are vital as well. But to ignore the population factor is dangerous and irresponsible.

In the final analysis, the key question is not how many people could theoretically be supported by the earth's resources. One can make fantastic assumptions about social and technological change and environmental resilience and "prove" that many tens of billions can be supported, or one can make more static assumptions about human and environmental adaptability to "prove" that population has already surpassed the sustainable carrying capacity. A more germane question is, What are the costs—ecological and human—of attempting to sustain ever more people? And, ultimately, what kind of world do we want for ourselves and our children? Short of all-out nuclear war, the human race could in some fashion survive the gross disruptions of the biota and natural cycles that will accompany large increases in population. But humankind would be poorer, both economically and spiritually, than it could be if population stabilized at lower levels.

The longer countries wait to address rapid population growth, the more stringent and less humane their ultimate responses are likely to be. China is in this regard instructive. Having determined that the attainment of a decent quality of life for its people requires a drastic slowdown and even reversal in population growth, the Chinese government has embarked on what many regard as a draconian birth-control program. In support of the goal of a one-child family, severe social and economic pressures are applied and personal privacy is intruded upon; even forced abortions are reported from some areas. Such measures may, in long-term perspective, constitute the only realistic path available to China, given the size of its population in relation to resources and level of development. But China's predicament stands as a warning of the varied potential costs of procrastination in confronting high birthrates.

Rapid population growth, grinding poverty, and destructive consumption patterns present three interrelated challenges. Progress against each is possible and will facilitate progress against the other two. Progress against all three is essential to a better future for humanity.

Notes

1. FAO, *Review and Analysis of Agrarian Reform and Rural Development in the Developing Countries Since the Mid-1960s* (Rome, 1979). See also Milton J. Esman, *Landlessness and Near-Landlessness in Developing Countries* (Ithaca, N.Y.: Cornell University Centre for International Studies, 1978).

2. John M. Cohen, "Land Tenure and Rural Development in Africa," in R.H. Bates and M.F. Lofchie, eds., *Agricultural Development in Africa* (New York: Praeger, 1980)

3. International Labour Office, *Employment, Incomes and Inequality: A Strategy for Increasing Productive Employment in Kenya* (Geneva, 1972)

4. M.W. Holdgate, M. Kassas, and G.F. White, eds., *The World Environment 1972-1982* (Dublin: Tycooly International, 1982)

5. Erik P. Eckholm, *Down to Earth: Environment and Human Needs* (New York: W.W. Norton, 1982).

6. J.P. Lanly, *Tropical Forest Resources* (Rome: FAO, 1982).

7. Norman Myers, *The Sinking Ark* (New York: Pergamon Press, 1979); *Entering the Twenty First Century: The Global 2000 Report to the President* (Washington, D.C.: Government Printing Office, 1980).

8. *Desertification: An Overview* (Nairobi: U.N. Conference on Desertification, 1977); Eckholm, *Down to Earth.*

9. Calculated from figures in WHO, *Sixth Report on the World Health Situation* (Geneva, 1980).

10. Centre for Science and Environment, *The State of India's Environment 1982: A Citizens Report* (New Delhi, 1982).

Reshaping Economic Policies

by

Lester R. Brown

One need not be an economist to sense that we are living in difficult times. Economic growth over the last four years has been less than in any comparable period since the thirties and there have been no gains in per capita income for the world as a whole since 1979. In countries such as Argentina, Brazil, Mexico, and Poland, massive external debt is strangling economic progress.

A projection of Brazil's economic future by Data Resources, Inc., indicates that the country should be able to pay off its debt, but that doing so means its depressed industrial output will not regain its 1980 level until 1990. By this time 37 million Brazilians will have been added to the 1980 population of 119 million, greatly reducing output per capita. Unfortunately, this projected interaction between external debt, economic output, and population growth is not atypical. It confronts dozens of developing countries, large and small.

The budgetary deficits and external debts that confound policymakers today derive from more fundamental shortcomings—outdated population policies, inappropriate economic policies, and misplaced priorities. In all-too-many countries, population policies belong to another age, a time when rapid population growth slowed but did not prevent improvements in living conditions. Economic policies, too, are a carry-over from a past when energy was cheap and resources were abundant. Existing priorities in the use of public resources were fashioned in an age when incomes were everywhere on the rise, when more guns did not preclude more butter.

Policymakers often lose sight of the relationship between the economic system, whose performance is monitored in great detail, and the resource base on which it depends. Glowing economic reports—with key indicators such as output, productivity, and export continually setting new records in the short run—are possible even as the economic policies that generate them are destroy-

Lester R. Brown is president of the Worldwatch Institute, Washington, D.C. This article is excerpted from A Worldwatch Institute Report on Progress Toward A Sustainable Society *(W.W. Norton, 1984).*

ing the resource base. Indeed, one reason for the bullish indicators might be the consumption of the resource base itself.

The need for a new accounting system is now evident. Existing economic indicators need to be supplemented by others that distinguish between self-defeating and sustainable growth. Most fundamentally, the world needs a system of economic accounting that reflects more completely the effects of economic policies on the resource base and, conversely, the effect of changes in the resource base on the economy. This system must account for more than the short-run "bottom line"; it must incorporate values that maintain economic life.

A Revised Accounting System

The lack of a more complete economic accounting system has led many governments to adopt ill-conceived policies in the management and use of resources. It has permitted governments to focus on production, while largely ignoring the effects on the natural capital that makes production possible. In some instances the accounting gap has led to a more or less permanent loss of productive capacity. Governments' shortsighted approach can be seen in one case after another: topsoil, water supplies, grasslands, forests.

Few annual accountings of soil formation and soil loss have been attempted, so national political leaders often do not know whether soils are being farmed or mined. Lacking data on soil erosion, governments cannot compute either the on-farm cost of soil loss or the off-farm costs of, for example, hydroelectric reservoir sedimentation. This in turn precludes complete cost/benefit analyses of soil conservation programs.

Resource accounting could help manage other resources intelligently as well. Water demands often exceed renewable supplies, leading to falling water tables, dwindling river flows, and shrinking lakes. Grasslands are being converted to desert in many areas of the world, but there is no effort to relate desertification to excessive livestock numbers and the loss of grazing capacity through overgrazing. And little accurate annual data on changes in forested areas exist, so in many situations trees are being felled faster than they are regenerating. Many countries simply do not know when they begin consuming the resource base itself. By the time it becomes physically obvious that they are doing so, it can be too late to act.

Changes in a few resource stocks are carefully monitored at the global level. For example, governments annually record the amount of oil produced and newly discovered, making it easy to determine changes in reserves. This information helps policymakers decide how rapidly the remaining oil reserves should be exploited. When aggregated at the global level, the sum of these national data provides information of great value to decision-makers everywhere, from individual consumers to political leaders.

At the national level, only Norway appears to have adopted a comprehensive resource accounting system. In 1974, the Norwegian Stortinget (Parliament) instructed the Ministry of Environment to prepare an annual review of natural resource stocks, their annual consumption, and any proposals for their future use. Work on the methodology for this assessment began in 1975 and a preliminary study was presented to the Stortinget in 1977. It included an accounting both of material resources and of basic biological life-support systems. Other countries, including Canada, France, Japan, and the Netherlands, have experimented with alternative accounting systems, but none has progressed as far as Norway in developing a comprehensive accounting.

Norway's goal in resource accounting is to maximize the "social profit" of resources and to prevent depletion or degradation wherever possible. In a United Nations Environment Programme review of the status of environmental accounting, Edward Weiller observes that "the concept of 'natural capital' is at the heart of the Norwegian resource accounting system." Its early architects decided, probably wisely, not to attempt to integrate it with the national economic accounts. In part this was because the latter are kept in monetary units, whereas resources are measured in physical units.

The Norwegian experience illustrates the value of a modest but realistic approach to accounting. It also demonstrates that each country needs to design its own system, one that is suited to its particular circumstances and needs. Japan, for example, a heavily industrialized and densely populated country, has focused on the costs of mitigating environmental damage, in particular the effects of air and water pollution on human health. South Korea, in a somewhat similar situation, has patterned its approach after that of Japan.

In the Third World, the primary need is to identify and measure the resource-degrading consequences of economic activity. Governments in these countries, where "natural capital" is so overwhelmingly important, need to know what is happening to soils, forests, grasslands, and water resources. If a desert is expanding, for example, policymakers in the areas affected want to know how fast it is spreading and what can be done to reverse the process.

Occasionally a country will institute a detailed accounting system when a resource is of particular value or when its stock is known to be diminishing, which would have potentially serious long-term economic consequences. It was precisely these concerns that led the U.S. Congress to pass the Resource Conservation Act in 1977, which required the Department of Agriculture to conduct a national soils inventory, focusing particularly on the relationship between soil erosion and new soil formation. The first assessment, in 1977, drew upon some 200,000 samples from croplands across the country and provided the most detailed information ever on U.S. soils. The survey was repeated again in 1982, but with even greater detail. Relying on close to a million individual samples, it represented the most exhaustive inventory of soils ever undertaken by any country. The completion of the 1982 assessment provided U.S. soil scientists with two data points that can be compared to establish long-term trends.

A resource accounting system provides a means of incorporating the costs of "externalities" such as acid rain or soil erosion into decision-making. The goal is more intelligent policymaking and a more enlightened public and private management of resources. Much more than a resource accounting system is needed, of course, for intelligent environmental and resource management, but this is a necessary yardstick for measuring a system's effectiveness.

New Economic Indicators

As the emphasis in economic policymaking and planning shifts toward sustainability, the inadequacy of many widely used economic indicators becomes obvious. As the goal of economic policy is redefined, new indicators are needed to measure progress. Central to this new definition is Kenneth Boulding's observation that "it is stocks of goods that contribute to human well-being while flows contribute to gross national product." Under the existing national accounting system, the production of shoddy goods that have to be replaced or repaired frequently raises the GNP, whereas a modest additional investment in high-quality engineering that greatly extends the lifetime of products lowers the GNP.

A set of economic indicators designed to measure progress toward a sustainable society should include data, for example, on the recycling of major resources such as steel, aluminum, glass, and paper. The throwaway society evolved when energy was cheap, raw materials were abundant, and there were far fewer people competing for resources than there are today. Societies failing to realize that these days are over are likely to pay with a falling standard of living. The release of monthly data on materials recycling would help highlight the importance of this process for both the general public and key decision-makers. Such indicators are not particularly difficult to develop; recycled scrap steel, for instance, is processed through mills just as iron ore is and thus can readily be measured.

Changes in the relative values of the various factors of production also call for new economic indicators. From the beginning of this century until 1973, energy became progressively cheaper while labor became more expensive. That trend has since been reversed, with energy costs rising much more rapidly than those of labor. With extensive and growing unemployment in industrial as well as developing countries, these new relationships suggest a need to focus more on energy productivity, specifically on that of oil, the scarcest fossil fuel. The barrels of oil needed to produce $1,000 worth of GNP is a useful way of determining how well a society is doing in weaning itself from this versatile but dwindling energy source. Similarly, since cropland area is essentially fixed, the value of land is increasing relative to that of labor, making land productivity relatively more important. This is not to imply that labor productivity is unimportant; rather it recognizes that raising the productivity of energy and of land increasingly holds the key to raising labor productivity

In a world where the rate of population growth is often the principal determinant of efforts to improve living conditions, data on population growth becomes an important measure of progress. The need here is not for a new indicator but for the more systematic gathering and dissemination of data on birthrates. Reporting this data monthly, just as governments already do for employment and inflation, would remind people how much remains to be done in order to achieve population stability.

As pressures on the global resource base intensify, spurring the shift to development strategies focused on basic needs, indicators other than income may prove more useful in measuring living standards. Given the basic need for food, particularly in low-income countries, per capita grain consumption or caloric intake may be more telling measures of well-being. Indeed, Bangladesh has begun to define poverty not in terms of per capita income but in terms of caloric intake. In 1980, the government reported that 85% of the people were living below the poverty line, defined as 2,122 calories a day, and 54% below the extreme poverty level of 1,885 calories.

In a world where resource scarcities make rapid economic growth more difficult or less desirable, designing development strategies that focus more specifically on basic social indicators such as life expectancy or infant mortality may be useful. The Overseas Development Council has devised a Physical Quality of Life Index (PQLI) based on three social indicators—life expectancy, infant mortality, and literacy—as an alternative to per capita income. The profiles developed with this new index suggest that rather high levels of social well-being can be attained at rather modest levels of resource consumption, providing an appropriate development strategy is followed.

Progress toward a sustainable society requires changes that will reduce the value of GNP as an indicator—underscoring the need for new economic indicators. For example, if the construction industry begins to incorporate the basic principles of climate-sensitive architecture, new buildings will require far less energy than existing structures. In effect, architectural design and engineering know-how will be substituted for energy, leading to much lower energy use and a decline in gross national product, but also to an improvement in the standard of living.

Similarly, as planned obsolescence is abandoned in favor of high-quality goods emphasizing durability, this too could lead to a decline in apparent economic output. Stated otherwise, many of the practices that have led to such enormous increases in gross national product do not necessarily correlate with improvements in quality of life. In moving toward a sustainable society it is quite possible to have a short-term decline in GNP while living conditions are improving. A new set of economic indicators keyed directly to basic social needs could help guide the effort to create a sustainable society.

Economic Policies for Full Employment

Economic analysts now put rising unemployment and international indebtedness at the top of the list of world economic problems, both having at least temporarily superseded inflation as an issue of concern. Unemployment and underemployment have been growing steadily for more than a decade in the Third World as more and more young people reach working age. In some developing countries, the unemployed and underemployed combined may constitute a third or more of the total labor force.

Even Western industrial societies are plagued with rising unemployment. In the United States, the United Kingdom, and several countries in Western Europe, unemployment reached double-digit levels in the early eighties. A ratchet effect can now be seen in the growth of unemployment in these societies. During recessions unemployment increases, while during economic recovery the number of unemployed stabilizes or declines only modestly, leaving the total number of job-seekers little changed. Thus with each economic cycle unemployment moves higher.

Theoretically the factors of production—land, labor, and capital, which includes energy—should combine in the marketplace in optimum combinations. If a given factor is not fully used, its price should drop. But market rigidities such as minimum wages and fixed salaries for many categories of workers have overpriced labor relative to other productive factors, leaving many people without jobs. The result is a waste of labor and a less-than-optimum combination of the basic factors of production.

Neither national governments nor international development agencies have proved very proficient in devising economic policies that will take full advantage of a country's labor force. No government would consciously idle part of its energy flow or capital assets. Putting money in a mattress would be unthinkable because it would not contribute to productive capacity or earn interest. And yet labor is used as unproductively as money in a mattress as a result of poorly conceived economic policies. Governments can avoid this by systematically seeking opportunities to use unemployed labor to increase a country's energy output, to conserve energy, or to increase food production.

One of the more imaginative efforts of this kind is South Korea's reforestation campaign. In the early seventies the government launched a national effort to replant the denuded hillsides of the country, land that was otherwise useless. By the end of the decade, seasonally unemployed villagers had planted an area in forest that was two-thirds as large as that in rice. This "greening of the countryside" was achieved by combining fast-growing pine seedlings from government-run nurseries, the organizational capacity represented by village-level cooperatives, and seasonally unemployed labor

In effect, South Korea has created a major energy resource, one that will provide fuelwood in perpetuity with a minimal expenditure of funds. Reforestation in this setting amounts to ecologic rehabilitation. By reducing runoff, forested lands reduce soil erosion and help recharge underground aquifers. South Korea's efforts, which have added to the country's resource stock and reduced its unemployment, are a model for other countries. Maintaining, culling, and harvesting the planted trees will provide employment to thousands of villagers for the indefinite future.

Another activity particularly important in rural areas is the construction of small dams that can be used for electrical generation and for water storage and irrigation. Small dams, which can be built almost exclusively with hand tools, can also reduce runoff and potential damage from flooding. China, which has some 89,000 small, locally constructed dams with a combined electrical generating capacity of nearly 3,000 megawatts, is the unquestioned leader in this resourceful use of labor.

A closely related effort that can capitalize on rural seasonal employment is the construction of terraces on hillside cropland. Where population growth is rapid, farmers have moved up the hillsides so fast that time has not permitted construction of the terraces needed to stabilize and preserve agriculture on these sloping lands. Mobilizing seasonally unemployed workers for this task could ensure both that soil on this land is retained and that rainfall is captured and used to good effect.

In a world where water is becoming increasingly scarce and a constraint on food production, reducing water loss from canals can yield a robust return. Even in advanced industrial societies such as the United States or the Soviet Union, irrigation canals are often dug in the bare earth without the benefit of any lining. Using stone, brick, or even a layer of plastic can sometimes virtually eliminate seepage, which can siphon off up to 40% of irrigation water supplies. In addition to reducing waterlogging, often a problem in irrigated areas with canal seepages, the investment of unemployed labor in this water conservation effort would also expand the irrigated area.

The broad-based effort to develop renewable energy substitutes provides an abundance of job opportunities. The shift from gasoline to alcohol as an automotive fuel in Brazil illustrates this potential. The increase in cropped acreage needed to produce sugarcane for the distilleries is a source of direct employment in agriculture. At the same time, the construction of alcohol distilleries in the countryside near the cane fields provides a form of industrial employment in the countryside. Although petroleum refineries need only a handful of workers, alcohol distilleries employ many.

A similar advantage exists in the development of wind power, an energy resource that is widely available compared with coal or uranium. Turning to the wind rather than nuclear power in the Third World also creates manufacturing jobs locally since virtually all developing countries have the industrial capacity to produce wind-electric generators, while they would have to import reactors.

Another energy source that can be exploited largely by indigenous labor is biomass, which can be converted into methane by using locally built methane generators. Every village in the Third World has a certain amount of organic material—human and animal wastes, household wastes, and crop residues—that can be converted into methane by an anaerobic digester. These methane generators extract the methane from organic material while leaving a nutrient-rich sludge that can be used as fertilizer. In effect, methane generators combine the production of energy and the recycling of nutrients, which is certain to become an appealing combination as fertilizer prices continue to rise.

As electricity rates and oil and natural gas prices rise, a prime opportunity exists to substitute solar collectors for these conventional sources. A concerted worldwide effort to shift to this method of water heating, a move that makes more and more economic sense, would create millions of jobs in the fabrication, marketing, distribution, and installation of solar panels.

The manufacture and marketing of more-efficient stoves for cooking in the Third World is another industry ripe for development. Food cooked on an open fire uses several times as much firewood, cow dung, or crop residue as that cooked in more efficiently designed closed stoves. One advantage of several new varieties of stoves is that they can be made entirely from local materials and produced by village-level industries. The social contribution of the reduced pressures on forests and of additional employment would be substantial.

Within the United States, one of the most promising areas for employment expansion is materials recycling, which has the advantage of reducing energy requirements, consumer costs, pollution, and materials use. The use of virgin ores for the production of throwaway containers and other materials is capital- and energy-intensive but uses relatively little labor. Recycling, by contrast, is a labor-intensive activity that requires far less capital and energy.

One sector in which all societies can increase employment while reducing energy use is transportation. One of the attractions of the 55-mile-an-hour speed limit in the United States, in addition to the energy and lives it saves, is that it increases employment in both freight and passenger transportation. Another variation on this basic theme of exchanging energy for employment lies in the design of public passenger transport systems. In some developing countries, such as Indonesia, the Philippines, and Turkey, small vans that carry 6 to 10 passengers are driven on established transportation routes, providing passenger transport that is easily competitive with buses in terms of cost but that uses less energy and more drivers

In some cases, a combination of the initiatives cited above multiplies job opportunities. For example, the construction of a local water storage pond or reservoir in a rural community can permit double cropping. In many Third World countries an increase in water supplies during the dry season will make year-round cropping possible. In the Philippines, for example, a new rice-production system has developed in areas with continuous water supplies. A farmer with, say, four acres of land divides it into small plots that are in rice continuously except during the few days between harvest and replanting. Each week another plot is harvested and replanted. With such intensive rotation, the work load is distributed evenly throughout the year. Labor is used with maximum efficiency and the land yields three or four crops of rice annually.

Mounting unemployment is not inevitable in either industrial or developing countries provided national leaders understand what needs to be done and have the political will to carry it out. In most situations the limiting factor is imagination and the capacity to organize people at the local level to achieve common social goals, whether the objective is planting and maintaining a village firewood plantation or building a small dam to store water and generate electricity.

Equity and Stability

As long as the world economy was expanding at 4-5% per year, the question of how equitably wealth was distributed was largely defused. It was assumed that the rising economic tide would raise living standards everywhere, and in most countries it did. But now that economic growth has slowed it becomes more difficult to dodge the distribution issue.

As economic growth lost momentum during the early eighties it fell behind population growth in many countries. For hundreds of millions of people, income levels in 1983 were less than in 1980. For this segment of global society the exhortations to be patient, that their lot would improve, are becoming less acceptable. As world population moved from 3 billion in 1960 to 4.6 billion in 1983, it outstripped the growth in many basic commodities on which humanity depends. When the per capita supply of a commodity is stagnant or falling for the world as a whole, if some people consume more, then others must consume less. Patterns of income distribution within and among societies must be considered against this shifting global economic and resource backdrop.

One common measure of the equity of income distribution within a society is the ratio of the income received by the wealthiest one-fifth of population to that of the poorest one-fifth. This provides a means for comparing income distribution regardless of the level of development. In the more socially progressive countries, such as those in Western Europe, the income ratio of the top one-fifth to the bottom one-fifth ranges from 4 to 1 to 6 to 1. Two other major industrial societies, Japan and Australia, are also within this income distribution bracket. Within the Third World, India, Bangladesh, and Sri Lanka stand out, with income distribution ratios of 6 or 7. Other major industrial countries with somewhat less equitable income distribution patterns include France (9 to 1), the United States (10 to 1), and Canada (11 to 1).

At the other end of the spectrum are countries in Latin America and the Middle East. Brazil, which has by far the greatest concentration of wealth of any major country, is at the bottom of the scale, with a ratio of 33 to 1. This explains why Brazil is sometimes described as "a Belgium and an India" within the same boundaries. For the upper 10% or roughly 13 million people, incomes are comparable to those in northwestern Europe; for many remaining Brazilians, incomes and living conditions are much closer to those in India. Mexico, the second largest country in Latin America, also has a highly skewed income distribution pattern. The wealthiest one-fifth of its population has an income 20 times as great as the poorest one-fifth. In Mexico, as in Brazil, this puts the poorest segments of society at a meager subsistence level of existence.

For governments wishing to achieve a more equitable distribution of income, there are numerous public policy instruments that can be used. One of the most common, of course, is a progressive income tax, a principle of taxation that has been widely adopted throughout the world. Education, or more precisely access to education, can also play an essential role. To be an effective equalizer, the educational system must be accessible to all people regardless of their economic or social standing.

When policies to redistribute income do not adequately reduce inequalities, governments can turn to the redistribution of productive assets, relying on land redistribution or employee stock option plans. In largely agrarian societies, land redistribution is often the key to redistributing wealth. Prominent among those using this device are Japan, South Korea, and Taiwan, countries that implemented thorough land reform programs as part of the reconstruction following World War II. Other countries, such as the United States, have brought about land redistribution indirectly through initiatives such as the Homestead Act. Although land reform is often the key to both wealth redistribution and successful rural development, it is also a politically formidable undertaking.

The selection of technologies often has an indirect impact on the distribution of wealth. For example, when Pakistan was granted a large loan by the World Bank to purchase four-wheel tractors of the sort used in Europe and the United States, the larger farmers, who were able to afford this equipment, acquired an advantage. With this tillage capability, many began looking for additional land to add to their holdings, often absorbing smaller farms, whose owners lacked mechanical power. The net effect was a further concentration of land in the hands of wealthier landowners. A more equitable alternative would have been to use the resources to import or domestically manufacture smaller two-wheel power tillers of the Japanese variety, an approach that would have helped smaller farmers remain competitive.

A similar situation exists with transportation planning. Given that there is not enough oil or other fuel to permit automobile fleets in the Third World to achieve the near-saturation levels of the United States or Western Europe, it is a mistake to invest heavily in an extensive automobile infrastructure that will benefit only a small fraction of a country's population. Social equity is better served by investing these same resources in an extensive public transportation system augmented by bicycles, mopeds, and motor scooters. Motorized three-wheel rickshas of the sort pioneered in India could be used as taxis.

Similarly, the selection of medical technologies influences the distribution of health-care services. If a country invests in a large modern hospital in its capital city it will be able to serve a small elite rather well but will lack the resources to provide any medical services at all to the bulk of the population. In the Philippines, for example, a $50-million heart-surgery center has been constructed at a time when many Filipinos lack access to even rudimentary health care. The waste is even greater because those Filipinos who can afford open-heart surgery prefer to fly to the United States for the operation rather than entrust themselves to local surgeons. Investing $50 million in village clinics and the training of paramedics could measurably reduce infant mortality and raise life expectancy in the Philippines.

In many Third World countries there is a particularly strong bias against rural areas that must be addressed. Urban areas invariably manage to command the lion's share of investment in public services. Development economist Michael Lipton points out that in India, for example, a youngster born in an urban setting is eight times more likely to gain admission to college than one born in a village. Similar contrasts can be found throughout the world in investment in basic social services such as education and health care.

As it becomes clearer that the world economy is not likely to resume the rapid growth of the last few decades, the emphasis in economic policymaking and development planning needs to shift toward efforts to satisfy basic needs if living conditions are to improve. The "basic needs" development strategy concentrates on nutrition, literacy, and health care. Social planners will need to acknowledge that for a person with a loaf of bread an additional crust is of little value, but for someone who has only a single crust of bread, a second crust can greatly improve the quality of life.

Countries with severely skewed income distribution patterns often lack social cohesiveness, making it difficult to mobilize for the achievement of specific goals. South Africa is facing this dilemma as it confronts a threatening population explosion. When commenting on a recent governmental commission report on projected population growth in South Africa, Professor David Welsh of the University of Capetown observed: "Reading the somber unemotive facts piled up by the science committee, one is made aware that we have a time bomb ticking away in our midst. If future populations are to control population growth the old order of racial supremacy and discrimination, of forced migrancy and poverty, of inadequate housing, and unequal education will all have to go." Without these social adjustments, the report concluded, it would be virtually impossible to bring fertility down fast enough to avoid a Malthusian catastrophe.

Given the grossly inequitable income distribution patterns in many Third World countries, the potential for social unrest and political unstability is high. This is painfully evident in Africa, where incomes are now falling in so many countries, and in Latin American countries with large external debts, where severe belt tightening measures are required to maintain credit-worthiness. At issue, as former U.S. Assistant Secretary of State C. William Maynes observes, is whether "the economic strains that Third World governments are experiencing are proving too great for existing political structures to sustain." In a world experiencing economic stresses more severe than any since the thirties, political stability may depend on reducing income disparity to a range that is morally acceptable and politically tenable.

Now Guns or Butter

The past generation has witnessed an unprecedented militarization of the world economy. Prior to World War II, military expenditures claimed less than 1% of gross world output. In 1983 they consumed 6 percent. In real terms, military expenditures increased some twentyfold between the early thirties and early eighties.

The militarization of the world economy, initially spurred by U.S.-Soviet rivalry, has spread to the developing world as well. Increasingly, countries are seeking security in military power. In 1983, this translated into global military expenditures of $663 billion, a sum that exceeds the combined income of the poorest half of mankind. This trend threatens society in two ways. As militarization and modernization have proceeded apace over the past generation, new weapons have evolved that possess an unprecedented destructive capacity. Much of this destructive potential is vested in some 50,000 nuclear weapons, 98% of them in the hands of the two superpowers.

The second threat to society from militarization is less direct, stemming from the diversion of resources away from pressing social needs. Swedish Under-Secretary of State Inga Thorsson, who chaired a U.N. group studying the relationship between disarmament and development, reports that the study "presents overwhelming evidence that contemporary military establishments significantly distort and undermine the very basis of sustained economic and social development in all countries." Every dollar spent for military purposes reduces the public resources available for other purposes. The implications of this are most evident at the national level. Although the United States leads the world in military expenditures, the military share of the Soviet economy is substantially larger, an estimated 9-10% compared with 6% for the United States. This drain of resources from agriculture and the consumer goods sector of the Soviet economy is leading to a markedly slower rate of progress than was achieved as recently as a decade ago.

For the United States, the diversion of investment capital to the arms-producing sector is depriving the remainder of the economy of investment capital. One consequence is that old plant and equipment is not being replaced, leading to a decline in the U.S. competitive position in the world economy. The competitive advantage in basic industries such as steel and automobiles is shifting toward countries with more modern, more energy-efficient plants and equipment. Economist Robert Lekachman observes that "the huge deficits engendered by imprudent tax cuts and even more misguided enlargement of the Pentagon rakeoff from the economy have turned the Treasury into a potential competitor for relatively scarce investment resources and contributed heavily to the skittishness of the financial markets."

At the global level, research expenditures devoted to the development of new weapon systems overshadow the strictly military share of the world economy. An estimated 23% of all investment in science and technology is designed to either improve existing weapon systems or develop new ones.

Some 500,000 of the world's finest scientists and engineers work in military research. Given the skill levels required in developing new weapon systems, it is likely that the share of top talent engaged in this destructive field of endeavor is well above the 22% of scientists involved overall. Not only do military expenditures dominate the global research and development budget, but they far exceed the combined research funds to develop renewable energy technologies, expand food output, and improve contraceptives.

Costly though these diversions of financial and scientific resources are, they may be matched by the claims that militarization makes on the time of political leaders. More and more of the working day of these individuals appears to be absorbed in attempts to resolve international conflict in one part of the world or another. Not only does conflict divert the energies of political leaders from other tasks, but the confrontational climate that exists, particularly between the two superpowers, is not conducive to the cooperative address of problems.

The progressive militarization of the world economy is also beginning to affect the stability and integrity of the international economic system. Weapons purchases have contributed to the burdensome debt with which many Third World countries are now saddled. Within the United States, growth in military expenditures during the early eighties has contributed heavily to the record fiscal deficits. It is certain to keep interest rates high in world financial markets for years to come, pushing debt-burdened Third World countries toward default. As of the mid-eighties the greatest single threat to world financial security may be the enormous U.S. fiscal deficit, part of it incurred in the name of national security.

The economic backdrop to militarization is changing. During the third quarter of this century, the world was able to have both more guns and more butter. Since 1978, however, world military expenditures have expanded at more than 4% per year in real terms, compared with 1.7% for the world economy. With per capita income for the world as a whole stagnating since 1979, increasing the military share of the gross world product has been possible only by reducing civilian consumption. It is this fundamental change in the economic backdrop against which resources are allocated between military and nonmilitary sectors that may force political leaders back to the drawing board in allocating priorities.

That military expenditures could expand when the economy is stagnating is an indication that the roots of militarization are deep in the body politic. Ruth Leger Sivard, compiler of the annual *World Military and Social Expenditures,* notes that "even long established democracies, where civilian control of the military is a firm tradition, are not immune to the effects of the military power they have created in the name of defense." Within national governments, departments or ministries of defense typically dominate the budgetary process.

Sivard notes that the arms-producing industry is "one of the most prosperous and powerful industries in the world today with unparalleled resources to influence political decisions. As sales agent for a burgeoning government sponsored trade in arms, it takes on important policy making functions which determine priorities both at home and in foreign countries." Countering the military-industrial complex that President Eisenhower warned about as he was leaving office will not be easy. Only when people become aroused in large numbers is the militarization of the world economy likely to be reversed. Rising public awareness of where current world military expenditures and policies could lead has translated into some of the largest political demonstrations and mass rallies ever held in Western Europe or the United States. New organizations are springing up on both sides of the Atlantic to counter what is perceived to be a dangerous drift of events.

Another possible hope for reversing the trend toward militarization lies with the International Monetary Fund (IMF) and the World Bank. The IMF in particular is gaining leverage in many Third World countries as they are forced to turn to it for investment capital. If their economic viability and capacity to service debt hinge on reducing military expenditures and foreign-exchange outlays for arms imports, the IMF may be able to turn national policies in a more rational direction.

Yet another possibility is the emergence of a strong national political leader or international figure who has the stature to turn the world away from militarization. An example of this process on a smaller scale is the way countries in Western Europe have successfully ended generations of enmity and conflict. In part this is due to postwar visionaries such as Jean Monnet who saw a European community as a solution. Exactly how the current worldwide conflict between the military goals of governments and people's aspirations for a better life will be resolved remains to be seen. But it seems clear that if militarization of the world economy continues, the social costs will be high.

One glimmer of hope in this field resides in Argentina, where the newly elected government, the first nonmilitary government in almost eight years, is planning to reduce military expenditures sharply. Shortly after his election on October 30, 1983, President-elect Raul Alfonsin announced plans to boost spending on education and welfare by cutting military spending. Should he succeed, he might be followed by other governments in similarly dire economic straits.

Priorities: Back to the Drawing Board

The mounting economic stresses of recent years make it clear that existing policies and priorities are not working well. In the absence of a massive reordering of priorities—one that shifts natural resources and political energies from the arms race to efforts to brake world population growth, to protect the agronomic and biological resource systems, and to spur the energy transition—economic conditions will almost certainly continue to deteriorate.

In many ways the human prospect is tied to two transitions—from primary dependence on fossil fuels to a reliance on renewable energy resources, and from an equilibrium of high birth and death rates to one of low birth and death rates. Completion of the former involves a restructuring of the global economy; the latter depends on basic changes in reproductive behavior.

As things are now going, the human prospect is being shaped by population growth, by the depletion of both renewable and nonrenewable resources, and by the arms race. Advances such as biotechnology, microcomputers, and the associated electronics revolution are sure to help shape the future, but the dominant influence will be the basic processes used to produce energy and food. German novelist Gunter Grass eloquently made this point in a lecture: "To be sure, we can make great new discoveries with our technological skill and scientific ability—we can split the atoms, see to the end of the universe, and reach the moon. But these milestones of human progress occur in the midst of a society sunk in a statistically proven barbarism. All those atom-splitters, those conquerers of space, those who punctually feed their computers and gather, store and evaluate all their data; none is in a position to provide sufficient food for the children of this world."

Faltering development strategies in the Third World can succeed only if they are reoriented. Auto-centered development models borrowed from the industrial countries and left over from the age of oil serve the needs of a small minority, an affluent elite. As Soedjatmoko, an Indonesian and rector of the United Nations University in Tokyo, has observed, industrial growth needs to be redirected toward meeting the needs of the majority. Such an industrial strategy would focus less on large tractors and more on two-wheel power tillers, less on automobiles and more on motor scooters and bicycles, less on nuclear power plants and more on simple solar water heaters. To be successful, each country needs to forge its own industrial development strategy, one responsive to its particular needs and circumstances.

A successful transition from fossil fuels to renewable energy will require a far more energy-efficient economy than now exists. In the past, developing countries everywhere could simply emulate the oil-centered energy economies of the industrial countries. Now, as they begin to move away from petroleum toward renewables, each country must tailor its energy plan to its indigenous endowment of replenishable energy resources. The transition to renewables can endow an economy with a permanence that oil-based societies lack. It could also lead the world away from the existing inequitable, inherently unstable international oil regime because renewable energy sources are locally available in all countries.

Completing the demographic transition—to low birth and death rates—is clearly possible, as a dozen countries have demonstrated. These societies have eliminated population growth as a source of ecological stress and resource scarcity. Not surprisingly, these 12 countries with zero population growth have highly equitable income distributions, all ranking near the top internationally. Their improvement in economic and social conditions has been so pervasive that no special effort was needed to bring population growth to a halt. Other major industrial countries outside Europe, such as the United States and the Soviet Union, however, have not reached zero population growth and do not yet have a policy for doing so. Within the Third World, some countries are making steady progress in bringing down birthrates, but only a few have adequate programs. If these countries are to stop population growth within an acceptable time frame, vigorous national leadership and strong incentives for smaller families will be required. Governments that fail are likely to see their efforts to improve living conditions overrun by the growth in human numbers

Given the obvious impact of rapid population growth on human welfare, it is inexcusable that an estimated two-thirds of all couples in the Third World, excluding China, still lack ready access to family planning services. An estimated fourfold increase in family planning expenditures—from $920 million to $3,700 million—is needed to make population stabilization a realistic goal. This increase of $2,800 million represents less than two days' worth of global military expenditures at the 1983 rate.

In the simplest terms, we are in a race to see if we can slow, and eventually halt, population growth before local life-support systems collapse. And we are in a race to reverse the nuclear arms buildup before we self-destruct. For many, the threatened decline in living standards has become a reality. Some countries have tried to postpone such declines by going heavily into debt. But over the long term, only a basic reformulation of development strategies, including population policies, will save us. It is no longer a matter of tinkerng with priorities. Only a thorough reordering will do.

The future is both discouraging and hopeful. With whole continents experiencing a decline in living standards, there is ample ground for pessimism. The worldwide loss of momentum in improving living conditions is not encouraging. Yet the problems we face are of our own making, and thus within our control. On the optimistic side, every threat to sustainability has been successfully addressed by at least a few countries. Even without any further advances in technology every major problem can be solved, every major human need satisfied. The issue is not technology or resources, but awareness and political will. Whether the future is bright and promising or dark and bleak hinges on how quickly we can mobilize politically to bring about the changes in policies and priorities that circumstances call for.

The Farmer and the Market Economy: The Role of the Private Sector in the Agricultural Development of LDCs

by

Orville L. Freeman

and

Ruth Karen

By the year 2000 the world's population will total six billion persons. They will have to exist and coexist on a planet where resources are limited, however ingenious man's use of them may be. Facing these facts, some planners are seriously considering the concept of triage, under which some sections of the earth, and the people living in them, are written off because it seems impossible to save them and still maintain a sustainable society for the rest of the planet.

The *triage* concept is proclaimed as realism, touted as the hardheaded ability to set priorities. The authors of this paper consider it morally repugnant, socially indefensible, politically dangerous, and economically irrational.

They would have to concede, however, that at present it exists in fact, as demonstrated by the devastating, if not frequently faced fact that only a decade ago, in the years 1972-1973, an estimated 500 million human beings perished from malnutrition and starvation. And unless effective practical measures are taken, the existing supply and demand equation between people and

Orville L. Freeman is president of Business International Corporation, New York, New York. Ruth Karen is vice president, Corporate Public Policy Division, Business International Corporation.

Index of World Grain Security, 1960-80

Year	Reserve Stocks of Grain	Grain Equiv. of Idled U.S. Cropland (million metric tons)	Total Reserves	Reserves As Days of World Consumption (days)
1960	198	36	234	102
1965	143	70	213	80
1970	165	71	236	77
1971	183	46	229	73
1972	142	78	220	66
1973	47	25	172	51
1974	132	4	136	40
1975	138	3	141	40
1976	192	3	195	55
1977	191	1	192	51
1978	228	21	249	62
1979	191	15	206	51
1980	151	0	151	40

Source: Worldwatch Institute, derived from U.S. Department of Agriculture data.

basic food grains can, and indeed inevitably must, produce a *triage* of comparable and even larger magnitude at any time.

The Situation Now

The index of World Grain Security, described in the chart below, quantifies the danger. The carry-over of reserves, measured in days of world consumption, dropped from 102 in 1960 to 40 in 1980. Total reserves dropped in that same period from 234 million metric tons to 151 million metric tons, and the grain equivalent of idle cropland in the U.S., the world's main supplier, shrank from a potential of 36 million metric tons to zero. At the present reserve level, the world is literally living from hand to mouth.

The situation holds an ominous price implication as well. Anytime there is a production shortfall from bad weather in several producing countries such as India, the U.S., Canada, the USSR, and Australia—over the long term an occurrence both frequent and inevitable—the impact will be felt all over the world, not only in a shortage of supply, but in the cost of what supplies there are. The price impact will be of major magnitude, matching and possibly exceeding the 200%-300% increase that took place in grain prices in 1973, when the world found itself facing this problem for the first time.

An Evanescent Glut

The apparent glut of agricultural products in 1982, and the softening of prices resulting from this glut, is a short-lived phenomenon with three causes. First, two successive extraordinary crop years in some countries, especially the U.S., and to a lesser extent India. Second, the widespread economic depression around the globe, which has weakened demand but not need. The stark reality is that a number of countries, and millions of people, need food but cannot afford to buy it under present economic conditions. What we have, in fact, is another instance of *de facto triage,* this time caused not by production shortfalls as it was a decade earlier, but by poverty in the most basic and brutal sense.

The third reason for the evanescent nature of the glut of 1982 is that there exist no *global* buffer stocks that could cushion the effects, for both producers and consumers, of the inevitable fluctuations of supply and demand. Agriculture, more than any other activity, is almost by definition a feast and famine undertaking that needs to be managed more rationally than it is at present. At present, only the United States has a meaningful program of organized storage. Grain on hand in the U.S. in 1982, including substantial stocks in farmer-owned reserves, is in the neighborhood of 70 million tons. This is enough to cushion the shock of significant crop shortfalls of the major producing countries for approximately one year. The situation would be much healthier if this carry-over were not concentrated in the U.S. but were spread around the world and constituted a global reserve.

(India is the only other country that, as a matter of policy, provides for a grain reserve on a systematic basis, but its level is relatively modest and not a major factor in meeting the needs of countries outside the Asian subcontinent.)

The pertinent point is that while the level of reserves in the U.S. in 1982 is roughly the same as it was in 1961 when one of the authors of this paper became U.S. Secretary of Agriculture, there are one billion more people in the world today than there were two decades earlier, and the global population is expanding at a rate considerably higher than it did in the 1960s. What may look like a glut viewed from the perspective of the U.S. farmer is, in fact, a minor and temporary adjustment in the deepening imbalance between global need and global production. The danger of these evanescent gluts is that they divert attention and distract concentration from the fundamentals—the inescapable realities of global demand and supply.

Demand

It is dramatically clear that the increase in world population, now 70 million each year, means continued demand pressure. What is not quite so obvious is that economic growth, with higher incomes for more people, also adds up to enormous demand pressure. There seems to be an almost immutable law that, as people's incomes climb, their dietary desires grow and they diversify their eating habits. Intake of animal proteins expands, and it is their production that is so enormously expensive in terms of the amount of grain consumed. This is true not only in the Western world, but also for the command economies, and it has evidenced itself emphatically in the advanced developing countries as well. A few figures will illustrate.

Per capita consumption of poultry has risen 24% in the developing countries in the last five years. One person consumes about 180 kilograms of grain each year if eaten directly, but if he or she has a meat-intensive diet, the grain demand more than quadruples to 750 kilograms. Such a diet on a worldwide basis is clearly not sustainable. As a matter of fact, if one extends the per capita acreage required to sustain the American diet (since 1976, U.S. consumption of beef has dropped 17% to a per capita intake of 112.6 pounds) to the rest of the world, twice the acreage the world has available per capita today would be necessary. Actually, more grain is fed to animals worldwide today than is consumed by the 1.4 billion people living in low-income countries. The proportion of grain for livestock doubled from about 20% of the world grain consumption in 1960-1961 to more than 40% in 1981, and is growing at twice the rate as grain consumption for food.

The Role of the USSR

What makes the present and future situation even more precarious is the entry of the USSR into the global grain market as a buyer in erratic but major quantities.

Beginning in 1972, a change in policy of the Soviet Union resulted in massive Soviet grain purchases. That year, Prime Minister Kosygin announced that the USSR had set the goal of increasing the protein intake of its people from 25% of the U.S. standard to one-half of the U.S. level, primarily by making available animal proteins. This meant that the USSR would henceforth consume an additional 25 million tons of grain annually. In 1973, the Soviets had a major crop shortfall and moved into world markets, buying grain carefully and, in the United States, secretly. The impact on world supply that year was sharp, for the Soviets did in fact acquire 25 million tons of grain. There were modest crop shortfalls in a few other places around the world that year and these, combined with the new Soviet demand, caused a 200%-300% percent increase in the price of grain. Another result was that about 25 million additional tons of grain moved from the United States into export to fill the gap in demand, and the U.S. cattle industry suffered grievously as a result.

Since that time, Soviet purchases have continued to be a major ingredient of world demand, ranging from 25 to 40 million tons a year. And it is almost certain that Soviet import demands will continue to grow for the foreseeable future. Soviet agriculture is very inefficient, and there is no evidence that the structural changes required to improve efficiency will be made. The USSR will therefore constitute a serious drag on world food supply not only for the short term, but certainly for the medium term and, it now appears, for the long term as well.

Also in recent years, the People's Republic of China has entered the world market on the demand side. While Chinese purchases are for the present limited by foreign exchange constraints, the needs of the still-growing Chinese population clearly cannot be met by local agricultural production. Indeed, economic plans of China foresee increasing food imports. What the magnitude of this addition to the demand side will be is difficult to determine, but it is significant at minimum and at maximum staggering.

And the Developing World

Adding to the increasingly skewed demand/supply balance is the turnaround exhibited by the three developing-country continents—Asia, Africa and Latin America—from being food exporters to becoming food importers. The chart below tells the story.

The Changing Pattern of World Grain Trade*

Region	1934-38	1948-52	1960	1970	1980
North America	+5	+23	+39	+56	+131
Latin America	+9	+1	0	+4	−10
E. Europe & USSR	+5	0	0	0	−46
Africa	+1	0	−2	−5	−15
Asia	+2	−6	−17	−37	−63
Australia and N.Z.	+3	+3	+6	+12	+19

*Plus sign indicates net exports; minus sign, net imports.

Source: Food and Agriculture Organization, U.S. Department of Agriculture, and Worldwatch Institute estimates.

Supply

It is true that on an overall global basis, using cumulative figures, the world has increased grain productivity to match population, and may even have inched ahead on a global per capita basis. But the figures expressing this become both different and dismal when a substantial number of developing countries are examined. Such a review will show that well over a third of the nations of the world, primarily in Africa and South Asia, have lost ground over the past decade in the race to feed their people. In some of these countries the problem goes much deeper than the export/import balance illustrated on a continental basis in the figures cited above. In these countries, production has not only fallen on a per capita basis but has gone down in absolute terms.

The latest assessment of the situation comes from Edward Somma, director general of the Food and Agricultural Organization (FAO), who notes that in 31 of the least developed countries, agricultural production in the past decade crept up by a mere 1.6% a year, while population increased at a rate of 2.6%. It is in these countries, where starvation is a constant threat, that increased production is a vital and urgent necessity.

On a global basis, the worrisome fact on the supply side is that overall growth in recent years has not matched the historic level of 3% per year that was achieved in the period of 1950-1970. Instead, growth shrank to less than 2% during the 1970s. This worldwide loss of agricultural momentum is serious in itself. Even more serious are the gathering forces behind the decrease. Soil erosion is taking its toll on productivity. Returns on the use of chemicals and fertilizer appear to have reached the margin of utility in many high production areas. The promise of new agricultural technology is modest for the moment. The increase in the price of oil and energy will continue to have its effect on production, directly as an element of cost, and probably in the way of competition, as many countries move cropland into the production of ethanol.

The Limits of the U.S. Breadbasket

Even the almost miraculous capacity of North America to respond to demand may ultimately be overwhelmed. Cropland in the U.S. is under growing pressure. The program to use U.S. grain in alcohol fuel distilleries appears to command considerable public support and may become a strong competitor for grain supplies. A decline in irrigated acreage in key farm states threatens production levels. An increasing number of agriculture analysts and environmentalists in the U.S. are arguing, in an intriguing parallel with oil producers, that it makes little sense to increase U.S. productivity at the expense of undermining the soil with growing erosion from heavy production practices. This argument holds that the current generation of farmers has no right to press for increased production, when that production is the agronomic equivalent of deficit financing and of mortgaging the future of generations to come. This line of thought notes that what is taking place now is fraught with risk, both for those whose livelihood depends on the land remaining productive and for countries and people who are becoming dependent on food imports that may well be unobtainable if productivity drops in the U.S. from the current rate.

A Possible Solution

What then is the solution to the horror of widespread hunger and continued *de facto triage?*

The fact is that there *is* unexploited potential for food production in the world, and that new attitudes, new policies, and new strategies are needed to turn potential into production.

At present, only one-half of the world's good arable land is actually being farmed. Most of the other half does not have the necessary infrastructure, and opening it up will require major capital investment. Nonetheless, the potential is there. In many parts of the developing world, productivity is at a level of only one-third of demonstrated potential. The key question is where, and how, increased production can take place. To date, major increases in productivity have, for the most part, been achieved in the industrialized countries. Most projections predict a continuation of this trend, i.e., surplus production in developed countries and increasing deficits in developing countries. The world food problem cannot be solved if that happens. Only if the developing countries—especially the 60 countries pinpointed by FAO—where massive population growth is taking place, and where the majority of the planet's people now live, increase their production sharply can the food-people crisis be met and the food-people balance restored.

Harnessing the Dynamic of the Private Sector

How can such a production increase be achieved in time? The authors believe that it can only be done by harnessing the dynamic of the private sector, specifically by creating a symbiosis of corporate know-how, farmer devotion to the land, and sound government policy. Such a partnership, joining the profit disciplines of large companies, the industry of small-holders, and solid government support, would get the results that are so clearly, indeed so desperately needed.

As the Fourth Woodlands Conference on the Sustainable Societies notes:

> The importance of the private sector in the resolution of world problems is difficult to overemphasize. The private sector has resources and management talent that dwarf those available to most governments. Furthermore, the private sector has fewer constraints on innovation than does the public sector. The contributions and opportunities within the private sector have often been under-appreciated.

In agriculture, a private sector resolution of world problems means mobilizing small-holders—and in most developing countries this means families that cultivate 1-5 hectares—around a corporate core that effectively moves these farmers from subsistence agriculture into the market economy as both producers and consumers, with all the developmental multiplier effects this implies, socially as well as economically.

The Evidence Exists

A conscientious world survey of global agriculture would demonstrate beyond a shadow of a doubt that the private sector—ranging all the way from the providers of credit, inputs, and extension services, through the farmers who produce on their land, to entrepreneurs who store, process, and market agricultural products—has played the key role in accomplishing what progress there has been on the agricultural front. And, without belittling the contributions made by tropical plantation agriculture and, in some cases, large-scale operations in temperate zones, in the main the successes in agriculture have come from the efforts and accomplishments of the family farm.

The definition of what constitutes a family farm varies by country and culture, by the availability of land, the existence of infrastructure, and the technological and educational level of the rural population.

In the U.S., a family farm is defined as an enterprise run by one family, with no more than 1-1/2 man-years of outside labor, and large enough to utilize modern technology and production. Whatever the definition, two factors seem to be incontrovertible. One is that large production units and collectivism as a social and economic structure do not work well. The latest example of this is East Germany, where the regime merged 800,000 farming units, mostly family farms, into 4,000 "agricultural factories" averaging 5,000 hectares. This was done in 1955, with the result that today East Germany imports up to 4 million tons of grain a year, mainly from the U.S., since the USSR has none to spare. The imports eat up 20% of East Germany's hard-currency earnings and have prompted Chairman Erich Honecker to declare, in July 1982: "Today, one can compare the grain problem with the oil problem in terms of priority."

The second incontrovertible fact seems to be that something about the agricultural producer and his relation to the land is *sui generis*.

But the farmer and his land, however strong the bond between them, do not constitute an economic or social island. Fair market conditions, and access to technology, credit, the appropriate chemical inputs, the required physical infrastructure—in all of which government attitudes and policies inevitably play a role—are part of the system in which the individual producer can get the desirable results. Where such a system is in place; where the combination of access to supplies and to the market exists; where government policies recognize the importance of stable and reasonable prices, the individual producer, whose reward is clearly the product of his own effort, has demonstrated initiative and creativity that have delivered results unmatched by any other approach.

This is true not only in the United States, but in countries with different traditions and cultures such as Taiwan, South Korea, and Israel. In each case, however, the basic components of success were the same: a private sector encouraged by sensitive and effective government support to stimulate productivity.

The question, then, is how can the private sector be mobilized for action in the 60-odd countries that fall under the general rubric of "The Fourth World," and be motivated to create the productive agricultural sector that is so clearly needed? Specifically, how can small-holders, families that cultivate 1-5 hectares (which, for the present, is a working definition of the family farm in these countries), be organized and energized to increase their productivity?

The authors are convinced that the answer is an integrated system in which a corporate core serves to move individual farmers from subsistence agriculture into the market economy.

In this system, private sector companies—processors and/or marketers of foodstuffs and industrial crops—develop in areas of potential productivity an integrated operation. They reach agreement with small producers, guaranteeing a market at a fair price, providing credit, technology, inputs such as fertilizers, herbicides, and seeds, assistance in soil preparation, harvesting, storage, and, finally, services in moving the product to processing and market. In some parts of the world, where land is abundant, small-holders who participate in such a scheme develop the know-how to move out of their mini-plots and learn to manage larger tracts of land, graduating into larger family-size farmers. This is not a process that takes place overnight. It requires long-term planning, infrastructure in place, and dependable government support so that investments made by the private sector and responsibly carried forward are protected for the long haul. If it is to succeed, it requires, in addition, the involvement and support of the entire rural community.

The key is a holistic approach, with a broad involvement of people, particularly women, who do an estimated 78% of the farming in most developing countries and whose willingness and capacity to make necessary changes have been demonstrated time and again when they have been properly approached and mobilized. Once increased production brings money into the pockets of small producers, production techniques spread rapidly throughout the community, stimulating a host of related economic activities that, in turn, provide jobs for the landless and build new markets. The process can multiply wealth rapidly, creating a win-win situation with four dimensions:

1. A substantial increase in the living standard of small-holders.

2. An important contribution to the sound development of the host country.

3. A profitable undertaking for the core company.

4. An input into righting the precarious food demand/supply balance.

How It Works

There are at least a dozen case histories on the three developing continents of Latin America, Africa, and Asia to illustrate how such an undertaking of small-holders grouped around a corporate core works. Six are cited here.

In Latin America

Gulf & Western

A classic is Gulf & Western's sugarcane enterprise in the Dominican Republic, with a history of more than six decades. The Gulf & Western undertaking also illustrates how such ventures have evolved over time.

Gulf & Western's sugarcane operations now include a sugar mill and refinery, a nucleus plantation consisting of 50,000 acres owned by Gulf & Western, and an additional 24,000 acres owned by independent growers who have individual contracts with Gulf & Western. The company has organized small-holder production and trained Dominican personnel to help supervise and manage all aspects of sugarcane growing, cutting, processing, and manufacturing. Operations are so technologically and managerially advanced that the efficiency with which the sugarcane is produced, transported, and processed has made the Gulf & Western operation the optimum sugarcane refinery in the world.

Thirty-five percent of the land utilized for Gulf & Western's sugarcane operation is owned by independent growers. The company has a four-year contract with each grower, which guarantees purchase of the crop by the company at the market price. Payments due Gulf & Western for tools, fertilizers, insecticides, and other production or harvesting support are deducted from the payment made to the farmer at harvest time.

Independent growers on contract with Gulf & Western have strict terms under which their sugarcane must be grown. Specifications on the amount and type of fertilizers to be used are stringently enforced. Cultivation and harvesting practices are closely monitored to meet quality standards. Technological assistance is given to farmers from the beginning of the sugarcane season until the crop is harvested, including cane cutting techniques. Gulf & Western has a sophisticated Agricultural Investigation Department specializing in sugarcane. The technicians of that department work with the farmers in the field, training them how to utilize their land to the fullest and ensuring the finest quality of sugarcane.

Gulf & Western finances the farmers for all their sugarcane production. The farmers are free to raise other crops, and many of them do. These other crops are financed by the government-owned Agricultural Bank, and a number of commercial banks will also provide loans to farmers with multi-crop fields.

In the Dominican Republic, an important ingredient in sugar processing is the use of oxen. Gulf & Western utilizes approximately 16,000 head of oxen in the sugarcane fields at harvesting time. The company owns some 50,000-60,000 head of oxen, and many independent cane farmers also raise cattle. They are supported by the company's livestock department, which trains the farmers and provides financial backing for a program that sells calves at cost to cattle raisers who are also sugarcane farmers.

In the late 1970s, Gulf & Western formed an agricultural cooperative with the sugarcane growers. At present, 1,000 members own stock in this co-op. The co-op owns approximately 35,000 acres of land, which is utilized only for the production of sugarcane.

In the 1970s, the company also extended its activities both horizontally and vertically. The horizontal extension consists of social services, including medical, educational, and recreational facilities as well as housing projects. The vertical extension includes the creation of an Industrial Free Zone on Gulf & Western land, which by the early 1980s had created about 10,000 jobs, of which the overwhelming majority are held by women.

Philip Morris

Another relevant enterprise in the Dominican Republic now going through an interesting process of evolution is the joint venture subsidiary of Philip Morris International, E. Leon Jimenes, C. pro A.

E. Leon Jimenes has contracts with 136 farmers who grow tobacco. Contracts are renegotiated every two years, when prices are adjusted for inflation, production costs, and world market fluctuations.

The tobacco is brought to E. Leon Jimenes' warehouse facilities, where the farmer receives an established price after the tobacco has been inspected. The amount the farmer receives is credited to his account. Payments owed to Jimenes for production inputs such as seed, fertilizers, insecticides, etc., are deducted from the farmer's balance. At the end of the season, the farmer can choose between a monetary payment or a credit balance. If he has a debit balance, the company carries him into the next season.

To grow tobacco, each farmer needs an irrigation system. The company provides financial assistance for the farmer to purchase the necessary supplies and equipment to irrigate his crop. This assistance is usually made on a four-year basis, but, when necessary, is extended to six years.

E. Leon Jimenes purchases tobacco only from farmers who have received technical assistance on how the crop is to be raised. Agronomists from the company visit each section (13 square miles) every two days during planting, growing, and harvesting season to ensure the farmer is proceeding as instructed. Farmers have been taught how to use a specific kind of seedbed, fertilizer, and insecticides. In 1981, farmers associated with the company produced 1,800 pounds of tobacco at $1.16 per pound, which worked out to an income of approximately $1,300.00 per acre.

In the Dominican Republic, this constitutes an extraordinary economic return for a farmer, made even more extraordinary by the fact that tobacco is a seasonal crop with a growing season of only three to four months. The parent company, Philip Morris International, and the Dominican Government believe that farmers can, and should, double-crop their tobacco fields with food crops. The parent company points out that "the rotation of tobacco with food crops cuts down on disease build-up more prevalent in the one-crop field. Such rotation also allows the grower to take fuller advantage of fertilizers used for tobacco crops, thereby lowering expenses for food production."

E. Leon Jimenes is now working on plans to teach its contract farmers the complexities of double cropping.

Concurrently, the company's social contributions have been extensive, both in range and amount. The range runs from a visiting nurses program to the construction of farm-to-market roads, from the establishment of a retirement home, the first in the community, to the contribution of paintings to the local cathedral. Social contributions also include educational, medical, and recreational facilities; support of local artistic and athletic endeavors; and substantial ongoing support for the local university, particularly the faculty that teaches business, agro-economics, and agribusiness.

The amounts involved are in the vicinity of $300,000.

In Africa

BAT

In Nigeria, the British American Tobacco Co. (BAT) operates on the assumption that "developing countries will depend on the private sector to reach their objectives and multinational corporations will need to do their part to help. From the coporate point of view to create wealth and good will makes good commercial sense." BAT has had in place for decades a system of building and supporting a network of satellite farmers in Nigeria, constructed on much the same model as that of Philip Morris in the Dominican Republic.

In 1978, the company took the system one step further. It started a pilot project in the village of Ekwetso, in which the farmers, villagers, and chiefs agreed to the company's suggestion that better land utilization and crop yields could be obtained if a parcel of land, in this case 100 hectares, were to be made available for mechanical bush clearing and land preparation, rather than the traditional method of manually hoeing between shrubs and trees.

It was made clear from the start that the land would continue to belong to the community, but that each farmer and his family would be allocated his own hectare of land on which he would be solely responsible for all cultivation practices and that the individual farmer would then reap the results of his efforts.

This was not to be a cooperative farm, but a farm where individual efforts were rewarded by the increase in yield while, at the same time, cooperation between farmers was essential. Hence "cooperation" but not "cooperative." From the outset, the farmers were enthusiastic, and with the back-breaking task of hand hoeing and hand stumping removed from them, the farmers and their families were able to concentrate on the raising of seedlings in nurseries and the planting out, fertilizing, weeding, and cultivating of their crop, followed by the harvesting and marketing of their produce. In the first year, with 20 of the 100 hectares under the scheme and 20 farmers and their families involved, the yield per hectare more than doubled and the work of the farmers became easier and more interesting and, of course, much more rewarding.

At present, the company envisions such "Block Farms," utilizing 150-200 hectares, on a three-year crop rotational basis. The company has introduced new high-yield varieties of food crops, such as maize, millet, groundnut, cowpea, yam, and cassava, and in most areas two and even three different crops are grown on the same piece of land in the same year. In fact, farmers who previously only produced a single tobacco crop of half an acre, together with a minimal patch of maize and yams, now produce one hectare of tobacco followed by maize, with one hectare of cassava or yam followed by groundnuts, etc., on the second plot. The third plot lies fallow.

An interesting multiplier effect both in terms of encouraging local entrepreneurship and creating additional income for individual growers was witnessed by one of the authors in a visit to Nigeria to observe first hand the farm block system. He discovered that mechanical equipment had been financed by the company to be owned and operated by individual growers who, in turn, contracted with their fellow farmers for the performance of the required mechanized services. A conversation with the owner/driver of a tractor revealed that the man carried a substantial mortgage on his machine and was going to make certain it would get the best and fullest possible use.

The next stage in the BAT block farm system will be to encourage an adequate marketing structure to ensure that all farm produce can be sold at a viable price. Already a suitable and inexpensive grain storage system has been demonstrated and accepted by the farmers.

Meanwhile, the socio-economic multiplier effects are clearly visible. Local houses now have windows and permanent roofs. Participating farmers have acquired bicycles and even a few motorbikes. Most important, more of the community's children are going to school and attending school for longer periods.

Booker McConnell

Another example in Africa of small farmers organized around a corporate core is the Mumias Sugar Co. in Kenya. Majority equity in Mumias is held by the government of Kenya, a minority share by the UK Commonwealth Development Corporation, the British counterpart to U.S. AID, and a minimum share by Booker Agriculture International. The concept, the technological input, and the management are all contributions of Booker McConnell, a leading UK-based agribusiness firm.

The Mumias Sugar Corporation was formed in June 1971. Ten years later, 16,000 associated farmers produced 163,000 tons of sugar.

The historical background is instructive.

The government of Kenya's decision to establish a cane sugar industry in the Nzoia Valley of the Western Province was made in 1965. The objectives were national self-sufficiency in sugar and the economic development of one of the more heavily populated and impoverished areas of the country. In addition, it was clear by the mid-1960s that the existing cooperative organization of cane production and refining was seriously defective and that other means for project development and management should be explored.

At that stage, the government approached Booker McConnell to develop what became the Mumias Sugar Corporation (MSC).

From the outset, the paramount criterion for MSC was efficiency. Farmers were involved in MSC only if, first, they had at least 1.2 hectares of land suitable for growing sugarcane, while still having enough land to leave an equivalent amount to produce food crops, and, second if the farmer could, and would, join with his neighbors to form cane plots of at least six hectares to permit economic use of mechanical plows and reduce cane transport costs.

The functions carried out by MSC and charged to outgrowers when the crop is sold are:

1. Plot selection and surveying.
2. Plowing, harrowing, and furrowing.
3. Delivery of seed cane.
4. Fertilizer delivery, around 200 kg. per acre for initial dressing and 100 kg. per acre for use 3-4 months later.
5. Cane harvesting and stacking.
6. Loading and transporting cane to the factory.
7. Extension staff and other outgrower administration cost.

MSC was profitable in its first full year and from the beginning substantially exceeded expectations in all critical aspects. Cane yields on the estate and among outgrowers, total harvested area, and factory conversion rates were favorable, enabling the output, of milled sugar to be above the original estimates by 63% in 1973, 45% in 1974, and some 21% in 1975. Despite the additional production of cane and unforeseen inflation, costs of harvesting and transport were 26% under budget in 1973 and 4% in 1974. The 75,000-ton expansion of mill capacity originally intended for 1979 was completed during 1976. Permanent employees of MSC are now approaching 4,500. In addition, the scheme provides jobs for some 4,000 casual laborers, mainly for cane harvesting on outgrowers' land. In 1979, MSC was directly providing permanent or temporary work for over 21,000 people who, together with their families, probably represent more that 5% of the two million people of the Western Province.

An assessment of the Mumias enterprise made in 1982 by Simon Williams, president of the Center for Rural Development Inc. of Fort Collins, Colorado, concludes that, while some social problems had developed around the scheme—including the desire of more farmers than the company can absorb to become outgrowers for Mumias—"the design of MSC . . . provides an inspirational model, to be replicated, with sugar or other crops as the raw material base, in many parts of the world. . . . Agribusiness, particularly multinational corporations, could exercise a powerful new force in efforts to alleviate poverty, hunger and alienation."

In Asia

The interesting aspect of the case histories in Asia is that they have succeeded in countries such as India, with a socialist cast to their economic policies, and that at least two governments have emulated the system—Malaysia and Indonesia—with results that are initially encouraging but still inconclusive.

In Malaysia, a government resettlement scheme of Bumiputra (Malay) farmers, ambitious in scope, worked well in the beginning, but after about 10 years, bureaucratic administration seems to have gone slack, and a host of problems have begun to appear as a result. Whether and how these will be resolved remains an open question at this point.

In Indonesia, the government is using old oil palm plantations as the core unit for the resettlement of farmers from crowded Java. That scheme is still in a stage too early for useful assessment. Both the Malaysian and the Indonesian experiments have financial and technical backing from the World Bank.

Castle & Cooke

The classic private sector undertaking in an unimpeded market economy in Asia is Castle & Cooke's successful transfer to the Philippines of its experience in Honduras. In Honduras, a subsidiary of Hawaii-based Castle & Cooke, the Standard Fruit and Steamship Company, began banana production at the beginning of the century, initially on a plantation basis. The company shifted to a system of contract production in the late 1960s, contracting—and providing a broad spectrum of technical assistance (specialized agronomists; aerial fumigation; training in bulb treatment; installation and maintenance of packing plants in production areas; supplying packaging materials, transport, supervision, and quality control)—both to individual farmers and to a smallholder cooperative. In the 1970s, the company introduced the same system to the Philippines, in southern Mindanao.

In Mindanao, Standard established a Philippine corporation with substantial minority interests held by Philippine citizens. The company imported seed from its Central American operations, established and operated a seedbed and demonstration farm, and constructed packing sheds and a transportation system. It then contracted with individual farmers for the production of bananas, supplying these farmers with the specially developed seed, providing the required technical and agricultural services, and assisting in arranging the required financing. The company also developed irrigation and distribution systems.

The Castle & Cooke operation in the Philippines demonstrates the extra dimension of development created by the company's core processing facility. At that facility, unskilled Filipino laborers are trained in semi-skilled and skilled jobs such as mobile equipment operators, stationary equipment operators, mechanics, machinists, electricians, and other trade jobs, as well as in clerical and laboratory skills. Finally, production employees are trained in supervisory skills, and professional jobs are provided up to and through doctorate degrees to university graduates in the fields of agriculture, engineering, sciences, accounting, and management.

Richardson-Vick

In India, Connecticut-based Richardson-Vick, through its subsidiary Richardson Hindustan, pioneered the development of mentha farming, using the small farmer system.

After a nationwide survey, the company selected a tract of land in north India, which until recently had been jungle. Unlike most farm tracts in India, which, having been farmed for generations, have an entrenched ownership pattern, this one was settled by Army retirees. Since they had been exposed to a new culture and modern techniques, they accepted modern farming techniques more easily than the traditional Indian peasant. The company set up a research center and successfully developed an acclimatized variety of the plant, which until then had been grown mainly in Brazil.

In 1965-1966, the company went to the field. It persuaded the farmers to switch to the new crop, promising them an assured market—at prices competitive with other crops—and technical guidance to teach them how to cultivate mentha. Interestingly enough, it faced indirect competition from the World Bank, which had selected the area for production of hybrid wheat and paddy seed. The company responded by developing a unique method to permit crop rotation of mentha with the hybrid wheat.

Initially, the company had planned to work with a few large farmers, believing that they would be easier to convince to use new production techniques and that it would alleviate administrative problems. However, the company found that most large farmers were absentee landlords, and the actual farming was left to rather unmotivated managers. Since mentha is a management-intensive crop, the managers found it too much trouble. Also, the company's meticulous record-keeping of inputs and output sometimes clashed with the reports the managers made to the farm-owner and obviated opportunities for cheating. The managers discouraged the farm-owners from growing mentha.

At that point, the company reached out to small farmers, whom it provided with plant stock, fertilizer, pesticides, loans for other inputs such as tube wells, and, importantly, consistent and continued extension services. The company field force, most of them traveling by motorcycle, contacts each farmer every 10 days. Personal relationships have been established, creating trust between the farmers and extension service personnel. Some 8,000 farmers are now involved in the system, working about 20,000 acres of land. All of the mentha is grown either on a rotational basis with traditional food crops, or on a multi-crop basis. The incomes of the farmers have tripled.

In addition, the company pioneered the on-site processing of mentha by developing an energy-balanced, mini-distillation unit that uses mentha waste as fuel and the fuel waste as fertilizer. It sold these units at subsidized rates to groups of mentha farmers. Today, 120 of these energy-balanced miniplants are operated by the mentha growers, giving them additional income.

Lessons Learned

Global experience—with the case histories cited merely illustrative of some approaches and achievements—makes it possible to deduce a set of lessons learned that can constitute a framework for action. They are offered here, subsumed in four categories: Operations; Systems; Policies; and Essential Insights.

Operations

To achieve a successful symbiosis between a corporate core and a network of small-holder farmers, the following are mandatory:

1. A firm, clear agreement between the farmers and the company. Under this agreement, the farmer must commit himself to adopt the company's techniques and practices to grow the product. He must commit himself as well to prompt harvesting and delivery to make possible a continuous flow of product to the processing facility.

The company, for its part, must contract for the product at a fair and equitable price level and make a dependable commitment to provide credit, inputs, and technical assistance. The details of such agreements inevitably vary, depending on crop, conditions, country and culture, but the contract must conform as far as possible to local practices and values.

2. An efficient and specialized advisory service that constantly reviews the training and supervision of the farmers, as well as

the corporate staff, in the production, processing, and marketing facets of the operation. Such an advisory service can also interpret the organization to the community and can communicate to all parties the importance of performance and the advantages that will result to participants in the enterprise from performance. Conversely, it can advise the company on people and community problems that may arise.

3. Efficient management of the operation, from soil preparation to marketing of the final product, is, and must be seen to be, the responsibility of the company. Management is critical and, historically, has been the most serious shortfall in carrying such satellite farming programs forward successfully. Companies must make top level managers available to run these enterprises.

4. A comprehensive research facility that can explore the latest technology and instruct and assist farmers in the application of the best production practices. This is a vital ingredient in upping both farmer income and corporate profitability.

Systems

1. The most important systematic element for success is market orientation. The needs of the market must be rigorously identified and measured before a project is launched. There are many distressing examples of decision-makers concentrating on production capacity without identifying and defining the market. A project won't work if the cart gets before the horse, which is what happens when production takes priority over the market. Both production capacity and market capacity must be established at the outset of any project.

2. Overall management, including allocation and coordination of all inputs, whether for production, processing, marketing, social, or infrastructure purposes, must be in the hands of a single authority.

3. A long-term orientation is required from all participants. For the company this means a stretch-out of profit expectations; for the farmer it means accepting instruction and guidance for a protracted period.

4. All agricultural projects have a social and cultural dimension that is different from industrial undertakings. Management must recognize and address this dimension from the outset. Failure to do so will haunt the enterprise and can threaten its viability in the long term.

Policies

In the industrialized countries, aid programs focused on agriculture should secure maximum participation from the private sector to assure the most dynamic approach and the most effective results. The system of satellite farmers grouped around a corporate core is probably the most efficacious system extant, and the experience of companies that have successfully implemented this system can be made available to other firms to enlist their interest and abbreviate their learning curve.

Governments of industrialized countries with aid programs designed for the agricultural sector can actively approach agricultural and agribusiness companies with demonstrated records of know-how and performance, making clear to these companies that the government assigns high priority to effective agricultural undertakings in the developing world and is prepared to undergird this priority with credit facilities and perhaps also with insurance and other mechanisms that ameliorate the corporate risk in these long-term and often politically vulnerable undertakings. Specifically, the governments of industrialized countries should make clear to companies prepared to take the risk that the home government will do its best to see to it that host governments honor their commitments related to agricultural enterprise. In the U.S., the Bureau of Private Enterprise in the Agency for International Development is giving serious consideration to providing this kind of support to companies prepared to launch agricultural undertakings based on the small-holder satellite system. Other industrialized countries should adopt the same policy.

In addition to mobilizing and supporting their own private sector companies willing to undertake agricultural projects in developing countries, the industrialized nations should also support the host countries that welcome these enterprises. Such support could take the form of assistance to the host government for farm-to-market roads, irrigation, and social and educational services in the rural areas. It could include support of training for the agricultural sector at educational institutions and perhaps even on-site training provided by the companies under a special contract.

International institutions—particularly development banks, which have credit, prestige, and experience—should put their considerable muscle behind such undertakings. The World Bank, for example, can be a powerful force, with great influence on the host country, to facilitate the necessary follow-through on commitments made and to resist the inevitable political meddling that occurs in developing countries when real change takes place.

Host country policies are, of course, basic. Today, the political leadership in most of the developing countries recognizes that food production is a key to progress and that a healthy agricultural sector is an inescapable factor in sound economic development. The recognition was long in coming, and in too many cases. the gap is still wide between rhetoric and action. Each of the case histories cited in this paper did have a measure of host country support. In each of them, also, that support could have been more emphatic and more effective. It will be necessary to bridge the gap between rhetoric and action in the developing countries to attract companies with production and processing know-how and marketing expertise to commit themselves to the substantial risks involved in such agricultural enterprises with their complexities and long-term payouts.

Essential Insights

There are five keys to understanding the full meaning and impact of agriculture and the way in which agricultural effort can be made optimally successful. They are:

1. Agriculture is the key to economic development. No country, with the exception of a few city-states, has ever prospered and built a sound economy without a solid agricultural base.

2. Agriculture is different. The forces with which agriculture must contend and which it must mold and master are quite different from the forces affecting industry. Agriculture is subject to outside, uncontrollable elements such as weather, disease, and pests. Also, farmers, like other raw material producers, have a relatively weak bargaining position, falling short of the return that processors and marketers of raw materials get from the marketplace. Management in agriculture is difficult. It is much easier to manage and produce efficiently using 10,000 men in a factory on one acre of land than it is to manage 1,000 people on 10,000 acres of land. This is why large-scale producing units are extremely difficult to operate efficiently and profitably. The family farm, with a land holding adequate to apply modern technology effectively, is the most productive size. The incentive that results when the producer benefits directly from his efforts cannot be duplicated by large holdings, whether they are privately held, communal, cooperative, or state-owned. Results from the factory-size organization of state farms and large collectives in the USSR are dramatic demonstrations of how not to organize agriculture.

3. Sound agricultural policies are difficult to develop and carry out. The time span required to put into place an appropriate land-people balance; to make available credit and necessary inputs to the grower; and to construct storage, processing, and marketing capacity, is longer than the usual time span of a political office holder. In addition, carrying out a sound, meaningful agricultural policy calls for changes that, by their very nature, shake up traditional patterns, resulting in fierce resistance.

4. A system whereby the producer on the soil benefits directly from his efforts is the single most important element in increasing productivity. In most places in the world, this means producer-ownership and requires egalitarian land policies adequately supported by the government. Taiwan, Japan, and Korea are examples of success where this principle has been followed.

5. Concentration on the small farmer is the key to success in increasing productivity around the world and in meeting the threat of world famine.

Conclusion

It is clear that the world stands at an important crossroad as we move further into the decade of the 1980s. Half a billion human beings are seriously malnourished in a world that could banish hunger, that has the resources, both physical and technological, to do so. The authors of this paper hold that this situation is not only unnecessary, it is unacceptable—morally, socially, and politically. Yet, as this is being written, there is no meaningful approach that promises results in a reasonable time frame for the 60-odd least developed countries in which this human tragedy is taking place.

It is the contention of the authors that the traditional means of increasing productivity on the land, and of reaching out to develop new land, are not adequate to meet the need. The private sector can, indeed must, play a leading role. Management and technological know-how are the special strengths of multinational companies in the agricultural sector, where strong home offices can provide the necessary support for field operations anywhere.

The writers' on-site observations and research have led them to conclude that satellite farming, with small-holders in a symbiotic relationship to a corporate core, is operating successfully throughout the world and in a range of commodities. It has demonstrated its viability and desirability.

Particular methods will vary with time and place, but necessary always are supportive relationships that run from home and host country, through international organizations and local communities, to the company and the farmers directly involved in the enterprise.

In a world that has come to recognize that agriculture is the foundation of solid economic progress, there is reason to believe that this system, if applied widely and targeted primarily at the critical countries of the Fourth World, would produce meaningful results.

The initiative should come from the industrialized countries. If they conclude that the system outlined in this paper is viable and that it constitutes a realistic method of involving the private sector and its productive dynamic in the task at hand, they should give this approach primary emphasis in their bilateral aid programs.

The same reasoning applies to the world's multinational assistance instruments, such as the World Bank, the regional development banks, and the entire U.N. system.

There is little doubt that the developing countries would respond to such an initiative. It would be extremely difficult in such circumstances for the political leadership in developing countries to sidestep commitments made. The full glare of international attention would be focused on their living up to agreements. This, in turn, would make it possible for companies to run the risks involved in such enterprises without incurring the wrath of their shareholders.

On the corporate side, while a return on these investments can be adequate, it is likely to be relatively modest, and the payout will require time. The corporate approach must, like that of the political leaders in the developing countries, be one that can encompass the long term, recognizing that only if the challenge of world hunger is met will there exist the possibility of a stable world where trade, investment, and genuine competition can have a place. It is more than likely that the response of the world's agribusiness companies will be a positive one and that support of their shareholders for such a program would be forthcoming, so long as risk is contained by consensus and alertness and the possibility exists for companies to earn a reasonable return on their commitment and effort.

The challenge is clear. Agriculture is a vital key to building a peaceful future in an open world. The system outlined in this paper could open the way to dramatic progress.

Solutions to the Latin American Debt Crisis

by

Robert Grosse

No one seriously doubts that there is a crisis occurring in the international financial system, since the first warnings in 1980, through the refinancing of debt in all but five Latin American countries during 1983, and now with repeated renegotiations for Brazil, Argentina, and Venezuela. The debate currently focuses on the issue of whether the problem is a liquidity crisis, to be overcome with worldwide economic recovery, or a solvency crisis, which will continue until some structural change takes place in the lending process. This paper explores the nature of the debt and its manageability, and offers some recommendations for changes in the current process of coping with the crisis.

During the past 12 months, virtually all of the countries in Central and South America have been forced to reschedule at least portions of their outstanding debts to foreign lenders, private and public (with the exceptions of Colombia, El Salvador, Guatemala, Panama, and Paraguay). Brazil and Argentina, in particular, have repeatedly failed to meet payment deadlines for both principal and interest due. While these events do not necessarily foretell a more permanent default, they do point to the continuing uncertainty over borrowers' abilities to repay their loans. Figure 1 shows the flurry of rescheduling activities by Latin American borrowers in 1982-3.

These serious problems for borrowers and lenders alike are the latest ramifications of the oil crisis of the 1970s, in which the oil-exporting countries amassed huge quantities of funds (dollars, primarily) in payment for their cartel's output and then deposited much of this new wealth in the international banking system. The banks needed outlets for these new deposits, and they in turn looked to many borrowers, including Latin American governments and private firms. That "recycling" process left most of Latin America with new funding at a much higher level than before, but without a substantially increased ability to generate

Robert Grosse is associate director, International Business and Banking Institute, University of Miami, Coral Gables, Florida.

Figure 1

Latin American American Debt Rescheduling/Renegotiation in 1983
(as of November 30, 1983)

Country	Loan maturities included in refinancing	Percent of debt rescheduled	New loan period
Argentina	1982-84*	100	7 years
Bolivia	1983-85*	100	7 years
Brazil	1983-84	100	8 years
Chile	1983-84*	100	8 years
Colombia	none	0	—
Costa Rica	1981-84	95	8 years
Ecuador	Nov 82-Dec 83	90	7 years
El Salvador	none	0	—
Guatemala	none	0	—
Guyana	Mar 82-Jul 84*	100	NA
Honduras	1981-84*	90	5 years
Mexico	Aug 82-Dec 84*	100	8 years
Nicaragua	Mar 83-Jun 84*	87	NA
Panama	new IMF facility	0	—
Paraguay	none	0	—
Peru	Mar 83-Mar 84	100	8 years
Uruguay	1983-84	90	6 years
Venezuela	1983-84*	100	NA

*not finalized

Source: Compiled by the author from published and unpublished sources.

foreign exchange to make repayments (except in the cases of oil exporters such as Mexico, Venezuela, and Ecuador). The question today is whether or not the debtor countries will be able to generate this foreign exchange, so that the cycle of renegotiations and reschedulings can cease.

The Size of the Debt

The outstanding loans of commercial banks, government agencies, and international organizations to borrowers in Latin American countries are massive, by anyone's measure. Figures 2a,b,c,and d present data on indebtedness of borrowers in several countries.

These data are estimates of all lending, from all foreign sources, to public and private borrowers in each country, for the years shown. The bases for these estimates are data published by the Bank for International Settlements on commercial bank lending to the countries, and by the World Bank on long-term public debt, plus extrapolations of the figures using their relationships to trade flows for years not covered in the published series.

Figure 2a

Total Debt of 4 Largest Latin American Countries
(in billions of current U.S. dollars)

	Argentina	Brazil	Mexico	Venezuela
1973	6.4	13.8	8.6	4.6
1974	8.0	18.9	12.8	5.3
1975	7.9	23.3	16.9	5.7
1976	8.3	28.6	21.8	8.7
1977	9.7	35.2	27.1	12.3
1978	12.5	48.4	33.6	16.3
1979	19.0	57.4	40.8	23.7
1980	27.2	66.1	53.8	27.5
1981	35.7	75.7	67.0	29.3
1982	38.0	88.2	82.0	31.3
9-year growth rate, APR	22% per year	23% per year	28% per year	24% per year

Source: William Cline, *International Debt and the Stability of the World Economy.* Washington, D.C.: Institute for International Economics. 1983. (Adapted from Table B-1.)

Note that the rate of growth of nominal borrowing has been in excess of 20% per year in every country covered; unfortunately, pre-oil-crisis estimates are not available for this measure (though they are shown for long-term public debt in Figure 2d below). Just a superficial view of this growth rate is enough to see that it exceeds the growth rate of GNP for any of these countries, or even the growth rate of export earnings for any of them, oil exporters or not.

Figure 2b shows the most recent and earliest available semi-annual data from the Bank for International Settlements.[1] These data state commercial bank loans from banks in Group of 10 (i.e., industrialized) countries to all borrowers in selected Latin American countries. (N.B.: loans outstanding to four countries—Argentina, Brazil, Mexico, and Venezuela—account for almost 40% of these lenders' foreign exposure worldwide.)

Similar data are available from the Federal Financial Institution Examination Council concerning U.S.-based banks. Figure 2c shows the indebtedness of selected Latin American countries to these banks, and also specifically to the nine largest U.S. banks. (Notice that the borrowers' rankings are virtually identical in both U.S. and total private foreign loans.)

Finally, data are available for most Latin American countries from the World Bank, covering long-term lending (i.e., loans with maturities greater than one year) to public-sector borrowers. This series is the most comprehensive in length and country coverage, though it only includes loans to the government and government-

Figure 2b

Group of 10 Commercial Bank Loans Outstanding in Latin America

(in billions of current U.S. dollars)

	Total loans		Loans maturing in less than 1 year	
Country	1976	1982	1976	1982
Argentina	3,260	25,305	1,587	13,106
Brazil	18,461	55,300	5,163	18,663
Chile	985	11,757	596	4,877
Colombia	1,851	5,473	1,233	2,452
Cuba	1,003	1,285	528	657
Ecuador	779	4,674	393	2,487
Mexico	17,885	64,395	7,278	32,208
Peru	2,996	5,216	1,221	3,361
Venezuela	6,853	27,249	4,366	16,270
Total Latin America*	55,660	209,490	23,035	98,444

*Does not include Panama or the Caribbean Islands

Source: Bank for International Settlements, semi-annual report on commercial bank lending to non-members of the Group of 10 countries (June 1977 and December 1982).

Figure 2c

U.S. Bank Loans Outstanding in Latin America

(in billions of current U.S. dollars)

	Total loans		Loans from 9 largest banks
Country	1977	1983	1983
Argentina	2,640	8,398	5,215
Brazil	11,993	20,539	13,280
Chile	821	5,609	3,065
Colombia	1,293	3,331	2,263
Costa Rica	425	479	218
Ecuador	1,040	1,952	1,119
Mexico	11,213	25,441	13,422
Nicaragua	563	371	233
Peru	1,831	2,626	1,463
Uruguay	203	966	670
Venezuela	5,374	11,163	7,575
Total Latin America*	39,375	82,269	49,374

*Does not include Panama or the Caribbean Islands

Source: Federal Financial Institution Examination Council. Country Exposure Lending Survey. (December 1977 and June 1983).

guaranteed loans to the private sector in most countries. Figure 2d presents selected data from this source.

Is There a Crisis?

How can we interpret these data? Clearly, no bank can afford to lose the total value of its shareholders' equity (as some banks have committed in one or more Latin American countries) if some loans go bad. Even a loss of half that size would be devastating. Given the recent rash of payments arrears (temporary defaults, during which periods the loans are rescheduled or renegotiated) among Latin American borrowers, one wonders about the evident possibility of failure to correct one or more of the borrowers' difficulties. This possibility can be evaluated using a variety of

Figure 2d

Total Public-Sector, Long-Term Debt in Latin America
(in millions of current U.S. dollars)

Country	1972	1977	1981
Argentina	2,374.6	5,032.9	10,505.7
Bolivia	618.3	1,375.3	2,421.9
Brazil	5,739.8	22,114.2	43,998.9
Chile	2,589.0	3,664.5	4,422.8
Colombia	1,631.7	2,657.6	5,076.3
Costa Rica	207.2	735.4	1,854.2
Ecuador	309.5	1,143.5	3,391.7
El Salvador	109.1	266.0	664.0
Guatemala	105.0	275.2	684.1
Honduras	119.4	475.5	1,223.2
Mexico	3,917.1	20,758.1	42,642.2
Nicaragua	235.3	866.6	1,974.5
Panama	345.4	1328.8	2,367.6
Paraguay	131.7	335.5	706.6
Peru	1,054.7	4,711.0	5,973.7
Uruguay	326.9	736.4	1,311.6
Venezuela	1,419.1	4,426.5	11,352.0

TOTAL Latin America
    a. public and publicly guaranteed (i.e., same as above)

	22,089.7	73,351.3	145,080.3

    b. private, non-guaranteed

	14,976.8	27,205.3	58,070.7

Source: Adapted from World Bank, *World Debt Tables*. Washington, D.C.: World Bank, 1983.

measures; we will choose the *cash flow basis* as a useful indicator.

The cash flow principle considers the sum of all inflows and outflows of foreign exchange (e.g., dollars, for a Latin American country) during a given time period. For example, in a simplistic case, the net trade surplus (dollars received for exports minus dollars spent on imports) must at least equal the debt servicing requirement, unless some other source of funding is available (such as additional borrowing). This example can be extended to the full balance of payments: a country must generate adequate funds inflows in international business to pay the debt requirements. Additional funds may come from: exports of goods and services, receipts of gifts, incoming foreign direct investment, receipt of long-term loans and other portfolio investment, receipt of short-term loans and investment, and receipt of new official reserves (e.g., SDR's).

For example, Brazil's merchandise trade surplus in 1981 of $1,185 million was offset by imports of services, so the current account balance of payments was a deficit of $11,751 million. This deficit would have required an outflow of foreign exchange of equal value, without other transactions. Fortunately for Brazil, foreign investors brought in $2,313 million of direct investment, and foreign lenders made $9,506 million of long-term loans. Once short-term capital flows and inaccuracies of recording are counted, Brazil actually incurred a "bottom line" increase of official reserves of $750 million in 1981. Thus, including payments made on the foreign debt, Brazil managed to raise its availability of reserves to help support future debt payments during 1981.

Various ratios can be used to demonstrate quickly the adequacy of specific funds-generating activities to cover debt-servicing needs (i.e., interest and fee payments plus repayment of principal amounts falling due in the relevant time period). The ratio of debt-servicing needs to exports and the ratio of debt-servicing needs to the trade balance are two key indicators of this type; these and a few more are shown for selected Latin American countries in Figures 3a and b.

Clearly, in 1981, the debt servicing requirements of all Latin American countries on foreign commercial bank loans (Figure 3a) equal or exceed the cash flow from exports, so some additional support is necessary in every case (except Colombia). This compares with the situation in 1976, when all of the countries except Peru and Venezuela were able to cover debt servicing needs with export earnings. Similarly, Figure 3b uses data from the World Bank to look at debt-servicing requirements on public-sector long-term debt only, but for a longer time period.[2]

Given that public-sector debt often has received preferential terms (i.e., lower fees and interest), these data really understate the true debt-servicing needs. The approximately 30%[3] of total debt that is to private-sector borrowers should bring the total burden up to that shown in Figure 3a.

Measures of Debt-Servicing Capacity*

Country	Debt servicing ——— Exports	Debt servicing ——— Trade balance	Debt servicing ——— GDP	Interest payments ——— Trade balance
Argentina				
1981	1.77	22.70	0.21	4.30
1976	0.49	1.66	0.07	0.28
Brazil				
1981	1.09	21.30	0.12	5.60
1976	0.70	—	0.06	—
Chile				
1981	1.59	—	0.19	—
1976	0.33	1.13	0.08	0.16
Colombia				
1981	0.97	—	0.09	—
1976	0.63	2.45	0.10	0.32
Ecuador				
1981	1.20	16.70	0.21	3.10
1976	0.36	1.82	0.09	0.30
Mexico				
1981	2.01	—	0.18	—
1976	2.61	—	0.15	—
Peru				
1981	1.23	—	0.24	—
1976	1.12	—	0.14	—
Venezuela				
1981	0.98	2.50	0.29	0.42
1976	0.54	2.56	0.16	0.35

*These data assume an annual debt-servicing cost equal to all principal due on loans maturing in less than one year, plus interest and fees on all debt at a flat 10% rate for 1976 and a flat 12% rate for 1981.

Source: Computed from Bank for International Settlements semi-annual reports and *International Financial Statistics.*

Liquidity Vs. Solvency

There are several reasons why the picture in the previous section may be somewhat overdrawn. First and foremost, the borrowers (let us talk only about government borrowers and other borrowers who have government guarantees, who constitute approximately 70% of the total) are not going bankrupt in the same sense that a company can do so. The main problem for Argentina

World Bank Measures of Debt-Servicing Capacity
(considers only public-sector, long-term lending)
(total debt service/exports of goods and services)

Country	1972	1977	1981
Argentina	20.5	15.4	18.2
Bolivia	18.0	21.8	26.9
Brazil	14.2	21.3	31.9
Chile	9.9	33.8	27.2
Colombia	12.5	8.8	14.6
Costa Rica	9.9	9.0	14.1
Ecuador	10.5	7.3	17.9
Guatemala	10.3	1.2	3.3
Honduras	3.3	7.0	12.7
Mexico	22.3	43.3	28.2
Nicaragua	11.1	13.9	NA
Panama	10.5	11.6	11.5
Paraguay	13.4	6.3	NA
Peru	15.7	30.5	44.9
Uruguay	30.5	29.9	NA
Venezuela	6.2	7.6	12.5

Source: Adapted from World Bank, *World Debt Tables*. Washington, D.C.: The World Bank, 1983.

as a borrower of dollars from private foreign banks is that Argentina may, at any time, have a shortage of *dollars* to use for loan servicing. This does not mean that Argentina's economy has stopped functioning, however. The value of current and future output of products and services of that country far exceeds the payments needs that we are discussing. Unfortunately, the "cash flow problem" (or liquidity crisis) of inadequate dollar availability may persist for several years. Thus, the crisis may not dissipate as quickly as the lenders will want to accept.

A second reason for downplaying the crisis is that the government borrowers recognize their continuing need to function in the international financial community. By defaulting unilaterally on existing loans, they would jeopardize future borrowing capability from virtually any lenders in the world. (Though, by dealing together or even separately, the governments could force a better set of terms from the lending banks—this idea of a "debtors' cartel" has been dismissed often, but may still come to be seen as a partial solution to the current situation.)

A third reason that the debt crisis may be overstated is that the creditor countries and banks recognize their interdependence with the borrowers, who cannot simply be disassociated from the global system of trade and financial flows. The lending banks cannot substantially reduce their credit to Latin American borrowers without causing further costly cutbacks, as U.S. firms find fewer and fewer export opportunities in the region. Consequently, these former exporters will have to reduce their production and employment, leading to more domestic repercussions in the lending countries. Thus, lending-country governments see the need to avoid Latin American insolvency, and probably will act to extend more credit to the borrowers (as the United States did in November 1983 by lending 8.4 billion additional dollars to the IMF).

Perhaps the need for dollars should be viewed as a transfer problem (as were German reparations payments after World War I and the oil importers' payments to OPEC in 1973-4).

In the German case, the Allied countries demanded compensation payments for war damages to be paid over several years. The German economy needed to generate sufficient output to effectively transfer real resources to the Allies. That transfer was partially accomplished by payments, partially avoided by inflation, partially financed by borrowing from abroad, and partially forgiven by the Allies after several years.[4]

In the OPEC case, the oil-exporting countries unilaterally raised the price of oil shipments and amassed a large wealth of U.S. dollars in the early 1970s. The OPEC countries forced a transfer of real resources from oil-importing countries to OPEC, and the results are still being seen. Basically, oil importers have transferred ownership of some of their real property and other assets to OPEC, the importers have sold tremendous quantities of real goods and services to OPEC, the importers have borrowed "petrodollars" from OPEC, and inflation has dissipated some of the value of the dollars involved.

The transfer problem fundamentally involves an attempt to move goods and services (i.e., real resources) from one country or group of countries to another, in order to adjust an imbalance in prior trade and financial flows. That is, for any country that is a net importer of goods and services, the financial claims against this importer must be paid at some future date. When that future date arrives, the former importer will be forced to switch over to net exporting, in order to effect the transfer. The date can be postponed by more foreign borrowing that temporarily finances the trade deficit. Ultimately, however, net exports must be made or the financial claims repudiated. Economic growth in the creditor country(ies) makes the transfer much more attainable, since it leads to increased demand for imports (from the debtor) and thus higher income and ability to pay by the debtor.[5]

Bank lenders originally provided funds to the Latin American borrowers in return for a promise of later return of the funds plus additional purchasing power (i.e., interest and fees). Thus, borrowers need to return to the lenders some form of real purchasing power (e.g., hard currency or perhaps real goods) equal in value to the original loan contract. Argentina, in the present example, needs to find some means of transferring real goods and services to the lending countries. Alternatively, Argentina needs to transfer real purchasing power in the form of dollars to these lenders. One way to do this is to stimulate exports; another is to encourage foreign direct investment. A third way is for Argentina to issue long-term promises to repay, and inflation will take care of the rest. (Notice that peso devaluation or printing of more pesos does not help, since repayment must be in dollars.) All of these strategies indeed are being followed today.

These mitigating arguments seek to demonstrate the view that the international lending crisis is important, but not an issue that will in any sense destroy the system of private international banking activity that ties national economies together today. The problem should not be understated either. Consider again the case of Brazil: Realistically, it will be virtually impossible for Brazil to pay the interest and principal that begin to fall due in two years, as a result of the most recent renegotiation of that country's debt. The load will be about $26 billion per year, or close to the total value of Brazil's exports for last year. There is no foreseeable way for Brazil to earn enough dollars to pay that bill and to continue functioning without an economic miracle and/or discovery of some new natural-resource wealth that becomes immediately available. The solution of additional foreign direct investment and long-term loans could finance the current crisis, if the lenders are willing. It appears that the recent renegotiation has just postponed the day of reckoning for borrower and lenders alike.

It is for this last reason that the problem is called a "solvency crisis," rather than a "liquidity crisis." It does not appear likely that Brazil faces only short-term cash-flow difficulties, which will disappear when the world economy goes back to "normal." Rather, Brazil may be in the position of a bankrupt firm—unable to generate sufficient income to repay the loans from currently-used assets, and unwilling to extend liability to the ultimate owners of the firm (residents of the country) to fulfill the contracts. This is insolvency.

A Portfolio of Solutions

What direction can we go to truly reduce the burden, instead of continuing to avoid it? Two general steps can be taken at present, each of which will tend to alleviate the problem, and each for a different reason. First, and more difficult, the lenders can accept some less-favorable terms in their renegotiations than previously demanded. Second, the resources of the International Monetary Fund (IMF) can be increased, to generate more liquidity in the system and more confidence in it.

Lending banks originally evaluated their borrowers very carefully before committing to the loans that appear in jeopardy today. The banks have charged a premium to borrowers that looked more risky than others—and even refused to lend in some cases judged too risky. Nonetheless, the banks cannot be perfect judges of future ability to repay loans. When a sovereign borrower encounters an inability to repay according to the terms set in a loan contract, the bank must make the best of it. This has meant, during the past quarter century, charging a higher rate of interest and additional fees to cover the costs of renegotiation and the extra time of commitment of funds. There is no rule or law that says this is correct or fair. By contrast, a company that makes a risky decision and loses must suffer a reduction in profits as a result. Banks can just as well accept their risks—by charging a risk premium, and receiving lower profits when a borrower is hit by an inability to repay as contracted. Thus, the first useful direction for mitigating the crisis is for bank lenders to set lower returns (e.g., lower interest rates and fees) on their problem sovereign loans. In this way, they accept the risk that was implicit in their charging a risk premium to the borrower, and they increase the probability that the borrower will be able to meet the terms of the renegotiated loans.

While there is no current mechanism in the system to carry out desired reduction in loan charges (other than the accounting method of simply writing down the value of the loans, which does not reduce or eliminate the loans for the borrower), it would be relatively easy to create a department in the IMF, or in the Fed, which would buy the loans from lending banks at a discount, thus devaluing the loans themselves and reducing the burden on the borrowers, hopefully to a manageable level. Such a plan has been proposed by several analysts (including Peter Kenen of Princeton University, Felix Rohatyn of Lazard & Freres, and Peter Leslie of Barclays Bank), and its weakest point seems to be the institutional structure of the new department or division. This idea is discussed further below.

The second step that can be taken today is to increase the financial resources of the International Monetary Fund. The IMF is more-or-less a bank that lends to and borrows from the central banks of its 146 member countries. Each central bank deposits some amount of money (for simplicity, assume that the money must be in U.S. dollars), and then may borrow any currency from the IMF, up to three or four times its original deposit in several cases. If the strong countries today, especially the U.S., Japan, and Germany, will deposit more dollars in the IMF, then the Fund will have more ability to lend to the crisis countries such as Mexico, Brazil, and Venezuela. This part of the solution is substantially a finessing of the problem, since the borrowers still must repay new IMF loans. However, these loans can be offered at somewhat subsidized rates and for long maturities, because the IMF's main concern is stability of the financial system, rather

Figure 4

Partial Solutions to the Debt Crisis

A. Reduction of Contractual Charges
    1. Kenen's plan
    2. Rohatyn's plan
    3. Leslie's plan
    4. Grosse's plan

B. Increase in Official Lending
    1. Raise the IMF's lending
    2. Raise national (OECD) government lending

C. Create New Contractual Forms
    1. Allow payment in goods and services
    2. Lend with collateral to sovereign borrowers

D. Form a "Debtors' Cartel"

E. Do Nothing
    1. Hope for lower interest rates
    2. Hope for renewed confidence in Latin America
    3. Monitor/restrict U.S. bank lending

than profits on its loans. Also, as a multi-country organization, the IMF can dictate terms and conditions (to improve chances of repayment) to its government borrowers more readily than can private bank lenders. By shifting more of the total loan burden to the public sector, away from private banks, the pressures on private banks to play political roles can be reduced. Finally, the IMF may provide the appropriate forum for establishing altered rules of the game for sovereign lending.

While the above two parts of a solution to the debt crisis are feasible and reasonable, several other steps can be taken as additional parts of the whole package. Figure 4 lists a portfolio of partial solutions that may be useful.

The reasoning in this article supports solutions A-D, in the expectation that solution E will only prolong the crisis.

Solution C calls for creation of new instruments or contractual forms that would add to the existing sources of financing. If banks were to accept payment for some of their loans in goods instead of money, they could assure payment despite a lack of dollars in the borrower's Central Bank. This kind of loan contract has been rejected by the banks until now, but perhaps the pressure is adequate to make it work. (Certainly, the U.S. government has opened the door to such contracts by enacting the Export Trading Company Act, which allows banks to trade in goods as well as financial instruments.)

Another new contractual arrangement could allow sovereign lending with collateral, which has been avoided previously. If the government of Mexico sought a loan of $100 million, commercial banks could offer $120 million, with $20 million placed on deposit in a U.S. bank, for example, as collateral. This instrument would not create a new means of payment; rather it could increase the confidence of lenders to make new commitments in the borrowing countries.

Solution D calls for a debtors' cartel. This possibility has been raised repeatedly during the past year, and rejected thus far by the debtors. The borrowers recognize that unilateral renunciation of the debt would not only preclude their future borrowing from foreign commercial banks, but it probably would cause severe contraction of the developed-country systems (which would further exacerbate LDC trade and finance problems). Their unwillingness to apply such pressure on the lenders is self-interested, but if some measure of partial default were agreed upon, a cartel could be feasible economically (if not politically). That is, just as the plans mentioned earlier (Kenen et al.) call for reduction of the bank lenders' charges, so, too, could the debtors enact a similar plan. So far, unity among the borrowers for such a move has not been adequate, but the possibility remains.

The "do-nothing" solution is regarded as untenable by virtually all involved, though many banks appear quite willing to see this choice along with an increase in IMF funding to help the liquidity crisis. If interest rates were to fall substantially, clearly the borrowers would benefit—since almost all loans are variable-rate contracts, which call for payment of the base rate, LIBOR, plus a margin of about 1-3% in interest and fees. Judging from the data presented earlier in this paper, the do-nothing solution must be rejected as inadequate to solve the problem.

Grosse's Plan

This section presents a partial solution that follows the same general lines as those presented by Peter Kenen, Felix Rohatyn, and Peter Leslie in other places. Namely, it calls for a reduction of contractual charges by the lending banks that would be passed on to the borrowers, thus raising their ability to repay the debt.

The plan requires creation of an International Lending Agency (ILA) that would serve as a loan-broker between commercial banks and country borrowers. The ILA could (perhaps should) be attached to the World Bank, or even to the IMF, and it would be backed financially by Central Banks of participating lending and borrowing countries. The ILA's sole purpose would be to buy loans from commercial banks at a discount, and to negotiate terms with the borrowers that pass on the cost reduction as well as possible longer-term repayment schedules.

The International Lending Agency would negotiate discount rates for the loan purchases according to market conditions. That is, any commercial bank wishing to sell a foreign loan (made to a qualifying borrower) could negotiate with the ILA for terms. If, for example, Kenen's suggested 20% discount is acceptable to both the bank and ILA, then the ILA would buy the loan and subsequently renegotiate with the borrower.

The ILA would need to negotiate discounts and sufficiently large numbers of loan purchases so that the debt-servicing burden on the individual borrowing countries would be reduced adequately. Unfortunately, it is impossible to define here exactly what is an "adequate" reduction in the debt burden. However, the ILA would be able to draw up some guidelines as to the necessary help needed to end each country's crisis.

Perhaps equally difficult, the ILA would have to contract with the banks from which it buys loans to finance the purchases. That is, the ILA would need to pay the banks through term payments that would themselves be financed by the borrowers' repayments to the ILA (and by any new funding provided to the ILA by member governments.) The banks would be trading country risk for ILA risk. The ILA would be assuming country risk—and perhaps gaining a position that would allow it to press for sound economic management from sovereign borrowers, as currently is done by the IMF with its "conditionality."

This partial solution to the debt crisis possesses the very desirable characteristic that it is market-based, i.e., that banks can choose to sell (or not sell) their loans to the ILA at discounts negotiated between the banks and ILA. It should not affect decisions of bank lenders as to the uses of their funds, since the ILA's activities relate to sunk costs (loans already made) and not to new loan decisions.

A problem that remains even with the ILA is that commercial banks would not face any limits on extension of new credit to the same borrowers. Thus, a new debt crisis could easily arise in a few years, unless the banks somehow become much more risk-averse in their foreign lending or the borrowers become much better able to service their debt. In searching for guidelines for lending limits, perhaps the ILA could function as a sanctioning body, from which "problem" countries could seek approval for raising their level of indebtedness. Certainly, this solution faces great political hurdles, but just such a solution will be necessary to escape the crisis.

Notes

1. The Bank for International Settlements also publishes quarterly reports for the same categories of borrowers and lenders. The quarterly reports, however, do not include loans by some offshore affiliates of U.S. banks. The discrepancy between quarterly and semi-annual reports is sometimes large for Latin American borrowers—so the more-complete, semi-annual reports are used here.

2. Another measure, perhaps less concrete but equally indicative, is the fact that at least one story concerning country defaults or the international debt crisis more broadly has appeared virtually daily during 1982 and 1983 in the *Wall Street Journal*. Given that perceptions may be as important as

the underlying reality, this indicator shows that the crisis is perceived as very real in the international financial community.

3. The World Bank's *World Debt Tables* show that, during the past decade, total long-term debt outstanding (disbursed only) incurred by countries in Latin America and the Caribbean has been split from 60/40 in 1972 to 71/29 in 1981 between public (and publicly guaranteed) borrowers and private borrowers.

4. See, for example, Jacob Viner (1943).

5. Harry Johnson (1956), among others, presents the analytical views of the transfer problem. Keynes expected that (the German) transfer would be nearly impossible, because of the need to put all of the burden on a change in relative prices of the "debtor" country, to adequately stimulate exports. Metzler argued that it would be possible to carry out the transfer if the income effect of greater spending by the creditor countries would generate adequate demand for the debtor's exports, even without driving down the debtor's terms of trade.

Bibliography

1. Cline, William, *International Debt and the Stability of the World Economy*. Washington, D.C.: Institute for International Economics, 1983.

2. De Sainte Phalle, Thibaut (ed.), *The International Financial Crisis: An Opportunity for Constructive Action*. Washington, D.C.: Georgetown University Center for Strategic and International Studies, 1983.

3. Eaton, Jonathan, and Mark Gersowitz, "Debt with Potential Repudiation: Theoretical and Empirical Analysis," *Review of Economic Studies* (1981).

4. Johnson, Harry, "The Transfer Problem and Exchange Stability," *Journal of Political Economy* (June 1956).

5. Mendelsohn, M.S., *Commercial Banks and the Restructuring of Cross-Border Debt*. New York: The Group of Thirty, 1983.

6. Viner, Jacob, "German Reparations Once More," *Foreign Affairs* (July 1943).

7. World Bank, *World Debt Tables*. Washington, D.C.: The World Bank, 1983.

The Global Information Communications Fund: Strategy for Resolving Global Crises

by

Yoneji Masuda

In spite of many prolonged discussions and proposals, there are as yet no indications that the global crisis is being resolved. In fact, the crisis is growing worse with the passage of time.

My personal observation is that almost all discussions and proposals aim at trying to resolve the effects of the global crisis, but do not get down to the roots.

The global crisis results from the maturation, inherent contradictions, and breakdown of the system of industrial society itself. The most fundamental difficulties blocking the solution of various global problems are: 1) the aggrandizement of state power and the economic power of private enterprises; 2) the failure of parliamentary democracy to function properly; 3) the widening gap between industrial countries and developing countries; and 4) the diverse nature of human values.

At the same time, the world is now entering a period of transformation from the industrial society to the information society, which means that the global crisis is a transitional phenomenon of the transformation of human society. Seen thus, the only fundamental and effective measure for resolving the global crisis would be the steady and successful transformation of human society from the industrial to the information society.

It is evident that actualization of the Global Information Society is the absolute measure by which to resolve the global crisis, but the major difficulty in achieving this is that it will take so many years—maybe half a century or more. In view of this, the formation of a global information and communications infrastructure could prove to be a shortcut to resolving the global crisis.

In light of this basic need, I am proposing the establishment of a Global Information and Communications (GIC) Fund.

Yoneji Masuda is president of the Institute for the Information Society, Tokyo, Japan, and is the author of The Information Society as Post-Industrial Society.

Objective and General Principles

The basic aim of the GIC Fund is to create a global informational environment—the fundamental condition for resolving the global crisis—by formation of a global information communications infrastructure.

The GIC Fund would be established by donations from countries that support its purpose. The best way would be for the USA and the USSR to become joint proposers and for other advanced countries and rich oil-producing countries to take part as promoters.

The GIC Fund would be administered on the following general principles:

It would be global, its thorough globalism overriding national interests and differences of ideology and social systems.

It would be transformational: directed toward the transformation from the industrial society to the information society, and not for the prolongation of the industrial system.

It would be synergetic: directed to synergetic and functional cooperation, not for diplomacy backed by political and economic power.

It would be non-commercial: in formation of the plan, allocation of budget, supervision by a business manager, not by direct operation.

It would be participative: promoting participation by many interests (business, academic, labor unions, religious organizations, volunteer groups, students, etc.), not merely by governmental bureaucratic administration.

Major Activities of the GIC Fund

The following seven concepts form the most desirable and feasible activities of the GIC Fund from the viewpoint of transformational strategy for resolving the global crisis.

1. Global Telecommunications Highway. A Global Telecommunications Highway (GTCH) would form the fundamental infrastructure of the future Global Information Society. High telecommunications technologies—communication satellites, broadcasting satellites, optical fiber, digital communications—would be fully utilized in its construction. Any place on earth—capitals, other big cities, towns, and even isolated villages and islands—would be within its reach.

All communications media, including telephone, electronic mail, telex, CATV, and videotex, would be able to transmit by way of the GTCH. Advanced new communication application systems, such as LAN (local area networks), VAN (value added networks), mail box, tele-conferencing, etc., would be available. A global rate system would be established for all communications media, and differential rates by distance would be eliminated and unified into a single rate.

2. Information Communications Aid to Developing Countries: Economic and technical aid for developing countries to construct an information communications infrastructure is an essential condition in formulating the GTCH, in order to eliminate the information and communications gap between advanced and developing countries. First priority should be given to this subject because success or failure in this area will have a decisive influence on the existence of the GIC Fund itself. The most effective and economical plan for information communications aid should be developed by fully utilizing highly advanced information communications technology in preserving the balance in the GTCH project.

The total plan should include an intermediate and a long-range plan. The main aspects of the intermediate plan would be: construction of a domestic digital communications network between capital and major cities in each developing country; and establishment of an emergency communications system for isolated villages and islands. The main focus of the long-range plan would be a domestic digital communications network for ordinary citizens, enabling each person to communicate by any media to any person any place in the world from a home terminal by utilizing the GTCH.

3. Global Medical Care System. An Emergency Medical Aid System would be operated on a global basis. For this purpose, a global integrated network of Emergency Aid Medical Hospitals, Eye Banks, Blood Donation Centers, replacement internal organ storage units, and other necessary facilities would be established.

A Long-Distance Remote Medical Care System would be set up to serve isolated islands, no-doctor villages, and refugee camps. A man-machine automatic diagnosis system and increased training of health-care nurses and barefoot doctors are urgently needed.

A Global Influenza-Prevention System can become real. Since advanced countries have increasing numbers of aged people, a global anti-influenza center should be established and become effective, with popular influenza-prevention medicine developed (for example, interferon in the Soviet Union).

A Cancer Therapy Data Bank would be established, with the most advanced cancer-therapy data and records collected and stored in a data bank.

A Long-Range Plan for the eradication of endemic diseases would be established, making use of the success of the anti-smallpox drive. The ambitious goal would be the eradication of all endemic diseases, such as malaria and leprosy, by the year 2000.

4. A Global Education System. A standardized Global Information Literacy Education system would be developed. The aim of information literacy education is to improve the ability of the younger generation to live in the future information society. It would include not merely how to become familiar with computers, programming, processing, etc., but also how to utilize information to make optimum selections of action and to achieve one's goals. To make this effective, education and training for problem solving and for opportunity development would be the core of information-literacy education, rather than cramming knowledge and technology.

In developing countries, illiteracy-resolving education would simultaneously accompany information-literacy education. In this case, information-literacy education will have a multiplying effect in the promotion of illiteracy-resolving education.

Global-intelligence education would be available to ordinary citizens, enabling them to acquire skills and adapt themselves to the dynamically tranforming global and societal environment. Global-intelligence education is more than mere re-education and retraining. It is more crucial, in that it is deeply concerned with the transformation of value thinking, ethical standards, social behavior, and way of life. This kind of education is the only way by which to overcome the huge number of drop-outs.

Lastly, the importance of information democracy in education should be emphasized. Three kinds of information rights will become basic human rights in the coming information society: the right to protection of privacy, the right of access to information, and the right to participate in decision-making at all levels of government and social institutions. The spread and stabilization of information-democracy education all over the world will be a prerequisite for the steady growth of the Global Information Society.

5. Universal Communications Media. Research and development of Universal Communications Media is one of the fundamental needs to break through the cultural and language barriers of countries, promote common understanding and recognition of global problems, and encourage their solution jointly by all concerned parties. The epochal innovation of information and communications technologies has rapidly enhanced the possibility of creating new universal complex information and communications media.

An Automatic Translation System (ATS) will be a most practical solution. In Japan, the national project of creating a fifth-generation computer takes up this subject as an important component of artificial-intelligence architecture. The ATS should make translation possible between the languages of all countries, in any form: voice, letter, or symbol.

Global Image Symbols (GIS) is a new revolutionary universal communications medium that will be a substitute for Esperanto. The basic concept of the GIS is as follows:

● It will be designed to enable complex intellectual information to be expressed structurally as well as in time-sequence, and to appeal not only to reason but also to human feelings.

• GIS would be capable of communicating meanings and the substance of ideas without need for special training or learning on the part of the user, for which purpose the utmost consideration will have to be given to making an optimum appeal to human sensory functions, the capacity of recognition and understanding.

• Such information media as color, light, sound, and smell will be utilized, in addition to shapes and forms.

• All forms of information communication—movie films, animation films, photographs, symbols, and marks—will be utilized, but written characters will be excluded.

• These information media should permit disassembling, assembling, deformation, and free time-sequential development.

Development of the GIS will provide the groundwork for the creation of an international means of communication of a new type, matching the information society, distinct from language, and will be a major contribution to the formation of a global information and intelligence network.

A Global Watchdog Center. A Global Watchdog Center (GWDC) will be established to gather, analyze, and evaluate all kinds of data and information relating to the global environment and to issue an early warning as soon as any dangerous signal or trend appears that could cause a global crisis. Voluntary citizens' groups, university researchers, and research institutes would cooperate with the GWDC to gather various kinds of data and information relating to potential political, military, social, or economic global crises. Students in primary and middle schools all over the world, fully trained and equipped with advanced monitoring and measuring systems, would participate in the collection of original data and information about weather conditions, temperature, air pollution, natural disruption, epidemic diseases, etc. These kinds of participative activities in the GWDC would contribute to deepening the ecological and global awareness of students.

GIC Peace Corps. One unique characteristic of the GIC Fund would be the formation of a GIC Peace Corps. The aim of the GIC Peace Corps would be to enlist the participation and cooperation of a wide range of citizens, technicians of information communications, medical and educational experts, and students of primary and middle schools in promoting GIC goals.

Activities of the GIC Peace Corps would include various kinds and fields of work. Volunteer groups of information communications technicians would be sent to developing countries to provide technical assistance and training for governmental staff and other people. Retired systems analysts and programmers as well as housewives who have had programming experience would voluntarily cooperate in the development of global social systems. Students of universities and high schools would be encouraged to devote themselves to the activities of the GIC Fund for a certain period; their experiences would qualify them for higher-level school work.

Working conditions of participants in the GIC Peace Corps would be flexible and dynamic. Some participants would work full time for reasonable payment, and others would work full time, but without payment, just because they want to do such voluntary work. Some participants would work for a given length of time and others part time or for a flexible period. In the case of university and high-school students, it would be a semi-obligatory work system.

One can imagine a hundred thousand volunteers working in developing countries, devoting themselves to the construction of the information communications infrastructure and cooperating with the local people as one body. From this one example alone, the significance of establishing a GIC Peace Corps will be readily apparent.

Immeasurable Effect of the GIC Fund

The establishment of the GIC Fund will bring immeasurable benefits to human society on a global scale:

• The operation of the GIC Fund will contribute to the activation of the world economy by creating a huge demand and market, centering on information communications related industries.

• Building the information communications infrastructure in developing countries will promote the simultaneous resolution of the north-south industrial and information gaps.

• The formation of the global information and intelligence network will increase mankind's mutual understanding of complex global problems and provide important clues to the solution of the global crisis.

• The most fundamental effect of the GIC Fund will be to provide the basis for transforming human society on a global scale from the industrial to the information society in one effort.

The GIC Fund Is Both Feasible and Practical

The idea of the GIC Fund may be thought to be too idealistic and fantastic, but it is actually quite feasible and practical from both the technological and economic aspects. The actualization of the GIC Fund depends only on political decisions and human wisdom. There is no need to explain the technological feasibility of the actualization of the GIC Fund. It is enough to point out the tremendous advances made in space and defense technology by the USA and the USSR as a result of their competition in the expansion of armaments. Let us therefore examine economic feasibility. According to a broad trial estimate, the total expenditure for actualizing the main purposes of the GIC Fund would be around $400 billion for the 15 years from 1985 to 2000. This means a yearly expenditure of about $25 billion. We should remember that the total amount spent by all countries on armaments in 1982 is estimated at about $800 billion, according to

United Nations sources. This means that the total spending of the GIC Fund would be only 50% of one year's armaments by all countries. It should be emphasized that, if all countries uniformly reduced their yearly budget for armaments by only 3%, it would be enough to implement the GIC Fund's ambitious plan.

Speaking of Japan's circumstances, the Japanese government has formally pledged itself to increase the amount of yearly donations for economic aid to developing countries to 0.6% of the GNP by 1990. This corresponds to around $6 billion, and if Japan invested the full amount in the GIC Fund, Japan would be able to provide 3 global communications satellites, 150 domestic communications satellites, and 100 earth stations for developing countries every three years. This would cover the total investment in the GIC Fund for the construction of a global and domestic communications satellite network. These facts show that the economic feasibility of the GIC Fund would pose little difficulty.

Furthermore, the total cost of GIC Fund projects will be substantially reduced by the rapid progress of technological innovations for communication satellites. And if the GIC Fund faithfully promotes its synergetic and participative principles, and succeeds in obtaining the voluntary cooperation of citizens from broad areas on a global basis, it will result not only in a dramatic cost reduction, but also in unexpected performance results from GIC Fund activities.

The U.S. Academy of Peace:
Developing a Peace Ethic for the Future

by

Spark Matsunaga

As a United States senator, one of my most rewarding, but frustrating duties is the annual consideration of applications submitted by young high-school graduates seeking nominations to the military service academies. So many heed the call to "the profession of arms in the service of God and Country" but so few can be chosen. It is distressing to disappoint youth with a goal. It is gratifying to be able to encourage those with high promise for our nation's future.

The successful applicants generally are the "best and brightest" and we bestow upon them the boon of an outstanding education underwritten by the nation's taxpayers. If anything, the rising cost of such an education, coupled with the declining means of financing it, has enhanced the quality of candidates for nomination to the military academies.

There can be no real objection to the maintenance of outstanding U.S. military academies, for, as long as war is viewed as an acceptable means of settling international disputes, and as long as any other nation chooses to settle international differences with warfare, we certainly need military experts for our own defense and security. But, increasingly, in a nuclear age, war is seen as an unacceptable means of resolving international conflicts. Recent events, such as the failure of our military "peacekeeping" policy in Lebanon and the downing by the Soviet Union of a Korean airliner with 269 civilian passengers aboard, illustrate the need to move beyond an outmoded reliance on military power alone and to develop a new peace ethic for the future.

Along with our military academies, we need to have a United States Academy of Peace to train the best and brightest of our

Spark Matsunaga is a United States senator from Hawaii.

youngsters, the potential future leaders of this country and others, in the art of peacemaking. We need a peace academy to develop a peace ethic for the world of the future.

The concept of an academy of peace is not as new and revolutionary as it may sound. In fact, a "plan for a Peace Office" in the federal government was first proposed upon the founding of our Republic.

The author of that Revolutionary War era plan is believed to have been either Benjamin Rush, a prominent physician and signer of the Declaration of Independence, or Benjamin Banneker, a black mathematician who was the publisher of the popular almanac in which the plan appeared. George Washington also supported the concept of a proper peace establishment within the federal government. Since then, for over 200 years, Americans have continued to view world peace as a vital part of our national heritage and as an essential component in our national security. Proposals for a federal agency devoted to peace research and education have been advanced by men and women of vision and stature both in government and in the private sector. In the last 50 years, over 140 bills have been introduced in Congress calling for the establishment of such an agency. The first of these, introduced in 1935 by Senator Matthew M. Neely of West Virginia, provided for the establishment of a U.S. Department of Peace similar to the "Peace Office" proposed by Rush and Banneker. A Bureau of Peace and Friendship, to be located in the U.S. Department of Labor, was also proposed in 1935 by Congressman Fred Bierman of Iowa. The Bureau, to be headed by an eminent sociologist, was to carry out sociological research on matters pertaining to peace and war. Research was also the focus of two resolutions introduced in the House in 1945 and 1947 by then-Congressman Everett McKinley Dirksen, later a senator from Illinois. The Dirksen Resolutions would have established a "Division of Peace and Friendship" within the U.S. Department of State.

In later years, the concept of a federal institution devoted to peace was expanded. In 1945, Senator Alexander Wiley of Wisconsin introduced legislation to create a small, high-level Department of Peace with the secretary serving, among other things, as the U.S. representative on the United Nations Security Council. That same year, then-Congressman Jennings Randolph, now a senator from West Virginia, introduced a Department of Peace bill that incorporated for the first time the concept that the international exchange of people and ideas is an effective means of promoting peace.

Hearings were held on the measures introduced in 1945 and 1947, but the real developments during that era were the successful creation of the Marshall Plan and the subsequent addition of a technical assistance program in 1949.

In 1955, President Dwight D. Eisenhower pointed with concern to "the unprecedented destructive power of (the) new weapons and the international tensions which powerful armaments aggravate." He appointed a Special Assistant to the President for Disarmament. That individual, Governor Harold Stassen of Minnesota, was given cabinet rank and was often called the "Secretary of Peace."

Also in 1955, Senator Mike Mansfield of Montana, now the U.S. Ambassador to Japan, and Congressman Charles Bennett of Florida proposed the creation of a joint Congressional Committee for a Just and Lasting Peace, and Congressman Harold Ostertag of New York introduced a bill that included for the first time the concept of a national peace college.

Between 1959 and 1961, the proposal that eventually became the Arms Control and Disarmament Agency took shape in Congress. The two most prominent sponsors of the legislation in the Senate were Senator Hubert H. Humphrey of Minnesota, who proposed a national peace agency, and Senator John F. Kennedy of Massachusetts, who proposed an arms control research institute. Presidential candidate Kennedy, on the campaign trail, was caught by surprise at the favorable audience reaction to an appeal for arms control that he had attached at the end of one of his speeches. Later, in his 1963 commencement address at American University, President Kennedy made a very moving appeal for peace, noting that "the pursuit of peace is not as dramatic as the pursuit of war . . . but we have no more urgent task." He described peace as the "rational pursuit of rational men."

Shortly after being sworn into office as a U.S. congressman from Hawaii in 1963, I introduced a bill to create a Department of Peace, with a cabinet-level secretary, having the authority to establish an academy of peace. Its time in history had obviously not arrived, and the bill drew very little attention.

In 1977, with Senators Jennings Randolph and Mark Hatfield as co-sponsors, I introduced legislation providing for a study of the various proposals for new institutions devoted to peace research, training, and operations. Our bill was attached as an amendment to the Education Act Amendments of 1978 and passed the Congress in October 1978. An appropriation of $500,000 was provided in 1979 and a nine-member study commission was appointed. Members of the Commission were: James H. Laue, Representative John M. Ashbrook, Arthur H. Barnes, Elise Boulding, John R. Dellenback, John P. Dunfey, Representative Dan Glickman, William F. Lincoln, and the author; three members each were appointed by the President of the United States, the President Pro Tempore of the Senate, and the Speaker of the House. I had the privilege of being the only senator appointed, and then being elected chairman of the commission.

In the course of its study, the Commission held 12 public hearings in as many American cities, from Boston to Honolulu. Expert witnesses known for their special knowledge of conflict resolution were invited and testified. They included representatives of business, labor, state and local governments, community and ethnic organizations, educational institutions, and civil and human rights organizations.

In addition, the commissioners held more than 50 meetings with other organizations. They visited three military service academies and met with officials of the National Defense University, the Foreign Service Institute, the Arms Control and Disarmament Agency, the Federal Mediation and Conciliation Service, the Community Relations Service, and many other private-sector and community organizations. Existing literature relating to peace research and conflict resolution was extensively reviewed by the Commission members and staff.

In October 1981, the Commission on Proposals for the National Academy of Peace and Conflict Resolution presented its final report, entitled "To Establish the United States Academy of Peace," to the Congress and the President. In recommending the establishment of a U.S. Academy of Peace, the Commission declared that "America's heritage, power and prestige make the United States a major force for world peace."

The U.S. Academy of Peace, as envisioned by the Commission, would be a private, non-profit institution, headquartered in the District of Columbia. It would have three major functions:

1. Perform research on its own and support research at other educational institutions.

2. Provide graduate and postgraduate educational programs for which students at institutions of higher education could receive credit, and provide continuing education services, such as workshops and seminars for public and private sector individuals and organizations aimed at strengthening their conflict resolution skills.

3. Establish an information service to gather and disseminate information related to the field of peace learning.

A Center for International Peace would also be established within the Academy to which present and future potential leaders of this nation and other nations would be appointed to study; and the Academy would establish the award of a Medal of Peace, to be presented annually by the President of the United States.

In support of its recommendation that a U.S. Academy of Peace be established, the Commission made eight major findings:

1. The U.S. Academy of Peace would advance the national interest by developing peacemaking expertise that could reduce the chances that the United States, or any other nation, would risk nuclear war or allow itself to be propelled to the brink of war.

2. The United States government has a special capacity to promote peace in the world and the United States Academy of Peace would build upon and expand this heritage.

3. The U.S. Academy of Peace would strengthen our own national security and reduce the cost of settling international differ-

ences through its research and training in a range of effective options to conflict resolution other than military force.

4. Through its education, training, and information services, the U.S. Academy of Peace would sharpen the peacemaking capabilities of Americans in government, in private enterprise, and in voluntary associations.

5. The U.S. Academy of Peace would amplify the field of peace learning and extend peacemaking expertise by focusing national attention on peace research, education, and training.

6. The U.S. Academy of Peace could use both international and national peacemaking and conflict resolution experiences in designing its education, training, and information services, and could perform priority research on cultural differences in peace and conflict processes.

7. The absence of a coordinated national commitment to research, education, and training in the field of peace learning has caused neglect of peacemaking knowledge and skills to the detriment of the nation's effectiveness in international policymaking and policy implementation.

8. There is broad public and governmental interest in a federal institution devoted to this nation's peacemaking capacities that would have complementary programs of research, education, training, and information services for people in and out of government.

In November 1981, with great optimism I introduced legislation in the Senate to implement the Commission's recommendations. That bill, S. 1889, attracted 56 cosponsors. Six hours of public hearings were held on the measure in April of 1982 by the Subcommittee on Education, Arts, and Humanities of the Senate Labor and Human Resources Committee and, subsequently, the full committee on Labor and Human Resources favorably reported the bill. Unfortunately, the full Senate was bogged down with budget legislation and could not consider S. 1889 in the 97th Congress. A companion bill, introduced in the House by a member of the Commission, Congressman Dan Glickman, with more than 150 cosponsors, was the subject of public hearings in July 1982, but no further action was taken before the 97th Congress expired.

S. 1889 represented the first time that a peace academy proposal was ever favorably reported by a legislative committee, and the first time that such a proposal was ever sponsored by more than three or four members of the Senate. Buoyed by this strong evidence that we may be closer now to having a U.S. Academy of Peace than we ever have been in our nation's history, I reintroduced a similar measure, S. 5645, the U.S. Academy of Peace Act, in the 98th Congress, on February 23, 1983. This bill is cosponsored by 55 senators, more than enough to pass it on the floor. In September 1983, it was favorably reported by the Senate Labor and Human Resources Committee.

Despite my optimism, however, the road traveled by the peace academy proposal has not been completely without pitfalls. Although it has won the endorsement of over 40 national organizations, including the National Education Association, the American Association of University Women, the YMCA and YWCA, and the American Association of Retired Persons; despite the fact that it has the support of the Consortium on Peace Research, Education, and Development (COPRED), an organization representing 34 universities; despite the fact that it has the endorsement of highly respected individuals such as Nobel Economics prize winner Gunnar Myrdal of Sweden, former secretary of state Edmund Muskie, and General Andrew Goodpaster, the former superintendent of the U.S. Military Academy, there are those who say that the Academy would be too costly or that it would duplicate efforts already under way at a number of American universities and colleges. In truth, as expert witnesses testified during the hearings on my bill, there is almost a total absence of peace research and education at the graduate and postgraduate level. Moreover, my bill would authorize the appropriation of funds in the amount of $23.5 million for the Academy's first two years—less than one-sixteenth the cost of a single B-1 bomber. Yet it could ultimately save us hundreds of billions of dollars in defense expenditures and inestimable numbers of American lives.

In the twentieth century, the United States has fought in two world wars, in the Korean conflict, and in Vietnam. It has witnessed, or participated in, countless other potentially violent confrontations throughout the world. Today, as the possibility of a nuclear confrontation looms on the horizon, the need to focus and fully utilize our national resources in the cause of world peace is greater than ever before. It is a need that we dare not overlook any longer, a problem that, more than any other, will affect the future health and safety of all the world's peoples. The establishment of a United States Academy of Peace, to train people to wage peace and to promote the adoption of a peace ethic, would be a giant step in the right direction.

The peace academy is an institutional idea whose time has come. Personally, I believe that there is a need for training the best and brightest Americans in the processes of peace and conflict resolution. To those who say that we cannot afford to have an Academy of Peace—even a most modest one—I would respond that we cannot afford not to have one. History has made it abundantly clear that wars are started in the hearts and minds of men, and if we want to prevent future wars, we can only do it by developing a peace ethic accepted and practiced by all nations. Most importantly, future leaders of this country and other countries will learn at the U.S. Academy of Peace to look to the conference table as the final resort in the resolution of conflicts, not to the battlefield.

How To Take a First Step Toward Peace on Earth

by

Aurelio Peccei

The history of man is the history of his inquisitive mind and dexterous hands, and hence of his ideas, discoveries, inventions, and industry; of his love for life, and therefore of his arts, songs, and poetry; of his wonder about what may lie beyond, and thus of his faiths and myths; of his gregariousness, and then of his cities and empires, and also of his institutions and laws. It is also the history of his fears and ambitions, and consequently of his conquests and his teeter-tottering between peace and war. All these characters and manifestations of man are likely to continue and flourish—except one, which is no longer tolerable: war, and its quintessential element, violence.

Never before were the alternatives of man so global as they are now, and never before were they so extreme, because never before was his capacity for building and creation so limitless and his power of destruction so absolute as they are now. Henceforth, all will essentially depend on whether he is at peace or at war with himself and his world. We must therefore take to heart a few new basic exigencies.

• Each one of us and all peoples and nations must realize that the banishment of war and of military and nonmilitary violence from the parameters of human evolution has now become imperative if this very evolution is not to end in disaster.

• At the same time, as "development" seems to have become humankind's paramount goal, we must also convince ourselves that no really worthwhile development can possibly be attained unless peace prevails on earth.

• We must therefore see peace as the primary factor in this crucial equation, and understand it in its universal depth and breadth of nonviolence, not only at all levels and sectors of human society, but also in the relationships between human society and nature.

The late Aurelio Peccei, founder of the Club of Rome and a leading business executive in Italy, is the author of The Human Quality *(1976) and* One Hundred Pages for the Future *(1981).*

• We must clarify the concept of development anyway, in order to reconcile in our single world the aspirations of those who desperately want just to stay alive and not to fall into even more abject poverty.

To recognize these premises, a profound mutation is needed in our traditional outlook and values; and we must first of all free ourselves from the "complex of violence" we inherited from our ancestors. This complex is still usually considered part of human nature because it served our forefathers well during the long centuries of their ascent; but they were weak and on the defensive, and it was thus expedient for them to resort to violence to assert themselves, while now we have much more power than we are able to control or need to rule the entire planet. It is time then to recognize that violence, though once a means of survival, can now become the cause of our doom.

This cultural evolution, however, is made more difficult by the emergence of several huge new problems that intertwine with the many old ones that are still unresolved. The age-old problems of population, hunger, poverty, ignorance, injustice, and intolerance combine with new ones generated by the current international financial and monetary chaos, the unprecedented size and complexity of human systems, the gross abuse and misuse we make of technology, and the devastation we are causing to our natural environment. Our difficulties are further aggravated by the ossification and bureaucratization of our institutions, as well as by the decay of our moral values and civic virtues, and our loss of faith in ourselves or in a Superior Power.

We may call it the predicament of modern man. The cold war and armaments frenzy, local conflicts, civil violence, and the fatal temptation to resort to force in order to resolve situations that seem otherwise insuperable—all are results of it. And so is the stalemate that blocks all efforts to promote a more equitable order and development in the world community and threatens to condemn irremediably a majority of the humans to want and deprivation.

Our major flaw in approaching this entangled situation is that we invariably try to deal with all the major problems individually, as if each one of them could be isolated from the rest; and then we focus on symptoms of this problematique rather than going deeper to attack the ills and dysfunctions that lie at its origin.

The most blatant and tragic example of our mistaken attitudes is that we consider the life-and-death question of war or peace independently from its root causes. We approach it as if we had to deal with the more or less self-contained technical problem of the arms race vs. disarmament, and as if this problem could be separated out from all the others and treated in essentially military-diplomatic terms. In following this path so outside the reality of the world, the experts have had to bring into the picture so many intricate technicalities that not even they seem to understand anymore where they stand, while what they say is totally incomprehensible to people in general.

No wonder, then, that the disarmament talks have so far led nowhere. No wonder, too, that during the more than 30 years of these negotiations the thermonuclear arsenals have not ceased to grow; in fact, they are now a million and a half times more powerful than before.

It goes without saying that there should certainly be no slackening in efforts to try to reach some agreements on prevention of wars, solution of conflicts, arms control, establishment of nuclear- and chemical-weapon free zones, demilitarizations, and general disarmament by following this path. It would be foolish, however, to expect that such agreements would in any way be equivalent to peace.

No measure of military disarmament alone can bring about a warless world or stop overt or covert military research and development of new infernal weaponry that can boost our overkill potential; nor can it avoid balance-of-power agreements being much more than writing in the sand; nor yet can it put an end to the creeping proliferation of the means of mini-violence which in many countries are already transforming the rule of law and legitimate political or social protest into brutal government repression and torture on the one hand and bloody subversion and terrorism on the other.

More reliable ways to establish the conditions of peace on earth must be found. The Club of Rome is committed to contributing to the search for them, and this paper has been prepared with this purpose.

To reiterate, violence and its ideology of whatever sort must be viewed as remnants of a past that is no more. Indeed, they are cultural derangements and social pathologies as incompatible with the present-day world community as would be slavery or human sacrifice.

Quite evidently, then, we need a new philosophy of life to rid ourselves of our propensity for violence and replace it by serene, responsible recognition of the fact that our situation has changed and that we must restore balance and harmony in ourselves and our world. This philosophy of life will necessarily be different from that which guided our forebears in simpler times, when their problems were much smaller and their knowledge and means much more rudimentary.

We must realize that our new philosophy of life must be fully consistent with the singularities and exigencies of this new age, and that the imperative of peace and nonviolence is the principal of the "pillars of wisdom" on which it has to be established.

It no doubt behooves our generations, who have the good or bad fortune to live at these hinges of history, to bring humankind across this new threshold of vision and wisdom. But we cannot rely much for this on the world's politico-economic establishment, which almost everywhere is largely unreceptive to any such reasoning. And the two superpowers are so absorbed in their power games and each is so obsessed by the other's nuclear potential that for the moment they are basically opposed to any innovation that may even remotely challenge their self-concerned, self-righteous postures and schemes.

Public opinion, on the contrary, can by and large be a positive factor in many countries. It is so shaken by what it sees happening in the world, and so afraid of what comes next, that it would welcome a turn for the better even at the cost of some sacrifices.

Popular awareness of the paramount importance of these issues is vital because great societal changes cannot last if they do not win the hearts and minds of citizens.

What is particularly encouraging is the vast involvement of the young, who, having always been taught the martial arts by their elders, are now teaching their elders the arts of peace. The young are the principal animators of the peace movements and the "green" movements that, although having just surfaced here, while still simmering there, tend to converge into a popular groundswell grass-roots force that demands a more humane and responsible society right across the board.

To support these aspirations, The Club of Rome has promoted the *Forum Humanum* project. Based on an international network of young men and women, it calls them to explore what positive futures would be open to the human community if it becomes inherently peace-loving and peaceful. The prospects are most heartening and therefore some preliminary indications will be presented in 1985, on the occasion of the International Youth Year of the United Nations.

A decisive turning point is now being made with the realizations that, in the same way violence in relations among men must be repelled, so, too, a stop must be put to the senseless use of violence against the natural environments on which our life itself ultimately depends.

The recognition that worldwide peace with nature is as primary as peace among humans, and would remain indispensable even if the danger of war and all other threats and problems were miraculously to vanish, opens new avenues to improve the human condition.

We should first realize that the state of our planet is none too good. It offers a dismaying picture of depletion and degradation: wilderness, the treasure chest of nature, disappearing; deserts advancing; tropical forests rapidly destroyed; coastal zones and estuaries ruined; large numbers of animal and plant species condemned to extinction; waters, soils, and the very air we breathe contaminated; natural cycles, climate, and ozone layer tampered with (often irreversibly); human ecology directly affected by overharvesting, overgrazing, and overfishing.

These unwholesome conditions have been caused because we

have violated the unwritten law of nature that species are made to live together, complementing one another, and resorting to violence only when this is needed to feed themselves or to protect themselves. We thought ourselves to be an exception and virtually free to use our arms and tools for any purpose we had in mind, even for such questionable objectives as just acquiring prestige or satisfying greed and caprice. Thus, confusing might with right, we subjugated or eliminated all creatures we could lay our sights on—including our weaker fellow humans—and exploited the earth's resources beyond all reasonable limits. We are now paying the price for this cavalier attitude.

But the harm we have done so far to our world habitat is probably very slight compared with what we are likely to do in the future, turning the already critical situation in many regions into one that will be well-nigh dramatic. The facts speak for themselves.

• The world population, which is now at a record high of 4.7 billion, is expected to increase by 1.5 billion before the year 2000 (thus adding more people in barely 16 years than those who lived on earth one century ago).

• The present generations are expected to consume more natural resources during their lifetime than all past generations together.

• Individual demands are continually soaring, so that total demand will increase more rapidly than population, probably doubling in the next two decades.

Thus, if decisive steps are not taken while there is still time to protect and conserve the global environment, the danger that humankind will be choked slowly but surely because its own weight steadily decreases the planet's carrying capacity is no less real than the danger that it will be destroyed as a consequence of a nuclear clash.

Fortunately, thanks to their basic common sense, people are beginning to be worried as to how the earth can manage, in its present conditions, to accommodate all the newly expected waves of population without being literally trampled underfoot; and they are equally concerned about what might happen if it cannot.

They also know that major events occurring in one part of the planet are apt to have repercussions everywhere; and therefore they fear that one day an unexpected ecological crisis taking place somewhere in the globe will seriously affect the entire system. As a consequence, they feel that it is high time that, in everybody's interest, the nations of the world should evolve adequate common action to safeguard the natural ecosystems while the worst can yet be prevented from happening.

The perception of precisely what should be done to improve the situation among humans unfortunately is quite different—and the climate of violence much more difficult to dispel. Even in societies where the practice of violence is not widespread, the political and social atmosphere is too bitter and tense to be changed easily; and in the international arena the relations are so strained and conflictual that no great hope can be entertained that an effort of pacification will produce substantial results in the matter of a few years or even a decade.

Psychologically, then, the circumstances are relatively favorable to involve public opinion in a movement to search for ways leading to a safer future by focusing initially on our relations with nature. Peace with the world environment, as difficult as its attainment may be, seems to be an attainable goal, and it would prepare people for peace among themselves as well, because it would familiarize them with cross-border cooperation. At this stage, then, in order to take the right turn towards peace on earth and desirable futures, the good strategy is to aim first at peace with nature.

The initial move in this strategy would be to place squarely before world public opinion and its leaders the dramatic dilemmas of this end of the century:

• Almost one billion people live near or below the poverty line, while in the next few decades several more billions will be added to the world population. What should the world community do, starting right now, to accommodate all these new people and assure to the entire population, including the poor regions of the Third World, a life of modest well-being and dignity as befits a human being?

• As the construction of immense new physical and social infrastructures and the more than doubling of the world economy are needed to settle and serve this new outsize population, how can all the facilities required be provided in the limited space and with the limited resources available, while at the same time safeguarding the world's natural environments that are essential to sustain humankind on a permanent basis?

• What tragic consequences would we and our children have to suffer if the ever-larger human multitudes could not be settled decently on this planet, or if to settle them the very natural wherewithal of their life would be irremediably impaired?

These problems are overwhelming but must be faced without delay. No doubt several other and often conflicting exigencies must be considered. But problems related to land—the most finite of all finite resources—must be addressed first. It seems logical, then, that the first step should be the preparation, as soon as possible and at the highest level of knowledge and information available, of a broad-line feasibility study of integral space and land use, management, and conservation, region by region, for the world as a whole up to the year 2000 and beyond. Land, taken as the basis of the study because it is also the basis of human habitat, should of course be seen and appraised both in its present state, with its natural endowment (character of the soil, plant and animal life, water, climate, etc.) and human artifacts, and with regard to its potential for development.

The study will probably show how urgent and essential, though difficult, is the task of keeping the planet in livable condition at a time when a much larger human family will have to live on it. And this will help one and all to realize the key function that global solidarity and cooperation can fulfill to keep the best avenues to the future open and let all human groups, large and small, benefit from the synergies of partnership.

Under the present circumstances, then, a movement of most, if not all, peoples and nations acting in their self-interest but aiming collectively at establishing global ecological peace is likely to influence the political scene, too, showing the benefits of coordinated joint action, and can thus represent a first practical step to bring true peace to earth. This is why, at the Second World Congress on Land Use held in June 1983 in Cambridge, Massachusetts, I put forward a proposal that this study be started as soon as possible. The proposal was accepted in principle, and consideration is now being given to the possibility of carrying it out. The following is an outline of how it should be conceived:

Rationale of World Land Use Studies

The *biosphere,* the thin mantle of soil, air, and water on the earth's surface, is the only known corner of the universe fit for human life. Our species is part and parcel of the pool of life that thrives in it, and therefore should endeavor to maintain it in as healthy a state as possible.

The biosphere had been evolving for billions of years when man appeared one million years ago. He soon started to build his *sociosphere* in order to organize his associative life and then his *technosphere* to give it muscle. Human life is regulated by these three spheres, but their logics are often incompatible with one another. The fact that the technosphere has tried to impose its own logic, particularly at the expense of the biosphere, is at the root of many problems we face.

When man settled some ten thousand years ago, he chose the best lands; and then he progressively occupied ever more lands, but did it in disorderly fashion and without knowing how to conserve them properly. Therefore, several regions were degraded or depleted with consequences that are felt to these days. The situation is now that the *productive soils* available cover the relatively limited area of some 33 million square kilometers, i.e., only about one-quarter of the earth's total ice-free land surface, and of them only 20% are highly productive, while half the remainder are of medium productivity and the other half low. Together with the coastal waters, they are the only place where man actually lives, his *Habitat.* It is here that the additional populations expected from now on must also be settled.

The outlying landmasses, plus the seas and oceans, the atmosphere, and some surficial layers of the earth's crust—which may collectively be called the *Surroundings*—are no doubt very important, too. They constitute either an inherent part of, or provide indispensable support for, the biosphere, and supply many precious resources for human needs; but they cannot be the permanent home of man.

To understand how the new waves of population expected in the near future can be accommodated on earth, we have then to refer essentially to Habitat, and start by considering what man has done to it during all his centuries of expansion and ascent. In most regions he has in fact brought about true mutations for better or for worse—by felling forests, developing agriculture, spreading his cities and villages, displacing or wiping out other species, and even causing desertification. There are very few suitable places on the planet where his presence has been unimportant (namely, where "civilization" has not yet arrived in one form or another), and very limited indeed are the zones in which pristine wilderness still remains.

We must also realize that, from now on, man's impact is going to be incomparably greater. The explosion of both human population and its demands and the formidable growth of the technosphere can leave no doubts about this. Suffice it to note that today's world population of 4.7 billion represents a quite substantial part (probably about 6%) of the total number of human beings who have lived on earth so far (it is estimated that there have been 70 to 80 billion), and that the present generations are expected to consume during their lifetime more natural resources than all their forefathers together. With the need to fit into Habitat a few more billion people during the next few decades, the situation may get totally out of hand.

Yet we behave with not even a modicum of common sense and reason, as if the planet had no limits and had been made for our exclusive use—and thus let our rivalries, pettiness, and greed push us to deplete and contaminate its ecosystems and our own Habitat at an ever-greater pace. Moreover, we totally disregard the vital necessity of leaving part of our environments untouched so that nature may pursue its evolution undisturbed.

If we persist in these irresponsible attitudes, the earth will be greatly impoverished and we will lose culturally, economically, and morally. Moreover, its overall life-supporting capacity will be drastically reduced and large parts of our very Habitat laid to waste and unable to accommodate the growing billions who will have to live in it. It is therefore urgent that we change urgently and put order and discipline in how we use and transform our one and only planet. Land use and management studies have proved to be a first-class policy tool at the local level. But this is not enough. In a "shrinking" world of growing interdependence and integration, responsible use and management of our global Habitat are imperative. The first thing to do is to examine how our present experience about land use can be of avail and how it must be complemented if we move from the local to the world macro-level. The elaboration of a feasibility study for a world plan of integral land use, management, and conservation, carried out region by region, should therefore be undertaken as soon as possible.

Practically all the information, knowledge, and means to make this study are available. The sources from which elements can be drawn are abundant, indeed, and include:

- Earth scanning results provided by satellites.
- International research projects, such as Geophysical Year (IGY, 1957-58), Biological Programme (IBP, 1964-74), Upper Mantle (UM, 1964-70), Global Atmospheric Research Programme (GARP, 1970-80), Man and Biosphere (MAB, 1971-), World Conservation Strategy (1980, IUCN-UNEP-WWF), Agro-Ecological Zones Reports (1978-80, FAO).
- Population trends reports (UNFPA).
- Development decades reports.
- A thousand other specific studies and reports, including the "Global Ecological Balance" proposed by C.A. Doxiadis in 1974 and the SOS and ABC projects promoted by IFIAS.

The first World Land Use Study will no doubt be of a very preliminary character. Yet, it will certainly teach us a lot about how to put our relationships with the Habitat, and nature generally, on a more rational and satisfactory footing. It would also be the base for further, more advanced inquiries.

The philosophy that should inspire this entire enterprise is clear—if one just thinks of it. For the first time in history, all peoples and nations must actually share a planet that can offer them a limited Habitat only, and thereby they are also bound together by a host of other factors—so much so that, in fact, they will eventually share a common destiny, too. The fate of each one of them cannot ultimately be different from the fate that will befall the planet as a whole—a fate that none of them will be able to escape and that to a large extent is determined by the way in which the world Habitat will be used and safeguarded. Therefore every human group—whether living East, West, North, or South—has a vested interest not only in how the global Habitat and the Habitat of all other human groups will be managed, but also in how, and how soon, the preparatory studies to this effect are carried out.

The World Federalist Movement: Philosophy and Goals

by

Charlotte Waterlow

The World Federalist Movement aims at promoting the creation of a world order: legally, a system of world law; politically, a world government; and economically and socially, a world "community." It believes that these developments are in the logic of history, and that the probable alternatives are world chaos or world destruction.

The Nation State

In "olden days" almost all traditional societies, with the exception of those of Greece and Rome, were based on a social order supposed to reflect the divine order revealed by the prevailing religion, in which the purpose of each person's life was to fulfil his or her allotted function. God, or "the gods," were therefore the sovereign powers, the source of all political and legal authority. In Western Europe, this traditional system began to change at the time of the Renaissance. "Nation states" began to emerge, and within them individuals began to assert their "rights" as *persons*. This led to the secularization of government and law: It is significant that the United States, bursting fully fledged into the "modern" world, explicitly divorced religion from both spheres. The sovereignty of God, wielded through the "universal" Roman Catholic Church, was replaced by "power politics." For two centuries, these nation states have been called "powers," implying that their *raison d'etre* is the pursuit of power or self-interest, rather than of goodness or the brotherhood of humankind. For two centuries, their governments, whether democracies or dictatorships, have gained increasing powers to organize the lives of their citizens. Sovereignty, in internal and external affairs, has thus come to be invested, in theory and practice, in the governments of these secular nation states, although in democracies it lies ultimately with "the people" who elect these govern-

Charlotte Waterlow is chairperson, Education Committee, World Association of World Federalists, Godalming, England.

ments. Small wonder that the era of "power politics" has been an era of imperialism and warfare unprecedented in both nature and scale, partly because the ability of states and individuals to dominate and destroy has been totally transformed by modern technology, culminating in the construction of nuclear weapons.

Human Rights

The rise of the nation state can, however, be regarded as the result of an even more fundamental development: the emergence of the concept of human rights.

The idea that "people matter," as such, that the purpose of a person's life is to express his or her creativity, rather than simply to fulfill a social function, is embedded in the loftiest teachings of all the great religions. But the idea that every person—of whatever sex, race, or social background—has a *right* to conditions that enable him or her to "live in dignity" and to "promote the free development of his personality" (Article 22 of the United Nations' Universal Declaration of Human Rights), and that the essential purpose of political, legal, economic, and social systems is to implement this right for all men and women, is new in history. And so the age of power politics is also the age of Bills of Rights and Declarations of the Rights of Man, culminating in the United Nations' Universal Declaration of Human Rights of 1948. These rights constitute a *moral code,* which differs from all traditional codes in that it is both universal and secular, not explicitly stemming from any divine source.

The rights set out in the United Nations' Universal Declaration fall into two main categories: on the one hand the civil and political rights, and on the other the economic and social. Within nation states the urge to implement them has produced constitutional and democratic systems of government, legal systems that guarantee civil rights, and welfare states to fulfill the economic and social rights to a decent standard of living (see Article 25 of the Universal Declaration). In international relations, this urge has produced the groundwork for a system of international law; of international conflict-solving through discussion and arbitration; of international policing of trouble spots, and of an international welfare state. These developments are embodied in numerous international treaties and are being carried out through the United Nations and a host of entirely new international organizations set up since 1945. A crucial corollary has been the postwar decolonization process, adding, by 1983, 106 newly independent states to the 51 states that signed the United Nations Charter in 1945.

The Nation State and Human Rights

The twentieth century, and particularly the era since 1945, has witnessed a fundamental tension between these two urges: toward the amoral pursuit of national self-interest and security, if necessary through war (there have been about 150 wars since 1945), and toward the implementation of the moral concept of human rights. National power politics have, moreover, been complicated by the phenomenon of the multinational corporations, which pursue the economic interests of their shareholders in a number of countries, generally regardless of human rights and accountable to no individual government. This tension has been exacerbated, since 1945, by ideology. The communist countries affirm the primacy of economic and social rights at the expense of political and civil rights and deny the right to private property (which is not included in the Universal Declaration). The Americans affirm the primacy of civil and political rights, and assert the right to private property, at the expense, to some extent, of social rights. Each country tends to regard the other's ideology as wicked. In between are the West European democracies and some Third World countries, such as India, that are struggling to implement both categories of rights simultaneously.

World Federalism and Human Rights

The basic aim of the World Federalists is to promote a world society grounded on the political, civil, economic, and social rights. As indicated, they believe that failure to implement human-rights policies will lead to a breakdown of the fragile fabric of the world civilization that is now emerging—and quite likely its total destruction. It is a question of grow up or blow up.

Moral Issues

The political and civil rights are in a sense *negative*. They assume that freedom and personal responsibility are moral values; but, as the Canadian Federalist and peace researcher Hanna Newcombe has pointed out, they are concerned with freedom "from" something or freedom "to" do something you want to do. They leave open the question whether people will use their freedom creatively or destructively. Economic and social rights, however, are *positive* in the sense that they imply the creative use of freedom in fraternal action to care for others. Those people who tend to decry social and economic rights tend also to have a cynical view of human nature, asserting that man is inherently power-seeking, profit-seeking, and selfish, and that legal and constitutional restraints on his villainous tendencies, involving the use of force, are therefore all-important. Those people who attach supreme importance to social and economic rights tend to assume that man is, as Rousseau said, "naturally good," and that in a society which is organized to assure his economic and social needs he will spontaneously behave fraternally. According to Marx and Lenin, the state, in the sense of law backed by force, will then "wither away." Of course, in communist countries the state, far from withering away, has become a monstrous growth, while in the Western democracies many people have proved to be humanitarian sheep disguised in the clothes of cynical wolves. It would seem that the truth lies between these two extremes: that the majority of people everywhere are "mixed-up kids," motivated by both "good" and "bad" moral urges. At this moment in history it is essential that the "good" urges should gain the upper hand. A senior State Department official wrote in 1975, "For major world powers, the gut problems of interdependence will remain unsolved until some common norms are devised. At a minimum, finite supplies of both raw materials and of common shared 'spaces' require that the norms of greed and of growth for its own sake be altered. Norms of moderation, cooperation, sharing, and tension-reduction are logically called for by the evolving world situation. They will not be easy to attain in an age of resurgent nationalism."[1] In practical terms, the triumph of "the good" involves the implementation of both kinds of human rights. (In this context it is arguable that the right to private property is not a moral right. The people may decide democratically that some property—for example, public utilities, scarce raw materials, "commons" such as land, water, forests, and air— should be publicly owned, as was almost universally the case in olden days. This ancient principle is now embedded in the Law of the Sea Treaty.

World Federalism and the United Nations

According to its Charter, one of the two aims of the United Nations is the promotion of human rights, involving in particular the positive aim of promoting "social progress and better standards of life in larger freedom." Its other aim is "to save succeeding generations from the scourge of war." And these aims are affirmed by "We the *people* of the United Nations." But the Charter also institutionalizes the nation states, the practitioners of the power politics that is so often the enemy of human rights. In theory, the United Nations cannot intervene in the internal affairs of member states in order to protect or promote human rights. (See Article 2 of the Charter.) There is, therefore, a contradiction at the heart of the United Nations. Is it a collection of national "powers" struggling to live together uneasily in order to avoid mutual destruction; or does it represent, however inadequately, the *peoples* of the world who yearn to be endowed with their human rights? The answer must surely be that it is both these things. As realists, World Federalists are therefore working at both levels. On the one hand, they are working for a legal and constitutional world order to control the "bad" impulses of the national powers and of wicked individuals such as terrorists, dictators, and those in high places who promote "institutionalized violence." On the other hand, they are working for a world economic and social order in which nations will collaborate creatively to promote social and economic rights for all. Such concepts as "world government" and "the surrender of national sovereignty" are relevant to the first objective. The second objective calls for a different kind of thinking, expressed in such terms as "process," "participatory planning," "community," and "common heritage of mankind." But both spheres must be *federal,* in the sense that they must comprise a plurality of tasks, to be performed at the global, regional, national, provincial, and local levels, as well as different units for different kinds of function, from world air traffic control to village bodies to deal with local planning.[2]

In the light of these general principles, the World Federalists' specific aims are essentially pragmatic: to build on the positive elements in today's institutions (positive in the sense of promoting human rights) in order to create tomorrow's world society, which will be both pluralistic and universal.

The Immediate Aims of the World Federalist Movement

At present the World Federalists are trying to promote these principles in certain specific directions: the reform and restructuring of the United Nations system; the promotion of the Law of the Sea Treaty; the promotion of general disarmament in the context of the creation of a system of world enforceable law; and the promotion of social justice in relation to the distribution of wealth between the rich and the poor countries.

The measures that the World Federalists are supporting include:

1. The establishment of a permanent United Nations peace-keeping force—a development from the existing *ad hoc* peace-keeping forces that the United Nations has been sending, on request, to trouble spots around the globe since 1956. The United Nations should have the power to interpose such a force without an invitation from the host country. Its control would endow the United Nations with governmental powers.

2. The development of specific procedures for dispute settlement by the United Nations, already provided for in principle in Article 33 of its Charter. A precedent for compulsory and binding arbitration procedures has now been established in the Law of the Sea Treaty.

3. The strengthening of the International Court of Justice, which deals with disputes between nations.

4. The establishment of an international taxation system in order to endow the United Nations with a secure budget, especially to finance the peace-keeping operations and aid to developing countries.

5. The modification of the great powers' veto rights in the United Nations Security Council, perhaps as a trade off for:

6. The modification of the United Nations voting principle— one nation, one vote—in order to make the organization more genuinely representative of the *peoples* of a world where a state's population may range from over a billion (China) to a few

thousand.

7. The establishment of an International Criminal Court to try terrorists and the leaders of countries that commit acts of aggression—as in the precedent set by the Nuremberg trials of 1945. (In 1928, for the first time in history, to wage aggressive war was declared by international consensus to be a crime, in the Pact of Paris signed by 68 nations).

8. The strengthening of the international procedures for dealing with violations of civil and political rights. The United Nations Commission on Human Rights is essentially an investigative body. The Human Rights Commission and Court of the Council of Europe (a body that includes all noncommunist European states) have powers to condemn and expel countries that violate political rights (as has happened in Greece and Turkey), and to hear appeals of individuals against the violation of their personal civil and political rights by their governments. The establishment of the right of an individual to appeal to an international court over the head of his own government is a precedent that should be developed at the regional and world levels.

9. The setting up of international bodies with *executive* powers to perform certain functions—for example, the International Seabed Authority to operate the mining of the deep sea minerals (already a basic component of the Law of the Sea Treaty); an international disarmament organization to organize and supervise universal disarmament; executive bodies to administer international food stockpiles and pools of commodities whose export is basic to many of the developing countries' economies; a "central bank of central banks" (to use Keynes's term) to control international credit and administer the "Special Drawing Rights," a sort of international reserve currency created by the International Monetary Fund; an executive body to administer the Code of Conduct for multinational corporations that the United Nations is drawing up.

These immediate aims show that it is *not* the policy of the World Federalist Movement to clamp down on the world a constitution for a world government. Rather, its policy is to build on and extrapolate from the existing developments that are taking place in our complex and confused world. The trend of events since 1945 is imperceptibly complementing the development of legalistic steps towards the rule of world law with innovative federalist processes. The model developed by the European Community, that of the *evolution* of the Community through gradually expanding its powers, its functions, and its membership—this may be described as "creeping federalism"—would seem particularly appropriate.

While proponents of "national interests" rant and rage, it just seems sensible for certain tasks to be performed at the regional or global levels. And it is significant that while working together on non-military matters, the European Community countries, the cockpits of World Wars I and II, have created a climate in Western Europe in which war between themselves is unthinkable.

These piecemeal aims and developments conceal a basic trend: the international order is moving from the stage of international consultation, discussion, and research into the stage of international executive action. In the regional and functional spheres, it is being found necessary to establish bodies with powers to execute policies. There is a creeping transfer of sovereignty—or a creeping expansion of sovereignty. So what the World Federalists are doing is essentially to push history along, both in practical actions and in radiating a philosophy grounded in faith in the inherent brotherhood of man.

Notes

1. U.S. Department of State, Special Report of the Bureau of Public Affairs No. 17, July 1975.

2. This concept of "subsidiarity" has been stressed in the series of Papal Encyclicals on economic and social matters, starting with that of 1893.

Responses to Technological Change

Federal Foresight:
Achievements and Aspirations

by

Audrey Clayton and Timothy C. Mack

Foresight has been defined as the ability to deal with long-range issues by first anticipating future developments and then formulating policies and programs that will minimize potential problems or exploit potential opportunities.[1] The purpose of foresight is to improve the information base for decision-making. It is particularly appropriate for legislators to exercise foresight, because many of their decisions tend to have long-term implications, remaining in effect until new decisions, laws, or regulations replace or amend the old. *Both* forecasting and assessment are essential components of the foresight process. What is needed is an institutional capacity to project long-range trends, both national and global; to assess their consequences; and to use these projections as inputs in the process of strategic assessment, policy development, and decision-making. Such a formal, systematic capability for comprehensive long-range foresight is becoming increasingly important in this information age of technological acceleration. A recent quote in the Congressional Record noted that:

> in the new Information Society . . . we need a nation-wide system of more timely and reliable social, economic, cultural and political indicators. These can provide a stronger factual basis for democratic planning, budgeting and implementation and for open and informed debate throughout the country.[2]

Hugh Heclo illustrates very effectively the growing need of decision-makers for effective assessment capabilities in an increasingly complex society:

Audrey Clayton is with the U.S. General Accounting Office, Washington, D.C. Timothy C. Mack is a consultant to the U.S. General Accounting Office.

In 1954 President Eisenhower could propose a new interstate highway program that was just that: a plan for building roads. The issue was initiated, debated, and executed with minimal attention to non-highway considerations. Today we would expect, almost without thinking about it, that consideration of such an issue should include the implications for private-car versus mass-public transportation, energy conservation, environmental impacts, effects on urban development and neighborhoods, regional economic development programs, minority hiring by road-construction contractors, and on and on. We may disagree about how trade-offs among these various concerns should be struck, but few would deny the legitimacy of their presence in any agenda of highway building.[3]

Despite this growing need for organized, purposeful "planning ahead," there is not at present a structured and integrated capacity for federal foresight. While outyear budgets, multi-year goals, etc., provide Congress and the executive branch narrow windows on certain fiscal and programmatic aspects of governmental operation, and a number of federal agencies do use sophisticated models as tools of long-range analysis and planning, a broad systematic approach is lacking.[4]

Obstacles

Why is this? Why is comprehensive, systematic foresight not a formal component of the governmental process? There is no one simple answer. Some of the reasons can be identified, however, and it is these we propose to discuss.

The preparation of forecasts is an essential first phase of foresight, but forecasts are frequently criticized because they do not "come true." While examples abound, some lesser known, subsequently invalidated forecasts include:

"...it is highly unlikely that an airplane, or fleet of them, could ever successfully sink a fleet of Navy vessels under battle conditions."— Franklin D. Roosevelt, then Assistant Secretary of the Navy, 1922.

"Stocks have reached what looks like a permanently high plateau"— Irving Fisher, professor of economics, Yale University, October 17, 1929.

". . . we don't like their sound. Groups of guitars are on the way out."—A Decca Recording Company executive turning down the Beatles, 1962.[5]

A focus on the relative accuracy of a forecast ignores one of the essential rationales for forecasting, namely, that it provides an opportunity for intervention: for purposeful action to change what would otherwise happen. A commonly quoted example is that of two planes in flight patterns indicating imminent collision. Once the present situation is perceived and the aircraft's progress extrapolated to the logical conclusion (intersecting paths), a forecast can be made (collision). At that point, evasive action can be initiated. The focus is on responsive options rather than on the actual fulfillment of the prediction. As another example, "future history" authors such as Huxley *(Brave New World)* and Orwell *(1984)* published their pessimistic forecasts primarily to influence decision-making on contemporary social policy—and thereby to preclude the occurrence of the situations they described.[6]

Another factor contributing to the relatively low utilization of forecasts is a lack of consensus among the forecasters. There is rarely a single voice, "crying in the wilderness." Instead, the voice is one among many straining to be heard, each with a different message. It is easy to look back and identify the "true prophet"— such as M. King Hubbert, who anticipated the oil crisis. But what criteria would have enabled us at the time to accept his analysis, while rejecting the contrary views of so many others? During the early 1960s, Hubbert developed a cogent argument that U.S. oil and gas production were about to peak and that substantial downtrends could be anticipated in the 1970s.[7] Unfortunately, "numerous other forecasters were available to support the case for alternatives to Hubbert's prediction. Anyone who had a specific energy future in mind could pick and choose the information needed to support his case."[8] The point to be emphasized is the difficulty of making a correct choice in this area, except in hindsight. The situation in this regard is not improving. Not only the forecasts, but the data on which they are based, are frequently the subject of contention, [9] and concerns over integrity of data must remain critical to effective forecasting.

Yet another reason for the widespread perception of inconsistency among forecasts springs from the uneven utilization of forecasting in the public arena. Policymakers sometimes prefer to disregard forecasts that appear to support priorities other than their own, or, on the other hand, may emphasize potential future problems largely because the political liabilities of current concerns are too intimidating.[10]

This brings us to the final impediment to the establishment of an effective federal foresight capability: the failure of prior attempts. A major causal factor is the nature of government itself. Government usually has to react to crisis rather that having the ability to study, analyze, and anticipate critical issues. While governments often acknowledge the need to plan for world changes in the years ahead, most have developed relatively little capacity to do so. A government obviously must survive the present if it is to reach the future, but if it concerns itself *only* with the present it may find itself without the resources to cope with the future. Today's crises often arise because organizations are too busy with yesterday to deal effectively with problems that are not yet perceived as critical.

The Congressional Research Service has noted that, 120 years ago, all federal functions fell into one of five simple categories: postal, customs, defense/diplomacy, new lands, and Indian affairs.[11] In the last century, the roles and responsibilities of government have expanded enormously—and with them the duties of the public servant. With this growing complexity, it is very difficult for contemporary elected officials and representatives to focus on the long-term. Their constituents want action on current problems and deficiencies in the system; their time is taken up more and more by the "routine" processes of government.

A number of specific obstacles to congressional foresight have been cited frequently:

1. There is little or no executive support for foresight.
2. The "best talent" has never worked on broad, long-term issues.
3. Bureaucratic rigidity, compartmentalization, and specialization have frustrated attempts to promote cooperation among departments and to take a broad, long-term view.
4. Time pressures restrict vision to the short run.
5. By the time models or forecasts are developed, policy-level officials have either moved on or lost interest.
6. Policy-level officials lack the knowledge and experience to use models properly.
7. The products of modelers' efforts are incomprehensible or irrelevant (to practical policy concerns), or both.
8. There is poor communication among those who contract for models and forecasts, those who develop them, and those who are supposed to use them.
9. Congress does not care about the long-term future.
10. The public does not care about the long-term future.[12]

Some congressional observers also complain of a perceived anti-analysis attitude in Congress,[13] while congressmen complain of the failure of forecasting to focus on essential political issues.[14]

Achievements

Acknowledgement in Congress and the executive branch of the need for systematic planning and forecasting has been intermittent. Ad hoc efforts have been made in specific subject areas, such as the 1969 National Environmental Policy Act (NEPA), which mandated an interdisciplinary approach to examine the effects of short-term uses of resources on long-term productivity. NEPA remains a model, although the intervention of the judiciary produced some unforeseen results. This sort of effort, however, too often tends to focus on substantive issues while neglecting methodological and data issues. Attempts have been made to institutionalize some analytical capability to identify long-term trends, by the establishment of the Council of Economic Advisors (1946), and to examine the potential future impacts of contemplated legislative initiatives, through the Office of Technology Assessment (1969). As a rule, however, these efforts have been episodic and uneven, focusing on specific issues or data sets. At present, foresight comes from widely scattered and insular sources, and widely shared methodological assumptions are uncommon.

Much more promising among efforts to increase federal forecasting ability are initiatives focused on Congress's own decision-making process and abilities. (Indeed, there are those who argue that "futurism" has been so successfully institutionalized and integrated into the legislative process that no one sees it.)[15] In 1970, the Congressional Research Service was charged with systematically providing to Congress information about trends and emerging issues; helping congressional committees incorporate foresight into their proceedings; assisting legislators in looking at future consequences of decisions made today; and involving citizens in the anticipatory processes of government. In 1975, a House Rule was established requiring each committee to undertake, on a continuing basis, futures research and forecasting on matters within its jurisdiction. The Senate was less specific, but did recommend, in 1976, the establishment throughout the authorizing committees of a responsibility for early identification and analysis of possible major policy problems. Mandates were also issued for the various congressional support agencies (the Congressional Budget Office, the Office of Technology Assessment, the General Accounting Office, and the Congressional Research Service) to undertake systematic futures research. Another move designed to focus legislative thinking upon the future was the establishment in 1975 of a legislative service organization, the Congressional Clearinghouse on the Future, whose purpose is to coordinate and promote futures activities.

Executive branch interest in forecasting has focused less upon institutionalization and more upon one-time studies and the appointment of commissions. The first apparent use of a distinct, non-issue-specific forecasting approach by the federal government occurred in 1929, when President Herbert Hoover created a Presidential Research Commission on Social Trends. The techniques employed by that body, and the findings that resulted, played a significant role in the New Deal process of planning and decision-making, and laid the foundation for subsequent methodological developments in forecasting.[16]

While such institutions as the National Science Foundation and the Council of Economic Advisors do pay some attention to long-term trends, no current institutionalized, comprehensive forecasting function has been clearly identified in the executive (or the legislative) branch. Proposals for creating an institutional focus for long-range global policymaking in the executive branch usually recommend that it be placed in the Executive Office of the President. The Reagan administration has apparently taken a small step in this direction by creating a new "national indicator system," directed by a Special Assistant to the President. This is viewed as "a system for providing social and demographic information to the policy people in a systematic and regular way, in advance of policy debates."[17] In a similar vein, a recent development at the state level looks hopeful. In Delaware, the governor and legislature recently agreed to use revenue forecasts from the Delaware Economic and Financial Advisory Council (DEFAC), an independent group established by the previous governor but virtually ignored. The 24-member council includes legislators of both parties and 13 persons from the private sector, many of them economists representing companies doing business in Delaware. "In many states, revenue forecasting is a very political process whereby the group in power will choose the forecast they like best," says Eleanor Craig, an economics professor at the University of Delaware who chairs DEFAC. "That's why so many states are in trouble now. They can't agree on numbers. Now we can, and we've had one of the most successful revenue-forecasting programs in the country."[18]

Some of the more prominent ad hoc federal efforts were summarized in the Appendix to Volume One of *The Global 2000 Report to the President* (which is itself an example of such a project, initiated by President Jimmy Carter in 1977). This study was a significant attempt to establish trends in population, resources, and the environment worldwide, from 1975 to 2000, and has focused much-needed attention not only on a number of critical issues, but on the continuing need for some type of ongoing forecasting capability on a national or even a global scale.

It is in relation to this now "classic" forecasting effort, however, that the extent of the obstacles to effective federal forecasting begins to become evident. Even Gerald Barney, director of the Global 2000 study, was disarmingly frank in acknowledging its shortcomings. He stated that, although individual executive agencies possess impressive, if uneven, capabilities for long-range analysis and forecasting within their separate areas of responsibility and interest, the analysis shows that collectively, "they are not now capable of presenting the President with internally consistent projections of world trends in population, resources, and the environment for the next two decades."[19]

Julian Simon and Herman Kahn, in *Global 2000 Revised,* were even more critical:

> The staffs of government and their agencies are ill-equipped to produce sound assessments of long-run future trends concerning resources. Internal government assessments suffer because of the organizational forces that prevail in government no matter what the administration, as well as because the best scientific authorities are not usually found on government staffs. Insider-produced government reports must pass through reviews at various stages up the chain of command, and the final conclusions of a staff report therefore are likely to emphasize conventional views and to reduce the range of opinion expressed. The resulting work cannot then be attributed to individuals, and no individuals need take full responsibility.[20]

Another group of necessary considerations surrounds the role of "advisors to government," including planners and forecasters. During the 1970s, the long-cherished American concept of experts working with political leaders to optimize highly structured, carefully defined national policy options, priorities, and programs became an image of unobtainable ideals, rigid thinking, and elitist and dogmatic power. As a result, many felt that the purely rational non-incremental approach to decision-making declined in use during the 1970s. Weaknesses in the foundations of the rational approach—its information systems, political-science theories and methodologies, and analytical tools and activities— came under scrutiny from both theoreticians and practitioners. Rather than maintaining old emphases, concerns were shifting toward a more flexible, value-oriented, pragmatic, modest, and above all useful formulation and application of reasoned knowledge in a complex pluralistic political process.[21]

When turning to the examination of recent proposals for expanding federal forecasting ability, these considerations and the others detailed below must be taken into account.

Aspirations

Three bills introduced in the 98th Congress were intended to improve the federal government's capacity for long-range strategic planning. They were:

• S. 1025, and the identical H.R. 2491, the "Global Resources, Environment and Population Act," introduced by Senator Mark Hatfield (R-OR) and Representative Richard Ottinger (D-NY), respectively.

• H.R. 3070, the "Critical Trends Assessment Act," sponsored by Representatives Albert Gore, Jr. (D-TN), and Newton Gingrich (R- GA).

• H.J. Res. 248, proposed by Representative Nicholas Mavroules (D- MA) and 23 co-sponsors, calling on the executive branch to conform to the recommendations of the Global 2000 Report.

The first bill (S. 1025/H.R. 2491) would establish in the federal government a global foresight capability with respect to natural resources, the environment, and population; would establish a national population policy; and would establish an inter-agency council to provide the President and Congress with an annual analysis of current and foreseeable trends in global demographics. Based on this analysis, the report would evaluate the adequacy of available resources (as defined therein) to meet human and economic needs in the future.

H.R. 3070 would establish an Office of Critical Trends Analysis in the executive branch. The office would make recommendations to the President and establish an advisory council to promote public dialogue on critical trends and alternative futures. The office would publish a report every 4 years identifying critical economic, technological, demographic, political, and environmental trends over a 20-year period. The report, detailing the effect of existing and alternative government policies on these trends, would be submitted to both houses of Congress. The Joint Economic Committee would be required to publish every 2 years, beginning in 1987, a legislative branch report examining the Office's conclusions and submitting its own findings.

The joint resolution (H.J. Res. 248) is designed to "complement" the other bills and serve as a "fall back solution" that sponsors see as "more palatable to a cost-conscious Congress." The bill calls on the executive branch to "conform" to the recommendations of the Global 2000 Report.

The bills as they stand are certainly far from flawless. More significantly, however, they raise broad philosophical questions: Is it appropriate and feasible for the federal government to institutionalize some type of foresight capability? Does the present legislation reflect the most effective approach? Would it provide useful inputs to the policymaking process?

Observations and Recommendations

Various criticisms have been leveled at this type of legislation. Opposition takes three forms. First, "it won't pass": the bills are "doomed to failure" because of the "historic congressional pathology" of "top down" leadership that prevents public input in generating open-ended images of the future,[22] coupled with an unwillingness of many legislators to leave the foresight lead in executive hands. Second, "it won't work": centralizing even something so basic as government statistical projections into one office would also restrict the variety of "differing assumptions which enrich the decisionmaking process,"[23] plus reducing the role of specific operating agencies as advocates and audiences for specialized parts of these forecasts. Third, "it shouldn't be allowed": "an Office of Critical Trends Assessment would be the first step on the road to central economic planning," [24] i.e., the search for the one right answer.

Institutionalization of a federal foresight capacity could be useful. We recognize, however, the place of negotiation in the lawmaking process. To maximize the benefits and to calm the misgivings of opponents, we suggest the following modifications to the approach presented in the current bills:

• Separate the preparation of statistical trends from the formulation of alternative futures.

• Centralize the coordination of the government's forecasting capability, but de-politicize this part of the process, with an emphasis on quality control and compatibility of data bases.

• Provide explicit foresight assumptions to aid discussion and consensus building.

• Provide an institutional link with policymaking activities to ensure that the results are used.

The rationale for treating trend monitoring, projection, and critical trends assessment as tasks separate from the development of hypothetical future scenarios is that the former activities can be approached in a manner that is more value-free. This can provide a common point of departure for exploration of policy options. The second, avowedly political phase of the foresight effort would develop hypothetical futures corresponding to various assumptions as to controllable and uncontrollable influencing factors. There would also be a normative focus, including the identification of events or trends that should or should not be encouraged, and the policies and conditions that will promote the outcome desired by the particular administration in office.

Overall analysis and policymaking require consistent, integrated forecasts based on explicit assumptions and a unified database. This, in turn, requires the coordination of existing diverse agency capabilities and information resources. Such centralized coordination could be depoliticized by establishing, for example, an "Advisory Commission on Trends and Future Policy Issues for the Public Sector" outside the executive branch, with a director selected in a manner similar to the statutory process used to appoint the Comptroller General (a unique appointment process for a 15-year term, established under the General Accounting Act of 1980, [25] with the legislative branch proposing candidates and the executive branch making a final choice). Such an appointment could provide continuity across administrations.

The commission would be charged with producing critical trend reports at regular intervals for executive and legislative branch comment. These reports would be a consolidation of existing capabilities throughout the government. It could draw on the expertise of the Bureau of the Census, National Bureau of Standards, General Accounting Office, and Office of Management and Budget, which already have statistical oversight, as well as centers of statistical and forecasting functions in other agencies. Centralization of trend identification already exists in Canada, and coordination as described would introduce more discipline and coherence, and help avoid duplication of effort, which has been a matter of some concern since the abolition of the centralized guardian of federal foresight data, OMB's Statistical Policy Branch, [26] and general weakening of the role of Chief Statistician. The commission, therefore, could provide technical assistance and function as coordinator and an advocate for forecasting functions throughout the executive branch.

This is not to advocate a "forecasting czar" to dictate methodological dogma and exclude heretics, but rather to recommend a centralized coordinating function that would increase efficiency and enhance the availability, quality, and consistency of data from a broad national viewpoint. The executive and legislative branches, and other users, could then develop their own individual scenarios or alternative futures as a background for assessing and proposing specific strategies for achieving desired goals.

In addition, we share the concern of some members of the legislative branch that the placement of forecasting responsibilities solely in the executive branch may result in the loss of important inputs from elsewhere in the government. We therefore suggest that some expansion of H.R. 3070's joint and interactive responsibilities approach be utilized between executive and legislative forecasters.

Finally, institutional links with policymakers are essential if foresight capabilities are to be useful and to be used. The regular provision of critical trend reports, as proposed in H.R. 3070, to both executive and legislative branches would ensure the access of the decision-makers to the information base. Promoters of specific issues or policies could also be relied upon to disseminate their own perceptions of one or more alternative futures. It seems safe to assume, at least initially, that pressures would arise for action, comparable to the Mavroules Resolution calling for the executive branch to "conform to the recommendations of the Global 2000 Report," or the similar letter from Senator Charles Mathias to the President, cosigned by 84 other members of Congress, which strongly urged that he give the implementation report *Global Future: Time to Act* [27] his thoughtful consideration and that he put into motion the machinery that would translate these recommendations into action. Thus, we are optimistic that a formal linkage process need not be institutionalized, provided that the foresight process itself gains credibility through the balance-of-powers dynamic, coupled with a recognition of the difficulty of effectively "mandating" such a link.

Conclusion

The very fact that three bills addressing various aspects of the foresight issue have been introduced in the current session of Congress indicates continuing congressional concern in this area. The Council on Environmental Quality's Global Issues Work Group is in the process of updating and following up on the *Global 2000 Report to the President*. The Congressional Clearinghouse on the Future has already drafted a schedule of critical issues recommended for congressional analysis in 1984, based on the Future Agenda Project conducted jointly with the Congressional Institute for the Future. The stage has thus been set for a renewed thrust toward institutionalization of a federal foresight capability.

Although the problems of actually implementing such foresight legislation will be immense, that does not detract from the importance of such an effort. The credibility of federal forecasts could be enhanced through two related efforts. The first involves education of both the government at large and the public concerning the underlying value and purpose of forecasting, which lies in the opportunity for intervention. The Congressional Clearinghouse on the Future is presently addressing this problem in the legislative branch. The second effort centers around the establishment of an integrated nonpolitical approach to data-base unification and forecast generation, which would formulate a single, explicit set of assumptions on which its forecasts are based. This should reduce the confusion that is generated by conflicting forecasts from multiple sources with no accompanying rationale for the discrepancies.

Past attempts have failed in part as a result of the problems noted above. While there is no guarantee of success with any approach, the separation of trend analysis from policy analysis, combined with the generation of several alternative futures, seems to hold promise. This should enhance the objectivity of the trend analysis and thus reduce the vulnerability of the effort as a whole to charges of political bias and distortion.

Notes

1. *Global Models, World Futures, and Public Policy: A Critique* (Washington, D.C., Office of Technology Assessment, April 1982), p.5.

2. Gross, Bertram, "Grassroots Planning in a Global Perspective," as quoted by John Conyers, Jr., *Congressional Record,* October 20, 1983, p.E5025.

3. Heclo, Hugh, "One Executive Branch or Many?," in Anthony King (ed.), *Both Ends of the Avenue: The Presidency, the Executive Branch, and Congress in the 1980s* (Washington, D.C.: American Enterprise Institute, 1983), p.33.

4. This need is now being more widely recognized in the literature. For example, an excellent discussion of the problems surrounding the creation of the Office of Technology Assessment can be found in Coates, Vary T., "Establishing Governmental Forecasting and Assessment Institutions: Common Problems and Lessons Learned" (presented to the IEEE Conference on Systems, Man, and Cybernetics, December 30, 1983-January 17, 1984).

5. Cerf, Christopher, and Victor Navasky, *The Experts Speak* (N.Y.: Pantheon Press, 1984).

6. Becker, Harold S., "Scenarios: A Tool of Growing Importance to Policy Analysis in Government and Industry," *Technological Forecasting and Social Change* 23, 1983, p.195.

7. Hubbert, M.K., *Energy Resources: A Report to the Committee on Energy and Commerce,* National Academy of Sciences, NRC Publication 1000-D, 1962.

8. Congressional Research Service, *Strategic Issues: Historical Experience, Institutional Structures and Conceptual Framework* (Washington, D.C.: Government Printing Office, 1982), Committee Print 97-KK p.16.

9. U.S. Congress, *Federal Government Statistics and Statistical Policy: Hearings Before the House Committee on Government Operations, June 3, 1982* (Washington, D.C.: Government Printing Office).

10. Ascher, William, *Forecasting: An Appraisal for Policymakers and Planners* (Baltimore, MD: Johns Hopkins University Press, 1978), pp.18-25.

11. Congressional Research Service, *Strategic Issues: Historical Experience, Institutional Structures and Conceptual Framework,* (Washington, D.C.: Government Printing Office, 1982), Committee Print 97-KK, p.11.

12. Richardson, John M., Jr., "Towards Effective Foresight in the United States Government" (prepared for the U.S. Department of State, June 1979),

pp.13-18.

13. Schick, Allen, "The Supply and Demand for Analysis on Capitol Hill," *Policy Analysis,* Spring 1976, pp.215-234.

14. Sarbanes, Rep. Paul S., in the U.S. Congress, House Select Committee on Committees, *Panel Discussions on Committee Organization in the House of Representatives: An Inquiry Under Authority of H.Res. 132,* June-July 1973, 93rd Congress, 1st Session, 1973, p.514.

15. Shribman, David, "Now and Then, Congress Also Ponders the Future," *The New York Times,* March 14, 1982, p.10E.

16. Little, Dennis L., et al., *Long Range Planning* (Washington, D.C.: U.S. Library of Congress, Congressional Research Service, 1976), pp.384-390.

17. Beal, Richard, Special Assistant to the President, and Director of Planning and Evaluation, quoted by Phillip S. Hills, "White House Uses Social Sciences, But Cuts Funding for Research," *Washington Post,* June 29, 1981, p. A8.

18. Fitzgerald, Randy, "The Little State That Could—And Did!" *The Reader's Digest,* December 1983, p. 189.

19. Barney, Gerald O., *The Global 2000 Report to the President: Entering the Twenty-First Century* (Washington, D.C.: U.S. Council on Environmental Quality and Department of State, 1980), Vol. 2, p.454.

20. Simon, Julian L., and Herman Kahn, *Global 2000 Revised* (Washington, D.C.: The Heritage Foundation, 1983).

21. Wilson, David A., *The National Planning Idea in U.S. Public Policy* (Boulder, Colorado: Westview Press, 1980), p.224-5.

22. Coates, Joseph, as quoted in "Global Foresight," *Foresights,* No. 10, July 1983, p.3.

23. Boggs, Danny, as quoted in "Global Foresight," *Foresights,* No. 10, July 1983, p.3.

24. McKenzie, Richard B., "The Future File," *The Washington Post,* August 22, 1983.

25. PL 96-226, Section 104.

26. For a thorough discussion of the abolition of OMB's Statistical Policy branch, see U.S. Congress, *Federal Government Statistics and Statistical Policy: Hearing Before a Subcommittee of the Committee on Government Operations, House of Representatives, June 3, 1982* (Washington, D.C.: GPO, 1982).

27. Yost, Nicholas, Staff Director, *Global Future: Time to Act, Report to the President on Global Resources, Environment and Population* (Washington, D.C.: U.S. Council on Environmental Quality, and Department of State, January 1981).

King Canute and the Information Resource

by

Harlan Cleveland

Some people collect coins or stamps or snuffboxes or forgeries of Salvador Dali paintings. I have taken to collecting Canutes—instances of behavior reminiscent of the legendary Danish monarch who stood on the beach and commanded the tides to stand still as proof of his power.

The information environment created by the explosive convergence of computers and modern telecommunications is full of examples of Canutish behavior. The trouble seems to be that, in our thinking about information, we have carried over concepts that used to work pretty well for the management of material things. But information (enhanced by modern telecommunications and fast computers) is such a different kind of resource that our inherited wisdom is somehow transmuted into folly.

Unlike coal or uranium or steel or automobiles or food or clothing, information is expandable (it grows with use, enhances its value through dissemination), diffusive (it leaks at nearly the speed of light, and is therefore harder to hide), and shareable (if I give you food or sell you an automobile, you have it and I don't; if I give you a fact or sell you an idea, we both have it).

In the United States, still the most "post-industrial" country, about half of all work, as defined by the Census Bureau's employment categories, is now information work—not only writing and calculating, but what executives, salesmen, advertisers, lawyers, accountants, secretaries, programmers, consultants, and hundreds of other kinds of workers do. And, though the Census Bureau doesn't say so, the ratio of brainwork to drudgery in nearly every job keeps rising. What are the implications for our inherited social wisdom of this sudden dominance of the information resource?

Harlan Cleveland is director of the Hubert H. Humphrey Institute of Public Affairs, University of Minnesota, Minneapolis, Minnesota. Portions of this article have appeared in Technology Review *(January 1984) and* Intermedia *(January 1984).*

151

even a separate discipline. It's something like the early reaction to space exploration. When the Mercury and Apollo programs were projected, it seemed at first that outer space might become a new principle of organization. But it soon dawned on us that space was not a new subject but a new place where all the old subjects—physics, biochemistry, medicine, military science, law, economics, politics, even art and philosophy—took on interesting new dimensions.

In a similar way, the convergence of computers and telecommunications doesn't resolve the ancient puzzles about human rights and responsibilities, Man and Nature, liberty and authority, productivity and fairness, pursuit of the common good in a world full of individuals, and protection of the global commons in a world full of nation-states.

But the new information environment, what the French call "the informatization of society," does change the context in which these durable dilemmas present themselves in the 1980s and 1990s. Out there in the marketplace of ideas, this expandable, leaky, shareable resource is creating a lot of confusion as it undermines our inherited wisdom. Out of a hundred possible examples, consider what's happening to our ideas about "control" and about "ownership."

The Nobody-in-Control Society

Knowledge is power, as Francis Bacon wrote in 1597. So the wider the spread of knowledge, the more work has to get done by horizontal process—what the Japanese call consensus, the Indonesians call mushyawara, communists call collective leadership, and Americans call teamwork. If the Census Bureau counted each year the number of committees per thousand population, we would have a rough measure of the bundle of changes we call "the information society."

The King Canute prize for 1981 was easily won by Secretary of State Alexander Haig. Shortly after the attempted assassination of President Reagan, Haig announced on television from the White House that "I am in control here." That produced neither reassurance nor anger from the American people but nervous laughter, as in watching a theater of the absurd. We, the people, know by instinct that in our pluralistic democracy no one is, can be, or even should be "in control," that by Constitutional design reinforced by information technology we live in a nobody-in-charge society.

We all know other Canutes whose absurdities don't get on national television: executives who give orders when they should be asking questions, managers who think of their co-workers as superiors or subordinates, impatient doers who don't have time for lateral consultation—in sum, the builders of bureaucratic pyramids who haven't adjusted to the new information environment.

In an information-rich polity, the very definition of "control" changes. Very large numbers of people empowered by knowledge—coming together in parties, unions, factions, lobbies, interest-groups, neighborhoods, families, and hundreds of other structures—assert the right or feel the obligation to "make policy." Decision-making proceeds not by "recommendations up, orders down" but by plural improvisation on a shared sense of direction. Secrecy goes out of fashion, because secrets are so hard to keep. Participation and public feedback become conditions precedent to decisions that stick. And "policy" widens out to become what Paul Appleby called it a generation ago: "the decisions that are made at your level and higher."

Information As Property

The openness that the informatization of society brings in its train is bound to raise fundamental questions about the idea that information "belongs" to a person or an organization. The propensity of information to leak is, like waves eating away the foundations of a seashore condominium, eroding the doctrine that information can be owned, exchanged, and monopolized the way "real" resources can. Those who persist in treating information as property are likely to get wet.

Two kinds of waves are rolling in. Dynamic high-technology keeps developing better and faster techniques of piracy—xerography, videotape, the backyard dish for picking up signals from satellites. The knowledge explosion also produces new kinds of works (computer software) and means of delivery (microfiche, videocassettes, computerized data bases). Laws written to protect books and phonograph records and broadcasts, the products of the past, are getting harder and harder to apply. Laws that address technologies not yet invented are hard to write.

Yet the Canutes persevere.

The Association of American Publishers sued New York University and nine professors for infringing copyright when they helped students learn by copying useful literature. They had to settle for vague promises to be good, at least for four years; the publishers didn't even get their court costs back.

The tasteless folks who own Home Box Office think it's bad taste for homeowners to build receiving stations on their roofs to capture HBO signals floating in the public's airwaves.

The Columbia Broadcasting System seems to believe it can establish a proprietary right to what it reports on CBS News. "They think they can 'own' history," says one outraged scholar.

And Universal City Studios is still trying to get Sony to ban the sale of Sony videotape recorders for use by people in their living rooms. Not only that, but a panel of federal judges in the Ninth Circuit agreed with Universal, in an opinion that for sheer effrontery to common sense rates the King Canute prize for 1982. Their ruling: " 'Off-the-air' copying of copyrighted materials by owners of videotape recorders in their own homes for private noncommercial use constitutes an infringement of copyrighted audiovisual materials."

Sometimes the law seems to be like Kipling's Elephant's Child, its nose pulled out of shape by the crocodile of reality. I have struggled through the densely legalistic prose of Universal City v. Sony, and diagnosed the appeals judges' problem: a dynamic technological environment makes them acutely uncomfortable. In the tradition of the law, which looks backward at precedent and past legislative intentions, they hitched their wagon to what Congress, in its ignorance, meant to say about technologies it couldn't yet imagine.

Courts are inhibited (though not precluded) by training, tradition, mandate, and structure from recognizing the nontraditional. The great dissenters such as Holmes and Brandeis were willing to peer into the future, but their dissents didn't become "the law" until, much later, the future arrived. Where there is no past to cling to, some judges become disoriented—and the resulting obscurity of their language doesn't really hide the fact that they are at sea.

The Supreme Court recently overturned the lower court ruling against Sony, thus showing that horse sense is not necessarily incompatible with the law. Perhaps they heeded the advice of Lao Tzu: "To know that you do not know is the best. To pretend to know when you do not is a disease."

The nervous breakdown of copyright protection may be retarded to some degree by technological fixes. Satellite broadcasters can scramble their signals to prevent pirating. Elaborate codes have been devised by the creators of some computer programs, though teenage "computer hackers" have been showing how inherently porous they are. Recording your unique insights on videodiscs may keep them secret at least from people who cannot afford videodisc technology.

When I first acquired a home computer, I found the ethical dilemma right up front; it came with the instruction manual. On its opening page I was threatened with litigious mayhem if I copied any of the instructions. On the very next page, I was told that before I did anything else I should make at least two copies of the floppy disk provided with the manual. Since then, the technological fix is increasingly in vogue: a couple of more recently purchased software packages contain floppy disks that self-destruct after the first backup copies are made, so they can't be replicated ad infinitum and furnished to my friends.

But the leakiness of the information resource seems destined to overwhelm the Canutish efforts to imprison it. The history of arms control, and the teenage computer pirates, teach us that there is always a technological fix for a technological fix.

Is the doctrine that information is owned by its originator (or compiler) necessary to make sure Americans remain intellectually creative? In most other countries, creative work is over-whelmingly controlled by organizations and carried out by salaried people. In Japan, even the most inventive employee is likely to have a lifetime job and receive salary raises in lockstep with his age cohort, his morale sustained not by personal owner-ship of his ideas but by togetherness in an organizational family.

Most U.S. patents are held by organizations (corporations, uni-versities, government agencies), not by the inventors. Many copyrights, perhaps most, are held by publishers and promoters, not by the authors and songwriters the Founding Fathers may have had in mind when they sewed information-as-property into the U.S. Constitution.

An author or songwriter who helps a publisher make money should certainly participate in the profits. But direct agreements about profit-sharing or joint venture arrangements (the movie industry is already full of relevant examples) seem a less fragile basis for such cooperation than fraying fictions that the author "owns" the words in a book and that shared information is being "exchanged."

In U.S. universities and research institutes, creative work is already rewarded mostly by promotion, tenure and tolerant trad-itions about teaching loads and outside consulting. We generate a respectably innovative research-and-development effort in pub-lic-sector fields such as military technology, space exploration, weather forecasting, environmental protection, and the control of infectious diseases without the scientists and inventors having to "own" the ideas they contribute to the process.

In the private sector, the leaders of industries on the high-technology frontier are already saying out loud that their protec-tion from overseas copyists doesn't lie in "trade secrets" but in healthy research-and-development budgets. John Rollwagen, chief executive of Cray Research, which produces the world's most powerful computer, puts it this way: "By the time the Japanese have figured out how to build a Cray 1, we have to be well along in designing Cray 2—or we're out of business."

The notion of information-as-property is built deep into our laws, our economy, and our political psyche—and into the expec-tations and tax returns and balance sheets of writers and artists and the companies, agencies, and academies that pay them to be creative. But we had better continue to develop our own ways, compatible with our own traditions, of rewarding intellectual labor without depending on laws and prohibitions that are disin-tegrating fast—as the Volstead Act did in our earlier effort to enforce an unenforceable Prohibition.

Governments and Secrecy

In international politics, the doctrines affecting information are in maximum disarray. Every newly miniaturized recording or micrographic device, and every new satellite launched for communication or photography or remote sensing, makes it more difficult to sustain the doctrine that national governments can own, or even control, their information resources.

In 1979 the U.S. government sent two delegations to two world meetings about the control of information. At a UNESCO conference in Paris, the instructed delegates righteously advocated the "free flow" of information—information furnished by U.S. news agencies, U.S. television producers, and U.S. movie studios. At the U.N. Conference on Science and Technology for Development in Vienna a few weeks later, an equally righteous group of instructed Americans came out against the free flow of information— information as technology we were anxious to hoard.

Both principles are authentically American: the right to choose, the right to own. In international discourse, we will hardly be able to have it both ways. Yet there is no evidence that the two groups of delegates, and the government that instructed them both, perceived the irony or the contradiction.

If information is inherently hard to bottle up, policies based on long-term information monopoly are likely to have a short half-life. For the 1980s and beyond, the principle of action is clear: if the validity of your action depends on its continuing secrecy, watch out!

In our generation-long arms race with the Soviet Union, successive U.S. administrations have managed to persuade themselves that each new U.S. weapons system—its made-in-America technology a continuing mystery to our adversaries—would enable us to stay "ahead." In the most Canutish of these actions, the United States in the early 1970s decided to stuff multiple independently targetable re-entry vehicles (MIRVs) into single missiles. Despite elaborate secrecy on our part, the Soviets very soon figured out how to do likewise. But since they (for other reasons) had built much bigger missiles boosted by more powerful rockets, they were able to stuff more MIRVs into their canisters than we could. Thus did we outsmart ourselves by taking an action that depended for its validity on technological secrecy, and created the famous "window of vulnerability" instead.

A prime example of Canutish behavior in my personal experience was U.S. reluctance to tell our NATO allies what we knew from satellite reconnaissance about Soviet deployments of missiles aimed at European targets—when they were bound to learn about them sooner or later. A wave of common sense inundated that policy when in 1966 Robert McNamara, as Secretary of Defense, handed to allied defense ministers, in the top-secret precincts of the Joint Chiefs' War Room, the satellite photos we had been withholding until then. That was 17 years ago, but I can still vividly recall the shocked expressions on the faces of the security men lining the walls as McNamara dove into his briefcase and tossed onto the table for international inspection the prize examples of our space-based photography. After that it became routine to share with our NATO allies what our declared adversaries already knew.

In the management of mutual deterrence, the overclassification of information about what we could do if we had to may actually increase the danger of war by miscalculation. The core of the nuclear deterrent, that remarkably stable if unattractive substitute for peace, is the Soviet leaders' uncertainty about what the U.S. president would do in the event of Soviet moves against our allies or ourselves, combined with the Soviet leaders' certainty that we have the means to retaliate no matter what. Keeping our intentions credibly uncertain is easy: we cannot know what we would do if, until we know what the if is. But keeping from our adversaries full knowledge of our capabilities merely adds another element of madness to the "mad momentum" of the nuclear arms race.

Our own government has for three decades engaged in half-hearted and demonstrably inefficient efforts to bottle up "strategic" U.S. science and keep foreign nationals out of "sensitive" university research. In our mostly open society, it never has worked very well. Americans have no corner on the market for brains; scientists talk across frontiers to each other; our European and Japanese allies never had much enthusiasm for controlling transborder information flows (because sales of equipment mean jobs for Europeans); and Soviet technological espionage has long been a thriving industry.

Keeping our R & D to ourselves is a policy that depends for its validity on secrecy; as the informatization of society intensifies in the post-industrial world, it can be expected to work less and less well.

Similar government behavior used to work better for dictators and totalitarian bureaucracies in societies where keeping information from spreading is honored by doctrine and practiced ad absurdum. Xerox machines are still licensed by the government in the Soviet Union; in Bulgaria, even typewriters are closely controlled. Ideas are harder to license: Russian youngsters readily learn about blue jeans and hard rock, and scientists on both sides of the porous Curtain seem to know how far along their peers are in unraveling (for example) the puzzlements of rocketry and space travel.

The good news is that information is leaky, that sharing is the natural mode of scientific discovery and technological innovation. The new information environment seems bound to undermine the knowledge monopolies that totalitarian governments convert into monopolies of power. In the horoscope of the USSR and the "Soviet bloc," a future looms where nobody is in charge.

Information and Wealth

The informatization of society may destabilize more than the Soviet bloc. It may help undermine the systems that keep two billion people in relative poverty, and more than a third of them in absolute poverty.

In the industrial era, poverty was marked by an absence of things—minerals, foods and fibers, manufactures. In the post-industrial era, these physical resources are joined at center stage by information, the resource that is harder for the rich and powerful to hoard. But whether the informatization of the globe will make for a fairer distribution of its resources depends on the extent to which people in the traditionally poor nations are motivated (and allowed by their own suzerains) to educate themselves for full participation in the information-rich environment.

The key that unlocks "growth with fairness" in this changing context is thus the widespread delivery of relevant education.

More than any other one factor, it was that prescient nineteenth-century decision to offer free public education to every citizen that enabled the United States to pull itself out of underdevelopment. It was another wise educational policy, the Morrill Act of 1862—using federal land grants to set up university-based agricultural research stations and build a county-by-county extension service to deliver the resulting science directly to the farm—that created the productivity miracle that is American agriculture.

Today, around the horizon of the developing world, in Asia, Africa, and Latin America, the close connection between education and "growth with fairness" is now crystal clear.

The growing importance of information in creating wealth has to be good news for countries less favored by geology and arable land than the early arrivers in the industrial age. The poor can get rich by brainwork—the Japanese have amply illustrated the new wealth-creating theorem, and the hustling, educated peoples of South Korea, Taiwan, Singapore, and Israel have more recently provided a similar demonstration. Not only have they grown faster than other developing countries, they have spread the benefits of that growth more fairly among their people than most countries that are favored (as they are not) by oil or hard minerals or soil or climate.

Around the developing world, indeed, the striking paradox is that the most successful countries are precisely those blessed with rich natural resources.

A country such as Japan, with virtually no fuels or minerals, with a short growing season and much farmland we would call marginal, is forced by physical poverty to bet on the only sure resource it has, the brains of its own people—by getting them all, not just an elite few, educated. That turns out to be the most profitable investment of all. The educated brains seem able to pull in from the global information flow the data, knowledge, and insights needed to create a development strategy of their own.

Even if the richer countries are not very good at helping the poorer ones—even if we ourselves act in Canutish ways (limiting access to our markets, trying to hoard our technologies, starving our educational exchange programs)—the developing countries that bet on universal education for their own people, and thus learn how to seek facts and ideas about technology, management, markets, and governance, can readily secure these hardest-to-hoard resources.

By contrast, in the countries whose people have been kept in ignorance (by colonial policies, or their own leaders' mismanagement, or first one and then the other), it doesn't seem to matter what riches lie in the ground they occupy. Most of their citizens become the peasants of the global information society—along with the dropouts of the post-industrial world. The physical riches get siphoned off to the educated folk huddling in the affluent sections of their central cities—and to the information-wise foreigners who come in to do good and do well.

The excuse for poverty in the industrial era was that there weren't enough resources to go around. If the rich and powerful believe that it's only at their expense that resources can be shared with the less fortunate, they will cast themselves as the Canutes of world politics: that is, they will dig in and resist spreading information around through education. But if information, the increasingly dominant resource, is really expandable, diffusive, and shareable, there will be less excuse in the future than in the past for depriving whole populations of the benefits of positive-sum development.

The modern King Canutes will be wise to assume that the information tide is coming in—and adapt their behavior accordingly. Knowledge is power, and let's not forget it.

Notes

1. The King Canute legend is actually a bum rap. Magnus Magnuson's *Vikings* (E.P. Dutton, 1980) and other authorities make clear that Knut "intended the tide to give him a wetting, as an object lesson in humility for the benefit of the assembled courtiers," who thought him all-powerful. But his name has gone down in history as a metaphor for efforts to avoid unavoidable tides of change, and it is in this sense that we evoke his memory here.

2. The unique characteristics of information are spelled out in the author's "Information As a Resource," *The Futurist,* December 1982.

3. *L'Informatisation de la Societe* (Paris: La Documentation Francaise, 1978) was a report commissioned by Valery Giscard d'Estaing while he was president of France. Written by two civil servants, Simon Nora and Alain Minc, it became a bestseller. Its lucid analysis, its vigorous nationalism, and its hard-hitting proposals for decentralization in a country where decisions have always been unusually centralized in Paris seem to have been influential in the framing of some of Francois Mitterrand's early program after he became France's president in May 1981. The book was published by M.I.T. Press in 1980 under the mistranslated title *The Computerization of Society,* but with an excellent introduction by Daniel Bell.

4. The often quoted phrase "Knowledge is power" is taken to be the trans-

lation of "Nam et ipsa scientia potestas est," in Francis Bacon's *Meditationes Sacrae* (1597). *Bartlett's Familiar Quotations* calls attention to a similar, much earlier formulation in the Old Testament (Proverbs 24:5): "A wise man is strong; yea a man of knowledge is more than equivalent to force." Samuel Johnson, *Rasselas* (1959), ch.13.

5. Paul Appleby's definition of policy is in his *Policy and Administration* (University of Alabama Press, 1949), p. 21.

6. The legal argument between the Association of American Publishers and New York University is quite fully covered in the *Chronicle of Higher Education:* December 8, 1982, and January 5 and April 20, 1983.

National Service:
A Structural Response
to Structural Issues

by

Donald J. Eberly and Michael W. Sherraden

As the United States faces the last years of the twentieth century, the youth and young adult populations face serious problems. Several million young men and women are out of work and looking for jobs. Hundreds of thousands of others have given up in despair and are no longer offically counted as unemployed. Many of those who are employed are working in dead-end jobs such as pumping gas and pushing hamburgers—jobs that provide low wages, few benefits, and hold very little promise of career advancement. Even young people in colleges and universities often do not know why they are there. They have not had enough experience to know what they are interested in, what major to pursue, or what courses they should be taking. Many are in college simply because they cannot find a good job otherwise. And even for college graduates, employment is no longer a certainty.

As a result of unemployment and uncertainty about the future, many young people—students and nonstudents, rich and poor, white and nonwhite—have grown disenchanted and are culturally disengaged. Their emptiness and frustration have been expressed in many ways. During the 1970s the nation witnessed among young people sharply increased crime and vandalism; markedly decreased national election participation; increased drug abuse, alcoholism, and alcohol-related deaths; record numbers of out-of-wedlock pregnancies and childbirths; and bleakest of all, record numbers of suicides. These unfortunate trends indicate that the path from youth to adulthood today may be more difficult than ever before.

The traditional prescription for maturity, "getting a job and settling down," is now a long and complex process. The labor market, undergoing radical transformation both technologically

Donald J. Eberly is with the National Service Secretariat, Washington, D.C. Michael W. Sherraden is assistant professor, School of Social Work, Washington University, St. Louis, Missouri. This article includes material adapted from their book National Service: Social, Economic and Military Impacts *(Pergamon Press, 1983).*

and demographically, is shifting employment opportunities away from unskilled and low-skilled jobs to technical positions requiring extended education. In addition, a larger number of adult women are entering the labor force and competing with young people for jobs. As a result, many young people are unable to find a place in society. Many have little hope of success from the beginning. Others get sidetracked along the way. And this is not a short-term problem that will disappear in the near future. These dominant trends in the labor market are likely to continue in the years ahead, and young people will continue to be pushed aside.

Many observers lament the familiar list of teenage problems—drugs, crime, suicides—and conclude that young people are "growing up too fast, exposed to too much, too soon." But this is a misleading and useless interpretation. The real problem in America is that young people are not encouraged—and often not permitted—to grow up soon enough. The unrelenting forces of the labor market thwart conventional employment and independence, and how else is one to be "grown up" in this society? There are currently few alternatives. Many of the social problems affecting young people are manifestations of the energy of youth gone sour for lack of constructive outlets. Young people do not have sufficient opportunities to assume responsible roles in society. The message they are receiving from society is, "What you have to offer is not needed."

The nation can no longer blindly assume that, left to itself, the labor market will effectively channel the enthusiasm and creativity of youth into the constructive contributions of adulthood. The labor market does not do so today and, in all likelihood, it will not do so tomorrow. There is a clear need in our post-industrial democracy for alternative structures to augment traditional education and employment in shaping active and responsible citizens. And this is true for young people in school as well as for those who are not.

National service is one such alternative. As a general term, national service refers to a period of work and service given by the individual to the nation or community, with appropriate recognition in return. National service embodies two complementary ideas: one, that some service to the larger society is part of each citizen's responsibility, and two, that society should provide opportunities for and encouragement of such contributions.

What would these contributions be? National service projects could include work in resource conservation, disaster relief, environmental clean-up, infrastructure repair, health, education, and social services. There are a vast number of labor-intensive projects in these and other areas that are in the long-term interests of the nation but that will not be undertaken by the private sector because the projects are not profitable for individual firms on a short-term basis. Young people could perform many of these labor-intensive jobs and do so with creativity, enthusiasm, and productivity.

Society would send a new message to young people. Instead of the current message, which is "Uncle Sam needs you only in case of a war," the new message would be: "The country needs your help today. You can help when there are floods and tornadoes. Children in day-care centers need the stimulation and instruction you can offer. Older people living alone and in nursing homes need your companionship and your assistance with small chores. People who are disabled or mentally retarded need your help to learn to live a more constructive life. The nation's forests and parks need millions of person-years of effort in natural-resource conservation. The nation's houses need insulation and weather proofing. You are asked to volunteer for these and other important tasks according to your choice. The work will be hard but rewarding. The pay will be small but adequate. You will be entitled to a year of education or training for every year of service you contribute."

National Service Model

What would national service look like? To address this question, it is useful to identify key lines along which national service models vary. Ten important issues are (1) voluntary vs. compulsory service, (2) universal opportunity, (3) diversity, (4) control, (5) size, (6) unit cost, (7) emphasis on constructive work and services, (8) employment implications, (9) educational value, and (10) relation to the military. Taking these considerations one by one, we propose a program along these lines:

• National service would be voluntary.

• Opportunity would be universal, which would require administrative and financial arrangements so that nearly every young person—including the disadvantaged and the disabled—would have a chance to serve. There would be only minimal mental and physical standards, less rigorous than those of the military.

• The program would offer many diverse service opportunities, including conservation work, construction projects, social services, education, and work in government agencies.

• Much of the program would be operated at the local level under the control of private not-for-profit and public agencies. A quasi-public foundation would be established to receive appropriations, approve applications, and maintain standards, but decision-making would be largely decentralized to the local level and responsive to local needs and conditions. In this way, the program would remain flexible and adaptive, and projects would be meaningful to local communities.

• The program would be allowed to grow in size depending upon demand and support at the local level. Because local organizations would bear some costs, individual projects would either work well or they would not be supported. If, for lack of local

163

support, the overall program did not grow, that would be appropriate. There would be no attempt to push projects that did not meet genuine needs. If successful, the program would grow to perhaps one million participants.

• Costs per participant would cover direct compensation at or slightly below the minimum wage, administrative overhead, and post-program educational benefits. This would be about $11,000 a year in 1983 dollars. (By comparison, the annual cost of maintaining one person in the military or in a correctional institution is more than double this amount.) Costs would be shared by participating agencies and the federal government. Educational benefits would be covered by funds currently spent on other student-aid programs; by cutting back on these educational subsidies, funds would be available to national-service participants.

• There would be a strong primary emphasis on productivity. National-service projects would be expected to pay their own way by providing genuine benefits. Participating agencies and individuals would sign service contracts outlining performance expectations. If these were not fulfilled, the agency or individual would be fired. Only high performance expectations and visible benefits would warrant continued public support.

• Employment implications would vary depending on the project. Job training, while not the primary goal, could be a frequent by-product. Successful job training programs, such as the Jobs Corps, could be adapted to national-service purposes. Especially important for the millions of unemployed young persons would be the assured opportunity for at least one year of work experience.

• Beyond the direct and substantial educational value of the service experience itself, national-service participants would earn a period of post-high-school education and training. Much of the current federal aid to education would be shifted to support those who had participated in national service, either civilian or military. As with the old GI Bill, educational benefits would be proportional to length of service.

• Civilian youth service would exist independent of the military establishment because the need for national service transcends military recruitment policies. Should a military draft be needed, persons volunteering for civilian service would bear a relationship to the draft comparable to those volunteering for military service.

National-service models similar to the above description have been studied and tested sufficiently to establish that there is plenty of important work to be done and that there are large numbers of young people prepared to volunteer. An experimental national service pilot project conducted in Seattle in 1973-74 is one prominent example. In the ACTION-funded Seattle project, any person between the ages of 18 and 25 who was a resident in the specified area could apply for service with a local community

164

project. Within a few days, interested individuals were invited to a one-day orientation where, if still interested in serving, they received a voucher. Individuals then carried the voucher and agreement form with them to agencies where they wanted to serve and completed these forms when they found a match. The sponsoring organization agreed to provide necessary training, supervision, and about 5% of the stipend in cash. The whole process, from the initial postcard application to the first day of work, normally took less than one month. Individuals were matched with jobs with an absence of bureaucratic paperwork. Volunteers assisted those who had difficulty with the matching process. An independent evaluation found that the value of the service performed by the average participant was nearly double the cost of ACTION in funding the program. Moreover, the unemployment rate of participants fell from 70% at entry to 18% six months after completion of service.

To launch a national service, a Seattle-type option could be joined by already existing programs such as the Peace Corps, VISTA, and a new Civilian Conservation Corps. Thus, young people would seek service at home, in the parks and forests, in central cities, in depressed rural areas, on Indian reservations, or overseas. In deciding where they wanted to serve and what they wanted to contribute, young people also would have a strong voice in defining the nation's response to social, economic, and environmental needs.

Implementation

The first step would be to establish a National Youth Service (NYS) Foundation. It would be a quasi-public organization, similar to the Corporation for Public Broadcasting, and receive appropriations from Congress. The foundation would invite units of state, regional, and local governments to submit grant applications, outlining plans for the operation of NYS projects within the specified guidelines. The foundation would award grants on the basis of merit and the funds available. In considering proposals, the foundation would give particular attention to the priorities allocated to job placement, accomplishment of needed service, education and training, and youth development. The ideal proposal would reveal a balance among these goals supported by participation of the respective agencies in program administration.

Grants would run for periods up to three years. Upon receipt of the grant, the grantee would announce the program and invite participation by persons ages 18 to 24. At the same time, the grantee would invite participation by public and private not-for-profit organizations interested in becoming NYS sponsors.

In addition to encouraging participation in the existing youth service programs, NYS would offer participants major options (for example, Community Service and Environmental Service).

Applicants for Community Service would interview for a wide range of local service projects sponsored by public agencies or private nonprofit organizations. Those who wished to travel in search of Community Service projects would do so at their own expense and register with the local NYS agency. Most sponsors of the Environmental Service option would be federal, state, or local agencies. Most environmental projects would require travel costs as well as expenditures for supplies and equipment. Such costs would be the responsibility of the sponsor, not of the foundation. If lodging and food were provided by the sponsor, these expenses would be reimbursed by the NYS grantee from whose jurisdiction the participant was recruited.

Sponsorship of NYS projects would be open to public and private not-for-profit agencies for positions meeting certain criteria, including (1) no displacement of regular employees, and (2) no political nor religious activities. The latter criterion would not exclude political and religious groups from sponsorship; they could engage participants for such tasks as non-partisan voter registration or non-sectarian day care.

The sponsoring agency would certify that it is prepared to contribute 5% of the participant's stipend per work-year of service and to provide the necessary supervision and in-service training. Also, the sponsor would agree to participate in a one-day training session before receiving any NYS participants. The 5% contribution would be in cash, but might come from outside organizations such as businesses and churches.

Sponsors' requests would be open to public review for a period of one week. Where challenges were made, the grantee would investigate them and make a determination. Those position descriptions which successfully passed through this process would be entered into a computer listing, where they would be immediately accessible to NYS applicants in the area. It is from this listing that applicants would arrange interviews and the agreement process would go forward. Should there be more than negligible abuse of this clearance process, it would be necessary to set up formal review committees, including union officials, to pass on each application for any NYS participant.

Decisions affecting the retention or dismissal of NYS participants would have to be made individually. Still, guidelines would be needed. The guiding principle would be the participant's willingness to serve. The written agreement would spell out the duties and responsibilities of both participant and supervisor. If a participant were repeatedly late for work or neglectful of agreed-upon duties, he or she would be giving a clear signal of the absence of a willingness to serve. Dismissal would be in order. By contrast, another participant who simply could not master an assigned job, even while making every effort to do so, would be provided in-service training or offered placement in a simpler job, accompanied by a renegotiated contract.

When sponsoring organizations failed to live up to the terms of the agreement, the participant would be assisted in securing another placement and the sponsoring organization would be removed from the computer listing. Participants, either individuals or organizations, dismissed for failing to comply with the terms of an agreement normally would be ineligible for reenrollment in NYS.

By relying on the best interests of the persons and organizations at the heart of the program to undertake most of the monitoring function, the need for red tape would be correspondingly reduced. For example, the use of vouchers and agreement forms would achieve placements satisfactory to both parties, would provide a basis for handling complaints, and would reduce costs and administrative oversight. If the service worker did not show up for work or failed to perform the duties agreed to in the contract, the sponsor would be motivated by its investment to report the service worker to the local administrator for discipline and possible discharge. Similarly, if the sponsor assigned duties to the service worker that were not in the agreement or otherwise violated the agreement, the service worker would be motivated by his self-interest (e.g., loss of anticipated work experience) to report the sponsor to the local administrator for discipline and possible discharge.

Use of the agreement form also would facilitate the process of incoming NYS participants building on the work of their NYS predecessors. New NYS enrollees could interview outgoing participants, read their reports, and review their statements of objectives. With this background information, incoming participants could better negotiate a set of worthwhile activities.

As indicated earlier, NYS would be a transition program. It would not be a lifetime job, nor would it guarantee employment upon completion. Still, NYS would include certain features that would facilitate future employment and further education. First, NYS would be a source of information about jobs and education. This information would take the form of newsletters, job information sheets, opportunities for counseling, and referrals to such institutions as the State Employment Security Agencies and the Community Education-Work Councils presently in operation in a number of communities. Second, NYS would certify the work performed by the participant. Certification would be descriptive, not judgmental, and would enable outgoing participants to get beyond the initial hurdle to jobs for which they are qualified. Third, NYS would award an education and training voucher to the departing national service worker. The voucher, a kind of GI Bill for National Service, would be good for one year of education and training for each year of service. Fourth, the Joint Action for Community Service and Women in Community Service programs of the Job Corps would be adapted for utilization by NYS. These volunteer programs are currently very successful in recruiting, counseling, and placing Job Corps enrollees. Community placement services would provide post-NYS assistance to young people with special needs as they completed national service.

Adaptability

National service would have to adapt to changing social, political, and economic conditions. The NYS program would prepare for adaptation by allocating 5% of its budget to experimental projects. A systematic program of experimental projects would be the best way to meet unforeseeable contingencies five or ten years in the future. The NYS Foundation could foster experimentation by supporting such initiatives as (1) a college incorporating a year of national service in its curriculum, (2) a labor union supervising national-service work projects while giving specialized training to participants, (3) a sponsor such as the Red Cross contracting with national-service participants for emergency work on an intermittent basis, (4) a sponsor such as a nursing home contracting for participants on a part-time basis, and (5) national-service participants taking the initiative to be their own sponsors or organizing their own national-service teams.

The basic NYS model could be adapted with very few changes to meet different conditions. Should a peacetime military draft be reinstated, those in NYS could be placed at the end of the draft queue, where they would be drafted only after those who had not served at all. Should a military draft be reinstated during a limited war, the public and Congress would probably insist that the risk of being drafted be equalized. In this case, a lottery would determine who was conscripted; others would be free to enter NYS or might, as an extension of equity consideration, be required to serve in NYS for a year or two. In the event of total mobilization, NYS would probably be limited to those young people who failed to meet the physical and mental standards for entry into the armed forces.

Taking a different perspective, national service could be adapted to older adults as well. As the population of the United States ages, and especially as the baby-boom bulge enters retirement in the next century, it may be necessary to ask older adults to participate in productive activity to meet the great expense of their own support. A flexible and diversified national-service program could help meet this challenge and take advantage of the wealth of experience in our older population.

There is also no need to be constrained by national boundaries. International service would be a desirable option. In a world of great interdependence and international tension, the value of international projects is apparent. There are secondary benefits as well; for example, the positive impact of the Peace Corps in influencing participants toward diplomatic and other international careers has been well documented.

Altogether, national service is a broad and flexible idea that can be adapted to fit local, national, and international needs as well as changing social and economic circumstances. National service is also a constructive idea, focusing on what people have to offer rather than on problems and deficiencies. It is a practical idea, moving beyond wishful thinking to workable solutions. And it is a comprehensive idea, an idea that faces structural issues, not with social tinkering, but wih a structural response. In the last years of the twentieth century, national service should be placed alongside education, employment, and the military as a new cornerstone in youth policy.

Note

National service has strong support from all segments of the population. A 1981 Gallup Poll reported that public support had risen from 66% in favor in 1979 to 71% in favor in 1981, with the greatest growth in support coming from persons 18 to 24 years of age. In the legislative arena, both the Senate and the House of Representatives have held hearings on national service. The Senate passed a bill in 1980 that would have created a Presidential Commission to study national service. A similar bill passed the House Committee on Education and Labor in 1982, was defeated by the full House in November 1983, and is expected to be reintroduced in the next full session of Congress.

The Second American Revolution: Redefining Capitalism for the Information Age

by

William E. Halal

Capitalism is changing. The old economic system of the "industrial" past that thrived on the use of physical technology to produce an abundance of material growth has passed its zenith and is in decline. Now modern economies must pioneer a far more difficult "post-industrial" frontier of social, intellectual, and political challenges that loom immediately ahead as the explosive growth of information technology promises to make the computer the central tool of a knowledge-based society. This historic transition to an Information Age represents a passage from adolescence to maturity in the life of nations.

Crisis of the Old Capitalism

It is this transition that is primarily responsible for the chronic symptoms that mark the crisis in economics. A strange malady of stagflation cripples sound economic growth, natural resources like energy remain critical, the problem of environmental pollution persists, and there is a decline in physical science and technology. In spite of the Reagan revolution, big government goes on unabated to stifle productive enterprise, while a tenacious malaise pervades the management of auto making, steel, appliances, and other traditional industries.

Enormous confusion reigns over these issues because the crux of the problem cannot be resolved at the macroeconomic level alone but requires nothing less than a transformation in the "fine structure" of the economy itself. The creative power of enterprise has been lost among large business corporations, government agencies, universities, hospitals, and other institutions that remain fiercely preoccupied with beliefs from the past—physical

William E. Halal is professor of management, George Washington University, Washington, D.C. This article is adapted from his book The New Capitalism: Democratic Free Enterprise in Post-Industrial Society *(Wiley, 1985).*

growth, hierarchy, authority, profit, efficiency, etc. This outmoded ideology of the "Old Capitalism" now poses the main obstacle to a vastly different future, causing the national economic infrastructure to be dominated by failing institutions that are collectively seized in a sort of "organizational gridlock."

A New Capitalism Emerges

Like all crises, however, great opportunities are presented as well as great problems. Rising like a phoenix from the ashes of a dying epoch is a new economic ideology being invented by creative entrepreneurs who are leading the way through this transition. Executives of progressive corporations are redefining the role of business to form a "New Capitalism" consisting of a few key strategic concepts—soft growth, organic networks, participative leadership, human goals, and strategic management.

An age of "less is more" has arrived in which vast opportunities for progress are opening up in a different new frontier of "soft growth," a good example being the historic GM downsizing decision. Innovative firms like Dow Corning, Armco, and 3M are developing manufacturing processes that save energy, recycle waste, and avoid pollution—while also making bigger profits. Others like GE, IBM, and Bendix are automating factories and offices to shift labor from tedious, routine jobs to more challenging and productive tasks. Many pioneering firms are developing "soft markets" to improve education, communications, health care, and other unmet social demands, and they are using "customer-driven marketing" that focuses on serving such personal needs. These are far more complex and more subtle challenges, but they constitute unlimited prospects for future growth in an "inner" domain of "human economy."

Old hierarchical pyramids are shedding their bureaucratic inertia as they become transformed into "organic networks" to handle this exploding complexity and to survive the intense competition caused by the deregulation of AT&T, air travel, and banking, as well as growing foreign competition. The microcomputer, telecommunications, optical cables, and other breakthroughs in information technology are converting entire organizations into "integrated information systems," thereby decentralizing decisions, eliminating the middle ranks of management, and shifting attention to the need for innovation. IBM's Personal Computer, for instance, took the lead from Apple by using a small, self-contained "Independent Business Unit" to provide entrepreneurial flexibility. As a result, large companies like IBM, GE, TRW, Dow Corning, DEC, and 3M are becoming "confederations of entrepreneurs," launching a boom of countless small ventures to pioneer the frontier of soft growth.

Within these organizational networks, a great wave of "participative leadership" is rising to enlist the committed energy of a new breed of employees from the "me-decade" who seek self-fulfillment. Many corporations like MCI, Delta Airlines, Motorola, and Ford are developing labor-management relations that contract "pay-for-performance," share profits, collaborate on decisions, improve working conditions, and safeguard employee rights. At Lincoln Electric, worker participation raised productivity to twice that of its competitors, making the company the leader in its field and rewarding employees with bonuses that average $15,000 apiece. These more productive and satisfying arrangements are creating a major shift in power that extends democracy to the workplace.

Not only are employees becoming enfranchised, a broader "political coalition" is slowly evolving among other business "stakeholders" to create various forms of "democratic" corporate governance that serves "human goals" while also enhancing profit. The Europeans, Japanese, and avant garde American companies like ARCO, BankAmerica, Aetna, Dayton-Hudson, Hewlett-Packard, IBM, and Kollmorgan are learning that economic success now hinges on enlisting the support of investors, labor, government, customers, suppliers, distributors and other critical constituencies. Lee Iacocca saved Chrysler from bankruptcy by uniting these groups to see that their mutual interest lay in working together. Even competitors are collaborating, as in the partnerships between auto makers and their foreign counterparts and the research consortiums among computer companies. This "open-system" view of business is leading enlightened executives to develop a role as "economic statesmen" to integrate these political interests into a stronger "social contract" that expands the role of big business to create "social wealth" as well as financial wealth.

A form of "strategic management" is emerging to adapt large institutions to the massive discontinuities posed by this transition to a new era. Most companies like GE, IBM, and TRW now use strategic planning, issue management, and participative strategy formulation to form a more adaptive "strategically managed organization." Many cities and states are also gaining control over their future using planning programs that involve the community. The result is an "organization-environment symbiosis" that *uses* external forces for change to create more effective strategies—much as the oriental martial arts convert the strength of an aggressor to one's own defense.

The Synthesis of Democracy and Free Enterprise

These elements of the New Capitalism offer an unusually fruitful approach to resolving the economic crisis because they bring to fruition the two central principles of Western societies—free enterprise and democracy. Although these ideals are usually thought of as incompatible in economics, there is a "revolutionary" quality to information technology that urges both entrepreneurial innovation and political collaboration. Nobody fully understands such unprecedented evolutionary changes, of course, but the Information Age seems to be relentlessly driving these two great forces to new heights of development and uniting them into a powerful synthesis.

As the above examples show, the strategic concepts of the New Capitalism represent fresh new forms of enterprise. Myriad small ventures in the frontier of soft growth, the market structure of organic networks, the innovation spurred by participative leadership, a stronger form of enterprise using stakeholder coalitions, and the adaptive power of strategic management—all comprise a resurgence of entrepreneurial vitality. This rebirth of enterprise is restructuring the old oligopolistic economy of big organizations into a dynamic system that exemplifies the creative responsiveness of free markets.

The New Capitalism is also propelling business toward a remarkably different "democratic" posture. Soft growth transcends materialism to improve the quality of life, organic networks preserve individual freedom, participative leadership recognizes the rights of employees, stakeholder coalitions lead to corporate democracy, and strategic management fosters a benign relationship with society. A quiet revolution is under way as this surge of democratic spirit slowly redirects modern economies to serve human welfare as well as financial interests.

Although such changes are controversial and still in their infancy, they seem to be moving inevitably toward a more mature economic system that I think of as "Democratic Free Enterprise"—not out of altruism or dedication to principles, but from sheer self-interest as exploding competition and a turbulent era demand these changes to survive. The productivity of entrepreneurial freedom is being united with the legitimacy of democratic values to create a unique form of economy that offers huge potential for rejuvenating the power of creative business.

A Business-Government Partnership

This more innovative, socially responsive nature of the New Capitalism is also redefining the old adversarial business-government relationship. Partnerships are occurring among many corporations, cities, entire industries, and states where progressive business and civic leaders are joining together to convert the difficult problems that plague society into opportunities for sound growth. Wang Laboratories worked with the community in Lowell, Massachusetts, to turn that decaying mill town into a model of high-tech prosperity. A coalition of banks, hospitals, and universities brought new life to Indianapolis as an international cultural center. Firms like Control Data have opened facilities in some of the nation's worst ghettos, alleviating poverty while also earning handsome profits. Many other such pioneering joint business-government ventures are spreading into a modern renaissance that could release great reservoirs of energy to revitalize the nation.

At the national level, these trends may lead to a new system of political economy. The social role of big business seems likely to erupt into a heated political issue over the next decade or so—just as the role of big government became a major issue recently—leading to three main choices. The recent "neoconservative" attempt to restore a laissez-faire past can only provide modest help in recovering the strength of big business, and it is provoking a sense of injustice that will foment a rebellion from the left. Conversely, a return to liberal big government could regain social justice, but it would also stifle business innovation and productivity.

A far preferable third scenario is possible in which both the right and left wings of the nation are united to form a partnership between big business and big government. Signs of a growing political center are already visible—the surge of support for Gary Hart offers a good example—which could easily swell into a powerful wave of centrist politics based on the concepts of the New Capitalism. If the large quasi-public corporations that dominate the economy were to extend their governance to include key constituencies, they would become more productive and they would "internalize" the social impacts of business—which would then permit a "decentralization strategy" whereby the federal government shifts the responsibility for managing the economy from the public to the private sector. The benign, "self-regulating" nature of these "soft corporations" would eliminate much of the present maze of government regulations, and many of the social programs that have led to the mushrooming growth of the welfare state could be reduced as unemployment, poverty, and other social ills are alleviated.

Freed from the burden of policing the abuses of business and cleaning up "externalities," government could turn to the critical challenge of redefining the economic system for a new era. One point both Republicans and Democrats agree on is the need to form political bodies represented by business, labor, consumers, and other major interests to guide economic policy. If Americans were to use such political arenas to address major economic issues "democratically," the nation could renew that vital sense of community which holds the key to implementing a variety of badly needed structural changes: "market supplements" using taxes and credits to internalize social costs and benefits in lieu of regulations; "indicative planning" to provide the information needed to run a market system efficiently; "privatized" government functions that can be contracted out to business more effectively; programs to spur technological progress and training; incentives that aid the flow of investment capital; and other crucial reforms.

As such business-government partnerships become more fully

174

developed, the Old Capitalism that produced such bitter antagonism between business, government, labor, consumers, and other political interests would be transformed into a far more sophisticated form of political economy that engages the collaboration of various economic actors to enhance entrepreneurial innovation, develop economic resources, and spur technological progress. Most importantly, it would serve all of these collective interests that are inextricably intertwined.

Global Corporations and the New World Order

A similar metamorphosis is under way in Europe, Japan, the Third World, and even socialist nations. The tension between the two superpowers has left a barren "no-man's land" in world politics that prevents resolving a growing world crisis. But recently, variations of these two polar ideologies have been flowering around the globe, producing hybrid economic-political systems that steer a middle path between the exploitive image of the "Old Capitalism" and the dictatorial inefficiency of the "Old Socialism." The immutable fact is that the spreading of industrialization to the populous Third World will inevitably magnify the problems of energy, environment, economic competition, and world conflict by about a factor of 10 over the next decades, forcing economies in the general direction of the New Capitalism that may also represent a "New Socialism."

Some global corporations like Phillips are developing enlightened forms of enterprise that create profitable ventures which assist in the economic development of hybrid economies like India. If large numbers of multinational corporations could apply the New Capitalism abroad to fill the vacuum between the two superpowers, they would realize enormous opportunities while simultaneously uniting the nations of the emerging global economy into a network of working relationships that form a coherent world order.

Democratic Free Enterprise: The Visible Hand of the Market

Many of these prospects are as yet mere visions, but they are realistic possibilities that all flow from the Western heritage of democracy and free enterprise that is urging Americans toward a new economic system that may foster a higher order of wealth, personal freedom, and public welfare. This mature form of political economy—Democratic Free Enterprise—is the New Capitalism that is beginning to revitalize modern nations. It offers the hope of creating an unusually powerful type of economy based on *both* cooperation and competition— collaboration among major economic parties to build a more effective economic infrastructure that nurtures healthy competition and equitable, prosperous growth. This "Second American Revolution" would redefine capitalism for the needs of the Information Age so that the "invisible hand" of Adam Smith becomes a "visible hand" that guides business in directions that are both more productive and more just.

Management and Futures Research in Our New Economic Era

by

William Lazer

Businesses here and abroad are now confronted with a new world economy that will require tremendous shifts in management thinking, strategies, and actions. To evaluate the factors that are requisites for management success in the new environment, I have organized the discussion around three main areas:

1. Our new emerging world economy, including comments on the current world situation, the transition that is occurring, the nature of competition and cooperation, and the role of government.

2. Key factors for business success, particularly the perspectives, actions, management requirements, and management changes involved.

3. Lessons for future management from the point of view of management perspectives, actions, and required changes.

Briefly, my plan is to highlight and summarize rather than to explore a few areas in depth. I shall attempt to develop a broad perspective and present an overall view, leaving detailed considerations for another time.

Let us turn first to the new world economy.

The Emerging New World Economy

Our world is undergoing very rapid and marked change, as is reflected in the titles of such current best-selling business books as *The Next Economy, The Next Frontier, In Pursuit of Excellence, Megatrends,* and *The Reindustrialization of America.* Ours is not only a turbulent age, but one of great introspection on the part of business executives who are reassessing their own business operations and decisions in the light of the evolving world around them. Among the topics now being widely discussed are: the decline of the smokestack industries, the new economic order,

William Lazer is Eugene & Christine Lynn Eminent Scholar in Business Administration, Florida Atlantic University, Boca Raton, Florida.

economic revitalization, the government's role, our information age, new consumer values, the next society, the new industrial order, changing demographic and lifestyle factors, international trade, high-technology industries, reasons for business successes and failures, and the desirability of adopting industrial development policies.

Business is now in the midst of a major transition in which some of its most cherished beliefs, prerogatives, methods of operation, and dogmas, which have served so well in the past, are being questioned and challenged. Those basic industries that once comprised the backbone of our major industrial sectors, such as steel, autos, chemicals, and heavy machinery, are in a state of relative decline. Our fundamental industrial premise of concentrating on rigid, set, high-volume, low-cost manufacturing processes is being reassessed. The new world economy is resulting in preferences for high value-added industries that embrace low-volume, automated production.

Our world is no longer one of international dominance on the part of one or two highly developed countries that establish the "rules of the economic game." Instead, several highly industrialized economies have emerged, and they will be joined by others as they, in turn, mature and are able to compete effectively in international markets.

Ours is now a world of instant global communications linking countries throughout the four corners of the globe. And they have become so intertwined that economic difficulties in one nation, such as Brazil or Mexico, or the decisions of various cartels, such as OPEC, have effects that reverberate internationally.

The very nature and scope of international markets are being transformed by the mobility of technology, people, companies, money, and products that move more freely across national boundaries. And ours is truly an era in which international trade is assuming ever-increasing importance for Europe, South America, Japan, the Third World, and the United States.

Today, all nations have rising lifestyle expectations and actively seek the attainment of a larger share of the world's total outputs. And despite recognized global interdependence, each nation still pursues its own goals and interests and eagerly supports its export thrusts while limiting imports and ignoring the global economic impact of its own actions. The increasing strains of the broadening gap between the "have" and "have not" nations, between the highly industrialized and Third World countries, is being felt as it affects international monetary systems and, indeed, international markets.

A fundamental change is also occurring in international competition, for it is no longer competition among individuals, small businesses, or even fairly large companies. International competition is now competition among nations and among complex multinational company consortia that cut across a broad spectrum of nations and interests. Economic success is often more dependent on collaboration, cooperation, negotiation, teamwork, group cohesion, commitment, and collective judgments than on devastating and debilitating keen competition. In such an environment, questions can be raised whether an emphasis on individual self-interest and personal competition, as is the case in free markets, can be effective in the light of new developments.

We are currently seeing the development of true global multinational companies, with allegiances that are not traceable to any country but, instead, involve managers, markets, employees, directors, governments, and assets of many nations. This contrasts sharply with past and current multinationals, where most—whether of Dutch, British, French, German, Japanese, or American origin—are really home-country oriented. The strategic implications of this change are most significant, because companies will no longer be able to promote the economic goals of just one country, nor will they be under its exclusive jurisdiction. Rather, they will seek the most profitable markets, the lowest costs, and the greatest returns from among worldwide market opportunities.

Our new era will likely result in a reassessment of the effectiveness of the free market as a superior organizing institution and as one that promotes the greatest common good. Presently, arguments about the desirability of free vs. government-directed markets seem to fall into two opposing camps that are usually described as a choice between prosperity or freedom, social justice or economic prosperity, business investment or social investment, and free markets or government control. They suggest a dichotomous choice—either one or the other.[1]

The realistic choice in our new world, however, may just be the relative weights to be placed on the respective free-market and government-control components. For the effective use of resources in the future will require cooperation and coordination among government and business, as well as labor, resulting in a blurring of the public and private spheres. Business in our new world context must accept the fact that private industry affects government and that government, in turn, affects private industry, which means closer cooperation for both to function effectively. Under a free-market approach, great latitude is given to individual initiative and responsibilities, with the result that individual business success means wealth, and failure means poverty. Questions are now being raised, however, whether such a pattern is acceptable in a modern society where almost all individuals are dependent on complex organizations that in turn are affected by government actions. Individual families and consumers now feel the impact of international disruptions, of the pricing decisions of cartels, of droughts and famines that occur in far-off places. And that oft-used trade ploy of the past, of trying to export one country's problems to others, or of taking care of national and personal needs at the expense of those in other countries, may no longer be an acceptable policy.

In this regard, the United States seems to be questioning whether it should abandon its traditional commitment to international free trade as a cornerstone of its trade policy. Suggestions that various forms of protectionism, such as trade and tariff barriers, should be adopted are gaining supporters among businesses and unions alike. Many seem to feel that a policy of free trade is outmoded and should be dropped in favor of one emphasizing nationalism and protected markets.

Most of the world today does not believe in keen international competition and free trade. Instead, rising protectionism abounds, and this could eventually mean the collapse of the current trading system and even the appearance of trade wars.

Businesses should be concerned about such developments and may well ask whether every nation will be forced to protect its own economy; if so, by what measures? A fundamental issue to be faced is whether protectionism is always undesirable, or are there market conditions under which it should be used?

Historically, free trade seems to be supported by countries when they have comparative advantage and, conversely, to be abandoned when they lose it. This occurred in Holland, England, and in some United States situations. Should this historical trend continue, we might raise the intriguing possibility that in the future the United States might abandon free trade as a cornerstone of its trade policy, while Japan might embrace it.

In the past, American marketers often tended to ignore major international shifts, for international trade was not deemed to be very important. And they clung zealously to the posture of opposing government interference in the marketplace. In our new world economy, altering the posture need not mean that more government intervention is required, and certainly not that central economic planning is desired. Rather, the new world economy needs a redirection on the part of both business and government. Business must be redirected to pursue more flexible, higher value-added, skill-intensive, high-technology industries, which, in turn, means significant changes in manufacturing and marketing as well as the development of a labor/government/management coalition. It requires business acceptance of a more open, explicit, and strategic government role so that government can make social investments and can negotiate effectively with other governments on behalf of industries and businesses.

For government, the future role in the new economic order is not to obstruct trade and protect home markets and declining, inefficient industries from global competition. Rather, it should render assistance so that industries can become more efficient and competitive. The government's role is to assist in increasing productivity and living standards rather than merely to protect outmoded businesses and the "home turf."

At the present time, we are in the midst of an economic transition that will result in major adaptations of our institutions, products, and processes. Some believe that this transition will result in adjustments of great magnitude similar to those brought about by the industrial revolution. The result, they feel, will be major changes in our marketing, manufacturing, and trading systems.

Our new world economy is likely to be a mix that links business and social objectives, economic and social change, economic progress and social justice, and closer ties among labor, government, and business, thereby legitimizing the more active involvement of government in business. If this occurs, then the United States in this new economic order may move to models that in many ways more closely approximate those of Japan and Western Europe.

Human capital in our emerging economy will be recognized as a critical major business resource, an important determinant of wealth. A management premium will be placed on developing people and on such human qualities as effective collective action, cooperation, participation, job security, adaptation, and equality, as well as creativity, rather than on strict creative individual initiative and "dog eat dog" competition. In a sense, business may become a center of various human and social services.

Global managers must ask whether our current management concepts, ideas, and institutions, born of a different age, are attuned to the new economic era, which is geared to flexible, low-volume, high value-added, skill-intensive, mobile, globally oriented, high-technology production? Or, do they apply to well-behaved, stable, fairly predictable, ever growing and expanding markets that are the assumptions of the past? They seem to favor the latter, since they assume mass markets being served by high-volume, low-cost, standardized production.

In the light of our changing economic order, companies have but two choices. They can become reactive, resist change, and continue to do business in the comfortable way by clinging to the old approaches, acting as though the new situation is but a slight variation of the old. Or they can recognize the new market realities and the major shifts, determine their implications, and make the changes required to adapt effectively. That, of course, is a difficult posture, for it requires creativity, innovation, and shifts in marketing approaches, organizational patterns, management attitudes, and values.

Paul Hawken, in his book *The Next Economy*, notes that a major transition is under way: we are moving away from the industrial age that lasted roughly from 1880 to the present and was characterized by the substitution of fossil fuels for human energy in order to mass produce goods for mass markets. As the cost of energy decreased, consumption rose, resulting in an unprecedented accumulation of goods and property, and our mass-production, mass-consumption, acquisitive, materially oriented, thing-minded economy developed. But this mass economy is now being replaced by an *informative* economy, an economy emphasizing the information contained in goods and services, where information is defined to include quality, durability, utility, design, craft, increasing functionality, and longer-lasting and easier-to-repair products.

We can summarize some of Hawken's insights by comparing the qualities of the mass and informative economies, noting the shift from expansion to contraction, replication to differentiation, accretion to mutual interest, affluence to influence, consumption to conservation, entropic to information-rich, high wages to low wages, and specialization to broad skills.[2]

While one might question some of Hawken's observations and conclusions, even if he is only somewhat correct, management will be challenged to adapt to changes in consumer wants, needs, habits, and consumption patterns and to alter marketing mixes and marketing strategies accordingly. Hawken implies that marketing will play a critical role in the next economy, for he states, "Business success comes from the ability to perceive wants and needs and that perception depends upon sensitivity to people and their environment." That, of course, is the essence of the marketing philosophy, the creed of modern marketers.

In continuing our discussion of the new world economy, I would like to turn to international trade. Trade issues today are particularly important, and businessmen and unions have given them too little attention. This is an arena in which government and business should cooperate, since a single line in a trade agreement, whether multilateral or bilateral, can exclude companies from international markets or give them immediate access. And while most businessmen and unions seem to focus on the restrictive nature of quotas and tariff barriers, those non-tariff barriers that are most restrictive and exclusionary are largely ignored. In fact, such marketing institutions as distribution channels have been used as invisible trade barriers, and that euphemistic term *orderly market agreements,* regardless of the image it conjures, refers to government-arranged barriers to limit competition.[3]

In the United States, the government's role in international trade is now being reassessed and many constituent groups are suggesting the initiation of an industrial development policy. A Presidential Commission on Industrial Competitiveness has been created to study the situation and make recommendations. Such a policy usually includes adopting a growth philosophy, selecting and targeting industry sectors for economic growth, providing financing for research and development, protecting emerging industries, and aiding and assisting industries that are in difficulty. What a radical departure that would be from the current philosophy.

Although Japan and the United States have the most important trading relationships, comprising almost one-half of all noncommunist production, and even though the United States is Japan's most important trading partner, great misunderstanding and disagreement often exists between them. A common American belief is that if Japan would engage in "fairer" competition by opening its markets wider to United States imports and reducing pressures on its own exports, then most American trade difficulties would be resolved. But I don't believe that would really happen, for such actions alone, at best, would be only partial, short-run, stop-gap measures—and not very good ones at that.

While current Japanese trade surpluses and successes in international markets are not mainly attributable to government intervention, the direct protection of markets, or even MITI's operations, nevertheless, that is a widely held image. It is an image based on actions of the past, the actions of the 1960s. And marketers know well how important perceptions and images are—and the importance of taking actions to correct them.

The main international trade problem facing the United States and, of course, many other countries, is simply one of becoming more competitive in world markets. The situation is, indeed, exacerbated by trade barriers erected by a host of countries. The remedy, however, is not the adoption of countervailing trade restrictions and, indeed, marketers should strive to reduce trade barriers and to open markets.

Japanese competition is now forcing a discipline on American and European management that is inducing them to take actions that they should have taken previously on their own initiative. In turn, however, American and European reactions, stemming from the current economic scene, are stimulating Japan to do what it, too, should have done earlier, namely, to open wider the doors to its domestic markets and to reduce non-tariff as well as tariff barriers.

International businesses should become more directly involved with the vexing problems of competition, trade friction, and protectionism. They are too important to be neglected or to be left to the whims of government, for they lie at the very foundation of international business. And, as the president of the Japan Marketing Association noted in a 1983 address to the American Marketing Association, detailed analysis of the trade approaches of different countries will reveal "that these problems are not confined to trade, but have much deeper roots extending to differences in economic systems, social structures and cultural values."[4] At the heart of the problem is a lack of the communications between countries that is required for frank and flexible top-level business and government interchanges that can result in sensible approaches to trade issues. Conferences such as this can be important vehicles.

Presently, we are witnessing the globalization of markets, which is sometimes interpreted to mean the homogenization of markets throughout the world. Some observers have noted that we are now in the midst of the Europeanization of America, and that we have already seen the Westernization of Japan. But I have great difficulty accepting such sweeping generalizations, for they mask important fundamental factors.

It is true, of course, that Japan has successfully introduced some Western customs, concepts, technology, and products; but that does not mark the Westernization of Japan. Rather, Japan has borrowed what applies, absorbing the borrowings into its own fundamentally unchanged culture by massaging Western things to adapt them to Japanese society. What results is the Japanization of Western culture rather than Westernization of the Japanese culture. Similarly, I do not believe that we are witnessing the Europeanization of America, as some suggest, although the United States does, indeed, represent a fine market for many European products.

Key Factors for Business Success

Having discussed a few of the dimensions of the new world economy, I would like to turn to the second area dealing with some implications, namely, key factors for business success. To do this, my plan is to summarize a few observations dealing with the perspectives, actions, lessons for future management, and changes required.

Regarding perspectives, a major management responsibility is to adjust continuously to changing future environments, to manage change—and that, of course, is where futures research fits in, for it provides a firm's immediate link to its environments. Businesses must become more concerned with monitoring future environments through the use of futures research and by developing effective approaches for dealing with emerging problems. In this regard, developing a futures orientation is very important.

Yet, many academicians and business researchers have difficulties with futures research. The comment is made that, since no one can foresee the future, why bother trying to research it. Also, futures research does not lend itself readily to quantification and, for the most part, rigorous mathematical and statistical tools and models are not applicable. Its methodologies use such techniques as Delphi analysis, interactive competitive analysis, cross-impact analysis, scenarios, expert opinions, and simulations, which lack the rigorous scientific theoretical approaches. Futures research data depend on insights, judgments, opinions, and informed guesses, which are hardly factual and certainly do not please statisticians, mathematicians, and rigorous marketing researchers. Yet, futures research is emerging and developing as an important management tool.

I have often wondered why so few companies seem to be committed to futures research and to incorporating the results into their marketing activities on a regular basis. Experience suggests that it is not a matter of the industry orientations, such as high tech vs. low tech, consumer goods vs. industrial goods, products vs. services, highly competitive vs. less competitive, or international vs. domestic. Rather, one factor seems to dominate, which is the existence of a futures research sponsor at top corporate levels. In almost every instance I know of where futures research is actively used, a top-level executive has pushed the thrust and has taken a direct interest in the results and in getting others to consider them. Also, it is evident that well-managed companies exhibit a concern for the future: future trends and opportunities, future competitors and challengers, future problems and issues, future resources, and future consumers.

It is, indeed, easy to understand why futures research is neglected by most marketing managers and their staffs, for they are concerned with current operating issues and problems. They are "in the trenches" and keep their eyes on the profits and losses for the next quarter and the current year rather than on developments 5 to 10 years hence. Performance evaluations, after all, are tied to present accomplishments and not to future results. The greatest acceptance for futures research seems to occur when the findings can be related to the more immediate future—such as product or distribution channel implications for the next two or three years.

Besides a futures orientation, other important perspectives include: a vision of the business mission, a long-run orientation, a global view of markets, and the recognition of social responsibilities.

Actions that are keys to business success are developing an entrepreneurial spirit, acceptance of change, a commitment to human resources, and a productivity emphasis.

All of this requires management competence in the form of identifying and delineating markets, tailoring the marketing mix, developing and utilizing standards, organizing effectively, and stressing quality, service, and social factors. Management changes require an emphasis on long-run perspectives, society, employees, flexibility, and globalism.

In light of the above, what are the lessons for future management? Let us briefly summarize them under 12 points.

Lessons for Future Management

1. To understand the business, understand customers. Work back from the marketplace.

2. Avoid analysis paralysis. Don't substitute analysis for action. Analytical techniques and computers are just tools. Action brings results.

3. Remember that employees are the company. Top management is not the company. Productivity depends on people, respect for the individual, trust, harmony, and loyalty. Treat employees

like partners and adults.

4. Develop an innovative climate. Entrepreneurship is important. Foster creativity, risk and losses, authority for new products.

5. Set high standards. Strive for excellence, quality, and service. Mediocrity breeds decline. Be realistic.

6. Diversify carefully. Bring something to the merger. Make sure values are shared. Make sure you know the business and the complementary marketing factors. Eliminate paper management.

7. Clearly state company values. Communicate the mission to all. State objectives. Don't compromise.

8. Seek clarity and simplicity: Form follows function. Don't just add on. Avoid haphazard organization. Maintain lean staffs.

9. Obtain centralized decentralization: Values provide direction, and stable expectations are required. People need to know what is expected. Focus on quality, service, growth. There is no need to dictate—delegate. Develop flexible organization.

10. Rethink the business continually. Accelerating rates of change in technology and environments—international, legal, and social—require this.

11. Assess likely futures, the opportunities, your preparedness, and expected change.

12. Accept social responsibilities: Recognize them, budget for them, and develop plans and action.

What is the leading management factor for success in the new world economy? I believe it is the effective management of market change—that is the future challenge.

The world economy, as we have noted, is in the throes of a major transition. Businesses in the future will be confronted with vastly different environments than they saw in the past. New world economy management will have to be viewed from its true perspective of a company change agent that develops new products, creates new marketing strategies and mixes and cultivates new markets. Management will have to recognize that one of its fundamental responsibilities is to capitalize on future market opportunities inherent in the changes fostered by our new world economy. It must learn to manage change effectively. That is the key.

Notes

1. Robert B. Reich, *The Next American Frontier,* Time Books, New York, 1983, p. 5.

2. Paul Hawken, *The Next Economy,* Holt, Rinehart and Winston, New York, 1983, p. 188.

3. Mitsuaki Shimaguchi and William Lazer, "Japanese Distribution Channels: Invisible Barriers to Market Entry," *MSU Business Topics,* Winter 1979, p. 49.

4. Michio Torii in a speech before the Annual Meeting of the American Marketing Association, New Orleans, May 10, 1983.

Form Follows Function:
A Technological Vision
of Higher Education in the
Humanities by the Year 2000

by

Suzanne E. Lindenau

Once upon a time there was a certain king who kept an astrologer to forewarn him of future events—and especially to tell him whether or not it was going to rain when he wanted to go on hunting expeditions. One day, when the king had started off for the forest with a train of lords and ladies for a grand hunt the cavalcade met a farmer who was riding a jackass on the road. "Good morning, farmer," said the king. "Good morning, king," said the farmer. "Where are you folks going this morning?"

"Hunting," said the king.

"Lord, you'll get wet. It's going to rain today," said the farmer.

Ignoring the farmer and trusting his astrologer, the king went into the forest. But, by midday, there came a terrible storm that drenched and buffeted the whole party. When the king returned to the palace, he had the astrologer decapitated and sent for the farmer to take his place.

"Law's sake," said the farmer when he arrived. "It's not me that knows when it's going to rain; it's my jackass. When it's going to rain, that jackass always carries his ears forward."

"Make the jackass the court astrologer," shouted the king.

The moral of the story: to prophesy is extremely risky and difficult, particularly in regard to the future.

Appearing in numerous versions since 1863, this irreverent anecdote anticipated by more than a hundred years the difficult challenge the World Future Society's Fifth General Assembly set for itself, namely, to identify and debate potential future solutions to our global problems. Those who accepted the summons to participate in this unique discussion forum represent the finest

---

Suzanne E. Lindenau is director, Language Laboratories, University of Georgia, Athens, Georgia.

minds in the professions—concerned individuals who today are grappling with the very difficult yet necessary task of dealing with current and emerging dilemmas and seeking visionary solutions to problems ranging from crime and justice to science and technology.

For my part, I thought it might prove profitable to examine the problematic state of today's higher education in the humanities and how the Information Age technologies—interfaced with the learning needs of society—could provide solutions to the problems confronting American society.

Liberal-arts education in America is in trouble. Today, in a nation fascinated with technology and marching to the beat of the electronic drummer, the liberal-arts graduate is not king. Unless their diplomas are in computer science or business administration, the nearly 1 million graduating seniors this year will find it hard to get a job in a manpower market tightly gripped by the computer-oriented information age. Acutely aware of this problematic state of affairs, colleges and universities all over the United States are rushing to revamp their programs to give students more "practical" education. According to *U.S. News and World Report* (Solorzano, 1983), technology is changing traditional liberal-arts education in four basic ways:

1. Traditional liberal-arts colleges from Wellesley in Massachusetts to Willamette in Oregon are adding computer-science courses to their humanities curriculums.

2. Nearly a dozen schools, under a project sponsored by the American Association of Colleges, are collaborating to re-define the meaning and purpose of the baccalaureate degree.

3. Faculty at schools such as the University of Iowa and St. Olaf College (Northfield, Minnesota) are helping students in the humanities to see their degrees in a more marketable light by breaking them down into job skills, such as analytical ability.

4. More and more schools (including Clarkson College in Potsdam, New York, and Drexel University in Philadelphia) are requiring students to own free-standing, personal computers.

These changes were not initiated by the colleges and universities; they came about as responses to the demands of the public and the realities of the computer-oriented information age.

A 1982 survey by the Group Attitudes Corporation found that 86% of adults rated preparation for a career as the most important reason for going to college (Solorzano, 1983). It is therefore not altogether surprising that, at last count, 42% of all bachelor's degrees were issued in occupation-oriented fields such as business and engineering, up 23% from the number given in the mid-1960s. Liberal-arts degrees as a share of all bachelor's degrees have fallen to an all-time low. Down from over 20% just 15 years ago, degrees in the liberal arts currently stand at a little more that 7% of all bachelor's degrees granted. A shaky economy has persuaded students and parents alike that pursuing the only bright spot in the job market—technology—makes good sense.

In part, the attractiveness of careers in technology is due to the fact that they promise financial rewards. Among this year's freshmen, about 70% said that being able to make money was a very important reason for going to college. In 1971, only 50% felt that way. Fewer than 50% of the freshmen entering college this year were concerned with using their college experience to help them develop a meaningful philosophy of life. In the 1960s, over 80% felt that going to college was the best way to develop a meaningful philosophy of life.

In larger part, however, the attractiveness of careers in technology is due to the realities of the computer-oriented information age. The most important reality facing American society today is the turbulence that comes from being a nation in transition. According to John Naisbitt, who—together with the Naisbitt Group—monitors events in every corner of American society, about 60% of the labor force currently works with information processing, and by 1985, well over 75% of all jobs will involve computers. In sharp contrast, whereas 67% of the labor force was involved in some type of manufacturing occupation in 1950, presently, only 13% of the labor force is still employed in manufacturing (Naisbitt, 1982). Even on the assembly lines of the industrial manufacturing centers, sophisticated computerized methods of production have displaced over 10 million workers in the past two decades (Warnshuis, 1983).

In addition, the computer-oriented information age is also changing the parameters of the U.S. labor force. By making blue-collar skills—for the most part—obsolete in the coming decades, technology is displacing U.S. production workers from their factories. Unequipped with the technical skills that employers need, auto and steel workers—whose counterparts in the entire industrial sector may suffer a similar fate—are being reduced to accepting menial, low-income jobs or chronic unemployment. Meanwhile, the more than 30 million highly-literate and technologically astute workers needed by industry and service enterprises by 1990 are nowhere in sight. If we exclude those who use the computer solely for entertainment, probably fewer than 4 million Americans are "computer literate" (Stewart, 1983). Even though American industry is spending close to $40 billion to help train and retrain workers, and the American government is spending over $20 billion, training and re-training needs are not being met (Heines, 1983). If there is one, single, cataclysmic reality that has come with the computer-oriented information age, it is the need for continuing, life-long education, training, and re-training. In fact, this need is so great that, according to Peter Drucker (Drucker, 1981), continuing education for the professional, highly skilled, and mid-career adult is America's fastest-growing industry.

Given the reality of an economy shifting from manufacturing

to information processing, the reality of a critical need for highly literate and technologically astute workers, the need for life-long learning for non-traditional students, and the existing and emerging information technologies that have ushered in the Information Age, what has been education's response? All too often, it is and has been a case of too little, too late.

Do we in the humanities really believe that adding computer and business courses to the curriculum will prepare society for the shift from manufacturing to information processing?

Do we really believe that re-defining the B.A. degree will produce the highly literate and technologically astute workers needed by 1990?

Do we believe that requiring traditional students to own computers will help the large and growing body of nontraditional learners train, retrain, and upgrade their skills?

Do we in the humanities really believe that making the liberal-arts degree look more marketable is an effective way to use the existing and emerging technologies in the instructional process?

If our response to the computer-oriented information age is no more than what it has been, then the vision our critics have of where education will be in the year 2000 is bound to be accurate: an obsolete educational system, manned by unprepared educators who did not recognize their own obsolescence and were consumed by the microcomputer revolution in one gigantic megabyte (Sommerfeld, 1983).

Fortunately, pessimistic critics are not the only ones with vision. All of us, in and out of education, need vision to survive. My vision of education is based on the certainty that:

1. The humanities will survive.

2. Instruction, teachers, and institutions of higher education will not disappear.

3. The heart of teaching will still be student learning.

4. Technology alone will not be *the* answer; rather the intelligent application of technology will lead to success.

5. The form of education will follow its functions.

If education is going to be a solution to the problems of the society it serves, all of us in education who believe and want our liberal-arts colleges and universities to continue as mainstays must begin now to plan how the existing and emerging information technologies can make a college education attractive to anyone willing to pay for it—and how these technologies can deliver education, training, and retraining to anyone, anywhere, anytime.

To make a college education attractive to people other than the shrinking numbers of 18-24 year olds, our colleges and universities will have to become major producers of quality software and giant databases. Like the over 1,000 commercial databases today, the educational databases of the future will store the entire corpus of human knowledge. People at home, at school, and at the office will be able to access the databases and learn everything from English composition to auto mechanics.

To deliver education, training, and retraining over time and space to anyone who wants it, colleges and universities will provide such services via satellites owned and operated by the schools and accessible to cable and non-cable viewers. Today, the major drawback of satellite communications is the tens of millions of dollars required to build and launch a typical communications satellite. An emerging technology, the incredible space mirror (Onosko, 1983)—a signal reflector that weighs 1/280th of an ounce, is 30 feet in diameter, and is suspended by an invisible radio beam—will be the solution for institutional ownership of satellites in the near future.

By the year 2000, the humanities will revolve around a humanities communication laboratory where existing and emerging technologies can be used to produce courseware and programs, and allow learners to learn by doing. Such a laboratory will be equipped with parabolic antenna and cable TV. Television programs transmitted by satellite from all over the world will be fed to various locations. News, drama, and cultural programming can be used by learners in the humanities as well as other disciplines. Such a laboratory will have in-house, closed-circuit TV facilities where foreign-language students, for example, can enhance their language skills by dubbing and subtitling programs. In such a communications laboratory, computer and computer-enhanced technologies will provide electronic dictionaries for language study, arrays of simulations for anything and everything, and electronic databases.

By the year 2000, our over 3,000 institutions of higher education will join with business and industry to form an education-business partnership. Such a link-up will provide constant "information-in-motion" networks beneficial to both.

And finally, by the year 2000, our teachers will be self-employed and their services will be contracted for by the institutions of higher learning. This will be cost-effective for the schools, and people tend to do a better job when they work for themselves. Like large construction companies today, our institutions of higher education will subcontract for the services they provide tomorrow.

We in education can be like the anecdotal king; we can trust the voices that tell us everything will be just fine. The solutions to the crisis of education are really quite simple: just add computer and business courses, re-define the B.A., and make the liberal-arts degree look more marketable. Or we can listen to the voices that tell us everything is not fine—that education and we who are in it are obsolete and about to be consumed by the electronic information age in one gigantic megabyte. There is, however, a third alternative. We can listen to our own voice—a voice that tells us that if education is to remain the mainstay of learning and serve a society marching to the beat of the electronic drummer, all of us must begin now to plan for long-term solutions that will address current and future needs of the information society in the computer-based electronic learning age. We must plan now to become major producers of software and databases of knowledge; we must become involved in the communications satellite business; we must develop education-business partnerships to share information; we must build the humanities curriculum around a communications laboratory; and we must support efforts to free our teachers to become self-employed.

The electronic learning age with its existing and emerging information technologies is not just another passing fad. Learning is taking place electronically and more of what we know, store, and recall will come to us from electronic sources. The time is fast-approaching when our society will be so integrally hooked into technology at home, at school, and at the office that those of us unwilling to use the new technologies will be the equivalent of people today who cannot read or write.

The information revolution confronts those of us in the humanities with an awesome choice: we can passively and ignorantly surrender to the information explosion—dig in our heels and hope that it will go away—or we can actively and wisely accept it—utilize its technological advances to revolutionize traditional education. In either case, let us remember that information is a two-edged sword that can work for us or against us. Today, time to choose is running out. Tomorrow, in the year 2000, and beyond, we will have no choice but to experience the consequences of what we did or did not choose today.

References

Drucker, P. "The Coming Changes in Our School System," *The Wall Street Journal,* March 3, 1981.

Heines, J. "Tomorrow's Classroom: The Changing Focus in Computer Education," *T.H.E. Journal,* 10(5), p. 101.

Naisbitt, J. *Megatrends.* New York: Warner Books, 1982.

Onosko, T. "The Incredible Space Mirror," *Video,* 7(2), pp. 63, 98.

Solorzano, G. "Liberal Arts Colleges Bow to the Future," *U.S. News and World Report,* 94(20), May 23, 1983, p. 67.

Sommerfeld, L. "To Byte or Not to Byte,"*Educational Horizons,* 61(3), p. 116.

Stewart, M. "Preparing for Our Future,"*Inc. Magazine,* March 1983, p. 134.

Warnshuis, E. "Challenging Opportunities or Insurmountable Problems," *Technological Horizons in Education Journal,* 10(5), p. 9.

Bibliography

American Productivity Center. *Output and Computer Literacy.* Houston, Texas, 1983.

Armacost, S. Address before the American Electronic Association. *Los Angeles Times,* January 1983, Section IV, p. 2, col. 5.

"Campus Satellite." Creighton University Systems Conference, May 19-21, 1983.

Chadwick, C. "Why Educational Technology Is Failing," *Educational Technology,* 1979, 19, 17-19.

Euchner, C. "Computer Firms Said Uncertain of Potential School Market." *Education Week* 1983, 2(35), p. 4.

Forbes, R. "Teaching for Thinking." *Educational Leadership,* 1983, 40(8), p. 3.

Howard, R. "Without Care, Schools Will Foster a Powerful Mismatch" (Editorial), *Electronic Education,* 1983 2(7), pp. 78-79.

International Resource Development. *Microcomputers in Education.* Norwalk, Connecticut, 1982.

Janko, E. "Education Fads That Have Come and Gone," *New York Times,* 1981, p. 23, col. 8.

Office of Technology Assessment. "Information Technology and Its Impact on American Education," Washington, D.C.: GPO, 1981.

Sturdivant, P. "School, Business Partnerships May Be the Answer," *Electronic Education,* 1983 2(7), p. 20.

West, C. "Computers in the 80's." in *Computers in Curriculum and Instruction.* New York: ASCD, 1983, p. 3.

Problem-Solving with the Forecasting Brain and Mind

by

David Loye

From our earliest appearance as a species on this earth into this time of mounting challenge to our very existence as a species, our survival has depended on our ability to solve problems. The chief instrument for this survival-oriented problem-solving has been the forecasting brain and mind.

At our beginning, for example, it was the operation of the forecasting brain and mind that made it possible for the early human to visualize the favorable consequences of living in a cave on high ground versus the unfavorable consequences of living in a lean-to on a sand bar. Now, as we near the twenty-first century, it is the forecasting brain and mind that make it possible for us to so visualize the consequences of nuclear war that increasing millions of us are taking to the streets throughout the world to protest the insanity of an escalation in nuclear overkill.

In both instances, we may see the situation of a problem to which the application of the forecasting brain and mind provides a way to find a solution. If, then, we may understand how this combination of a physiological and a psychological entity works as a general problem-solver, it should help us to understand how to solve all problems in particular. So this paper will present what recent neuropsychological research indicates is the way our brains and minds handle the future. We will do this in evolutionary terms because this seems to be a particularly effective way of bringing the forecasting brain/mind model to life.

The Brain/Mind Model at the Beginning

Many kinds of research indicate that the chief difference between how humans solved problems 100,000 years ago and how we do it now is a matter of complexity and differentiation of brain function. In the early years of our species, our brains and minds functioned in what could be characterized as a relatively undifferentiated, whole brain, and psychically sensitive way. We know

David Loye is co-director of the Institute for Futures Forecasting, Carmel, California, and author of The Sphinx and the Rainbow: Brain, Mind and Future Vision (Shambhala, 1983). He is also research director of the Program on Psychosocial Adaptation and the Future in the Department of Psychiatry, UCLA School of Medicine, Los Angeles, California.

this must be true because of what we can observe in lower-order mammals today in two regards. One is their relative lack of the kind of split in brain functioning for right and left brain hemispheres characteristic of modern humans. The other is the remarkable capacities of animals for the kind of psychic (or paranormal) sensitivities that modern humans only occasionally draw upon. It is, for example, well known that animals can sense impending earthquakes, that dolphins and other fish can communicate, and that lines of communication even run from animal to plant life in ways that remain incomprehensible to present-day science.

So at this early stage of human development we may picture the forecasting brain and mind operating according to a relatively simple two-level model. The more accessible level would involve the conscious cognition of what likely lies ahead through a relatively undifferentiated whole brain and mind. The less accessible level would involve the precognition of what likely lies ahead through another form of whole-mindedness operating on an unconscious level. The forecasts that the early human used as a guide to problem-solution and action would then be a composite of information from these two levels of brain functioning.

Now about 30,000 years ago something happened that radically changed this situation. We know this with some degree of certainty because of the work of Harvard brain researcher Marjorie LeMay. She found that before this time prehistoric fossilized skulls show no evidence of brain-half differentiation, but after this time a difference in skull configuration appears, apparently to accommodate a new difference in brain-half configuration.

As this happens around the time that humans would logically have begun to develop the complex languages that now so sharply differentiate us from lower-order animals, and because it is now well established that language is primarily a left-brain function in humans, it is further surmised that it was the need for a special accommodation for the new symbol processing that brought on the split in function for right and left brain hemispheres in humans.

What resulted from this pressure to split increasingly complex operations formerly handled by the whole brain into two sets of operations was the "partnership" arrangement characteristic of the modern brain. As is well established and well known, this difference is that of a tendency of language and mathematics to be dominantly processed by the left hemisphere, and music, art, and pattern-detection to be dominantly a matter of right-brain-half processing.

Specific to the operation of forecasting were (and are) these two fundamental differentiations. The left brain half is the base of operations for the serial processing of information that provides us with a main component of our "sense" of time. Specifically, it provides us with the framework of past, present, and future within which we visualize the future both as "time's arrow" and in the fine clocklike differentiations of seconds, minutes, hours, days, and so on.

By contrast, the right brain half is the base of operations for a simultaneous or parallel processing of information that provides us not only with the other great grounding dimension for our existence—our "sense" of space—but also a grounding sense for the detection of patterns that provides another kind of essential structure for our reading of the future.

In contrast to the early human, then, in our modern brains and minds we have these two major sources of information processing that provide decision-making centers with two basic ingredients for all our forecasts. The strength of this arrangement is apparent in the difference between seeing with one eye or with two eyes. Cover one eye and look ahead, and in the loss of depth perception and general "roundedness" of things you will see a radical loss of information that could, in tight circumstances, be the difference between survival or annihilation. Uncover that eye and in the way depth and roundedness spring back into place you will see an analogue of the advantage of the two brains that combine to form the modern mind. Now you can see not only what is approaching, but also how far away it is—and also gauge how quickly it is approaching in a way providing a far more accurate basis for taking action.

Higher and Lower Brain Power

Now it is at this point that a third component that was already operating in rudimentary form in the early human, but that now takes on special importance, comes into play in the modern brain and mind. This is the operation of the areas of the frontal brain lobes that brain research has shown act as the "mind's manager." Though other, lower brain areas are also involved, the chief higher brain area concerned with both the detection of problems and their solution through the involvement of forecasting and action to test and implement or accommodate forecasting is located in the frontal brain.

In problem-solving terms, the critical frontal brain functions include: 1) detecting the problem; 2) alerting right and left brain hemisphere areas to gather their radically different pictures of what the problem is and what it may portend; 3) consolidation of these two vastly differing inputs into a useful synthesis of inputs; 4) decision on whether to take action or not to act upon this information; 5) commands to the brain's motor centers to act in a way either to gain more information or to take action aimed at problem-solution; 6) build more forecasts based on more feedback; 7) order more actions—and so on, until the problem is solved or put on the shelf for a while, so to speak.

All this indicates why the frontal brain operations, which are so much like what is expected of a competent manager of any organization or industry, are the basis for characterizing the frontal brain as the "mind's manager."

In left, right, and frontal brain, and in their interaction, we have then the three components for the model for the operation of the forecasting brain and mind developed more extensively in *The Sphinx and the Rainbow* and previous articles of mine in *The Futurist* and the *World Future Society Bulletin*. (See references at end of this paper.)

We have, up to this point, only dealt with the "top half" of what started out as a two-level model in the early human. We have only dealt with the cognitive part of the model more accessible to consciousness, dividing what was more of a wholeness originally into a splitting of brain functions into two and then three parts.

So far, while we are speculating, we are doing so on the basis of a considerable body of psychological, sociological, anthropological, and philosophical as well as neurological research. To state what probably happened, and is now likely operating, on the "lower half" of the model requires much more speculation with much less research support. It is a task worth doing, however, for two reasons: First, it provides us with guidelines for research to determine exactly what is going on here, and, second, we are at a juncture in human history when our existence is so threatened that we must call up every power of mind we can find—including this lost and buried ancient capacity—if we are to weather the storm of fate and sail clear into the next century.

We can speculate, then, that this is what happened to the ancient precognitive abilities we surmise from their operation in animals. Back there 30,000 years ago, when we began to program the left brain half to handle this wondrous new ability of ours to speak and write, we set in motion the long-range tremendous gain in problem-solving power that having words and numbers represents, as symbols to radically expand and more finely differentiate our thinking. But as this new left-brain power was set loose, we also at that time began to suppress more and more of the old input from what we now would call psychic sensitivity.

Now what could be our loss? There is a growing tendency today to downplay rationality and anything else that smacks of left-brainedness and to extol the neglected power of the right brain. But as anyone who has spent any part of a lifetime developing or involved with forecasting methods and systems knows, there is an inconceivably great advantage in being able to use numbers in the ways we do, to build mathematical models for forecasting, and especially to have the almost inconceivable power gain that the computer represents to implement them. Surely this represents an advance of some light years over the old animal way.

Why, then, should we seek now to go beyond this new left-brained, computerized forecasting power? For the same reason that 30,000 years ago we humans split our information processing into two brain halves, and for the same reason that two eyes are better than one. We need to draw upon all of the forecasting brain and mind's sources of power: the right, left, and frontal brain power of the model's upper half and the newly explorable psychic functioning power of the lower half.

How, then, might we apply this model to the problems of our time?

One example will have to serve here for many. We have identified the problem of de-escalating nuclear escalation that threatens our continued species existence. Our left brain provides all the grim words and numbers while our right brain provides the specific vision of how it would look and sound and feel to be annihilated. Our psychic sensitivity provides a presently unreliable but still additional powerful intuition of what can happen. The frontal brain areas then consolidate the three inputs into a forecast of disaster if the world's present leadership continues on its invariant threatening and bullying and macho-posturing course. This forecast, in turn, provides the fuel for whatever actions we take in trying to do what we can to change the situation and point our destiny in a life-enhancing rather than a life-destroying direction.

And so forecasting, and acting to test and modify the forecast, and again acting, and again forecasting, again acting, we proceed in this age-old way that, until now, has helped guarantee our survival and existence.

Perhaps the greatest advantage we have is in knowing not only that something of this sort operates within us, but that also every one of us has this kind of power to draw upon, if we will only take the time to understand it, and believe in ourselves and the future that can be ours if we begin to make more use of this neglected power.

Selected References

Loye, D. *The Sphinx and the Rainbow: Brain, Mind, and Future Vision.* Boulder, Colorado: New Science Library of Shambhala Books, 1983.

Loye, D. "The Brain and the Future: First Ripples of the Wave," *The Futurist,* October 1982.

Loye, D. "The Forecasting Brain: How We See the Future," *The Futurist,* February 1984.

Loye, D. "A Guide to Personal, Business and Social Forecasting and Survival, *World Future Society Bulletin,* September-October 1983.

Overcoming Unemployment: Some Radical Proposals

David Macarov

One of the most ubiquitous and persistent social problems in the Western industrialized world is that of unemployment. Despite continuing and massive efforts of various kinds to reduce the number of the unemployed to acceptable proportions, in most countries the problem of unemployment remains, and—with current advances in technology—may become a permanent feature of society. Long-term unemployment, particularly among youth, now commands the attention of many national and international bodies. Conventional methods of attempting to overcome unemployment are becoming more and more ineffective. Consequently, this article proposes some more radical attempts to overcome the problem of unemployment.

Unemployment in History

Unemployment is usually thought of in relation to paid labor— even if the payment is in kind—and consequently is not often linked to purely agricultural economies. However, in the days when such an economy was widespread in the form of family farms, there was no value to the farmer in producing surplus products; in the absence of roads, storage facilities, and accessible markets, a surplus would only rot (a situation that continues in some present-day developing countries [Macarov and Fradkin]). Hence, farmers produced only for themselves and their families and—despite the mythology of unceasing farm labor—had over a hundred workless days a year (Buckingham). Fearing the fruits of idleness, the State and the Church filled these days with national and religious holidays (de Schweinitz). Consequently, whether this constituted unemployment in those times is clearly a matter of definition. However, even today agricultural laborers, not to mention farm owners and their families, are omitted from most unemployment compensation programs throughout the

David Macarov is associate professor, Paul Baerwald School of Social Work, The Hebrew University, Jerusalem, Israel.

world (Macarov, 1980), and are not included among the unemployed no matter how the latter are counted, and regardless of how little work they find to do.

When people moved off the family farms, however, and began to work for others, unemployment in the modern sense became a constant and recurring problem. In fact, urbanization and unemployment were probably coeval. Mendelssohn explains the building of the first great Egyptian Pyramid as requiring 20,000 laborers for as long as 20 years. In the agricultural economy of ancient Egypt, the laborers were necessarily recruited from among farmers, who were transplanted with their families to the site of the building and sustained by the Pharoah. As the work progressed, however, and the structure became smaller as it neared the top, fewer and fewer workers were needed. The problem of the workers who were becoming "unemployed"—all of whom had been away from their farms for so many years that they no longer possessed land—became acute. Hence, according to Mendelssohn, the second and subsequent Pyramids were begun as the previous ones were nearing completion. In short, the later pyramids were actually public-works projects to combat unemployment, regardless of their subsequent usage.

Similarly, when the Second Temple was completed and Herod was faced with thousands of unemployed workers, a wide paved road around the Temple Mount was begun—a road that is still visible in the Old City of Jerusalem. Vespasian, too, was concerned about unemployment, and consequently refused to make use of mechanical devices for moving heavy stone columns for fear it would take jobs away from people (Garraty)—a fear that continued until and past the Luddites in England who destroyed textile machines that replaced people. Lord Byron's first speech in Parliament was against the death penalty for such acts. Unemployment has been combatted in other ways, too. Armies have sometimes been amassed and used more to give employment than for any other purpose; overseas colonies have been founded to get rid of unemployed populations; and land has been given to veterans to "get them off the streets," so to speak (Garraty).

Although at one time unemployment was seen as a purely economic question, and perhaps one that had political overtones in terms of possible social unrest and upheaval, work itself—and hence not working—began to take on various moral overtones. Martin Luther's postulation of work as a vocation decreed by God meant that those who did not work, or did not work hard at whatever job they had, were sinners, since God required people to work. The good works of Catholicism were replaced by the good work of Protestantism. It is no wonder, then, that employers saw themselves, and were sometimes seen by Church and State, as benevolent persons who were offering other people a chance to serve God. Hence strikes, labor unrest, or disaffection were not seen as purely social or economic manifestations, but as heresy if not blasphemy. Work and religiosity thus became intertwined.

Adam Smith added another moral element to work with his theory of the "invisible web" in a laissez-faire economy, whereby each was to compete with all in attempting to maximize his or her economic position. Such competition would create high-quality goods at low prices, thus benefitting everyone. Anyone who did not attempt to maximize his or her position—by not working, for example—became a hole in the net, damaging everyone else. Such people were not only immoral in the religious sense, they were harmful to the total community; they were bad neighbors.

The philosophy known as mercantilism, which put the wealth of the state above the welfare of the individual, added another negative connotation to not working. It was the national duty of the citizen to work hard at increasing the country's wealth, thus enabling it to compete with others—not only economically, but often militarily as well. Profits often went to pay soldiers, and therefore one who did not work injured his or her country. In short, he or she was unpatriotic for not working.

Finally, Sigmund Freud added another element of morality to working. His dictum that happiness consists of the ability "to love and to work" became transmuted into a formula for mental stability or, at least, normalcy. Freud not only influenced members of the helping professions; through the media and popularization of his theories, vast numbers of people in the West used his terms and absorbed his concepts. Interestingly, the fact that Freud also said that as a method of attaining human happiness work was not highly prized and that, indeed, there seems to be a "natural human aversion to work," was hardly noted. In any case, Freud placed the stamp of acceptance on work as both the vehicle for, and evidence of, individual normalcy.

Thus, through Luther, Smith, mercantilism, and Freud, work took on religious, civic, patriotic, and mental-health values, and soon became reified as a value in its own right. Clearly, not working was reprehensible, from both an individual and a societal point of view.

Together with the development of the concept of work, the development of society added to the picture. New opportunities in newly-discovered lands; seemingly limitless frontiers; rapidly increasing production; and growing affluence all lent themselves to the creation of a belief that anyone who really wanted work could find it, and even if it was dirty, difficult, or disagreeable, it was not only better than not working—it was probably temporary, the stepping-stone to greater things, a la Horatio Alger.

To be unemployed has generally been seen by the larger public as evidence of a personal failure. Except for times of deep recession or real depression, when the numbers belie the beliefs, this imputation of lack of incentive among the unemployed is clear (Macarov, 1970). Hence, the deliberately difficult procedures for collecting unemployment compensation, which is itself bounded with limitations and restrictions. Coupled with "blaming the victim" is the view that such aggregate unemployment as exists is numerically unimportant, is only of short duration, or can be overcome by relatively simple measures such as retraining or relocation.

Thus, unemployment is categorized as either "frictional," meaning people between jobs for short periods; "cyclic," which means that bouts of unemployment are offset—usually rather quickly— by periods of full employment, or even labor shortages; or "structural," meaning that the skills or location of the workers do not match the jobs open at a given place. These definitions serve to obfuscate the long-term, continuing, and growing phenomenon of permanent unemployment.

Defining and Measuring Unemployment

Unemployment has been simplistically defined by Lord Beveridge as fewer vacant jobs than people seeking work. A more complex definition is used by the Long Island Coalition for Full Employment: "The right of all persons able, willing and seeking work to full opportunity for useful paid employment at fair rates of compensation." This definition takes into consideration both the usefulness of the work (ruling out make-work) and payment (excluding underpaid jobs), and complicates measures to reduce unemployment. As the definition of full employment becomes more exacting, e.g., "interesting work at decent pay under good conditions producing socially desirable objects or services without deleterious side-effects on the worker, society, or the ecology," then possibilities of attaining full employment become almost impossible.

Further, since unemployment is defined and measured differently in various countries, comparative figures are quite unreliable. Common to most Western industrialized countries, however, is the political need to understate the extent of unemployment as much as possible, and for this reason definitional and statistical artifacts abound.

Some countries define unemployment as the number of people drawing unemployment compensation, thus omitting those not covered by the compensation program (often farm laborers, casual laborers, and domestic help); those who have not worked long enough to be eligible for benefits; those who are within a "waiting period" before becoming eligible (Griffiths); those who have exhausted their benefits; and those who—for various reasons— have never applied for them. Other countries count as unemployed everyone who registers as such, whether or not they receive compensation. This method, too, omits those who do not register—because of distance, ignorance, pride, inability to get to the office, limited hours of registration, etc.; those who are not eligible to register, such as non-residents or non-citizens, illegal aliens; and those who have never worked before and are therefore not considered to be unemployed, such as school leavers. Still other countries do not accept as unemployed anyone who will not take any job offered, regardless of salary, conditions, training, and suitability.

In the United States, unemployment figures are based upon a continuing survey in which people are asked basically two questions: "Are you working?" and "During the last week, did you look for work?" If the answer to the first question is negative and to the second is positive, that person is considered unemployed. It has been pointed out in a number of places that this method ignores persons who are working at (perhaps *very*) part-time jobs, only due to inability to find full-time work; and those who have become so discouraged at their inability to find work that they no longer look. There are also those who would like to work, but who live in areas or times where or when it is obvious that there is no work to be had. Unemployment figures in this case are subject to many other variables. Unemployment often drops after a deep snowstorm, for example—not because people are employed to clear the snow, but because it is impossible to get out and look for a job, thus fulfilling the criterion for being unemployed.

There are other methods of concealing the true measure of unemployment. One is to enroll the unemployed in various kinds of training and retraining courses. They then become—statistically—students getting educational stipends, rather than the unemployed drawing compensation. Sweden, for example, usually has more people in training courses than unemployed—a handy device for limiting the latter number. In Britain, there is a two-week waiting period and a six-month limitation. In this case, official unemployment can easily be reduced by lengthening the waiting period, or reducing the time compensation is paid, or both (Field). Then there are job-sharing schemes, in which two people each do half a job and are taken off the unemployment rolls (Best); "lay-offs," which are technically for a limited period and thus not unemployment; and administrative requirements, such as the Israeli demand that unemployed laborers report in person to the employment office *every day* and academics twice a week in order to continue to be considered unemployed. Another ploy is to characterize claimants as "unsuitable for full-time work" (Field)—a category that can be used almost arbitrarily, including those who are not polite enough to the employment clerk.

Finally, there is the time-honored method of "feather-bedding"—that is, maintaining unnecessary jobs, or maintaining unnecessary people in jobs, in order to keep labor peace or to reduce unemployment. This is becoming increasingly prevalent as technology takes over and unions (as well as entire societies) demand that human workers be kept on the payroll. Twice recently, in Israel, textile factories have been threatened with closure because their product is not profitable. In each case the government stepped in to subsidize the plant—not because there would be a shortage of cloth, but because there would be a loss of jobs. Threaten to close a shipyard in any Western country and the resultant outcry has nothing to do with the need for ships, even warships, but with the jobs that will be lost. Consequently, the introduction of new technology is often accompanied by a "no firings" pledge, and profits from the new machinery wait until attrition without new hirings has reduced the number of workers to those actually needed.

The Extent of Unemployment

Because of and despite the statistical artifacts and the societal/individual subterfuges used to conceal the extent of real unemployment, it has been estimated that the official figures—no matter how derived—are understated from 50 to 300% (Field; Kogut and Aron; Macarov, 1980). Consequently, an official figure of 8% unemployment really represents from 12 to 24 people out of every hundred ready, willing, and able to work who cannot find jobs. Within some groups, such as inner-city black youths, the figure may be 60% or even higher.

The unemployment rate in Western industrialized society has been rising sporadically but inexorably over the last 30 years at least. Even this rise in unemployment ignores the extent to which average hours of work have decreased within the same period. Over the past half-century, labor hours per unit of output have been reduced about 3% per year, and average hours worked per year have been reduced by close to .5% per annum (Kendrick). In the United States, hours of work have declined from 53 hours a week in 1900 to 35 hours a week in 1980—a reduction of almost one-third. In short, if work hours had not been reduced, a third of the people working now would be unemployed, in addition to those presently out of work.

Together with the rise in unemployment there has been constant revision of the "acceptable" rate of unemployment. From 4% official unemployment (which means 6%-12% actual unemployment), the figure has constantly risen—6%, 7%, and in some countries 8% is seen as tolerable, or even inevitable. Even those who stick to the "cyclic" theory—that returning prosperity will reduce unemployment—admit that many of the jobs, especially those taken over by automation, will not return, and that many of those made unemployed will remain so. This is called the "ratchet effect," and is epitomized by a *New York Times* headline: "The Jobs That Won't Come Back." The matter of youth unemployment has become one of special concern in a number of countries, for these are not people who have built up vestedness in compensation programs through previous work; nor acquired savings and/or pensions; or even attained job skills or work-related behavior patterns. On the contrary, there is fear that many of these young people will *never* find work, or, at most, only transient and temporary employment.

The Results of Unemployment

Since, as noted above, work has become overlaid with religious, human, patriotic, and mental-health values, it is no wonder that all the vehicles of socialization are brought to bear to induce, seduce, coerce, and aid people not only to work, but to see in work the path to happiness and self-fulfillment. Since the reality of work denies the expectations, various psychological devices are used to bridge the gap—cognitive dissonance, denial, and others (Macarov, 1970).

Consequently, the experience of unemployment—and especially long-term, hopeless unemployment—must have its effect on the psyche and the soma of the unemployed. And, indeed, in studies too numerous to list, in daily life, and through personal experiences there is testimony to the mental and physical ill effects of unemployment.

Not only is the effect felt by the individual concerned, in terms of being unable to cope, and—usually—being financially penalized, but these effects reverberate through family and social ranks, roles, and relationships. Neighborhoods or communities of mass unemployment tend to be shunned, and the previously noted assumption that the unemployed have themselves to blame begins to be shared by the individuals concerned.

On a wider front, unemployment leads to diminution of purchasing power, and therefore consumption, with consequent effects on the total economy. Conversely, the need to support the unemployed not only becomes a burden, but a source of social unrest and bitterness toward the victims. The assumed effect of unemployment on the voting patterns of those cast into that role is not lost on politicians, who assume that in the final analysis many people vote with their stomachs.

In short, as work is seen as an individual and social good, so unemployment is viewed as evidence of individual and social failure. Hence, the determined efforts to disguise unemployment, as well as to overcome it.

The Future of Unemployment

The likelihood of growing *permanent* unemployment is becoming more accepted as a reality among social planners as figures mount, and as palliative measures fail. Taggart, for example, examines the effects of tax cuts, wage subsidies, reduced worktime, public-works projects, public-service employment, and macroeconomic changes in a book entitled *Job Creation: What Works?* A careful perusal of these various options indicates that the most honest answer is: "Nothing." Similarly, the record of training and retraining courses to help the unemployed is dismal (Macarov, 1978). Consequently, the AFL-CIO's Committee on the Evolution of Work foresees a persistent job shortage, consisting of 4-6 mil-

lion Americans unemployed at all times *(World of Work Report).*
Rankin summarizes the situation:

> Of one fact . . . we can be sure, which is that outside the context of
> war we will not revert to a state of full employment in the foreseeable
> future: that era has finished. . . . More and more people (will) find
> themselves without the support of an adequate income and sense of
> worth, both of which were usually provided through full-time paid
> employment.

The future of work will be influenced by a number of factors,
including increasingly large numbers of women in the labor force,
the aging of work populations, higher levels of worker education,
the shift to services, and changing attitudes toward work
(Macarov, 1983). Reverberating through each of these areas, however, and having major impact on both the extent and nature of
work, will be the growing impact of technology.

Whether technology will erode the number of jobs available in
the future, or whether new industries and new work opportunities
will be created, continues to be hotly debated in the literature.
When one recognizes, however, that rising unemployment and
reduced work time are being accompanied by increased production and productivity—the latter averaging an increase of about
2.5% per year, or an aggregate of 32% in 10 years—it is hard to
identify any other factor that could be responsible for these developments. Certainly, people are not working harder every year,
nor does the modern worker put in more hours or energy than
did his or her grandfather. Even if they did, it would have little
effect, since the human factor is said to account for only 10% to
25% of changes in productivity. Increases come about in great
part through changes in methods, machines, and materials—not
manpower. Nor are new sources of energy or new natural resources discovered and exploited at the rate of 2.5% per year.
Technology is the only factor that can account for such sustained
productivity growth.

From 1948 throught 1969, technology accounted for 54.5% of
growth in national income per employed person. As a factor in
the postwar growth of the American economy, technology was
four times greater than business capital investment, 2.8 times
greater than investment in education, and 3.8 times higher than
improvements from more efficient use of resources (Wilson).

It has been estimated that technology decreases jobs in manufacturing by about 3% a year (Hull), and the growing productivity in the services—also about 2.5% per year—is almost entirely
due to technological changes (Carnes; Carey and Otto; Carnes
and Band). With growing productivity inevitably comes reduced
work times and unemployment. Consequently, if long-term
trends are considered, it seems that continued technical advances
will increase productivity and unemployment, despite reduction
of work times.

Even if technological advances slow down, the long-term trend will continue, albeit slower. There is no reasonable possibility of technological advance stopping completely, however, if for no other reason than that the demand for new products and services makes it impossible, as does the synergistic nature of technology—one change not only making possible, but requiring, other changes. On the contrary, there is every reason to believe that technological change will not only continue at its present pace, but that it will increase almost logarithmically. Speaking of microelectronics alone, Norman says:

> The microlectronic revolution could affect employment from steel works to bank; no technology in history has had such a broad range of potential applications to the workplace . . . products incorporating microelectronic devices generally require significantly less labor to produce the goods they replace . . . a third reason for apprehension is the speed with which technology is advancing.

The future impact of technology will be no different from its past—increased per-person productivity, leading to reduced work time as a palliative, and increased unemployment as a result.

The basic dilemma arising from this situation is the relationship between jobs and work. Although technology makes human labor more and more redundant, the growth of populations, together with rising expectations, requires that more and more jobs be provided. Reducing work time has been the traditional response to this situation, and will probably continue into the near future, but in the long term, a point will be reached when it is no longer technically feasible to subdivide tasks (Homans) not only mechanically, but from the point of view of supervision, coordination, record-keeping, and continuity.

It is not only that modern society does not need all of the work represented in the actual and potential labor force, it does not even need all the work of which people now holding jobs are capable. It has been estimated that people use 44% of their potential in their work (Walbank), and 54% of those asked said they could work harder than they do (Berg, et al.). A number of studies that interviewed workers in depth found that they do not "give their all" to their jobs (Lasson; Garson; Rubin; Terkel). Cherrington did an empirical study, sending observers to watch building workers erecting a structure. He found that the workers used only 49% of their work time doing the job—the rest was spent on late starts, early quits, waiting around, drinking coffee (among other things), and just loafing. This has been referred to in various places as "time theft," "unproductive work time," and "underutilization" (Sullivan).

Indeed, if everyone capable of working were to obey the strictures and work to the full extent of their ability, the result would be absolute catastrophe for society, which would not be able to provide all the work demanded, nor use all the goods and services provided. As it is, both planned obsolescence and mass advertising are necessary to create enough demand for the productive capacity of most Western countries.

The actual situation is the reverse: Society does not need all of the human labor available, and with the advance of technology, needs less and less. The current necessity to provide jobs means that the work available must be stretched, divided, invented, and expanded—a la Parkinson's Law —to meet the demand for jobs. This demand is one of the major factors restraining the further and more rapid advance of technology. The fear for jobs leads to the continuation of human labor even in situations where it is clear and/or demonstrated that technology can do the job faster, better, and cheaper.

However, technology will continue to advance, and consequently permanent unemployment for large portions of the population is a prospect that must be taken into consideration, if not confronted.

What's To Be Done?

As noted above, a number of devices are used to obscure the extent of unemployment or to reduce the number. Some of these, in addition to simply cutting work hours directly and through increased vacations, holidays, etc., are:

Job Creation: The direct creation of jobs, although much discussed and recommended, is too costly to be feasible. In 1978, it was estimated that each job created in Australia cost $16,000—a figure that rose to $23,333 by 1982 (Dasgupta; Jamrozik and Hoey). In 1979, it cost $16,000 to create a job in Germany, and that figure has probably risen like the Australian figure (*World of Work Report*, February, 1979). An American congressional proposal to raise $5.5 billion from gasoline taxes to create 320,000 public-service jobs works out to $17,188 per job (*New York Times*, December 12, 1982). To create 24,000 jobs in construction would cost $1 billion, or $41,667 per job (Ball); Sulvetta ups this to $50,000 per job. The gross cost for a public service employment job is $8,000, while one created through tax cuts costs $25,000 (Killingsworth and King). The amount necessary to create a million jobs was estimated in 1972 as $26 billion (Killingsworth and King). With about 10 million people unemployed in the United States, creating jobs for them would cost $171 billion. Providing them with construction jobs—often cited as the socially most necessary jobs—would cost $416 billion. This option is obviously not open for any large number of people.

Subsidized Jobs: Under this plan, employers are subsidized by government grants to offer jobs, usually to new workers, graduates of training courses, the handicapped and—in the case of Israel—new immigrants. The expectation (or rather, the hope) is that the employee will then become permanent. Rarely does this happen. The employee represents cheap labor to the employer (and unfair competition to other job seekers, as well as union members), and a succession of such short-term subsidized workers is the usual pattern. This has overtones of the famous Speenhamland plan in eighteenth-century England in which workers received government subsidies to bridge the gap between their salaries and the cost of food—whereupon the employers lowered salaries, making more profit as the subsidies grew larger. In the CETA program in the United States, subsidized people were substituted for regular employees for as long as the subsidies lasted, so there was no net gain in jobs created (Pierson). In general, job-creation subsidies have disappointing results, as Buck points out regarding Holland and Ireland, and Hanby and Jackson as regards Germany.

Work relief: Work relief is a method of making relief payments through the mechanism of work. It selects workers according to need, rather than ability; engages in programs for maximum employment, rather than maximum efficiency of production; and often pays according to amount needed, rather than a standard salary. The WIN program of AFDC was an American example of such an effort—with very meagre results. Indeed, work relief is not designed to overcome unemployment, but rather to get some return for welfare expenditures. Inasmuch as most of the work done under such programs is make-work, of little intrinsic value, it has little employment potential.

Public works: Public-works projects differ from work-relief programs in that they usually pick workers for competence (at least to some degree), pay according to a standard scale rather than according to individual need, and usually have some intrinsic values as to results. Ideally, public-works projects consist of valuable work that has not hitherto been done because either the workers were not available or funds to pay for the work were lacking. Unemployed workers and budgets to pay them make up the combination that brings such programs into being. Such programs suffer from a number of limitations, however. For one thing, unions often insist that if there are jobs available, their own unemployed members should get them; nor do they want pay scales established within public-works programs that are below those for which they have fought for doing the same work. Nor do commercial firms want goods produced or services performed at prices lower than they charge. Hence, both relief work and public works tend to be marginal jobs that nobody else will do, or will do for the money paid.

Perhaps the most salient example of pubic-works programs in the United States was the post-Depression WPA. Despite the impressive accomplishments of this program—evidence of which is still with us in terms of bridges, murals, plays, and successful artists—2.5 million people eligible for the program were never assigned, due to lack of useful work for them (Charnow), while everyone who lived through that experience remembers mostly the great bulk of WPA workers who were going through a slow charade in order not to use up the work available. Make-work projects today are no longer as harmless as WPA leaf-raking, but tend toward the manufacture of armaments and other large-scale items of dubious value, if not danger, which are defended as much in terms of their job-creating potential as concerning their intrinsic usefulness. Fechter summarizes: "Common sense would suggest that public service employment will produce output of marginal priority or value since, presumably, if it had higher priority or value it would have been unnecessary to stimulate it production by subsidization," and "There is no evidence to suggest that we can create 1.5 to 2 million (public employment) jobs."

Work-sharing: One of the latest methods of fighting unemployment is work-sharing (Best)—i.e., dividing a job (and its salary) between two people. Thus, two people doing half-a-job each is seen as better than one person working full time and another not working at all. Obviously, work-sharing for purposes of overcoming unemployment entails a number of problems. For one thing, it requires two people, each of whom are content with half a salary. If they work in this manner for lack of alternative, then what actually exists is part-time work used to conceal the extent of unemployment. It also requires the kind of work that can be done in parts, either by dividing the time put in, or the output. Insofar as the participants are sharing one salary, rather than earning a full salary, it increases poverty while decreasing unemployment—a doubtful gain.

Work-sharing is a positive factor when it is used to enable people who prefer part-time work—retirees on pension, the handicapped, those with independent means—to find it. It also serves a very useful purpose in the case of couples who share a job in order to also share household duties and/or childrearing tasks. In the latter case, it is more a phenomenon arising from the need for a new lifestyle, or from (usually women's) career desires than from an effort to overcome unemployment. Actually, insofar as half-salaries are paid for half-jobs, work-sharing can be seen as another device for concealing unemployment, since the normal desire to reduce work hours is linked to continuation of income at the former rate, not to take a salary cut. In any case, cutting both jobs and salaries in half may technically reduce or eliminate unemployment, but at a cost that neither the economy, the society, or the individuals involved will tolerate.

Universal service: One of the ideas for which trial balloons are regularly launched is some sort of voluntary or compulsory national service that will act to take large numbers of people out of the normal labor market. Military service sometimes serves this purpose, but is not usually presented in this manner. However, plans for services like the Civilian Conservation Corps of Depression days continue to surface. The plan is to physically remove people—usually young people—to a setting where they will not compete for jobs in the labor market, supporting them with food, clothing, housing, and minimal wages doing work that is intended to be both useful and educational. The details of such plans are not usually presented in full, since matters such as voluntary versus forced participation, finding really useful work, and teaching skills that will be usable in the normal labor market are not readily solvable. Hence, such plans usually bear the earmarks of hopes, if not fantasies, rather than of programs.

Reducing retirement age: An indirect proposal to ease the problem of unemployment is to reduce the age of mandatory retirement—or to make voluntary retirement at a younger age more attractive. The removal of older workers from the labor force would free jobs for younger people, goes the argument. However, on the one hand the decreasing need for human labor might simply mean that such attrition would reduce the labor force in the aggregate, without opening up job opportunities. On the other hand, reducing the retirement age goes counter to the entire trend of present social movement, which is to abolish mandatory retirement, or move it up in the age bracket. It would be seen as negating the movement toward greater personal freedom and choice concerning lifestyles.

Increasing the attractiveness of early retirement is a more likely scenario, especially given all the evidence that people who retire with enough income to enjoy it are happy that they retired, wish they could have done it earlier, and are enjoying life. Parnes, for example, found that a very large majority of retirees report that their experience in retirement has equalled or surpassed their expectations.

Using voluntary retirement as a method of reducing unemployment, however, would be a very costly—probably too costly—method. If retirees' incomes are not to be allowed to drop enough to discourage retirement, substantial additions to their post-retirement incomes will have to be made. Schulz estimates the replacement rate for a hypothetical male worker with 30 years of service and a nonworking wife, drawing both Social Security and a private pension, as 59% at best. That is, he will receive only 59% of the income necessary to maintain his previous living standards—or, conversely, he will reduce his income by 41%. And, as Schultz points out, this is only for those who have long and uninterrupted work histories, and most workers shift jobs, reducing their retirement incomes.

Government As Employer of Last Resort: This proposal posits the government as the residual employer for everyone who cannot find work otherwise. When this is proposed as a general solution, it encounters the same problems as do work relief, public works, and other such programs. In no known case has this been tried as a general solution. There are, however, countries such as Egypt that guarantee a government job to every university graduate who cannot find one otherwise. The result is a horde of overtrained government clerks in every office, with absolutely no work to do (Vigilante).

In summary, none of the proposals put forth to date for overcoming mass, permanent unemployment has the potential for accomplishing that goal. Not even a combination of all of them will solve the problem of a world in which human labor is not only increasingly unnecessary, but beginning to be understood as an inefficient substitute for advanced technology. It is time to consider some more radical proposals.

Some Radical Proposals

The failure of current attempts to do away with unemployment, or even to reduce it to a minimum, arises from unwillingness to recognize that the amount of human labor available is much greater than that needed for the production of goods and services. The assumption that there is work for all if only the right formula or combination could be found leads to self-defeating activities. These activities include labor-intensive industries and services, when machines could do the job better, faster, and cheaper; condemning people to difficult, demeaning, unsatisfying work as a condition for financial maintenance; and stigmatizing those who don't work, even through no fault of their own, with all of the attendant physical, mental, and social consequences involved.

What is needed to cut this Gordian knot is a planned, conscious movement, of all deliberate speed, toward the highest technology possible, replacing human effort in every area for which changes in methods, machines, and materials can be found. In short, the goal should be that which Griffiths calls "full unemployment." Paradoxically, the elimination of that which is today considered unemployment requires that it be widened to include the majority, if not nearly all, of society; whereupon it will perforce be changed into, and seen as, a social good, rather than a social ill. As Cunningham puts it, when 10% of the population produces all the goods and services needed, "Shall we continue to regard the other 90% in the same light in which we viewed yesterday's 4% or 5%? The question answers itself."

A prerequisite, then, for overcoming unemployment is that we cease trying to find work for people to do, and instead bend every effort to replace them with machines. Then we can pose the questions: Assuming a society in which automation has taken over the bulk of work (and therefore jobs) and in which the results of automated work are available to society in the broad sense; through what mechanisms will people be supported? How will their situations be defined so that they will feel free of stigma? What activities will structure their time, give them identity, cause them to feel needed and wanted? These are the questions that proposals to eliminate unemployment must seek to answer.

Guaranteed Incomes: The proposal to guarantee everyone at least a minimum income, whether they work or not, was originally designed as a method whereby social workers could avoid inflicting the presumed stigmatizing "means test" on their clients (Schwartz). It was later proposed as a simplified method of aiding those who could not, or should not, work—the aged, the handicapped, single parents of small children, and the unemployed and unemployable. Milton Friedman typified conservative economists who favored the plan because they felt it would replace what they saw as the hodge-podge social welfare system. Liberals rallied to the idea because it promised to wipe out poverty, with all its attendant ills. The program was proposed to Congress by President Nixon as a "Family Assistance Plan." The plan came very close to adoption (Moynihan), but finally failed, mostly because liberals saw the benefits as too conservative and conservatives viewed it as too liberal. However the real problem with the proposal for a guaranteed minimum income was called the "notch" provision: At any given level of benefits, and any given percentage of permitted income above the benefit level, there would be a number of persons for whom the plan would be more financially beneficial than working. Hence, the basic difficulty in adopting any guaranteed income plan, be it Family Assistance, Reverse Income Tax, or any of the other titles assigned, was the fear that people would not work if given money. The presumed work disincentive, although later found to be minor (Rossi and Lyall), was, and continues to be, the major sticking point to giving money to people—be it through this plan, normal social welfare channels, or private charities (Macarov, 1970).

However, in a situation in which work incentives would not be an issue—the almost completely automated society—the proposal to guarantee a minimum or adequate income to everyone does not raise these questions. Consequently, the questions that must be resolved are of a different kind. First, there is the problem of the mechanism for income distribution. One possibility is for the kind of family or children's allowance that is common in almost every Western country, but instead of paying the money based on number of children, or to a legally defined family, grants would be made to every individual—a personal-allowance scheme, so to speak. A second problem to be tackled has to do with the level of payments. If everyone is given the same amount, in accordance with the theory of equality, then people with special or additional needs will suffer. If payments are made on the basis of categories of people—the aged, parents, middle age, etc.—the question of special individual needs continues. If payments are to be based on individual need, in accordance with the theory of equity, then need determination may be extensive, expensive, and complicated.

A third question has to do with the manner in which society acquires and distributes the fruits of automated production —via taxes, insurance, nationalization, or other means. Finally, there is the question as to how people will spend their time. This is not just a matter of avoiding boredom, which may require an enormous expansion of leisure-time skills and activities; but has to do with what will replace work in terms of prestige, time-structuring, personal identification, etc. Kaplan, for one, holds that people are already increasingly identified by their leisure-time pursuits rather than by their work.

These are difficult, but not insoluble, problems. In fact, devising answers to the questions will be the simple part of the problem; finding methods of implementing them in a manner that will not create social unrest and upheaval is more difficult.

Redefining Work: A simpler way of arriving at a satisfactory workless society is to redefine work, paying people to engage in activities that are presently unpaid. The most obvious example is paying housewives for what they do—a suggestion recently made by the Vatican in a Charter of the Rights of the Family (*Jerusalem Post*). A less obvious example is to pay people for engaging in socially desirable activities, such as studying, playing games or sports, entertaining others, playing musical instruments, and writing; or more intangible activities such as parenting, neighboring, tutoring (including one's own children), gardening, exploring, etc.

In this way, people could be given income for a wide variety of desirable activities, and could avoid the stigma and other consequences of unemployment. Payments could be scaled to performance—good students being paid more; and not only could musicians be paid according to ability, but also composers, conductors, and even those who tune musical instruments, print the music, and turn the pages.

Although at first glance this proposal seems fanciful, if not fantastic, a moment's reflection will indicate that society already pays certain people to engage in just those activities. Baseball, football, and basketball players are well-supported, but only when they have achieved a certain level of skill. Why can't everyone who wants to play ball be supported by the fruits of automated production, even if the level of skill determines the level of support? Musicians are certainly paid in our society, and entertainers of various kinds are not only paid but paid lavishly—including those who write for them, do their clothes and make-up, etc. Students are supported by stipends, and some of these already make academic attainment a condition of continuation.

Since foster parents and staff in child-care agencies are paid to take care of other people's children, why should natural parents not be similarly compensated for their time and ability? Again, this is not simply fantasy—as noted above, most Western countries, and many developing countries, pay family or childrens' allowances, sometimes in very sizable amounts. The United States is a notable exception in this regard, although as early as 1898 New York State agreed to pay parents of children released from institutions the same amount they had been paying to the institution for the child's upkeep. The bill was vetoed as being morally repugnant, in that it paid parents for taking care of their own children (Coll)—perhaps the reason that there is no children's allowance in the United States.

Similarly, helping one's neighbors is not necessarily restricted to unpaid activities. Many countries use "paid volunteers" on a community basis to bring service to those needing them. Israel has an "Aged Helping the Aged" program, which supplements the income of the elderly helpers, gives them the (justified) feeling that they are useful, and gives service that the social-welfare system is not large enough to offer. Community health aides are used in other countries, as are agricultural assistants. Other examples of paid neighboring abound.

Canada supports aspiring writers through direct grants and grants to supporting agencies. In many countries, grant organizations make possible the careers of people, from artists to researchers. In Israel, for example, the heads of religious groups—rabbis, kadis, preachers, priests—are supported by government, as civil servants. This could be extended to many other kinds of consultants, counselors, advisors, etc., who presently act on a volunteer basis.

In short, in the automated society, it would be possible to pay people for doing what they enjoy, within the limits of socially approved behavior. Such a program overcomes the problem of time-structuring, since the activities undertaken would clearly require some sort of time commitment. Similarly, with payments linked to achievement, it would be a spur to ambition. With special payments for creativity and originality, many wellsprings of progress might be uncovered. Positive self-images and social identity would be linked to the activity performed.

There might remain the problem of those with neither interests nor skills. For these, a basic payment might still be provided, even if their activities consisted of watching television, drinking beer, and playing cards, as long as it was not anti-social.

Cooperatives: One method of overcoming malaise at work, spurring ambition, and meeting needs has been the recent growth of cooperatives in the world of work. Although some countries have long used and encouraged cooperative endeavors in neighborhoods, and some—such as Israel—even in business, transport, agriculture, and other areas, only recently have industries in many Western countries begun to organize worker/management co-ops, cooperative work groups in factories, or even worker-owned businesses on a cooperative basis.

Insofar as the problem of unemployment is concerned, even when the co-op member has little to do, he or she is not considered unemployed as long as they are members of the group, and they are supported by the income of the total cooperative. Widespread ownership of automated industries and services by co-ops would make the members, in a sense, owners and thus—curiously—not unemployed even if they do no work. Again, this is not outside the realm of the possible. Many current writers speak of the possibility—even the desirability—of workers purchasing robots to replace themselves, and leasing these out to employers, living on the profitability of the robot as compared to a human laborer. A $41,000 robot, lasting eight years, will cost less than $5 an hour to buy and operate, as compared to $15 per hour paid one employee in the auto industry (Casner-Lotto). In Japan, a robot leased for $90 can turn out work that would cost $1,200 if done by humans (Lohr). Schrank also suggests that workers buy robots and lease them out—a possibility increasingly feasible as the cost of robots is reduced. Bylinsky says that, by the turn of the century, robot labor may be down to about 70 cents an hour. The purchase of several robots by co-ops of (former) workers may be more feasible than on an individual basis, while diversification of kinds of robots might avoid seasonal or other types of fluctuations.

Even without regard for automation or the future, one method of overcoming unemployment, or its effects, is through ever-widening circles of cooperatives, in which the income is divided among members, including those not working. With the merging of co-ops, ever-larger units can be included, until income from all work done is shared equally among everyone.

Cooperatives, too, are not a dream. There exists an extensive literature on both industrial and agricultural co-ops, and a smaller literature on service-rendering co-ops (Case and Taylor; Teselle). In Israel, "moshavim" (cooperative farm villages) have existed for at least 50 years and are now including industrial projects in their economy. Other countries, notably in Scandinavia, have used cooperative industries extensively, with good results. Indeed, the spread of cooperatives until they encompass the total economy is not even dependent upon the advent of the technological society. Co-ops, by their nature, obviate unemployment as it is now understood.

Collectives: Going beyond cooperatives, which divide proceeds among members, there is the possibility of collectives, which provide for all their members' needs (and many of their wants) from the income of the group. Perhaps the best known example of the large-scale permanent collective is the Israel *kibbutz* (pl. *kibbutzim*). Too well-known to require more than a few words of description, the kibbutz is a voluntary collective in which all of the property is owned by all of the members in common, and in which all of the members' needs, including childcare, education, health care, housing, necessities, amenities, vacations, care of parents, etc., are taken care of by the group. Perhaps the most salient difference between the kibbutz collective and other social forms is that the type and amount of support are in no way linked with the kind or amount of work done by the member. Income is based purely on need, and although there are differences in work patterns among kibbutz members (Macarov, 1971; 1982), the total economy of the kibbutz has been found to be no less efficient and productive than that in the private sector.

Although originally founded as agricultural communities, kibbutzim now include many industries and services, and some of the kibbutzim are now in their fourth generation, being over 75 years old (Weingarten; Criden and Gelb). The history of collectives other than the kibbutz also has deep roots, including a number of so-called Utopian communities, e.g., the Oneida community; religious groupings such as the Hutterians, the Amish; and communities that had their origins in the social movements of the sixties (Peters; Hostetler; Melville; Kephart).

A recent phenomenon in some of these groups—notably the kibbutz—has been in the inroad of technology. Originally founded with a very heavy emphasis on human—or, rather, individual—labor, finding work for all the members has become a problem for some kibbutzim, particularly those that have moved heavily into industry. Accepting life without work as it is presently defined has been difficult for them, but since their inception kibbutzim have supported members to paint, be musicians, engage in the plastic arts, and—to a lesser extent—to write. The number of such people is now growing, and increasing amounts of leisure are not only being accepted in the kibbutz, but—as in many other places—are being viewed as a problem that must be addressed.

The formation and spread of collectives throughout economies and countries is another way in which unemployment can be overcome. By definition, there is no unemployment in the collective. In the final analysis, collectives support their members on the same basis that Smith calls for society to support everyone— simply because they are alive.

Overcoming Unemployment

Overcoming unemployment will require basic changes in current societal values concerning work, which will have to be dethroned from its present central position in the pantheon of values; and basic changes in societal structures, to achieve a basis for income distribution other than through jobs. Paradoxically, these changes will probably come about only when massive increases in the number of the unemployed make them necessary—a situation of "full unemployment." Technology is rapidly bringing this situation into being, despite palliative and rearguard actions such as retraining courses, wage-sharing, job-creation, and others.

Traditional methods of meeting the new situation will not suffice, and more radical proposals need to be examined and tested. Among these are a guaranteed income for everyone, regardless of their activities; redefining and paying for work as anything that people like to do; forming cooperatives on an ever-widening basis; and encouraging voluntary collectives.

If the experience of the past is any indication, the workless society is not to be feared. In ancient Greece, which was a complete welfare state for citizens (Gouldner), the work was done by slaves—free men were neither expected nor encouraged to work, since work, according to Plato, Aristotle, and Socrates, made a person a bad friend, a bad patriot, and a bad citizen (Parker; Kranzberg and Gies; Anthony). What was the result of such a workless society? Only the beginnings of modern drama, dance, philosophy, mathematics, geometry, astronomy, sculpture, and many other arts and sciences too numerous to list. Freed from the day-to-day exigencies of making a living, people were able to be creative in widely different fields, enjoying life as they did so. There is no valid reason to believe that modern humanity will, or will be able to, do less. On the contrary, the workless society might usher in the most fertile period of imagination, creativity, and originality that the world has yet seen, raising mankind to a new threshold of self-fulfilling, happy lives.

References

Anthony, P.D., *The Ideology of Work.* London: Social Science Paperback, 1978.

Ball, R.M., *Social Security Today and Tomorrow.* New York: Columbia University Press, 1978.

Berg, I., M. Freedman, and M. Freeman, *Managers and Work Reform: A Limited Engagement.* New York: Free Press, 1978.

Best, F., *Work Sharing: Issues, Policy Options and Prospects.* Kalamazoo: Upjohn, 1981.

Buck, T., "Experiments with Job Creation Subsidies," *Industrial Relations,* 8(Winter, 1977/78):12-18.

Buckingham, W., *Automation.* New York: Mentor, 1961.

Bylinsky, G., "The New Robots: Nimble—and Far Brainier." *Fortune,* (December 17, 1979).

Carey, J.L., and P.F. Otto, "Output per Unit of Labor Input in the Retail Food Store Industry," *Monthly Labor Review,* 100(January 1977):42-47.

Carnes, R.B., "Laundry and Cleaning Services Pressed to Post Productivity Gains," *Monthly Labor Review,* 101(1978):38-42.

Case, J., and R.C.R. Taylor (eds.) *Co-ops, Communes & Collectives: Experiments in Social Change in the 1960s and 1970s.* New York: Pantheon, 1979.

Casner-Lotto, J., "Robots Expected to Boost Productivity: Labor Unions Accept Use With Caution, Insist on Job Security as Condition." *World of Work Report,* 5(March 1981):17.

Charnow, J., *Work Relief Experience in the United States.* Washington: Social Science Research Council, 1943.

Cherrington, D.J., *The Work Ethic: Working Values and Values That Work.* New York: Amacom, 1980.

Coll, B.D., *Perspectives in Public Welfare.* Washington: Department of Health, Education, and Welfare, 1969.

Criden, Y., and S. Gelb. *The Kibbutz Experience: Dialogue in Kfar Blum.* New York: Herzl Press, 1974.

Cunningham, R.L., *The Philosophy of Work.* New York: National Association of Manufacturers, 1964.

Dasgupta, S., "Facing the New Era: A Plea for a New Approach to Human

Well-Being," in *Human Well-Being: The Challenge of Continuity and Change*. New York: International Council on Social Welfare, 1978.

Fechter, A., "Job Creation Through Public Service Employment Programs," in R. Taggart (ed.), *Job Creation: What Works?* Salt Lake City: Olympus, 1977.

Field, F., *The Conscript Army*. London: Routledge and Kegan Paul, 1977.

Garraty, J.A., *Unemployment in History: Economic Thought and Public Policy*. New York: Harper and Row, 1978.

Garson, B., *All the Livelong Day: The Meaning and Demeaning of Routine Work*. Harmondsworth: Penguin, 1975.

Gouldner, A.W., *The Hellenic World: A Sociological Analysis*. New York: Harper and Row, 1969.

Griffiths, D., *Whither Work*. Bundoora, Victoria, Australia: Preston Institute of Technology Press, 1977.

Hanby, U.J., and M.P. Jackson, "An Evaluation of Job Creation in Germany," *International Journal of Social Economics*, 6(1979):79-117.

Homans, G.C., *The Human Group*. London: Routledge and Kegan Paul, 1951.

Hostetler, J.A., Amish Society. Baltimore: Johns Hopkins Press, 1968.

Hull, F.M., N.S. Friedman, and T.F. Rogers, "The Effect of Technology on Alienation from Work," *Work' and Occupations*, 9(1982):31-57.

Jamrozik, A., and M. Hoey, *Workforce in Transition: Australian Experiences*. Bradford, U. L.: MCB Publications, 1982.

Jerusalem Post, "Wives Should Be Paid for Home Duties," November 28, 1983.

Kaplan, M., *Leisure in America: A Social Inquiry*. New York: John Wiley, 1960.

Kendrick, J.W., "Productivity Trends and the Recent Slowdown," in W.E. Fellner (ed.), *Contemporary Economic Problems*.

Kephart, W.M., *Extraordinary Groups: The Sociology of Unconventional Life-Styles*. New York: St. Martin's, 1982.

Killingsworth, C.C., and C.T. King, "Tax Cuts and Employment Policy," in R. Taggart (ed.), *Job Creation: What Works?* Salt Lake City: Olympus, 1977.

Kogut, A., and S. Aron, "Toward a Full Employment Policy: An Overview," *Journal of Sociology and Social Welfare*, 7(1980):85-99.

Kranzberg, M., and J. Gies, *By the Sweat of Thy Brow*. New York: Putnam, 1975.

Lasson, K., *The Workers*, New York: Grossman, 1971.

Lohr, S., "New in Japan: The Manless Factory," *New York Times*, December 13, 1981, p. F-1.

Macarov, D., *Incentives to Work*. San Francisco: Jossey-Bass, 1970.

Macarov, D., *Work Incentives in an Israeli Kibbutz*. Jerusalem: Paul Baerwald School of Social Work, 1971 (Hebrew).

Macarov, D., *Design of Social Welfare*. New York: Holt, Rinehart and Winston, 1978.

Macarov, D., *Work and Welfare: The Unholy Alliance*. Beverly Hills: Sage, 1980.

Macarov, D., *Worker Productivity: Myths and Reality*. Beverly Hills: Sage, 1982.

Macarov, D., "Changes in the World of Work: Some Implications for the Future," in H. Didsbury (ed.), *Working Now and in the Future*. Washington: World Future Society, 1983.

Macarov, D., and G. Fradkin, *The Short Course in Development Training*.

Ramat Gan, Israel: Massada, 1973.

Main Economic Indicators: Historial Statistics, 1960-1979. Paris: Organization for Economic and Cultural Development, 1980.

Melville, K., *Communes in the Counter Culture: Origins, Theories, Styles of Life.* New York: Morrow, 1972.

Mendelssohn, K., *The Riddle of the Pyramids.* London: Sphere, 1977.

Moynihan, D.P., *The Politics of a Guaranteed Income: The Nixon Administration and the Family Assistance Plan.* New York: Free Press, 1969.

New York Times, Saturday, April 3, 1982.

New York Times, "The Jobs That Won't Come Back," December 12, 1982, Weekly Review, p.1IE.

Norman, C., "The New Industrial Revolution: How Microelectronics May Change the Workplace," in J. O'Toole, J.C. Scheiber, and L.C. Wood (eds.) *Working: Changes and Choices.* New York: Human Sciences Press. 1981.

Parnes, H.S. (ed.), *Policy Issues in Work and Retirement.* Kalamazoo: Upjohn, 1983.

Peters, V., *All Things Common: The Hutterian Way of Life.* New York: Harper, 1965.

Pierson, F.C., *The Minimum Level of Unemployment and Public Policy.* Kalamazoo: Upjohn, 1980.

Rankin, M., *Strategies for Mutual Support Among Unemployed People.* Paper delivered at Third World Congress on Social Economics, Fresno, California, August, 1983.

Rossi, P.H., and K.C. Lyall, *Reforming Public Welfare: A Critique of the Negative Income Tax Experiment.* New York: Russell Sage Foundation, 1976.

Rubin, L.B., *Worlds of Pain: Life in the Working Class Family.* New York: Basic, 1976.

Schrank, R., *Ten Thousand Working Days.* Cambridge: MIT, 1979.

Schultz, J.H., T.D. Leavitte, and L. Kelly, "Private Pensions Fall Far Short of Preretirement Income Levels," *Monthly Labor Review,* 102 (February 1979):28-32.

Schwartz, E.E., "A Way to End the Means Test," *Social Work,* 4(1963):3.

Schweinitz, K. de, *England's Road to Social Security.* Philadelphia: University of Pennsylvania Press, 1943.

Sullivan, T.A., *Marginal Jobs: The Underutilization of American Workers.* Austin: University of Texas, 1978.

Sulvetta, A., "Comments," in R. Taggart (ed.), *Job Creation: What Works?* Salt Lake City: Olympus, 1977.

Taggart, R. (ed.), *Job Creation: What Works?* Salt Lake City: Olympus, 1977.

Terkel,. S., *Working.* New York: Random House, 1972.

Teselle. S. (ed.), *The Family, Communes, and Utopian Societies.* New York: Harper, 1972.

Vigilante, J. L., School of Social Work, Adelphi University, Garden City, New York. (Personal communication.)

Walbank, M., *Life in a Kibbutz.* New York: Reconstructionist Press, 1955.

Wilson, J. O., *After Affluence: Economics to Meet Human Needs.* New York: Harper and Row, 1980.

World of Work Report, "Industrialized Nations Create Jobs for Hard-Core Unemployed in Broad Range of Programs, Says ILO." 4(February 1979):12.

World of Work Report, "Not Enough Jobs." 8(November 1983):81.

The Creative Utilization of Mature Intelligence and Experience

by

Esther Matthews

There is an urgent need for the utilization of mature intelligence and experience in the service of amelioration of world problems and in the expansion of positive change in all aspects of the human condition.

The entire age spectrum needs to be utilized in the service of a safe, just, and ethical world order. However, the focus here will be upon one segment of the population—older persons.

The term *older persons* is used here to describe individuals moving beyond total concentration on an occupation or on intense family commitment. The term *retirement* is inappropriate for many people because it does not incorporate the idea of transition to a new and different level of existence. Older people, worldwide, form a vast pool of potential energy that can be more widely and creatively utilized.

The Aging Population

The sheer size of this age group and its dramatic proportional increase merit careful consideration as a force in human affairs. The number of older persons in the population is steadily increasing and will continue to increase into the next century. The United States Bureau of the Census in 1983 reported that the number of Americans 65 and older is projected to double between 1980 and 2020. According to United Nations figures (Vienna International Plan of Action for Aging, 1983) persons over 60 worldwide will have increased by 224% from 1950 to 2025.

The landmark Vienna Plan contained many recommendations. Two of these recommendations are especially pertinent: 1) that the wisdom and expertise of elderly individuals be considered (Recommendation 22); and 2) that the elderly be utilized as "teachers and transmitters of knowledge, culture, and spiritual values" (Recommendation 44).

Esther Matthews is professor emerita of education at the University of Oregon, Eugene, Oregon.

Older people have already exerted considerable political pres-
-sure in gaining special legal, economic, medical, and social
privileges and protections. This defensive position is understandable. However, it is also necessary to consider how part of the
energy of that age group may be increasingly turned toward service to the general welfare of people everywhere. A core problem
is how to steadily bring to bear the vast, untapped reservoir of
knowledge, experience, and insight resident in this age group
directly into policy and decision-making from the local community
to the global arena. At present, we tend to depend mainly upon
experts in all fields of endeavor.

Prior to making specific suggestions, it will be useful to: 1)
recognize the present services of older people; 2) note how older
people utilize their time and energy; 3) indicate how recent knowledge of the psychology of late life has changed our views in a
more positive direction; and 4) illustrate how specific needs,
strengths, and assets of some older people relate to the focus of
this paper.

Services of Older People. Older people the world over, to
varying degrees, help to care for young children and for still older
people. Millions work until they die at advanced ages. Untold
numbers volunteer uncounted hours, over many years, to help
out in hospitals, schools, churches, and other institutions. The
quality of human services would decline markedly without their
help.

Time and Energy Utilization. Older people are as diverse
as any other age group. This particular age cohort includes the
ill, the deprived, the pleasure-seekers, and the learners and natural scholars. The last group is especially likely to be interested
in translating thoughtful study into individually determined and
collective action.

Psychology of Late Life. The field of psychology is at last
recognizing that life development is an ongoing, dynamic process
and that significant positive changes can occur in people's lives
from birth to death. Certain individuals reach stages of development in late life characterized by Erik Erikson as generativity
and integrity. It is important to remember that true maturity is
a difficult personal creation and not an automatic consequence
of aging.

As human beings move through the life cycle, the focus of their
energy shifts from exclusive concentration on the self to the foundation and evolution of the family and occupation and, finally,
to an awareness of oncoming generations. It is this final stage of
life that provides the framework for these ideas.

Erikson looked at the life cycle as a series of stages, each presenting a developmental challenge. Each stage seems to illustrate
the need for some level of resolution of ever-more-complex deriva-
tives of the concept of trust vs. mistrust. In infancy, the baby
needs a basically trustful environment that ensures physical and

emotional support. The alternative condition of basic mistrust can result in a negative life beginning. As the infant moves toward childhood, adolescence, and adulthood, development finds expression through school, work, and family. The concept of trust vs. mistrust is expressed through ever-more-intricate translations of trust (or mistrust) in others outside of the family, in learning, and in creating. It is important to remember that no stage of life is perfectly or permanently resolved. One hopes for a reasonable resolution of each stage. Earlier life issues rise again in larger, more complex forms and require more mature resolution. Change and challenge are inevitable until the moment of death.

Here we are most interested in the final challenges described by Erikson in terms of generativity vs. self-absorption and integrity vs. disgust and despair. Erikson uses the term *generativity* to convey the growing sensitivity to and concern for oncoming generations, in contrast to the negative and nearly exclusive concentration on the self. The term *integrity* is more difficult to explain. It involves the acceptance of one's life and the surety of one's beliefs and values as guiding principles of existence. The negative polarity is represented by a sense of disgust with life and an overwhelming feeling of despair.

Here we are seeking to understand the characteristics and powers of people who have achieved a relatively positive resolution of later life stages in contrast to those who have moved through life in ever more self-centered, fearful, and nonproductive directions. At present, it seems that the world tends to view power in terms of money and force. Yet brain power, experience, ethics, and wisdom represent the real wealth and hope of the earth.

Needs, Strengths, and Assets. The foundations of late-life contribution to society lie in the combined and overlapping needs, strengths, and capacities of mature adults. Some older persons have a continual thirst for new knowledge and a need to translate that knowledge into productive action in commitment to a cause or effort beyond themselves. Many crave transition to a more meaningful level of existence through understanding the meaning, pattern, and significance of their total lives.

Some of the strengths that mature persons may bring to the final stage of life include:

- Decades of life experience.
- Independence of judgment.
- Clarity of ethical vision.
- An integrated value system.
- Insight into good and evil behavior and their consequences.
- Decreased egocentricity.
- Increased capacity to transcend self-interest.
- Heightened compassion for oncoming generations.
- Expanded capacity for philosophical thinking.
- Growing awareness of the interrelatedness of all fields
of endeavor and of all people.

- Acceptance of the need for balance between reality, hope, and intuition (i.e., the synthesis of the objective and the subjective).
- A workable philosophy of life (whether articulated or not).
- Powerful intelligence capable of being magnetized to purpose.
- Greater ease with ethical and spiritual concepts.

A few of the assets of some older people include: unrestricted time and energy to think, learn, and plan; reasonably good to excellent health; minimal or sufficient economic security; less need for personal success and achievement; expert knowledge of one or more occupations; and a life-time habit of service to family and/or occupation.

In sum, numerous older adults possess personal, emotional, intellectual, and occupational capacities that can be utilized in expanded forms of service. What kinds of activities and actions might absorb some of this precious resource of energy? What types of organizations could be involved? On the eve of doomsday, is it futile to even suggest that we can still turn back? Some have no choice but to try, regardless of the odds. As the suggestions that follow are considered, it is necessary to suspend attitudes of skepticism and fatalism. The old proverb is the guide—"It is better to light a candle than to curse the darkness."

Ideas and Actions

1. Elderhostel Potential. The mature adult's fascination with learning is amply demonstrated by a study of Elderhostel. As many of you know, Elderhostel is a low-cost enterprise opening up all kinds of college and university courses to people 60 and older. The phenomenal growth of Elderhostel illustrates that the hunger of older people for learning is insatiable.

Elderhostel was founded in New Hampshire in 1975 with an initial enrollment of 200 people. The only requirement for enrolling in Elderhostel courses was (and still is) that the registrant has reached the age of 60 (or is married to a person who has). Five years after its founding, the enrollment had reached 20,000. In 1982 the figure jumped to 55,000 and in 1984 the expected enrollment figure is 110,000.

Recent statistics indicate that 634 colleges and universities participate. Most of the institutions are in the United States and Canada, but there are at least 46 participating institutions in 11 European countries. The range of course topics is enormous. Professors are universally impressed with the infectious enthusiasm and serious commitment of the participants.

How could the Elderhostel experience be utilized in service to world problems? One suggestion would be to encourage the Elderhostel organization to conduct a study, or to encourage some participants to plan their own study. Some of the suggestions for study may already be available. There are many questions of importance, such as:

1. What are the enrollment patterns by type of course and location?

2. What proportion of people re-enroll each year?

3. What patterns of interest do returning students show?

4. Why do they enroll in Elderhostel?

5. Do they express any need to translate their learning into any form of action or service? Have they done so?

6. Would some, or many, like to teach as well as to learn in Elderhostel?

7. What ideas or solutions do they have with respect to our ever-present problems (war, poverty, disease)? It would be extremely important and enlightening to see what a group of Elderhostel students would find out as their own researchers and action takers.

2. Utilization of Past Peace Corps Volunteers. A survey of early Peace Corps volunteers might produce realistic ideas for dealing with specific problems in various countries of the world. An older volunteer might decide to undertake such a project and raise such questions as: Who were the early volunteers? Where did they serve? What did they do in their country of service? What did they learn? Did their term of service change their lives? In what way? Do they still have ties with their country of service? How do they view their experience in retrospect?

After this information has been gathered and tabulated, it might be possible to discern worldwide patterns and commonalities that could be of use to many organizations and countries. Perhaps this kind of research has already been done by the Peace Corps. However, mature, nonprofessional researchers might ask quite different questions and receive entirely different answers. It is now reluctantly conceded that professional interviewers, project directors, and polltakers often receive minimal and/or inaccurate information. Some of the reasons seem to be a lack of trust, a feeling of being manipulated, and an uneasiness about the purpose and use of the research.

Older people might become similarly involved in studying VISTA participants or any national or international service group.

3. World Institutes and Think Tanks. World institutes and think tanks need to be surveyed in order to understand how they could benefit from the wisdom of older people. The design and purpose of such organizations naturally result in staff selection from the highly educated, expert class of society. In addition, nominations to serve as members or consultants are made by senior staff who may tend to select people who are not in conflict with their views. This situation can result in a rather closed, self-perpetuating condition antithetical to the consideration of new and creative ideas to deal with old, persistent problems.

Perhaps many such organizations are open to experimenting with more than token lay persons. One way to proceed would be for a few older people to concentrate on one institution by studying annual reports and other publications. Many questions are worth asking: What are the stated purposes of the institution? How are participants selected? What is the male/female ratio, the age cohort balance? Are the participants exclusively professionals? How is the board of directors selected? What kinds of problems are studied? What becomes of reports? What impact do they have? What kind of duplication of services is evident?

An investigation of this kind may be very difficult to conduct, because many organizations of this kind are privately funded, endowed for specific purposes, and not interested in being studied by anyone. Think tanks funded by business interests might also be reluctant to receive attention. Yet these kinds of organizations sometimes have powerful impact upon the shaping of legislation by governments. Older people with time, energy, and experience could make a valuable contribution as objective participants or as thoughtful researchers.

4. Television—Educational and General, Local and Global. Educational television is a mighty source of education for those denied advanced education as well as for those craving new challenges or wishing to revive old interests. It is important to find out what proportion of older people take advantage of home TV courses. Perhaps they could be encouraged to contact others taking the same course. Some may be capable of teaching different types of courses. Many may be intrigued with the idea of planning integrated, personal learning programs by concentrating on study of the language, culture, and history of a particular country. Commmunity-college counselors would be particularly helpful as advisors. The end result might be traveling to the country studied and making new friends to invite back to this country. The idea of international friendships, on an individual basis or through "sister cities," is not a new one. It is an idea deserving of extensive application by older people, who are in a life stage of greater freedom and of mature generativity. We have long supported the international exchange of high-school and college students. It would be interesting to see what might result from greatly increased exchange of older people who are, hopefully, keenly aware of the utter interdependence of all countries and people.

Housebound adults could provide a much-needed service in analyzing general television. For example, they could systematically study local, national, and global news broadcasts. An individual might decide to study all items on a particular topic, government, country, etc. Modes of analysis would include assessing cultural sensitivity or insensitivity; level of congruence or contradiction; factual accuracy or inaccuracy; indications of trust and understanding or evidences of mistrust, ridicule, and contempt; "straight talk" or "double talk"; viewer involvement or manipulation.

The persistent pooling of such information could conceivably alter local TV news broadcasts and eventually cause national repercussions. TV news broadcasts are based heavily upon the words and actions of leaders. Continual attention to the type of analysis described could be highly informative to all voters.

Another appealing and compelling focus would be to study TV's presentation of the children of the world and potential hopes for them; such a focus would engage the generative capacities of older people and emphasize human likenesses rather than cultural differences. There is little doubt that emphases on cultural, political, economic, and religious differences have been manipulated to divide and fuel aggression under a screen of apparent objectivity.

Another service of TV could be a program called World Voice. Satellite-assisted television capacity makes possible instantaneous global communication. The prototype of Voice would be the Voice of America, but the purpose would be nonpolitical. The purposes would be to convey life-giving rather than life-destroying information and to provide accurate information about the possibilities for a more cooperative world. At present, TV news coverage is basically fixated upon recording war, violence, crime, and natural disasters. Incidents of peace, cooperation, justice, etc., seem to come as surprising deviations from the norm. We live with a negative world view shaped partly by communications media. We need a continual and powerful reshaping of negative, defeatist, nonproductive viewpoints. This does not mean ignoring problems or drifting into a pleasant state of naive inertia. It does mean the persistent reporting of positive action on every level, from village to nation to world.

The gradual accumulation of examples of positive attempts to deal with crucial problems could shift the balance toward a recognition of the possible instead of the continual focus upon our failures. One example will illustrate the idea. In Jerusalem, the Martin Buber Institute for Adult Education draws Arabs and Jews together to learn each other's language and to come to know each other as individual human beings.

All of these ideas would be in service to Buckminster Fuller's conviction that, if ordinary people of the world had access to any approximation of the truth about human possibilities and about the present world political situation, they would demand that their governments move in more peaceful directions.

5. Networks and Study Groups. Many older people are involved in informal networks established to accomplish a particular purpose and to dissolve when their task has been accomplished. The concept of the network is fully described by Marilyn Ferguson in *The Aquarian Conspiracy* (1980). A network avoids some of the disadvantages of an established institution, especially those related to hierarchical power structure and need for self-perpetuation. A network usually forms locally but may expand regionally or even nationally. The purposes of networks are as varied as saving the trees on a hometown street to protesting nuclear warfare. Networks are especially important for older people. Joining with all age groups provides a sense of generational solidarity and promotes a sense of involvement and usefulness.

Local study groups may be founded for more general, ongoing purposes. Regardless of the original reason for forming any group, the members draw support, encouragement, and affirmation that can enrich their lives in many ways.

The possibilities for the establishment of useful, creative groups are endless, limited only by the needs, scope, and vision of the participants. Small groups offer wonderful opportunities for older adults to become their own leaders and teachers; to draw upon their own experience and creative potential; and to move their lives to new levels of existence.

A few examples may be useful. A small group might focus on a topic like human courage, as a springboard for deciding the direction of their own risk-taking. Three references would trigger their own recollections of personal acts of courage. *Profiles in Courage* (1955) by John F. Kennedy illustrates the need that people have for drawing strength from examples of courage and forbearance. More recent examples include Geraldo Rivera's *A Special King of Courage* (about children) and Margaret Truman's *Women of Courage* (1976).

There is a surge of interest, especially among older people, in writing one's autobiography and in studying biography. Through photographs, diaries, recorded incidents, and study of family chronology, people are learning to understand and accept their lives. The warm, friendly, nonjudgmental acceptance from a small group, whose members have also lived through those times, can change a person's life view.

6. The Computer and Older People. Increasing numbers of older people flock to enroll in computer courses. At first they seem motivated by curiosity and by a desire to feel a part of this technological revolution. They experiment with the practical application of the computer to their own lives—for example, organizing financial and tax records. Some are learning to use the word processor to compose books or articles. This useful tool will greatly expand their productivity and release more time and energy for new creative endeavors.

In the near future, operations and functions undreamed of will be carried out via computer. The field is changing with astounding rapidity. For example, in January 1984 the California Institute of Technology announced the development of a small-sized super-computer prototype, capable of rapidly performing many functions simultaneously and at less cost. The prototype can carry out three million operations a second. It is predicted that its capacity can be increased until it has 1,000 times the power of the present costly Cray 1 computer, which can do 20 to 80 million operations a second.

The analysis of many of the ideas in this paper hinges upon older people developing a high level of computer literacy and sophistication. The storage and retrieval of large masses of information needs to be followed by the construction of computer programs that can detect trends, patterns, and commonalities—and even postulate consequences. Manual search and study is not feasible. The life experience and wisdom of older people may provide new dimensions of understanding. They could prove capable of sensing new patterns and possibilities in large amounts of data.

One of the most exciting frontiers is to be found in the dawning field of computer ethics. There is no doubt that computers, like all inventions, can be used unethically. For example, it is now possible to monitor the number of keystrokes per second of employees. What are the consequences in employee morale? How do we begin to build a system of computer ethics? The qualities apparent in some older persons, discussed earlier, make them logical possibilities for this complex task.

7. Town Meeting Format. Moving from computers back in time to a town meeting format may seem like a regression, but it is not. The old New England Town Meeting was a remarkable institution. Each year all citizens of a town assembled to discuss and legislate their common affairs. Any citizen was free to express his or her view, however different. The barriers between rich and poor, educated and uneducated, young and old were held in abeyance. The town meeting is still the form of governance in some parts of New England. Anyone who has participated in a town meeting can recall the skilled role of the respected (usually elderly) moderator.

During the period of history when radios performed a major communications function, the "Town Meeting of the Air" flourished. In the present era of television, the town meeting deserves revival. The Donahue program is somewhat comparable to a town meeting. However, there are important differences: each program focuses on one topic, usually a controversial social issue; the purpose is really entertainment; the audience is largely female; the reactions are in response to the opinions of experts.

Older people could be instrumental in experimenting on a local TV level with a real town meeting format. Simultaneous meetings throughout a state or region could result in common patterns of ideas. Again the analysis of such meetings could be carried out by older people with time, energy, and computer skill. The results would provide one more contribution to a persistent groundswell of influence by ordinary people that might reshape politics and government, at least to some extent.

At present, people organize to be heard, chiefly around immediate crises (land usage, school budgets, freeway construction, etc.). Such issues are important, but there are many long-term questions that deserve persistent public consideration, lest we continue to be completely surprised and appalled by events that were really predictable.

8. Talent Pool. Older people could perform a fine service by taking the initiative to build a talent pool of potential speakers, workers, consultants, reporters, and natural teachers who believe we can change our present doomsday perspective. The talent pool would first be developed locally and then through surveying many types of large organizations, such as the World Future Society (WFS) and the American Association of Retired Persons (AARP). The role of WFS will be explored, in more detail, in a later section.

The AARP is a large (approximately 15 million) and powerful organization. At present, its mission seems to be chiefly aimed at politically influencing all legislation affecting older persons. Perhaps the board of directors and the membership may be open to exploring their role in other areas of human concern. In any case, the AARP, with its national power and local networks, could supply many names of people for a talent pool. The importance of the formation and utilization of a talent pool lies partly in the ever-present need to reduce the presumption of apathy and dependence often attributed to older people and to further utilize their experience and insight.

9. Fuller's World Game. Buckminster Fuller's World Game concept captured his basic philosophy about the necessity for combining advanced technological knowledge and ethics in the service of mankind. Fundamental to his idea is the belief that solutions to problems can be envisioned and expedited, and further, that these solutions can be growthful, life-enhancing, and protective of all people. His gaming theory (in contrast to war-gaming theory) was based on "everyone win, no one lose" demonstrations. Fuller's advanced theories were not the product of naive, impractical, simplistic thinking. Instead, they were forged, with difficulty, over the 50-year span of his brilliant, original, and unremitting labor. At last, on the verge of global destruction, many people are coming to realize that his core idea, the synthesis of advanced technology and ethics, is our only reasonable course of action. The World Game is one of the most thorough and compelling paths to survival.

Basically, the World Game is a concentrated effort to assemble all available information about a particular problem; to consider all possible solutions; and to analyze the probable effects of various solutions, in terms of human welfare. One example of a World Game focus is the study of available and potential world food resources. Of course, the capability of advanced computer technology and programming is an essential element.

Older people may be particularly intrigued with the World

Game concept. It gives them an opportunity to utilize a lifetime of experience in a stimulating, interactive, purposeful group and to share in a sense of shaping the future.

10. The World Future Society. The World Future Society is an especially important and appealing group for older people to consider. All of the WFS publications and conferences carry a sense of life, vitality, and possibility—all needed stimulants in a society that frequently ignores or discounts the talents and life experience of older people. WFS also has a tradition of soliciting ideas and reactions on controversial issues from its members. The local chapters provide a forum for discussion and action.

Perhaps WFS might become interested in developing a pilot project aimed at older members. The first step could be an open invitation in *The Futurist* for people over 60 to identify themselves (including mailing address and telephone) and to express their interest in a list of areas such as the 25 themes of the Worldview '84 Assembly. In a later stage of such a project, it would be important to elicit suggestions for local to global solutions and actions. The responses of people could be summarized and analyzed by computer. In this way, concentrations of interest would become apparent as well as both the commonality and originality of solutions.

Perhaps a general membership survey has already been accomplished. The age factor may or may not have been considered. Surveys routinely seek information about level of education and training. Such inquiries usually rule out involvement of potential participants without advanced education. Many people from ages 60-80 did not have the opportunity for advanced education. Many feel sensitive about their lack of formal education. When society stubbornly equates wisdom with years of formal education, we lose the insights and services of millions of people. A basic emphasis throughout this paper has been the need for identification and utilization of an additional group of potential problem solvers—the mature natural teachers and scholars of all societies.

Conclusion

In summary, we have suggested the need for the creative mobilization of the huge population of older people in service to the amelioration of world problems. This aim can be achieved in many ways and through various kinds of organizations, institutions, networks, and groups.

The life-stage potentiality of some older people has been described in terms of generativity and integrity—both characteristics fundamental to positive change. Our problems have been described endlessly. The technological capacity to resolve them is at hand. The means must be rooted in powerful conceptions of justice, compassion, and ethics. We have yet to understand and accept the fact that ethics can and must become the basis of personal and global peace and survival. A workable definition of ethics, in this instance, is a set of underlying principles that, when applied to any action, large or small, results in the greatest good to the greatest number. It is eminently possible to determine such outcomes. We have the record of history spread before us— with its frightful examples of the futility of war as a means of solution for any crisis.

World communication, technological advances, and computer capability all provide potentially new ways to understand and resolve old conflicts. The millions of ordinary, and extraordinary, older people could help to direct us in ways of peace, justice, and honor—if we will but listen.

Technological Change
and Employment Policy

by

Peter J. Monk and J. Verner Wheelock

The application of new technologies to the process of economic production is synonymous with changing employment patterns. This is not a new phenomenon; the quality of technology has been a prime determinant of the distribution of employment opportunities since the start of the Industrial Revolution. The evolution of the food system is an excellent example of the extensive changes that do occur in employment patterns. In farming, the enormous increases in output and productivity have only been achieved by the application of a wide variety of technical innovations. As a result there have been improvements in animal breeding and feeding, plant breeding and soil fertility, and control of disease, weeds, and pests combined with the use of sophisticated machinery to name but a few examples. Consequently the labor released has been available for the establishment of new industries. Initial developments were closely related to agricultural production, e.g., milling and wool textiles. These were followed by the evolution of other major industries such as engineering and chemicals, all highly dependent on technological innovation.

It should also be noted that, even where the job function has not changed, the actual work demands can be quite different. For example, today's sophisticated farmer has to be able to control very complex systems and equipment; the skills required bear no relationship to those of peasant or subsistence farming.

Since applied technology defines the set of available methods of economic production, it must also partly determine producers' demands for labor and capital. The relative demands for labor and capital depend very largely on the relative prices of these two factors of production: prices that in turn depend on the potential productivity of the two factors. In addition, demands for labor and capital are also determined by the pattern of demand for their products. Technological progress increases the range of foods and services that it is possible to produce. This process—by definition—increases the range of potential patterns of demand

Peter J. Monk and J. Verner Wheelock are professors at the School of Science and Society, University of Bradford, Bradford, West Yorkshire, England.

for products. If the rate of technological progress is high, changes in both final demand and the relative positions of capital and labor will be rapid and disruptive.

The crux of the matter is that changes in the products and processes of economic production, brought about by changes in technology, alter the structure of demand in the labor market. Since people are not perfectly mobile between different occupations, and there can be no guarantee that new demands for labor can be met from the existing distribution of skills in the labor market, some additional unemployment must occur. Even if the existing supply of labor could fill all the vacancies created by new industries using new technology, the level of short-term "frictional" unemployment would still increase.

A temporary increase in short-term unemployment might be seen as an unwanted economic problem but it would not constitute a significant challenge to the economic mechanism of employment. However, the implication of the accelerating development of information technology (IT) is that, unless there are significant shifts in attitudes, frictional unemployment will become a recurrent experience for a high proportion of the labor force. As changing technology demands new skills of labor, and continues to increase the rate at which the distribution of employment opportunities changes, members of the labor force will need to retrain and to find new jobs more often than they do now. In this way, the rapid and widespread changes in employment patterns that will be required to facilitate the use of IT must lead to increased levels of unemployment.

Therefore, unemployment will rise as a result of changing employment patterns irrespective of whether IT has the potential to displace labor on a broad scale from all forms of economic production. (Early commentators on the implications of IT concentrated their arguments on the labor displacement issue and paid little attention to the problems of occupational mobility). However, it is certain that a wide variety of production tasks—in all economic sectors—could be automated or rendered unnecessary by automation elsewhere. Moreover, as IT-based production methods are developed to increasing levels of sophistication, the range of automatable tasks will grow, and will not be restricted to current production activities. In other words, the production of new types of goods and services made possible by the development of IT is highly likely to be automated. It would be both ironic and inefficient to produce IT-based goods and services by means of outdated and expensive production methods.

IT and the Creation of Employment

The diffusion of new technology into an economy can happen in a number of complementary ways. Demand for new products may be stimulated by advertising; existing products and processes may be changed to include the new technology; and new production processes may be adopted by producers. In the case of relatively minor technical innovations—for example, the development of synthetic ropes and cords, or the use of plastics in electrical components—the diffusion of new products and processes need not disrupt existing employment patterns. Although changes do occur, the structure of employment and the limited nature of incremental advances in technology ensure that conventional technological progress does not lead to serious imbalances in the labor market. The development of IT, however, does not represent merely incremental technical innovation.

The rate at which IT is adopted by producers—for both product and process innovation—will crucially depend on the availablity of suitably skilled labor, the level of demand for IT-based goods and services, and the rate of new investment in IT-based capital. Of these three factors, demand for new or enhanced goods and services appears least likely to cause major difficulties. (Markets for video and personal computer products had to be created; the market for industrial and office automation products has the added advantage of providing enormous financial returns on investment.) The remaining two factors are related, and together they form the substance of the economic mechanism of technology diffusion.

Changes in employment patterns occur for two main reasons. Firstly, demand for goods and services may change, so altering the structure of the demand in the labor market. Secondly, the diffusion of new technology into the economy causes changes in the distribution of demand for labor skills (to operate new processes, to design and make new products, and so on). The demand for labor is also affected by changes in the relative prices of labor and capital, which occur as the diffusing technology alters the potential productivity of both production factors. In the case of IT, radical changes in both the relative prices and potential productivity of labor and capital provide the key to both labor displacement and employment creation. Consider two examples: robotics and office automation.

A robot is a general-purpose, programmable device with four or more "degrees of freedom" for the manipulation of tools, parts, or raw materials. Because it is programmable, a robot's performance depends as much on the quality of the software used as on the physical limitations of the machine. Hence, it is quite feasible to increase the productivity of a robot by improving its software, as well as changing its type of use by reprogramming. One of the principal areas of current robotics research is to increase the extent to which robots may be reprogrammed for even more sophisticated tasks.

The labor displacement effect of the use of robots in industrial production is quite straightforward: since robots can operate continuously at a constant level of efficiency, their potential productivity is several times that of human workers doing the same tasks. As the cost of robots continues to decrease—to an estimated $10,000 per unit by 1990—the incentive for producers to employ robots rather than people will increase. Although existing production methods may persist for some time, new production facilities must incorporate the most efficient methods available. As the cost of capital decreases relative to the cost of labor, IT-based automation will become the only economically viable method of production for many types of goods. Moreover, as robotics software becomes more powerful and sophisticated, the increasing flexibility of robots will allow them to perform an ever-greater range of production tasks.

The production of services is typically a labor-intensive process. In many service industries, the level of capital investment per worker has been very much lower than in manufacturing industry ($2,000 per worker in services; $25,000 per worker in manufacturing). In addition, IT-based office automation equipment is not expensive, and it is becoming cheaper at an estimated 10-15% per annum. The consequent redundancy of many office workers— even under conditions of expanding demand for office services— seems inevitable. The size of the problem has become notoriously difficult to estimate, although predictions that 30-40% of present office jobs will disappear during the 1980s are certainly credible.

The significance of office automation goes beyond the immediate problem of labor displacement caused by the diffusion of new technology. As successive advances in technology have caused employment patterns to be centered firstly on the manufacturing sector and then, more recently, on the service sector, a crucial assumption in economic planning has been that the service sector would continue to expand, providing many new opportunities for employment. Office automation denies that assumption. In other words, the production of services is just as vulnerable to the labor displacement effects of automation (based on IT) as the manufacturing process.

However, the displacement of labor from service and manufacturing production need not result in permanent mass unemployment within industrialized societies. Just as the development of IT offers the possibility of vastly increasing the efficiency of traditional types of production, so it also offers opportunities for employment in new sectors of the economy and in the radical expansion of education, health, and welfare services. It is most important to realize that these new employment opportunities will need to be created and fostered if they are to provide work for labor displaced by new technology. One characteristic of the changing relationship between technological progress and employment creation is that the operation of private-sector markets alone can no longer guarantee sufficient new employment opportunities to maintain "full employment." Nevertheless, the private sector will continue to play a vital role in the employment-creation process.

The increasing pace of technological development has provided a continuing stimulus for the creation of new firms—particularly those that produce goods and services related to IT. The nature of IT products is such that an increasing proportion of their cost is derived from software rather than hardware. Software production is a labor-intensive process and—despite advances in programming languages and methodologies—it is likely to remain so for the foreseeable future. Thus, in the software industry, employment will expand to meet the rapidly growing worldwide demand for ever more efficient, flexible, and sophisticated products. However, software production is a skill-intensive process; the software industry provides a graphic illustration of how the creation of new employment opportunities will depend on the availability of suitable knowledge and skills among the labor force. There is growing evidence that the rapid expansion of the IT sector of private industry marks a change in the relationship between invention, innovation, and business prosperity. In particular, the need to increase the efficiency of the innovative process has led to the rebirth of the private entrepreneur. The resultant growth of new businesses will certainly expand IT-related employment and have a positive, even if indirect, effect on the creation of new employment opportunities elsewhere in the economy. However, that process by itself cannot solve the problems created by rapid and radical changes in employment patterns. Employment policy solutions will also be required.

Employment Policy Requirements

The deliberate creation of employment opportunities within industrial economies has been the subject of successive governments' economic policies since the Great Depression in the 1930s. Those policies have not, however, followed any consistent method or even shared common objectives beyond the notion that "full employment" was something that should be maintained. This diversity of policies has reflected a similar diversity of opinion amongst economists, as well as politicians. Recent economic debate has focused on the relative importance of "supply-side" and "demand-side" factors in determining the structure and level of employment. However, the problem of how to maintain employment levels—and why it may be desirable to do so—must now be resolved in the light of rapidly accelerating technological progress and its attendant effects on the processes and results of production.

What, then are to be the objectives of employment policy?

It is proposed here that employment policy within industrial economies should be centered on two concurrent and related objectives:

• That opportunities for employment should be created and encouraged to the extent of providing gainful employment for all who want it.

• That the productive potential of new technologies should make possible wider and freer choice as to modes and patterns of work and employment, and therefore of lifestyle.

All policy formulation involves normative value judgements and the proposals contained in this paper are no exception. The normative assumptions on which those proposals are based are, briefly, as follows:

1. It is considered neither desirable nor necessary that the transition to an "automated society" should require radical alteration of existing political structures or institutions as a precondition of success. Although social and political changes may occur, they are considered as effects rather than causes of beneficial techno-economic change.

2. Similarly, policy objectives and solutions should not require the violation of fundamental social or cultural values. Again, those values may change in the future but it is considered here to be unwise, unnecessary, and undesirable to rely on major alterations in social attitudes and values in order to solve the economic problems caused by technological progress.

3. Since the main cause of present and future employment problems is an extraordinarily productive technology, which offers growing opportunities for wealth creation, it is assumed here that part of that potential should be used to solve long-standing socio-economic problems. In particular, policy solution should aim to alleviate poverty, ill health, malnutrition, and poor housing, both in the domestic society and abroad.

These normative assumptions form a set of constraints on how objectives proposed above may be implemented. Additional constraints are imposed by the nature of IT and its potential for future development, and by the operation of existing economic mechanisms, both national and international. Therefore, it is also assumed in this analysis that rejection of technological progress is not a feasible method of solving current or future economic problems. Even without embracing the mechanistic philosophy of "technological determinism," it would be naive to imagine that any society can ignore the pressures of worldwide technological change, or insulate itself from the technology-transfer effects of international trade. Therefore, the assumption is made here that the solution of employment problems—particularly that of rapidly changing employment patterns—must rely on the effective exploitation of IT and other advanced technologies.

Employment Policy Solution

In designing solutions to problems of dynamic changes in the structure of employment, three major characteristics of those problems must be taken into account. Firstly, the problems are complex and cannot be isolated within the bounds of existing academic disciplines. Employment problems are not purely economic, are not solely determined by technological changes, and they are linked to social and cultural values. Secondly, these problems are dynamic and will change both quantitatively and qualitatively over time. Thirdly, these problems will develop differently within different societies. Therefore, a specific solution may be viable for one society yet not for another: solutions appropriate to the United Kingdom may not be applicable in the U.S.A., France, or Japan. To accommodate these factors, the proposals given below should be seen as solution elements, some or all of which may be combined to produce workable policies for specific contexts:

• **Active recognition of the changing relationship between employment, work, and income.** It is proposed that employment and taxation policies should be adjusted to allow individuals greater freedom to change their modes of employment and income acquisition. In particular, benefits would derive from easing transitions to and from self-employment, part-time employment, and temporary employment, by increasing mobility in the labor market.

• **Income independence policies.** The aim of such policies would be to allow individuals' incomes to be made partly independent of employment and work. There are two reasons for doing this. The first is that individuals are restricted by present income-distribution mechanisms (notably the wages system) from changing jobs, working patterns, and occupations, and undertaking retraining and further education. In a period when such changes will become increasingly necessary, the removal of barriers to labor mobility would increase the efficiency of resource allocation in the labor market. The second reason is that many individuals require considerable periods of time to adjust to new employment patterns. In particular, older people whose skills become redundant may find retraining difficult or inappropriate, and they may be disadvantaged in an increasingly mobile and technologically oriented labor market. Provision must be made for such people to remain active economic consumers if both social and economic difficulties are to be avoided.

• **Flexible work-pattern policies.** In parallel with recurrent changes of occupation, changes in the temporal pattern of work are likely to become necessary. The present temporal structure of employment—in which individuals typically work the same number of hours per week throughout their working life—will become increasingly inefficient as employment patterns change. Flexibility in work patterns will be beneficial, although policies to encourage it will have to be linked to changes in the means ot income distribution.

• **Geographical mobility policies.** In line with other policies to increase mobility—and thus efficiency—in the labor market, attention should be given to the desirability or otherwise of increasing geographical mobility. In particular, a thorough re-examination of housing policies and the housing and rented accommodation markets is needed. (There is, for example, little point in retraining a person for a new job in a new area if he or she is unable to live near enough to the new job.)

• **Private capital policies.** As technological progress accelerates, the rate at which new products and processes become available in the economy will increase. At the same time, existing production facilities will become redundant at an increasing rate. An important element in solutions to structural employment problems will be the encouragement of new businesses (both large and small) and the exploitation of new industrial and commercial opportunities. Again, changes in taxation policies may be required to achieve this, along with a reassessment of regional development funding by local, national, and international authorities.

• **Public capital policies.** In parallel with the encouragement of private firms, public authorities will need to provide a new and flexible information infrastructure. This will mean expenditure to guarantee adequate provision of digital communications facilities, public service information systems, semi-public goods such as new programming languages, plus facilities for fundamental research and development projects. These public capital policies would serve two purposes: they would underpin continuing technological development and they would create employment directly.

In conclusion, it should be recognized that these "solution elements" form only part of the overall effort that will be required by governments, private organizations, and individuals to overcome the difficulties created by technological progress. The problems faced by industrialized societies may be great, but if the challenge of technology can be met, the rewards will be much greater.

Human Dimensions

by

Perry Pascarella

My barber and I are talking about the tough economic times. Eleven million Americans are on the unemployment rolls. "But a lot of people aren't really working anyway," he says. "You know what I mean?" I nod my head as much as his comb and scissors will permit. But I'm not sure whether he means a lot of people are loafing on the job, or that a lot of people are doing dull, meaningless work. Either way, I would agree.

Some people can't work. Some people won't work. This dual problem was especially troublesome in the early 1980s when unemployment had become far more extensive than at any time in the memory of most Americans. But it wasn't the *problem;* it was the *symptom* of a disease caused by people who were employed but not working effectively.

By the early 1980s, the country was on an unhealthy "high"—high prices, high interest rates, high unemployment, a high rate of business failures, and a high level of imported goods. Working Americans suffered cutbacks in their paychecks, and the less fortunate became victims of reductions in government spending programs.

Spirits were low. Some industries seemed doomed to extinction soon. The auto and steel industries were setting substantially lower sales goals even for the better years ahead, wiping out many people's hopes of ever regaining employment. Even those persons who were better off felt they were on a sinking ship. They were no longer making the economic gains they once enjoyed; their dollars lacked the power to buy quality goods and services; and they could see the vital supports for a strong economy—such as roads, bridges, and other public facilities—crumbling day by day.

All the safeguards that were to have kept the U.S. from depression's door had failed to prevent us from slipping into the worst economic slump since World War II. Few people could escape the fear that they were worse off than they had been in previous years and that the future might be even worse.

Perry Pascarella is executive editor, Industry Week, *Cleveland, Ohio.*

Even more troublesome than the economic situation itself were people's suspicions about its underlying causes. The economic system wasn't working because not enough people were working as they should. The fascination for consuming goods and leisure-time activities had superheated the economy at one time, but now it seemed to have turned on us, crushing our expectations of further improvement—even of maintaining what we once had. The economic indicators were transmitting a message of something more sinister. We began to suspect that the economic system hadn't failed the people but that the people had somehow failed one another. Painfully, we accepted the possibility that the American character might have decayed to a critical state. If this was true, the chances for economic recovery were slim.

My barber and I, and millions of other Americans, for years now have been buying products that haven't seemed to meet the old standards; they seem less and less worth the price we are paying for them. Too often, the people selling them to us don't seem to care whether we are pleased with them or even whether we buy them at all. When we need help and attempt to buy services, we often encounter people who don't seem interested in serving us. They are either preoccupied or uninterested. Even when we are ill or injured we have to deal with service agency or hospital staff personnel who are more concerned about their clerical work than their caring work.

The economic malaise seems intertwined with rudeness, disrespect, immorality, crime, and poor government. The economic recession is only part of a more fundamental psychological depression. The total malaise is too pervasive to be the workings of some conspiracy. It is not the scheme of some skillful minority but the accumulation of the wrongdoings of an entire society that, we fear, is inept. However much people try to sort out the problems and find their separate causes, my barber and I and others sense that these problems are hopelessly interrelated.

America has lost many of the skills and attitudes needed to be a strong manufacturing nation, and our mounting resentment renders us less and less suited for becoming a service economy. The desire to be served is out of proportion to the willingness and ability to serve. Many of us lack the skill to convey respect for the provider. For every clerk, waiter, or service representative who performs poorly, there is a sizable number of customers who feel no inclination to make a kind remark when they do receive good service.

Many of us have condemned one another for not wanting to work—for not being interested in doing a good job. We fear that the economy has been crippled because so many fellow Americans have been spoiled by affluence and the assumption that they are entitled to certain comforts whether they work for them or not. We have convinced ourselves that the work ethic has been lost and, therefore, that there are no grounds for hoping we can head off decades of further economic decline, social turmoil, and personal pain. If people are coming to the workplace with attitudes and values that make them poor workers, how can we hope to restore our lost economic vitality?

Losing It All

We had it all once, but we feel we are losing it fast. Throughout American history, people had come to expect more and more from their jobs—better pay and more leisure time. The rewards for their efforts were good. Many people were able to find excitement or, at least, escape by consuming an unmatched wealth of goods and services. Pursuing their self-interests, Americans had built a fantastic economic machine. But the nation that once had been a super-producer now appears to have pumped itself dry. Frequent recessions, inflation, and the loss of jobs to foreign competitors have brought economic hardships to more and more of us. There is less justification for people to look forward to the automatic improvements in their standard of living or the easy upward mobility they had experienced in the past. Even the most dedicated and skillful workers feel that there is little an individual can do to reverse the ebbing tide of quality and the rising tide of prices.

We have inherited a tradition of steadily improving efficiency. The number of hours of work required to produce a given amount of goods and services has been steadily reduced through most of the nation's history. But in the late 1970s and early 1980s, this measure of productivity slipped downward. Failure to improve our productivity—the efficiency with which we convert work, materials, money, and machines into goods and services—means that we cannot improve our standard of living. Failure to improve productivity as fast as other nations means we will lose battle after battle in the world market, and that means losing jobs and falling backward in our standard of living.

The Human Dimension

There is a third reason for being concerned about poor productivity performance—one not measured by conventional economics. Productivity has human dimensions. It is more than the impersonal relationship of inputs to outputs. It reflects an individual's inventiveness and skills. To be human is to grow, to fight for significance, to distinguish oneself from others. When people cannot contribute to their own material and psychic well-being, they yield to frustration and hostility. When they cannot exert influence on the world around them, they feel less than human. When people are unwilling or unable to work effectively, they suffer the penalties of poor productivity in both economic and very personal, noneconomic terms. Even when they are productive enough to fill their stomachs, they may be unfulfilled in other ways.

We the people are both the victims and the cause of the productivity problem. Politicians and economists attack the economic problems with "hard" economic solutions, dealing with such things as tax incentives, interest rates, and levels of investment in plants and equipment. Round after round of economic and political remedies have failed to cool the American fever because the cause is not "the economy." We the people determine how productive we are in the use of our resources, of which we ourselves are the principal one. Manipulating the hard factors will not correct or compensate for human wrongdoings and weaknesses. How can we expect someone else to deliver expiation for our sins? We have developed a gut feeling that we are victims of our own complacency, carelessness, laziness, and selfishness. We may assume it's not our own but the other guy's fault. He deserves trouble. We smolder with resentment because we have to share his fate.

Tax cuts, government welfare programs, import quotas, and other political "solutions" can address only part of America's productivity problem. They will not solve the problems of people and people relationships. They will not reverse negative attitudes toward work or change work so that it meets people's expectations. Economic policies can only enhance the efforts of productive people. Government programs to reduce unemployment won't work when misuse of the employed—or underemployment—is the culprit.

Economic failure has been accomplishing what preaching and moralizing have not been able to do; it has sensitized us to the possibility that our values and our organizations are not sustainable in a changing world. Some people believe that industrialized economies carry the seeds of their own destruction. Our economic malaise and unmet human needs come as no surprise to them. Emphasis on consumption eventually weakens people's productive capability, they say. As it engenders values that create an increasing demand for the products of the system, it robs people of the ability to produce them. A cruel irony! If this line of thinking is being proved in modern America, can we hope to restore our industrial strength?

An even more troublesome question arises in the minds of some: If industrial systems create unproductive, materialistic people, should we really want to restore the system? Should we, instead, search for a way to dismantle the structure of our system and revert to some simpler, better way of life?

Restoring People

Attaining success in both economic and noneconomic terms will require more than modifying or undoing the system's structures, however. It must begin with restoring people, both as individuals and as members of the human community. In *An Immodest Agenda,* sociologist Amitai Etzioni points out the danger of blaming all our malaise on government and assuming that individuals would step forward to restore an energetic nation if government involvements were reduced.[1] Etzioni questions whether Americans are ready to stand on their own. They have been robbed of their individual initiative, and the natural community that would support individual action has been displaced by formal structures. The heavy intervention of government in people's lives has acted as a double-edged sword, wounding both the individual and the natural community.

In the late 1970s, Christopher Lasch, in *The Culture of Narcissism*, wrote that Americans were not simply the victims of affluence, but had been made helpless by the many third-party organizations and specialists who do things for them.[2] These mechanisms, designed for smoothing the rough spots of life, have replaced human contact and personal involvement in our lives.

The more economic progress Americans have made, the more they have delegated noneconomic matters to institutions and left only an economic box for the individual to occupy. They paid someone else, directly or through taxes, to perform human acts that they didn't care to undertake themselves. The prevailing attitude became "let the schools do all the teaching, the hospitals care for the sick, the insurance companies pay for damages, the psychiatrists deal with people's frustrations." In effect, people sold themselves piece by piece, narrowing the definition of what it means to be human.

Today's business, social, and political institutions make people feel more and more helpless. The individual frequently can neither exercise his own initiative nor rely on institutional help to get something done in a satisfactory manner. Whether it's repairing one's car, getting medical care, or protecting oneself from crime, the individual often feels he can't do the job himself, and he can find no effective help. Helplessness leads to frustration, and frustration leads to further helplessness. The box gets smaller and smaller.

Some people are trying to break through the artificial limitations imposed on them. Sometimes they assert their humanity positively; they go into business for themselves so they can do things their way, or they learn new skills so they can get a better job. Others assert themselves negatively; they evade work on the job, or they go to the extreme of injuring people or property. The challenge in the years ahead will be to direct this force toward individual and societal good.

In the 1960s and 1970s, a liberal challenge to the system, ironically, resulted in enlarging the system to take care of more individuals in more ways. With the dawning of the 1980s, a conservative trend in American social and political sentiments challenged the system by attempting to strip away some of the supports and programs. Included in the conservative swing were those who fought for the opportunity to allow for greater self-reliance. But Etzioni asks the critical question: If we were to get government out of business and our personal lives, would the individual come forth and do better?

It is doubtful that any overnight change would unleash a nation of individuals ready to operate more effectively than they are doing now under the controls, incentives, and guidance of government. Rather than the emergence of a healthy combination of self-reliance and community action, we might see a surge of senseless individualism that would block social and economic progress. Neither greater nor less government involvement, then, seems in itself to be central to the solution of the troubles gnawing at Americans.

Yet, if we look carefully, we can see around us today people grasping for ways to build a wholeness of self and to find a place in some greater unity—the neighborhood, the work group, the planet, the universe, or a supreme being. Perhaps at no time in history have people been so insistent on pursuing their search for meaning and significance. We are moving toward a "self-realization ethic," says futurist Willis Harman.[3] We are beginning to fashion a "self-development ethic," says psychoanalyst Michael Maccoby.[4] And after studying the results of many surveys—his own and others'—of American attitudes and values, social analyst Daniel Yankelovich suspects we are moving toward an "ethic of commitment."[5] These analysts, too, are saying that people are trying to break through the tight definition that has been imposed on them. People are turning inward, reaching outward, and looking upward. The drive toward personal growth leads many to commit to things outside themselves. For some, too, this means seeking a spiritual or transcendental connection.

The genuine searching for meaningful self-development is accompanied by random, undirected, irresponsible assertion of self on the part of some individuals who have not developed the values and skills that can lead them to meaningful lives as individuals and as members of society. What is worse, we seem to lack a vehicle for nurturing such values and skills.

Where can people look for help? If not to government, then to whom? Etzioni urges us to restore the family and the schools—the traditional vehicles for nurturing positive human values.[6] Much as I agree with his sentiments and hear his plea, I cannot hope that a plea will lift despondent people to action. Restoring the family and the schools is, unfortunately, too big an objective in itself to be a solution to the problems at hand.

The family has been on the decline in its influence on American values. The worker's mobility has taken his children from the influence of aunts, uncles, and grandparents. Instability of marriage itself has left millions of children with one or no full-time parent close by. Modern lifestyles put children in touch with numerous influences that rival those of whatever family they have. At the same time, the schools have been removed further and further from the values of business. Lost in the attempt to prepare people for roles in the economic system, they have done less and less to teach or reinforce any particular values.

Vehicle for Change

This would indeed be a time for complete despair if there were not some vehicle to support the development of the individual and give him the means for expressing himself in ways that are constructive both for himself and society. But such a vehicle is beginning to have a positive impact. Today the business corporation is making the first significant moves toward helping individuals realize their potential and enabling them to grow to their full measure. While further decline in the effectiveness of the family and school in shaping values is quite likely for some time to come, we can already see signs of people coming alive at work, acquiring life skills, and proceeding toward personal growth.

There are three propositions that can give us cause for renewed hope in restoring the individual and direction for individual action and social policy:

1. The work ethic is very much alive.

2. The business corporation can be the primary vehicle for nurturing positive human values and developing skills that will help people lead more fulfilling lives.

3. We need a new view of what it means to be human and the role that work plays in our humanity if we are to attend to both our economic and our noneconomic needs.

Meeting people's full range of needs runs counter to what the corporation has generally done for people and what people all too often expect of themselves. The rise of industrialization led to a narrow definition of man as an economic unit. In the earlier stages of the industrial era, the individual was reduced to an interchangeable part in highly structured work situations. In effect, the individual was eliminated as a consideration.

In recent times, work has been made a little less hazardous, a little less physically demanding, but often less and less intellectually challenging and individually rewarding. Sadly enough, not all people want to be challenged. They reject stimulation and challenge despite the pains of boredom and loneliness. They try to invest as little of themselves as possible to ward off boredom without going beyond a point of equilibrium. Work often gets in the way of what people are striving for in life, providing either too little or too much challenge. It forces some people to surrender the companionship they can find only off the job or on the work-break. It forces other people into more personal contact with others than they want.

People killing time in the neighborhood bar, taking time out for a smoke in factories, or chatting in offices may scoff at the suggestion that the workplace could be a vehicle for nurturing human values, giving meaning to their lives, or helping them develop skills for better living. For that matter, some would doubt that life has any meaning, and many would not understand the concept of human growth. The break they're taking at the moment is the best they hope for at work. Far too many workers have found work to be nothing more than a necessary evil. For them, it has meant sacrifice rather than gain. Whether an individual feels too challenged or not challenged enough, the mismatch between the demands of the job and his demands on it is so great that he feels he is a loser.

Those business organizations bold enough to innovate job structure and invite workers to participate in decision-making have already demonstrated that a positive view of people pays off, not only for the company, but for the individual. By building networks of decision-makers rather than hierarchies of order-followers, they are producing better decisions and building enthusiasm to carry out those decisions. They do not share the notion that the work ethic is dead. For them, the proposition that the corporation can be a vehicle for human growth is not preposterous. By neither sacrificing economic objectives nor unduly elevating them, they are attaining both economic power and human growth. They see that the two go hand in hand.

Workers fortunate enough to be in such new work situations are learning with management to reduce distrust and to cooperate since both parties realize that their economic fate is tied together. As one auto worker told me: "We don't care how long the problems existed in this plant or who is to blame. We realize now that we have to work together if we want to stay in business." In more and more workplaces, employees are enjoying a sense of victory rather than defeat and surrender. As others observe this taking place, they will find that there is more to life than they had expected. The press operator, the diemaker, the salesclerk—all can take an active part in the business rather than feeling that they are merely being acted upon.

Corporate efforts to nurture positive values and become involved in human development will often have to overcome the resistance of the very people who would benefit from it. They themselves assume the work ethic is dead. Many business managers would be included among those who would scoff at the assertion that the work ethic is alive and that people can make a real contribution to solving corporate problems. They are caught in the middle between unhappy customers and unhappy workers. They feel the same frustrations as the rest of us, plus the special agony of trying to keep their organization afloat. They are inclined to believe that economic improvement depends on developing better and better systems of control and eliminating the human factor wherever possible since people are coming to the workplace with negative attitudes toward work.

Having heard the situation discussed from both the management and nonmanagement points of view, I have found that many managers see the worker as the chief stumbling block for the improvement of goods and services. Those workers who are concerned about doing a quality job, on the other hand, see the manager and his systems as their biggest restraint. All too often, management views the worker as self-indulgent and rebellious—a carry-over from the 1960s. Workers, as well as the public at large, hold a nineteenth-century view of the corporation.

If we could peel away layers of misperceptions, false teachings, and unrealistic expectations, we would find that the work ethic is still very much alive. Despite the changing values swirling around us, we would discover that people have numerous reasons for wanting to work. We would see the makings of a strong, new, self-development ethic that has a producer—rather than a consumer—orientation. People's new perceptions of themselves and their intensifying fight for significance and fulfillment do not mesh well with the economic system, however. They do not lead to good work behavior in conventional terms. They do not fit the old notion of what a "work ethic" is.

The corporation must develop, rather than restrain, the individual in order to elicit greater commitment and creativity in the struggle to improve productivity and product quality. That means creating winners, not losers. We have reached a stage of industrialization that requires greater—not less—human input. Despite the mechanization going on in both goods-producing and service industries, more and more human touch, creativity, and dedication to detail are necessary for the corporation to succeed. This need coincides with growing insistence by some people that they be permitted to invest more of their human powers in the workplace. Since industrialization has reached a point where continuation of the dehumanizing trend in the workplace makes the organization a loser as well, further economic advance depends on reversing the dehumanizing process.

Members of the corporation, from top to bottom, are beginning to realize that the values that lead to personal growth are the very ones that generate economic growth at this point in U.S. industrial evolution. We are, then, at a stage when efforts to integrate economic and human considerations will be intensified. Industrialization will become a humanizing endeavor rather than the dehumanizing process it has often been in the past. Despite all the scorn heaped upon the business corporation, it is here of all places that we can look for the first steps in restoring American character. The workplace will increasingly become the place to nurture the very values that were once surrendered there.

The Response to Change

Leadership in the workplace will increasingly become dedicated to people development—not molding people to fit the organization, but enabling each individual to fulfill himself or herself. Management will lead some people to their first awareness that there is such a thing as human growth. It will enable members of the organization to move toward fulfillment by providing the proper job structure, work assignments, training, and environment for growth. Then it will have to respond to people's broadening range of skills and interests and deepening commitment.

People have been failing one another, and they have been failing themselves. They have been coming together in the workplace—sometimes reluctantly—to meet their material needs. But there are many other needs to be met by work. These forces constitute a work ethic (despite the many obituaries written about it), but the workplace and workers have changed in ways that thwart the conversion of this ethic into positive work behavior.

It is essential to understand the wave of changing values as well as some timeless truths, because managers who accept traditional, negative assumptions about people are not going to be the winners in the decades ahead. And workers who expect only the traditional rewards in the workplace will miss the opportunity for personal development and fulfillment. As a nation, we might continue the futile search for a strictly economic strategy for our economic problems and a strictly noneconomic route to human growth, not realizing that these objectives are bound together. There can be no significant economic advance without consideration of human growth and fulfillment, and there can be no human growth without attention to the economic aspects of life.

Agenda for Management Action

The process of humanizing the corporation is moving forward, but not as fast as it might; misperceptions on the part of the public and the members of the corporation itself obscure what could happen and even what is now happening. The opportunity for people to come alive at work is being unnecessarily limited by management's assumptions about people and the public's impression of what is going on in the corporation—both of which are out of date.

The workplace offers immeasurable potential for human growth and for attacking social and economic problems at their source. Management needs to capitalize on this potential in order to meet its economic objectives, and others need to appreciate this potential so they will not expect political contrivances that punish or protect business to get to the roots of people's failure to find fulfillment.

Members of the organization, at all levels, and the general public need to set aside outdated concepts of the corporation and set several new assumptions in their place:

1. The corporation's productivity has human dimensions beyond simple output/input calculations.

2. The corporation serves not just its owners, but a number of stakeholders—employees, customers, suppliers, and the public.

3. The corporation bears considerable responsibility for the

education of its stakeholders.

4. The corporation is a process—a human process—not merely a legal entity. Its primary obligation is to society for whatever purposes society chooses.

5. The corporation is involved in the ethical and moral issues surrounding it, whether it is so directed by laws or not.

6. The corporation plays a major role in shaping the values of its various stakeholders, and this role is becoming increasingly positive.

7. Nurturing a producer mentality produces both a healthier economy and more human growth than does a consumer mentality.

8. Cooperation by growing persons is more effective than competition among persons crowded into narrowly defined roles.

9. Work and the work situation can be a rich source of meaning, identity, personal development, and sense of community.

10. The corporation, led by managers who perceive the new image of man as well as the demands of the economic arena, is changing from within. Many of the corporate risk-takers and innovators are in the forefront of exploring the full dimensions of humanity and the new values.

"Business is a yeasty place for change," said Marilyn Ferguson at the 1982 World Future Society Assembly. Yet, the public has been slow to perceive the changes that are occurring and the potential that they suggest. It is generally unaware of the many new commitments to quality-of-life programs, quality circles, and other participative processes. It has heard little of the material riches accruing from such developments and practically nothing of the human richness pouring into workers' lives.

Management itself is not totally committed to the new assumptions about work and the workplace. Even those managers who are in the forefront of change may not know how to put their convictions and hunches into practice. They are in a central position for helping us relate to one another and to develop our full human potential; there are numerous actions that they can take to accelerate the trend toward humanization of the corporation and make those changes known to the public so it will support their efforts. To help them on their way, let us conclude our study of people coming alive at work by suggesting the following agenda for today's manager:

1. Take stock of your fundamental beliefs—what's important in your life—as well as any doubts that are important.

2. View your role and that of your organization in the largest possible context.

3. Continually assess the values of your organization's various stakeholder groups.

4. Tell others in the organization where you are coming from and where you would like to go.

5. Study the values and seek the vision of your stakeholders,

and then work toward building a common purpose.

6. Include employees at all levels in discussion of values issues related to what the company does and how it conducts its business.

7. Establish noneconomic as well as economic objectives for the organization, and make them widely known.

8. Set standards of excellence and make them known internally and externally.

9. Communicate purpose, values, and standards honestly and sincerely in terms that your audience can understand.

10. Invite customers and special-interest groups to discuss reactions to proposed products and production processes.

11. Explain to the public the cost, benefits, and risks of proceeding with or refraining from specific technological innovations.

12. Promote work as a rewarding and fulfilling activity.

13. Develop advertising programs that lead to a producer mentality rather than a consumer ethic.

14. Strive to develop *individuals* in your organization.

15. Make people "visible." Help them attain a feeling of significance.

16. Lead people to teamwork by helping them to realize their interdependencies and to respect the work of others.

17. Establish corporate training and development programs to enable individuals to evaluate themselves realistically and explore their potential for growth.

18. Ensure that each job is analyzed in terms of its true educational requirements so that unnecessary barriers will not be placed in the way of otherwise qualified people.

19. Commit to continuous educational programs that will enable workers to acquire both technical skills and skills that will help them in interpersonal relationships.

20. Encourage and support the educational sector in the development of people rather than seeking training for specific, short-term needs.

21. Provide educational opportunities for employees beyond those relating directly to their present jobs.

22. Encourage all workers to participate in problem-solving, doing everything you can to sustain the process once you have initiated it.

23. Work with labor representatives to reduce job classifications and create flexible, more rewarding work.

24. Bring workers, management, and labor-union officials together to discuss the impact of new technology well before its introduction to determine the impact on work content and working conditions.

25. Share corporate financial information and plans—the good news and the bad—so employees at all levels will know where the organization is headed, how it is doing, and how they can contribute more effectively.

26. Enable work groups to take over their own scheduling, administrative work, analysis of equipment needs, and facilities design.

27. Support work groups when they are ready to move beyond dealing with problems relating to their primary function to a broader role inside and outside the corporation.

28. Teach consensus-building skills rather than reliance on hierarchical power and politics.

29. Structure subordinate managers' duties to allow time and resources for dealing with values issues.

30. Evaluate managers on their contribution to long-term objectives and people development.

31. Reward managers for performance on quantifiable human-resource factors such as low levels of worker grievances, low absenteeism, development of worker skills, as well as improved quality of product and service.

32. Train managers in problem-solving, communications, and leadership skills.

33. Select and promote managers who have the capacity to appreciate and deal with values issues.

34. Encourage and reward managers for participation in community, regional, and national activities through which they can become sensitized to a broad range of interests, concerns, and opportunities for contributing to human growth.

35. Provide support and education for middle managers and first-line supervisors to overcome their reluctance to share decision-making responsibility with their subordinates.

36. Enable managers and supervisors to establish networks inside and outside the company through which they can share concerns and successes in implementing participative management practices.

Footnotes

1. Amitai Etzioni, *An Immodest Agenda,* McGraw-Hill Book Company, 1983, pp. 3-4.

2. Christopher Lasch, *The Culture of Narcissism,* W.W. Norton & Company, Inc., 1978.

3. Willis Harman, *An Incomplete Guide to the Future,* San Francisco Book Company Inc., 1976, p. 120.

4. Michael Maccoby, *The Leader,* Simon & Schuster, 1981, p. 49.

5. Daniel Yankelovich, *New Rules,* Random House, 1981, p. 12.

6. Etzioni, op cit., pp. 108, 131.

A New Game

Matthew J. Puleo

American buiness is out of touch with its work force. Things have changed so rapidly in the last 10 years that we've missed a very fundamental point. Work and workers in America are very different from before and they are now out of sync with each other.

Much of my time is spent with clients who are trying to improve their profits by increasing productivity. A major interest is in ways to make employees more committed, take more interest in their jobs, put out more effort, etc. All too often, managers say, "I don't understand these people. They're very different from me." Those managers are right—the work force is different, not only in terms of their attitudes but also in the nature of the work they do.

If you've been frustrated with these problems in the past, welcome to the club. In a recent survey, only 22% of the work force said that they were working up to capacity. So your frustrations are based on reality. Even worse, 44% say they are doing just enough to get by and not get fired. We do have a problem. But I don't think the solution lies in changing the American population. It requires that we seriously examine our assumptions about what is going on at work.

In particular, there are three general topics that, upon review, give specific insights into the issue:
- What work means today.
- The "social contract" between employers and employees.
- How the new definition of work requires a new way to measure productivity.

When looked at independently, they show dramatic change. If viewed interdependently, we can see how out of sync we really are. In fact, we could not have a worse possible combination of divergent trends because they feed upon each other to create an increasingly unmanageable situation—like Rubik's Cube. Management practices, in this scenario, simply are the last straw, the one side that never matches. But also like Rubik's Cube, the

---

Matthew J. Puleo is vice president, Human Resource Group, Yankelovich, Skelly and White, Inc., New York, New York.

problem is not impossible to solve. It's just complex—a complex puzzle with a logical solution.

I suggest that, if we look at how these shifts came about and what their components are, then we can develop a new perspective that will enable us to manage the work force and make us more productive.

Transitions

We all know that we are facing the challenge of a second transformation in our economy. The first, an industrial revolution, stretched from the 1870s to the 1970s. It brought about a shift in the main sector of the American economy, from an agricultural to an industrial base. The second new "revolution" is shifting the economy away from the traditional "smokestack" manufacturing industries to those based upon information, services, and new technologies. The first revolution took many decades, and it gave us time to make accommodations and understand the cultural and social implications.

The technologies that drive the new transformations are not as kind as those of the first era. They have created a pace that increases in speed by geometric progression. The resulting situation is one in which managers face serious stresses in coming to terms with the changes that are transforming today's workplace.

How the Old Definition Came About

America's rise to economic preeminence in the mid nineteenth and early twentieth centuries was due, in part, to our ability to create a radically new way of organizing work. The new approach skillfully blended the available human resources with the newly developed technologies into a low-discretion model of the workplace. By using the scientific management approach, it maximized productivity by minimizing the need for creativity, autonomy, and commitment on the part of individual workers.

The low-discretion model had several components. It contended that laws of the physical sciences were equally valid for managing people. Work was quantifiable and behaviors sufficiently projectable so that a "system" could be developed to completely control and predict output. It substituted science for individual judgment. It was as if the entire human element could be expressed in the common language of all physical sciences—mathematics.

Second, there no longer was a need for, or value placed upon, the skills of the craftsman. Molds and frames could be fashioned to reproduce in hours what formerly took months to create. The assembly line for automobiles is probably the single best example of how the process took over. The car, once the "creation" of skilled mechanics, could now be built by a work force with less than six months' training in a matter of hours.

In addition, the system, not the employees, was the company.

All decision-making authority resided in management. Workers were not expected, nor permitted, to have input into the process. Worse yet, it was intentionally designed so that there was no dependence or importance placed on any one person.

Finally, there was an adversarial view toward the work force. The school of scientific management developed a close theoretical relationship between discretionary effort, motivation, and productivity. It postulated that, if given the chance, workers would hold back and produce less.

The Need To Rethink Work

If we think America underwent a remarkable transition in the century between 1870 and 1970, it pales in comparison with the transitions that have occurred in the last decade. In direct contrast to the flexibility that allowed us to master the first revolution, we have responded with uncharacteristic rigidity. The result has been our loss of stature in the new international economy. The "rise and fall" of the most powerful economy in world history was, in part, caused by using old rules to play a new game.

Our assumptions about affluence as an American birthright and the vitality of our economy blinded us to the changes that were occurring. We failed to realize (or admit) in the business community that we were undergoing a fundamental shift that not only affected the marketplace we produced for, but also the systems and structures required within an organization. For this shift from an industrialized economy to an information/service economy simultaneously affected the nature of the products and the types of workers necessary to produce them. It produced changes in the definition of manufacturing—from a physical environment, where people performed tasks with their hands or with machines that transformed material, to the handling and processing of information with their minds.

Why do we ignore it? This distinction is neither subtle nor trivial. Physiologically, we use a different part of our body for moving an object than to change a thought, requiring a different way of controlling the activity. Similarly, since the emphasis has moved from hard work to smart work, we no longer are harnessing strength. We are harnessing the ability to develop and disseminate ideas. That is what requires rethinking of the basic definition of work.

More Evidence

Additional changes, both demographic and nondemographic in nature, also require this redefinition. Today, managers and professionals outnumber unskilled laborers five to one, in contrast to the turn of the century when only one in four was considered white-collar. Yet, the percentage of the work force that is blue-collar has decreased only 9% since 1920. What has occurred is the development of a new stratum of employees that are asynchronous to the low-discretion model. By job design, managers and professionals should bring autonomy, creativity, and commitment to their jobs. However, the low-discretion model does not allow for it because these behaviors do not occur in predictable ways.

The tremendous increase of jobs in the service sector also erodes the underlying premise of scientific management. From 1950 to 1981, the number of "goods producing" jobs decreased from 59% to 28% of the work force, while service-sector jobs concurrently rose to 72%. According to our research, in general, service-sector jobs require substantially more discretion.

Finally, the general increase of technology in the workplace has substantially altered routinization. We all have been affected by technology on our job, whether by its presence or absence. While technology has the potential of allowing managers to monitor employees' work more closely, the opposite is usually the case. In fact, more than half the American work force reports that technology has given them more independence in how to do their jobs.

There are also other indications that suggest that, because of factors such as changing technology, even traditional blue-collar jobs may have more discretion than they did in the past. This is particularly true in terms of the importance of the individual vs. the system. On the shop floor, computerization, robotization, and mechanization continually make for a leaner type of organization in terms of people. But the fewer people you have and the more sophisticated your technology, the heavier the reliance that must be placed on each individual. This is just what the low-discretion model was designed not to do.

The Result

In summary, the mega-shift is that now the major portion of effort is controlled by the job holder rather than by the employer or the inherent nature of the work. Daniel Yankelovich, in a recent study published by the Public Agenda Foundation, has named this phenomenon "discretionary effort"—that is, "the difference beteen the maximum amount of effort and care an individual could bring to the job, and the minimum amount of effort required to avoid being fired or penalized."

Simply put, it is the amount of effort over which an employee has greatest control. Today, it's the individual, not the system.

Social Change

The second shift was in the national consensus. The success of the low-discretion model was not only predicated on assumptions about the nature of work and the composition of the work force. The assumptions we just reviewed were about how jobs could be analyzed and broken down into simple tasks that could be confined within the hours of a time clock, controlled by an assembly line, and directed by the supervisor.

The next assumptions relied on a common work ethic. It was assumed that the labor force subscribed to a work ethic that supported the view that the low-discretion model was as attractive to workers as it was to managers. Workers were thought eager to buy into their role in the "system" and willing to sacrifice autonomy and to work hard at unsatisfying jobs in exchange for the material rewards, respect, and sense of belonging that come from subscribing to a commonly held set of beliefs.

There no longer is a consensus. The social revolution of the 1960s and 1970s has resulted in a work force that is not homogeneous but highly segmented. This necessitates that we begin to view workers not as the employees of the past with the traditional views of status, success, and material worth, but as something different. They are individuals with a variety of needs and attitudes, and they behave much like consumers do in the marketplace. They bring different values to work—different from the past and each other—which results in a complex situation to manage.

Possibilities for Tension

The concept of discretionary effort suggests that both the intensity and extent of an individual's performance are under his own control. The law of conservation of energy suggests that the effort will somehow be expended. With the absence of a consensus, the critical question now becomes, "On whose behalf will it be expended?"

Current trends indicate that professional Americans are very strategic in their decision-making. They weigh the alternatives and go in the direction of the greatest return on their investment of time and talent. Americans are no longer convinced that effort invested in their jobs will be rewarded. In fact, survey results show that the percentage who see a direct causal connection between hard work and a payoff for it has gone from 58% in 1968 to only 36% today. The situation is further complicated by the economic realities of today, making it more difficult for both employees and employers to make concessions.

For the individual, the question of best return on investment really translates into "How am I going to attain a 'better' standard of living?" Our economy no longer seems to be delivering as reliably on the implied promises of the past. Therefore, rewards are viewed from several angles. Entitlement programs, changing social attitudes toward job hopping and unemployment, and two-earner households have reduced the down-side risks. We have severely reduced the incentives to conform.

The New Social Contract

The result is a work force that sees "payoffs" in several forms of currency: (1) money; (2) work itself; (3) non-monetary rewards; and (4) opportunities. Work is no longer simply a commodity we

259

buy from people with a paycheck. The social contract between employer and employee has been altered.

The most startling change is in the value of money. I don't wish to underemphasize the importance of money, but rather reposition it in the social contract between employees and employers. Money is almost an entitlement. Our compensation systems are such that too many people are paid on a basis that is tangentially related to any measure of performance.

These passive pay systems where raises are semi-automatic and linked more to inflation than effort have had a surprising consequence. The response from the work force has been that money is the price of admission for the employer that allows him to expect that people come to work on time, stay late, and not take too many sick days. All that can be expected for money is physical presence.

In a work environment that fits the low-discretion model, physical presence may be enough. But in the current economy only one job in eight fits that description. It is for the other seven that the other currencies become important.

Turning the Tables

Therefore, it is important to create a workplace that induces commitment on the part of the workers by ensuring that the company's goals and the individual's goals are not mutually exclusive.

The way people are managed and rewarded with these other currencies will determine the amount, quality, and direction of their output. They are necessary today to buy the psychic presence that is required in the high-discretion model. Therefore, effort, in addition to no longer being automatic, may require varying methods of motivation.

The creation of a mutually beneficial system, however, creates dissonance with the traditional views of loyalty and commitment to the common good. Both sides must review what their rights and responsibilities are.

Productivity: The Wrong Yardstick

Given the shifts that have occurred, it is not surprising that we have so much difficulty improving productivity. The problem with measuring productivity is that it doesn't fit the new model. Productivity, as commonly defined in this country, typically looks only at efficiency—a short-term measure of cost-effectiveness—rather than effectiveness—a longer-term, macro view of an operation. Being efficient can be effective, but only under certain circumstances.

Productivity, as the measurement criterion for high-discretion positions, is accurate but not valid. Productivity is the wrong thing to measure. It looks at linear output in a multi-variant system where it is possible to do a lot but not contribute to the success of the individual's work unit. Performance is what we should look for.

The measurement of performance, in an environment where discretionary effort dominates, requires a new philosophy that focuses on structure and process rather than just trying to manage it in the narrow terms of cost efficiency. Improving performance is a business strategy—not an operating tactic.

Why Bother?

A company's ability to survive in the current marketplace requires not only an efficiently produced product but one that someone else is willing to purchase. Unless you have a wide circle of friends and relatives to buy all your products, correct market alignment is critical.

There are two ways to align your goods and services with your market. The first is to keep in touch with the marketplace and modify your offerings to reflect the changes that are occurring. The second is to try to convince your customers that what they really want to buy is what you produce—no matter how out of sync it is. We all know that most companies prefer the first method.

However, today's markets shift at an alarmingly quick pace, which heightens the need for innovation, adaptability, flexibility, and responsiveness—a readiness to compete. That means that the systems in a company must be designed with change in mind. Change in our economy is inevitable, and it may be our only constant. Just because a business is going well today doesn't mean it will continue to do so. As the shakedown continues in our shift to a new economy, flexibility will become the key to survival.

Therefore, we can no longer rely on pat models. We can no longer make the assumptions of the 1950s and the 1960s about continued growth, dominance in markets, predictable interest rates, and easily controllable inflation. There are many examples of companies that have excelled and failed in the last five years.

A Balance

There is a difference between flexibility and chaos. Systems and policies are designed to reduce judgment. This has been taken to the extreme in the low-discretion model. However, the reverse would be just as disastrous—letting everyone do their own thing. If we establish the goals and ways to measure how effective we are in meeting those goals, then we can allow individuals the freedom to work out the details for themselves.

This is where the value of an empirical management style lies—in the ability to provide a work environment that uses creativity and individual contribution as a way of encouraging commitment to corporate performance. The new manager now becomes the ideal catalyst for discretionary effort by helping subordinates obtain the payoff.

This necessitates a review of reward systems. Since there are many forms of currency, and a lack of social consensus, it is difficult to determine where the individual will see a payoff. If required performance is clearly part of an overall business strategy and the rewards are based on that business performance, then the discretionary effort can be harnessed. However, as the utility becomes more tactical and short term in nature, effectiveness will be decreased.

Summary

The challenge that faces American business today is two-fold. First, there is a need to appreciate and understand the changes that are occurring. Second, there is a need to properly use the technologies that are fueling the transitions. If the approaches we adopted in the past were successful, our adaptation would be easy. But they were unsuccessful and, unfortunately, have outlived their usefulness. The changes we have experienced in the last decade have totally revolutionized our society.

In retrospect, maybe the industrial revolution was the aberration in our society. The move toward discretionary effort and the need for flexibility are, perhaps, merely signs of the resurgence of the importance of the individual.

The Silicon Age:
Living and Learning
in an Information Epoch

by

Harold G. Shane

What is there in the list of strange and unexpected events that has not occurred in our time? Our lives have transcended the limits of humanity; we are born to serve as the theme of incredible tales to posterity.
— Aeschines (389-314 B.C.)

Some years ago Daniel Bell, the Harvard sociologist, coined the term "post-industrial society" to describe an era based on services, into which our industrial age was being transformed. More recently, however, it has become clear that the post-industrial world is not just a service society; it is an "information society"—one in which knowledge and the handling of information have elbowed aside the smokestack and the assembly line as symbols of America's prowess.[1]

When did the United States enter the information epoch? John Naisbitt argues persuasively that the "megashift" from industrial to information society occurred in 1956 and 1957. In 1956, white-collar workers—managerial, technical, clerical, and professional—for the first time outnumbered blue-collar workers. And 1957 "marked the beginning of the globalization of the information revolution: The Russians launched Sputnik, the missing technological catalyst in a growing information society."[2]

The unique opportunities (and demands) that accompany the information epoch require us to explore and to understand more clearly the myriad ways in which society is being influenced by the information sciences and microtechnologies. We must determine what social inventiveness and institutional repair work may be required because of 1) the enormous impact of the microprocessor and of telecommunications networks, 2) ergonomic[3]

Harold G. Shane is university professor of education, Indiana University, Bloomington, Indiana. This article originally appeared in the Phi Delta Kappan *(October 1983).* © 1983, Phi Delta Kappan, Inc.

responses to increasingly robotized workplaces and computerized homes, and 3) ubiquitous 24-hour television, which, in some areas, now allows access to more than 100 channels.

Learning To Live with New Realities

Change in our modern age takes place with bewildering speed. In recent decades the life sciences have produced clones of mammals, oral contraceptives, artificial life forms, heart transplants, and gene splicing. The physical sciences have given us lasers and holography, the computer, and landing on our moon and on Mars; they have even sent a probe into the infinite reaches of space that lie beyond the orbits of the outermost planets in our solar system.

One outcome of this rapid change has been social disorientation. The disorientation manifests itself in many ways—from worldwide assassinations, political kidnappings, and terrorism to alienation, drug and alcohol abuse, and teenage pregnancies and suicides. Correcting problems such as these—and a host of others—would be a prime task for humans to undertake in the information age.

Another challenge in an era of information overload or "infoglut"[4] is meeting the demands that will be placed on education. As Bentley Glass put it in 1968. "The educated man of yesterday is the maladjusted, uneducated man of today and the culturally illiterate misfit of tomorrow." Consequently, educated humans need to acquire much more knowledge than they needed to have 25 or 30 years ago. Traditional curriculum content and instructional practices are certain to change as educators begin to master the art of using knowledge to react promptly and wisely to the difficulties created by the demands that accompany an era of infoglut.

In the remainder of this article, I plan to outline some of the ways in which the world community is being transmuted by the electronic environment. Since "knowledge potential" is our one infinite resource, I have also suggested some ways in which we need to modify certain personal and educational values as we use this potential to thread our way through the maze of information that Daniel Bell estimated will soon be doubling every two years.

The Electronic Environment

The implications of microelectronic phenomena go far beyond the microcomputers that have captured popular attention. The steam-powered technology of the eighteenth and nineteenth centuries and the internal combustion/electrical technology that shaped the early decades of the twentieth century greatly reduced the need for arduous physical labor. However, because microelectronic technology has begun to supplant both physical and intellectual labor in the 1980s, significant changes are taking place at all levels of society throughout the world.

The effect of the microelectronic revolution on the military, for example, is dramatic and rather alarming. On the one hand, many of the most advanced developments in microelectronics lend themselves readily to military applications. On the other hand, the rapid developments in sophisticated communication and weaponry could further destabilize the nuclear arms race. Devastatingly accurate targeting, guidance, and damage assessment devices have been developed. A report from the Worldwatch Institute suggests that the new technology may make first strikes more tempting to an enemy that hopes to score a nuclear knockout.

One other factor adds a devastating element of uncertainty in a society that has begun to depend heavily on the power of microelectronics: the electromagnetic pulse (EMP) effect. Scientists believe that a nuclear device exploded over, say, Nebraska—even though detonated 250 miles above the earth's surface—would blanket the entire United States with an electromagnetic pulse that could completely paralyze much of the equipment powered by electricity—some of it permanently.[5] This EMP effect renders electronic gear—from toasters and telephones to transistors, computers, and even our airborne command posts—dysfunctional.

The changes wrought by the microelectronic revolution go far beyond the military, however; they affect all parts of society today, including the times and places where work is done, the range of foods available, the bewildering array of video- and audiocassette equipment, our increased mobility and choice of mode of transportation (more than 700 models of cars and trucks were on the U.S. market in 1982), and even new patterns of personal relationships. The microchip has created living quarters in which mail, information sources such as videotext and viewdata, security control, and the selection and ordering of goods and services are all handled electronically.

Health and longevity are also being influenced in our microelectronic epoch. Computerized prosthetic devices have already helped the paraplegic to walk, the voiceless to speak, and the brain-injured to function. It has even become technically possible to use brain-dead bodies, housed in a "neomortorium," to provide storage for living organs until they are harvested to replace the lungs, kidneys, hearts, or livers of those who need transplants.[6]

The growing use of laser-beam surgery represents yet another dramatic advance in medicine. Doctors can now snake a laser through tubing and reach organs in locations that heretofore were inoperable because they are out of the reach of traditional surgical tools and techniques.

And then there are the electronic media (particularly television)—possibly the most pervasive manifestation of the silicon age. The "tube" brings us visual mobility and instant information, as well as the phenomenon of "interactive TV," which enables viewers in some communities to express opinions on various issues and questions merely by pressing a button. TV also barrages us with manic ads, increasingly explicit sex, and gore-in-detail during the 1.5 billion hours Americans spend daily in televiewing.

Until recently, the TV programs available to European audiences were for the most part limited, and to some extent controlled, by the governments of the various countries. One cannot avoid speculating about the socioeconomic and political implications of a vastly increased public exposure to American-style TV with multiple stations and dozens of program choices. One European official, who requested anonymity, suggested that, to protect the public from garbage on TV, his government might consider forbidding the use of receiving dish antennae that pick up signals from satellites.

Charles Owen of the Illinois Institute of Technology is among a growing group who forecast the proliferation of in-the-home electronic equipment that ranges far beyond television. Among his images: robots to perform routine household chores; appliances responsive to voice commands; force fields to detect intruders; high-tech food processors to chop, mix, cook, and store victuals; and "holographic" TV to project three-dimensional scenes *outside* the confines of the tube.

Though experts disagree as to the merits and demerits of video games, it seems safe to conclude that they have pervaded our lives. In 1982 alone, 38 billion quarters clinked into coin slots, and home video vendors grossed $4.5 billion in sales. Some communities have felt obliged to set a minimum age for admission to video arcades. Others have forbidden their youths to enter such arcades during school hours, in an effort to stem absenteeism on the part of pupils who had become "video junkies." The most unusual—and alarming—information that testifies to the possible effects of "videomania" indicates that prolonged play—five or six hours at a stretch—has triggered epileptic seizures (both grand and petit mal) in young addicts.[7]

The Changing Workplace

The new microelectronic age is radically changing the workplace. This transformation has implications for education that we are only now beginning to understand.

The long-term impact of rapid technological change is nearly impossible to forecast accurately. The technological changes reported almost daily tend to threaten us with technogenic unemployment even as they open new employment vistas. In July, 1983, for instance, *Robotics World* announced that scientists at the Nippon Telegraph and Telephone Public Corporation had created a robot that could read the news with 99.5% accuracy. The robot's computer (programmed with a dictionary) can scan print, check its memory banks, and deliver a properly inflected sentence. The report suggests a future for news-reading robots on the radio and for robots as telephone operators and as readers for the blind.[8] Some innovations are already creating technogenic unemployment, as when, for instance, a factory is retooled and automated. Consider this example.

> The General Electric Company is investing $316 million over the next three years to revitalize its locomotive plant in Erie, Pennsylvania. When all of the robots, computerized machine tools, and other automation systems are in place, the Erie "factory with a future" will have increased its production capacity by one-third.[9]

Obviously, such investments should strengthen the nation's economy. As far as the work force is concerned, however, two workers in the future will do in 16 hours at General Electric what 70 employees did in 16 days before the plant received its electronic facelift.

Developments of this nature promise more major job-market shifts for the 1980s and 1990s. For instance, electronic mail promises to reduce the need for postal workers; linotype workers, elevator operators, and farm laborers will probably continue to dwindle in number; and our homes, as they become "electronic cottages," are likely to take less time to maintain.

On the other hand, the ranks of computer operators, office machine technicians, and tax-form specialists should swell, along with those of child-care personnel, geriatric nurses, social workers, and fast-food distributors. A volume prepared for the World Future Society forecasts a sampling of new occupations, the number of workers likely to be required, and average salaries as of 1990: energy technicians, 1.5 million at $26,000; housing rehabilitation technicians, 1.75 million at $24,000; genetic engineering technicians, 150,000 at $30,000; holographic inspection specialists, 200,000 at $28,000; bionic-electronic technicians, 200,000 at $32,000; and many more.[10] Educators from the preschool to the graduate school will need to be increasingly alert to shifting demands posed by a rapidly changing workplace.

Automated offices and an increase in stay-at-home workers have added two new buzz words to our vocabularies: 1) *telecommuters,* to describe people who "commute" to work via TV or computer terminals, and 2) *flexiplaces,* which refers to flexibility in the sites where one earns a living. The terms also suggest that new employer/employee relationships will continue to emerge and that many of our long- and dearly held images of work are obsolete. As Alvin Toffler observes in his most recent book, *Previews and Premises,*[11] the nature of work in the emerging Third Wave information sector that is superseding the industrial society mandates enriching and enlarging jobs. It also calls for increasing employee participation in policy making, devising more varied organizational approaches to the tasks performed in our workplaces, and—of particular importance to educators—graduating workers who are knowledgeable, literate, resourceful, empathic, and innovative.

The increasingly widespread deployment of industrial robots may prove to be the most important phenomenon to restructure industry since steam-engine technology appeared in the eighteenth century. James Albus, chief of the industrial systems division at the National Bureau of Standards, estimates that, as of early 1983, there were perhaps 5,000 robots in U.S. factories and that their numbers would increase by at least 20,000 and perhaps by as many as 60,000 installations per year between 1990 and the year 2000 if present trends continue. Since two to four person-years of work go into the installation of a system of industrial robots, a robot/electronic economy could be a welcome source of employment. However, these "steel-collar workers" will take jobs from a substantial number of human blue-collar workers. As Vary Coates noted, "Since robots have neither the flexibilities nor the restrictions of humans, a work environment organized for humans is not necessarily the environment that is best for robots. . . . To use robots most efficiently, the flow of work and the factory floor may have to be completely redesigned."[12]

Consider the challenge to education presented by 1) meeting new skill requirements of workers and of managers and 2) retrofitting or retraining the personnel displaced. In fact, as Toffler sees it, educators need to begin revamping our present system of mass education:

> Today's schools are turning out still more factory-style workers for jobs that won't exist. Diversify. Individualize. Decentralize. Smaller, more local schools. More education in the home. More parental involvement. More creativity, less rote (it's the rote jobs that are disappearing the fastest).[13]

Another development that may create spectacular changes in the workplace is examined by Colin Norman in his study of science and technology in the 1980s.[14] The potential impact of micro-technology and biotechnology is so tremendous that it seems unlikely that any new industries will even begin to approach the wallop that these two fields promise to have on our lives by the end of the century. Gene splicing, for instance, permits the gene for human interferon to be fished out of a cell possessing tens of thousands of other genes. Among other possible biochem/microtech contributions to the information epoch are self-fertilizing corn and wheat that draw nitrogen from the air. Other innovations include new ways to produce drugs and chemicals at modest cost, to produce fuel from waste materials, and to produce bacteria that clean up oil spills.

Let me mention one final development of the silicon age that could soon affect all our lives. Kenneth Hanck and Keith DeArmond, chemistry professors at North Carolina State University at Raleigh, have been working for more than four years to replace microchips with individual molecules. Such molecules would be capable of storing readable, coded information in approximately one-millionth of the space that even today's tiny computer chips require. To date, Hanck and DeArmond have identified chemical compounds with molecules that retain six electrons potentially useful as memory devices. Computers using molecular memory devices would be incredibly more powerful, tinier, and more efficient than anything now available.

Education in an Electronic Age

In recent months our entire system of education—kindergarten through college—has come under harsh scrutiny. In part, this is because governments, institutions, and individuals are discovering that dynamic developments in electronic information technologies, in biotechnologies, and in complex global communications are rapidly changing what they do, how they do it, and how they relate to one another. But the onrushing silicon age is already changing the entire landscape of education. According to the Office of Technology Assessment:

> The so-called *information revolution,* driven by rapid advances in communication and computer technology, is profoundly affecting American education. It is changing the nature of *what needs to be learned, who needs to learn it, who will provide it, and how it will be provided and paid for.*[15] (Emphasis added)

We cannot improve our schools without first determining how to cope with the silicon age; we need to develop strategies—both as professional educators and as private citizens—for living and learning in an electronic epoch, as well as future-oriented administrative policies, curriculum content, instructional practices, links with parents and community and other educational agencies—including the omnipresent TV set and its video-appendages.

Alternatives and Consequences

As the microelectronic boom enhances the information explosion, I see no cause for "technophobia" in public-school classrooms or on the college campus. However, we must recognize that in an information society the schools seem fated to find themselves no longer cloistered retreats but lively arenas in which an increasing array of conflicting social, economic, moral, and political ideas will collide. A good curriculum for the 1990s will be one that, among other things, helps learners understand the nature of an era of value conflicts.

Basic skills, clearly defined, are of even greater importance in the new knowledge society that we are entering. As we define "basic skills," we find that, in addition to the basic computer skills necessary to an information epoch, familiar basic elements—e.g., reading and writing, which have constituted traditional literacy—will acquire new meaning. In the language arts, for instance, an understanding of propaganda and the nature of and reasons for selected news is now basic. So is an understanding of ecological relationships, toxic-waste problems, and the subtle meanings of entropy in the natural sciences. As for the social sciences (e.g., history, political science, economics, sociology, anthropology), all must acquire new meanings that will be compatible with the demands of the era in which our young learners will spend their lives.

Perhaps above all, one of the basic qualities of good schools will be their ability to teach skills that are transferable from one job to another in a rapidly changing world of work. This has become an important direction for traditional career and vocational education to take.

In addition, the "mind workers" of tomorrow—many of them already enrolled in our kindergarten-to-university continuum—must be exposed to value choices by wise and courageous teachers who are themselves aware of contemporary ideological crises and who have clarified their own values. Educators must understand that the nature of the world of tomorrow cannot be forecast with precision; what tomorrow brings will depend on where our insightful, humane values—or their absence—will lead us as we move into the future of the information society. This is what living and learning in a high-tech/microtech age involves.

The societal tensions generated by microtechnologies and their impact on our world will not grow less. Schools must begin living in the future now, just as their young charges will have to do. Even amid rapid and often bewildering changes, I remain optimistic. I believe we are passing the crest of our Third Wave malaise and are ready to debate and to determine what the "microkids" of today and tomorrow need to know and how U.S. schools can best educate the "microelectronic generation."

Notes

1. See, for example, Yoneji Masuda, *The Information Society as Post-Industrial Society* (Tokyo: Institute for the Information Society, 1980).

2. John Naisbitt, *Megatrends* (New York: Warner Books, 1982), p. 12.

3. "Ergonomics" originally referred to the study of worker/machine relationships with the aim of reducing fatigue, strain, or discomfort. In the computer era, it has begun to be used to encompass psychological and social relationships. For example, the computer may begin to take the place of the imaginary playmate in the affections of some children; hence it has become the object of psychosocial analysis.

4. To the best of my knowledge, "infloglut" is a useful coinage by Michael Marien, editor of *Future Survey*.

5. For a more detailed report on EMP, see William J. Broad, "The Chaos Factor," *Science 83*, January/February 1983, pp. 41-49.

6. For compelling arguments supporting this rather unsettling proposal, see Willard Gaylin, "Harvesting the Dead," *Harper's,* September 1974, pp. 23-30.

7. T.K. Daneshmend and M.J. Campbell, "Dark Warrior Epilepsy," *British Medical Journal,* 12 June 1982, pp. 1751-52.

8. *Indianapolis Star,* 4 July 1983, p. 10-A.

9. The June 1983 issue of *The Futurist,* from which this illustration is taken (p.18), notes that further information can be obtained from the News Bureau, General Electric Company, P.O. Box 5900, Norwalk, CT 06856.

10. Marvin Cetron and Thomas O'Toole, "Careers with a Future: Where the Jobs Will Be in the 1990s," in Edward Cornish, ed., *Careers Tomorrow: The Outlook for Work in a Changing World* (Bethesda, Md.: World Future Society, 1983), pp. 10-18.

11. Alvin Toffler, *Previews and Premises* (New York: William Morrow, 1983).

12. Vary T. Coates, "The Potential Impact of Robotics." *The Futurist,* February 1983, pp. 28-32.

13. Toffler, p. 58.

14. Colin Norman, *The God That Limps: Science and Technology in the Eighties* (New York: W.W. Norton, 1981).

15. Office of Technology Assessment, *Information Technology and Its Impact on American Education* (Washington, D.C.: OTA, Autumn 1982), p.3.

Lifestyle Changes in the Future

by

Robert Theobald

What can be said about lifestyle changes in the future? A generation ago such a discussion would have seemed naive because we believed that our lifestyles would stay the same for an unlimited period into the future. To admit the possibility of significant lifestyle changes is in itself a profoundly new and important development.

We are essentially admitting that there has been a profound break in human history; we are seeing a shift from the industrial era to the communications era. This does not mean that the elements of the industrial era will vanish any more than the elements of the agricultural era vanished when we moved into the industrial era. It does mean that we shall build on the successes of the agricultural and industrial eras to create a new set of possibilities and problems.

The communications era has been coming into existence for the last 20 or 30 years. If we are to survive, its development must be completed by the end of this century. We therefore face a challenge without parallel in human history. Each of us as individuals, and all of us as a society, must shift our thinking so that we mesh with the new realities that we have brought into existence by our increased productive and destructive power.

What are the prime changes that have taken place?

First, there is the development of our productive capacity, which is now so great that it is straining the ecological capacity of the world. The most important development of recent years is that more and more competent ecologists are arguing that we cannot know at what point we enter an irreversible downward trend in the capacity of earth to support human and other life. We are therefore compelled to adopt a conservative policy. This means that we must try to decrease the number of births as rapidly as possible and at the same time limit the amount of production to that level which people need to be able to develop themselves and others. The strange climate patterns of 1983 are of growing concern to those who watch ecological issues.

Robert Theobald enables people to deal with issues of fundamental change through Action Linkage, Wickenburg, Arizona. He is the author of Beyond Despair *and* Avoiding 1984.

Second, levels of destructive power now place the survival of the human race at great risk. Nobody can prove that wars will escalate into nuclear wars and nobody can prove that nuclear wars would be so destructive that they would leave little behind them. On the other hand, nobody can argue that the risks of nuclear war are not significant and that the risk of an unleashed nuclear war could not destroy most of the human race. Again, we are forced to develop a more conservative policy to find new ways to settle international conflicts.

Conflict is inevitable, both internationally and domesticaly. We cannot expect to eliminate conflict. Trying to do so is unrealistic. We can, however, recognize that there are different ways to resolve conflict. These can be violent or we can work towards arbitration, mediation, and other means of settling disputes that allow for win/win attitudes of mind. We can only eliminate war if we recognize that warfare is simply an enlargement of our angry attitudes at home, in the neighborhood, in the community, and nationally. I sometimes fear that if neighborhoods had access to nuclear bombs they would be willing to use them on other neighborhoods!

The increase in productive and destructive power has put us into a new situation. This new situation is further changed by the human-rights drive in our society. We are no longer committed to excluding certain types of people because of their class, age, race, sex, etc. This growing psychic commitment has still not, of course, developed in custom or in law to the extent that is necessary. But those who deny the force of the human rights movement will find themselves in grave difficulties.

These new realities are being driven by emerging technological discoveries. The robot and the computer are having incredible impacts on society, which are still being far too widely ignored. The cost of computers is dropping very rapidly and a very complex and powerful computer can now be bought for far less than the annual cost of the minimum wage. The implications of this for employment are only just beginning to be understood. The office, where productivity has been low, will see rapid and dramatic increases in the amount of work that people can, and will be expected to, accomplish.

Similarly, the robot is going to have far greater and more immediate impact than people realize. The robot is not being blocked by its lack of technical excellence, but by social and institutional inertia. Robots cost as little as a quarter of the wage of the skilled worker that they replace. Already, in Japan, the development of high-technology industries is breaking up that famed level of cooperation between labor and management that has made the Japanese miracle the envy of the rest of the world.

It is already clear that many of the people who have worked in smokestack industries, particularly those who are older, will never get back to work again. They will not be able to compete with people who have been initially trained with computers. In addition, their self-perception is such that working with a computer is not seen as an appropriate activity for a male.

It has been calculated that if one counts all of the computers that are in cars and washing machines and telephone systems and other consumer and industrial machines, as well as those machines that we normally call computers, there are now more computers in the world than there are human beings. We must accept that the computer and robot will continue to dramatically decrease the amount of hours that a person spends on the job.

This decrease is far greater than most people understand. In the middle of the nineteenth century, a male would spend 40% of his total lifelong hours on the job; now the figure is down to 14% and it is falling. Not only are hours of work per week decreasing but the periods of schooling, of retirement, of holidays and vacation are growing all the time. Jobs were the center of life; they no longer are. The dramatic consequences of such a shift on the Western psyche, which has made the job the way we value human beings, are almost incalculable.

It is not only the robot and the computer that are changing the way we live. The robot and the computer are the technological driving force of the '80s but in the '90s biology will have consequences that are even more dramatic than those of the computer and robot. Biology coupled with the computer is going to change the way we produce food and clothing and shelter and the way we manage all of our resources.

In addition, biology is going to challenge all of our beliefs about what it means to be a human being. We are going to have to ask ourselves what rights we have to cope with failures in natural processes. We are going to have to ask whether knowledge of a damaged fetus warrants intervention. We are going to have to look at the whole issue of genetic engineering. Ignoring these issues simply ensures that the wrong decisions are going to be made.

Up to the present time, we have been trying to sweep under the rug many of the changes surrounding us. We have been ignoring the need for new social, community, and neighborhood policies. In many ways we have succeeded in doing this at the institutional level. People, on the other hand, have been adapting because they have had no choice.

The problems of poverty that surround us and have become worse in recent years, because of a combination of policy and recession, are also tied to dramatic changes in lifestyle and family structure. Poverty is increasingly concentrated in single-parent families. The consequences for the next generation are far more serious than we have yet been willing to face.

We now know that the future is going to be dramatically different from the past. Those who will do well in the future are those who recognize the inevitability of fundamental change and who

274

force themselves to struggle to discover what these changes will be and how they can benefit from them, individually, as a neighborhood, and as a community.

This is a quite different situation from that which existed in most of history. Normally, groups that have been left out of a society must struggle to force their way into that functioning society and demand their fair share of the rights of that existing society. On the other hand, if the society is shifting extremely dramatically, then the best way to benefit is to discover the direction of those shifts, to work to be the initiators of them, and thus to be well placed to become the leaders of the new periods of history.

What Do We Do?

With this background, we can now look at a few of the lifestyle changes that are going to be forced on us and where we can benefit from them if only we choose to do so. The most dramatic shift has already been mentioned. There will be a further continuing decline in the number of hours that people will spend on their jobs. This means that toil will not be seen by the coming generation as the center of their existence; rather we shall encourage people to think about their own development and that of others, their neighborhood, and the community. This is a dramatic shift affecting every part of our lives—and particularly our educational system.

We have an educational system that was designed for the industrial era—and indeed even still contains attitudes that were designed in the agricultural era. Our school pattern is related to the need for as many people as possible to be available in the fields during the summer. The times of our vacations have little to do with the needs of the industrial era and even less to do with those of the communications era.

The industrial era taught people to read, write, and figure so that they could do the repetitive jobs that were required at that time. Today, we need people who can think: the repetitive jobs will be taken over by the computer and the robot. Today, people no longer need to learn facts and data; they need to discover the skills that permit them to learn to learn to keep up with the rapid and fundamental changes in society. This requires a cooperative schooling system where many types of communication skills and styles are taught and effectively learned. The tests that we now use to measure success in schools are also related to the industrial era. We need profoundly new models and tests if we are to find out how effectively we are preparing people to live in a cooperative and creative society.

If the job is no longer to be the center of life, then patterns of income distribution, which are based on jobs, can no longer be effective or appropriate. As computers and robots become the producers of more and more of the wealth of the society, then we must extend the types of activity for which people can be paid. One of the most obvious areas in which we need to reconsider our policies as soon as possible is that of child raising. It appears clear that there are many people who would choose to stay home and raise kids if only their monetary income was sufficient and they did not feel forced to go out and hold a job. Introducing policies that would support people in the home is one of the priorities in adapting to the communications era.

Indeed, the issue of income distribution goes further. We have effectively adopted a policy of guaranteed income in the United States and throughout the rich world, but we are afraid to admit what we have done. We will not permit people to starve or freeze—but the mechanics we use to prevent this are an extraordinarily complex and messy set of arrangements, so the smart and the crooked can get very large amounts of money and the honest and the dumb are usually short-changed.

We need to set up a scheme that will permit everybody to get a basic income. This should be sufficient for survival and for basic needs. Neighborhoods and communities will then need to encourage those who are living on this basic income to do useful and creative things for neighbors and the neighborhood.

It must nevertheless be recognized that some people will continue to waste their time. This must be permitted for two reasons: First, once one creates a society in which some people are allowed to prevent other people from "wasting their time," one is already moving rapidly into a police state. Secondly, what one era defines as wasting its time may in fact be the most critical actions for the next era. As we move from the industrial era to the communications era, we must provide people with as much opportunity to do what they feel is important as we possibly can.

A guaranteed income, however, will not meet the needs of everybody all of the time. There must be provision for the availability of additional resources to cope with bad luck, with a run of problems. At the present time, we try to manage these types of problems through bureaucratic systems, and we have discovered that this is ineffective. The alternative we must now adopt is for neighborhoods and communities to have funds available to them to deal with the needs of people in the community. Each community's resources will always be more limited than the community's needs and there will have to be tough and difficult decisions made. Here, as in so many other areas, we cannot hope to cope with our problems unless the human race grows up. The levels of honesty, responsibility, humility, and love that will be required by those who take responsibilities of this type seem at present to be beyond us. But, humanity has now achieved such power that unless we make decisions at this level, we shall inevitably destroy ourselves. We shall only discover what our capacities are by testing them.

The model being proposed here will be rejected by those who

hope for a utopian system. There is no suggestion that we can tidy up the world so that there is equal justice for all at all times. All that we can hope to do is to struggle towards justice; to enable people to have a chance to create the sort of society they want; to place power as close to the individual as one can in each particular situation. Some communities will use their power well; others will use it badly. If one no longer relies on the federal government to intervene whenever things are going wrong, then some communities will work better than others. This is the inevitable consequence of an acceptance of local autonomy and decision-making.

There are far too many people who hope that communities will do an ideal job. Their arguments for enhanced local decision-making are based on the view that local human beings are far more perfect than those at the state and federal levels. I live in a local community. It is a community that I chose, but it is all too obvious that disagreements can flourish just as much in small towns as they do in big cities.

Another factor in the changing patterns of income distribution is the need to re-introduce barter or the exchange of goods without money. The industrial era moved more and more of the transactions in our society away from family, neighborhood, and community solidarity and toward money exchanges. We are now moving back to barter systems and this upsets the Internal Revenue Service, which cannot tax them as effectively as a money system.

Indeed, there is an enormous issue here—even the Internal Revenue Service does not claim a right to tax exchanges between husbands and wives and children. It does not claim a right to tax church suppers—when and where are the boundaries? Supposing a settlement house proclaimed itself a "family," would the Internal Revenue Service have a right to tax any of the exchanges that took place within that "family"? Could people babysit for each other as an expression of community solidarity with the currency being hours of work, rather than dollars?

This issue of barter is one that needs the attention of some of the best minds in our society. We need to look creatively and imaginatively at how barter can be introduced in ways that do not lead to legal challenges that disrupt the movement from the industrial era to the communications era. But, we must not forget that clashes are inevitable as a society moves into a new era Those people who believed in the agricultural era found the industrial era intolerable, and struggles continued for decades. Now our change from the industrial era to the communications era is being compressed into less than a lifetime, and each of us is having to change his/herself.

Let us look at two other critical aspects of lifestyle changes. One of them is the rapid movement toward neighborhood watch, block watch, and other similar programs. These programs have proved enormously effective in reducing the amount of crime in certain communities. Spokane, for example, has seen a dramatic drop in the crime rate as a result of the introduction of the program, and the police chief, like many others around the country, is more than willing to give credit to these programs. He sees them as a necessary, indeed essential, part of the way in which a community can be effectively policed.

The introduction of community and block watches is yet another way in which the neighborhood and the community must come together. Settlement houses are indeed communities; they have continued the tradition of solidarity for many years at times when it has been out of favor in the total culture. They now need to assert their leadership and to re-introduce some of the values and models that they know as well as any part of our society.

The other aspect is the shift from medicine to health. We have lived in a society in which we have expected to cure people by the use of medicine. We are now discovering that this is too expensive. Ten percent of the U.S. national budget is going toward medical care at the present time and the figure is still rising.

We are going to have to encourage people to stay healthy, but this, too, raises tough and difficult questions. What levels of social and community constraint are appropriate? Are we entitled to stop people from smoking when they want to and if so in what circumstance? Should we demand that people fasten seatbelts? And this in turn brings us back, of course, to the biological revolution.

In sum, we must recognize that we shall only be successful if we face the fact that we must change the whole ethic and values of our society in order to be successful.

Informatics-Based Mass Education for Solving Systems Problems in Cities, Industry, and the International Arena

by

Roberto Vacca

Modern large systems are organizations that include human beings (as operators and as users), machines, and infrastructures as well as communication and control apparatus. Postal systems, electrical power grids, telephone networks, complexes of banks, exchanges, financial institutions, and armies are examples of systems. A large city is another important example of a system. A nation-state is a system.

The efficiency of systems has always been fairly low, because it is very difficult to integrate and coordinate the different components of the system. The very structure of systems is often the cause of malfunctions and inefficiencies. In fact, most systems' structure has not been designed from scratch: it has proliferated for decades, or centuries, and construction was steered by different teams of experts at different times. The above is ancient history. It is also well known that the size of most systems in advanced countries has grown in the past to gigantic proportions. This has been due to population increase as well as to economic, scientific, and technological development, and it has compounded the difficulties of coordination and integration.

Increased size, on the other hand, produces entirely new effects as certain quantitative thresholds are exceeded. Redesign, retrofit, or management interventions assume, then, a counterintuitive character. The most appropriate appear superficially to be the worst and the intuitively more attractive ones may turn out to be quite disastrous. This is a new type of quandary in the long list of dilemmas that have forced humans to make decisions in conditions of uncertainty.

Roberto Vacca is a systems analyst in Rome, Italy. He is the author of The Coming Dark Age *(Doubleday, 1973).*

Decision-makers are often incapable of solving large problems because they have not even grasped the essential notion that systems exist; far less do they understand the systems approach or systems engineering methods. But many systems are linked together through many simultaneous channels and they interact, unleashing the effects of multiple feedback loops. Large quantities of energy are often part of the interactions, and the ultimate effects involve large masses of humans, Therefore a degradation in the level of service of systems—or even congestion—may have serious or even fatal consequences for entire populations.

Consequently, today's megalopolises, large technological systems, and economic, political, and military systems require competence levels of designers, operators, and users much higher than in the past. The competence needed also includes forecasting abilities. We know, however, that no generally valid forecasting procedures have been found so far. A knowledge of operations research, statistical methods, theory of dynamic systems, global models, econometric models, and physical models is certainly an asset for decision-makers. Nobody can claim, though, that the competent use of any of these tools—or all of them jointly—will guarantee optimal solutions to socio-economic, technological, or systemic problems.

The ultimate recipe for solving large systems problems is not known. But the risks don't go away; they tend to increase. Even a nonexhaustive list is impressive:

- Risk of nuclear war and holocaust.
- Overpopulation and hunger.
- Exhaustion of natural resources.
- Fragility of society caused by systems crises and social unrest.
- Energy crisis.
- Unemployment, economic depression, inflation, low productivity.
- Degradation and pollution of the environment.

Obviously, we cannot hope that a simple recipe could stave off all of these risks. Lacking the knowhow to concoct the ultimate systemic recipe, let us try to single out as many essential ingredients as we can. Putting them together will provide us with an empiric lower quality formula, which will have to suffice until better formulas are invented. I think that three of these vital ingredients are: mass diffusion of culture, organizational upgrading, and the theory of human cooperation.

Mass Diffusion of Culture

The population of a country can neither reach nor keep up a high level of economic prosperity unless its cultural level exceeds a given threshold. This includes, certainly, literacy for the large majority of the population. It does not include any depth of knowledge of the physical world except for scientists, technicians, designers, etc. The largest single factor of automatic demographic control has been growth above this first threshold. It was not planned consciously by statesmen or educators. It just happened, although it was made easier by improvements in schools and teaching methods.

But the cultural level reached in industrial countries is inadequate to ensure the continued existence and successful operation of large systems, whose complexity is proliferating. An upgrading of competence is needed for the designers and the operators of these systems—and most of us are aware of this. An upgrading of competence (in the sense of knowledge and understanding) is also needed for users—and this is hardly felt by anybody. User competence is essential to avoid congestion, to obtain appropriate use of systems, to avoid emergencies, and to minimize their ill effects. It is not enough to teach the public how to drive in urban areas or why life is easier if phone calls are kept short. The public should know that systems exist and learn how they operate. As many people as possible should form in their minds a model of the operation of the natural world and of the artificial man-made world. If this happens, the informed, responsible behavior of large masses of people will upgrade, in turn, the levels of service of systems.

At the same time, on the higher plateau of a better general cultural level, loftier peaks of competence will surge, represented by better scientists, technicians, and designers, who will improve system structures and—eventually—produce better recipes for overall systems optimization. The tools for a massive cultural upgrading already exist (radio and TV networks, audio and video recorders, computers, automated teaching aids). They have been used only marginally so far. Therefore we can trust that very impressive results will be obtained by stepped-up recourse to them. Many of us have learned vital abilities and acquired deep knowledge very economically—from a good teacher who used chalk and blackboard. Good teachers are rare. More should be trained. The exceptional ones, though, should not teach just to small classes. They should be recorded on video tape and should be shown to millions of students—even long after they are dead. This is a way to obtain high tuition quality at low cost.

Many of the abilities and knowledge bases needed in the advanced world are connected with informatics and computers. These tools, properly taught and used, do more than provide immediate advantages. They may extend the human intellect and make easier the acquisition of knowledge/understanding in many different sectors. Many of the disciplines that make up informatics are quite useful as training grounds for logical reasoning—a must for any activity aimed at understanding and improving any type of system.

Concrete steps are then:
- Implementation of radio and TV stations broadcasting round-

the-clock descriptions of the natural and the man-made world at all levels.

- Diffusion of computerized teaching aids: in schools, but also in arcades and in any public place.
- General improvements in traditional schools and teaching methods.
- Implementation of adult education programs and of comprehensive training programs for systems users.
- Continued advanced education for systems operators and designers, including general science and any discipline specially relevant for the type of system they are involved with.
- Continued advanced education of politicians in systems analysis, decision theory, informatics, logic, flowcharting.

Organizational Upgrading

It is well known that many criteria quite useful for upgrading organization structure, operation, and level of service have hardly ever been implemented with any degree of generality. Suffice it to mention two of these: time sharing (e.g., in communication and transportation systems) and real-time generation and diffusion to system users of information concerning the very system they are using. Since very little has been done in these areas, appropriate interventions are likely to yield considerable advantages.

The waste of human resources is quite often more grievous than the waste of natural physical resources. Rationally planned replacement of transportation with communication will produce large savings. The design of control systems for planning, monitoring, and reviewing human activities in large and small organizations—avoiding useless trips, canceling innumerable pointless meetings, aborting the generation of irrelevant written documents—can save much more valuable assets than any energy-saving drive.

The theory of social, political, and economic organizations is still in its infancy. Even the structure of market prices in mixed economies often appears to be governed by random phenomena. Price motivation and psychological motivation are two vital keys to the improvement of organization. Probably we shall be able to understand these keys only after a significant amount of culture has been massively diffused. It is to be expected that the ingredients for systemic upgrading interact with each other. Action items are:

- Establishing task forces for implementing overdue improvements (e.g., time sharing, information systems for systems users, etc.).
- Stepping up research in operational optimization of human resources.
- Establishing monitoring and control centers to avoid waste of human resources.

Theory of Human Cooperation

We don't need just competent operators and knowledgeable and well-informed users. It is also necessary that negative behavior (vandalism, egotism, greed) be avoided. Negative, possibly violent, behavior produces short-term benefits and long-term ruin. But conventional wisdom has taught for ages that violent behavior is advantageous, though reprehensible. This teaching is often not true, due to the increase in human and systemic density and to technological advances. An instance of high density forbidding any advantage sought with violent means is road traffic congestion. Even the most egotistic driver ends up damaging himself through tendentially violent behavior, An instance of technological advances making violence useless is given by nuclear arsenals. With mutual overkill capacity, it is well known that nuclear wars can only be lost, not won by either side.

Negotiations and decisions in commercial, political (national and international), and social contexts are bound to lead to dire loss if they are based on obsolete criteria. The modern theory of cooperation does not prove that altruistic behavior is always more advantageous in the long run. But it begins to explain the operation of positive and negative payoffs in certain simple competitive situations. Large efforts are necessary in order to build a cooperation theory really useful in social and political contexts. At present, a wide dissemination of elementary cooperation theory may already help to avoid the pitfalls, termed "social traps" by John Platt. Hopefully, in the future, larger conflicts also will become amenable to understanding based on advanced cooperation theory.

The action items here are:

• Stepping up research in cooperation theory, applying theoretical results to real-life situations in business, politics, social life, voting assemblies, etc.

• Disseminating and popularizing any useful results of the above research; of course, this can be done more efficiently within a large endeavor for the mass diffusion of culture.

In a high-density world whose complexity is soaring, no behavior can be ethical unless long-term consequences of actions are foreseen. Prevision ability has widely diffused knowledge/understanding as an obvious prerequisite. Also, correct prevision is impossible if random factors are too common in the environment. Organizational upgrading is a prerequisite to an orderly (non-random) environment. Finally, the behavior of social and economic actors can be foreseen only if they possess correct and timely information. The tenets and procedures of cooperation theory have to be widely known so that accurate predictions can be made of rational, constructive behavior of the majority of the public.

Early Warning Signals

Computers and the Future of Privacy

by

Robert L. Pisani

> *Every step you take,*
> *Every move you make,*
> *Every vow you break,*
> *Every smile you fake*
> *I'll be watching you.*

from *Every Step You Take* by the rock group The Police, the top popular song in the summer of 1983; copyright 1983 by A & M Records

In 1890, jurists Samuel Warren and Louis Brandeis, outraged by press reports on social events in the upper-class homes of Boston, wrote an article for the *Harvard Law Review* declaring the "right to be let alone."[1] Though they wrote the article in response to a specific series of events, they made it clear that the main support for their thesis lay in the common-law tradition stretching back over many centruies. Even then, Brandeis and Warren were bemoaning the "numerous mechanical devices [that] threaten to make good the prediction that 'what is whispered in the closet shall be proclaimed from the housetops.' "

Today, faced with government surveillance and the growing sophistication of data bases, the concept of privacy has evolved to reflect a different standard. The National Bureau of Standards defines "privacy" as "the right of individuals and organizations to control the collection, storage and dissemination of their information or information about themselves."[2] Clearly, this is much more than merely the traditional "right to be let alone."

While much has been made of the great benefits of the information revolution, little attention has been focused on the fundamental threat to our concept of privacy, both the "traditional" and "modern" type, that is inherent in the use of these technologies. Another area of great concern is the centralization of information that the federal government will attain as a result of the new technology, allowing power to flow into a single source. Senator Sam Ervin, who held some of the very first hearings on federal

---

Robert L. Pisani is executive director, International Legal Defense Counsel, Philadelphia, Pennsylvania. ©1984 by Robert L. Pisani.

data banks in 1970, expressed precisely this concern by noting that "the undisputed and unlimited possession of the resources to build and operate data banks on individuals, and to make decisions about people with the aid of computers and electronic data systems, is fast securing to executive branch officials a political power which the authors of the Constitution never meant any one group of men to have over all others. It threatens to unsettle forever the balance of power established by our Federal Constitution."[3]

Data-base linkage by both government and business is growing at such an alarming rate that it is outstripping our ability to comprehend or cope with the many privacy issues inherent in such systems. The inability to cope with the growth of these systems extends to all levels—intellectual, social, and legislative—and means that these systems will be in place for years before abuses are detected or before the full social impact of such systems can be evaluated. Of special concern is the explosive growth in surveillance technology, which the author believes will first be used to monitor "deviant" subgroups in which the government has an interest. Such surveillance has become significantly easier due to inadequate laws, recent court rulings, and technological advances.

To counter this threat, measures must be taken to protect privacy. The author discusses several such measures, including legislation, wholesale or partial dismantling of such systems, technological means to procure surveillance-free communications systems, public education, press involvement in the privacy issue, and the development of special-interest groups dedicated to the issue.

Data Bases

In the past, what was known about an individual was usually limited to his friends and acquaintances. Because most communities were self-sufficient, there was little need to rely on outside sources. Nor were there many to rely on—it has only been in the last century that the large government and corporate bureaucracies that we know of have come into existence. In 1816, for example, the total civilian employment of the federal government was 4,500 people, amounting to 0.05% of the total population—half of whom worked for the post office![4]

However, as time passed two things happened to change this relationship: (1) citizen need for services (health, education, etc.) increased; and (2) government and business began demanding more information to assess these needs. Not all of these "demands" were made as a result of citizen "needs," of course. The questions posed by the U.S. Census, for example, expanded almost exponentially in response to business demands to know more about marketing demographics. Whatever the relationship between citizen "need" and government "demand," American (and especially federal) involvement in formal governmental bureaucracies grew tremendously after the turn of the century. Because this relationship required that the government deal with virtually millions of anonymous people over an extended period of time, data bases were created to keep track of the complex relationships (taxation, Social Security, welfare, etc.) that were developing between citizen and state. The advent of the computer has enabled manipulation of these data and their linkage with other data bases.

Most of us do not realize that we leave a "paper trail" of our lives almost everywhere we go. Imagine if all the receipts we received, all the credit-card transactions, doctor's and dentist's visits, insurance policies, magazine and book club subscriptions, memberships in organizations, even a list of the type of food we bought, were available for inspection at a central source. Such a "paper trail" would enable the government to form a detailed composite of the type of person we are, permitting a fairly accurate determination of our personal tastes and lifestyle, including our health, where we like to travel, what we like to read or eat, our political beliefs, perhaps even our thoughts themselves.

Access to this kind of information would be invaluable to corporations seeking to gain marketing data on certain segments of the population, but it has even greater value to a government that may seek to keep track of real or potential "deviants" such as anti-nuclear protesters, homosexuals, those convicted of a crime, marijuana users, members of minority political groups, or anyone else the government views as a threat to either itself or "society."

Moreover, the growing sophistication of commercial data banks can hardly be viewed as a "benign" development. By way of example, consider that immense corporate data banks exist in the following areas:

Credit. The five largest credit-reporting companies in the United States maintain 150 million individual credit records in their computers, including an individual's marital status, place of work, salary, other sources of income, arrest records, lawsuits, etc.[5] The largest of these companies, Equifax, Inc., maintains a staff of 13,000 employees who work out of 1,800 offices in the United States and Canada and who produce over 25 million credit reports a year. It sells this information to 62,000 customers, including the federal government. Equifax grosses about one-third of a billion dollars each year from the sale of credit reports.[6]

Financial transactions. The records of financial transactions are becoming increasingly easier to access due to the use of Electronic Funds Transfer (EFT). EFT can make it considerably easier to disclose financial information to third parties and increase government or private surveillance of an individual and his or her activities. The inner workings of such systems are virtually invisible to customers, who have no way of knowing what information they contain and who is gaining access to the information. Moreover, there is almost no legislation protecting dissemination to third-party sources, nor requiring the institution to divulge that it is even disseminating such information. In a report on EFTs published in 1981, the U.S. Office of Technology Assessment concluded that:

> With increased use of EFT there will be a large number of points at which traditional norms of privacy could be invaded. More EFT terminals will be online, making electronic surveillance a more credible possibility. Single-statement reporting of all kinds of financial transactions will become common; more data will be aggregated and thus easier to access. At the same time, there could be broader and swifter dissemination of inaccurate data. Even if customer correction of data is facilitated, it will be more difficult for corrections to catch up with and replace faulty information[7]

Health records. Two out of three Americans have life insurance, nine out of ten working Americans are covered by individual or group health insurance policies. Americans make more than 1 billion visits a year to the doctor; millions visit hospitals each year.[8] The widespread availability of computerized health records makes unauthorized dissemination a growing threat. A doctor's ethical obligation not to disclose details of his patients' health is daily compromised by the demands of health institutions, insurance agencies, and government bureaucracies, all of whom regard detailed information on a patient's history as essential to the maintenance of their information system. As with EFTs, centralization of health records promotes greater ease of access. Health-insurance agencies have recently created a single computerized clearinghouse to process insurance claims. Called the National Electronic Information Corporation (NEIC), it will process up to 85% of all the claims handled by commercial insurance companies through a single computer.[9]

These three areas are only representative of the group as a whole. Other massive data banks are maintained by mailing list companies, employers, other insurance companies, investigative reporting agencies, educational institutions, cable companies, and others. All of this information on individuals is available on computers—computers that are simply waiting to be linked together.

The fact that so much information on individuals is available at a single source leaves the system wide open to abuses. Revelations of such records can intimidate, harass, and embarrass certain individuals if revealed at the right time. So pervasive is the public's fear about disclosure that the National Institute of Mental Health estimates that 15% of all Americans who have medical insurance and are undergoing mental therapy pay for therapy out of their own pocket.[10] That these fears are well-grounded would seem to be confirmed by the experience of Senator Thomas Eagleton, whose vice-presidential nomination was aborted when it was revealed that he had had therapy some years before.

Imagine if the manipulation capability inherent in EFTs were made legally available to government agencies such as the IRS. If the agency felt that you owed it money, why should it not be authorized to remove the money from your account using EFT, with or without your permission? If this sounds unlikely, bear in mind that parents who have reneged on their child-support agreement are now having this money removed automatically from the money that they receive from the IRS on their tax return. In 1982, the IRS used its computers to prevent the distribution of $168 million in refunds scheduled to go to 275,479 delinquent parents.[11] It does not require a great leap of imagination or technology to allow the IRS or any other governmental agency direct access to your account.

Even data bases containing what may seem like "benign" information can be used for questionable purposes. Consider two "up and coming" services that will, as an aside from their primary purpose, create a whole new series of "lifestyle" data banks:

Home banking. New York's Chemical Bank and the Knight-Ridder newspaper chain recently unveiled their home banking systems, known as Pronto and Viewtron, respectively.[12] Viewtron is the more sophisticated of the two, allowing not only home banking but also the ability to read help-wanted ads, order merchandise, check movie and sports schedules, find an airline flight, and more.

Videotex. Two-way interactive cable television, despite a slow start, is taking off. Such systems allow the subscribers to vote in opinion surveys, order products, choose topics of conversation, and in general to reveal important information on a customer's personal beliefs and preferences to the company. In addition, sophisticated videotex systems will soon be available via most popular home computers. IBM, CBS, and Sears recently announced a joint venture to have such a system commercially available within a year.[13]

Because both of these systems offer a variety of services in different areas, they are capable of creating new, more broadly based data systems that reveal a great deal about the subscriber's general lifestyle, a topic of intense interest to thousands of service-oriented businesses as well as a government intent on suppressing or monitoring select groups leading a certain lifestyle. For example, Warner-Amex's Qube interactive cable system in Columbus, Ohio, has a computer that "sweeps" the system every six seconds to determine, among other things, whether the set is on, what channel is being watched, what political opinions customers are expressing or merchandise they are ordering through their response buttons.[14]

Governments, too, can be intensely interested in this type of information. Consider the fact that the IRS is now advertising in business publications for "lifestyle" mailing lists that it can rent. The purpose? To compare tax returns with the lists to see if tax payers are paying taxes commensurate with their lifestyle.[15] The IRS recently obtained a computerized list of the estimated incomes of 2 million American households in Brooklyn, Wisconsin, Indiana, and Nevada and will be matching that list against a list of people who filed income tax returns for the tax year 1982.[16] Thus, a seemingly harmless practice such as a lifestyle data compilation can be turned into a surveillance instrument in the proper hands.

In addition, the creation of such "lifestyle" data bases can be so important to service-oriented industries such as Warner Communications and American Express that one could speculate that the primary purpose of owning such systems is to develop "lifestyle" mailing lists to use to market a company's other products, or to sell such data to others.[17] As *Privacy Journal* editor Robert Ellis Smith has remarked: "A single two-way cable television service in a mid-American community can be a gold mine of marketing information. . . . even if the company itself never produces a profit."[18] Even though three states—California, Illinois, and Wisconsin— have laws prohibiting dissemination of information to third-party sources, this apparently does not prevent the parent corporation from using the information as it wishes. [19]

Furthermore, although these corporate data bases are proliferating at an alarming rate, recent court cases have indicated that the Fourth Amendment does not extend to third-party holders of information such as insurance companies and credit agencies.[20] The U.S. government may thus have access to most of these third-party data bases without a warrant and without the need to notify the individual that such an investigation is occurring.

Even more extensive than the corporate data bases are those maintained by the government, especially the federal government. Though there are many, I will concentrate for the moment on criminal data bases, which I consider to be among the most insidious because of the effect that dissemination of these data can have.

The FBI has two large data bases: the Identification Division and the National Crime Information Center (NCIC). The Identification Division maintains the fingerprints of over 63 million people, fewer than half (24 million) of whom have a criminal record.[21] NCIC is a computerized network designed to link all the individuals who work with the country's 57,000 different federal, state, and local criminal-justice agencies.[22] The ostensive purpose of NCIC is to increase the efficiency of law-enforcement agencies by facilitating exchange of information.

The Attorney General's Task Force on Violent Crime has recommended that the federal government create a new data-base system called the Interstate Identification Index (III) that would allow the user to interact with all the other computers of criminal-justice agencies linked with the system, greatly expanding the data base of the system as a whole.

A police officer in a patrol car will thus have the entire FBI files at his disposal at any time. While a system that would inform a police officer about a potentially violent arrestee may seem appealing at first, the type of information transmitted through such a system should give us pause. There are two concerns here: (1) Is the information transmitted relevant information for the arresting officer to have? and (2) Will it really help the police improve the efficiency of their work?

The argument that such a system will protect police from violent professional criminals by giving them prior knowledge of their behavior might have merit if the whole concept of the violent criminal were not so terribly overblown. Most arrests are made at the local level and under circumstances that a district attorney can check by talking to the arresting officer. No such check could exist in this nationwide hookup. In addition, we are talking about *arrests,* not *convictions.* A large percentage of arrests (30 to 40%, according to some) are dismissed before coming to trial. In addition, many of the records in which an arrest is noted do not make clear what the final disposition of the case was. A recent Office of Technology Assessment (OTA) report noted that federal courts have found violations of civil and constitutional rights regarding the completeness or accuracy of criminal-justice records, particularly when arrest-only information is used in minority employment decisions and when arrest information without disposition information is used in criminal-justice decisions such as setting bail.[23] The same study noted that, on the average, only 66% of the files reported what the final disposition of the case was.[24] Such inaccuracies have not gone entirely unnoticed; the governor of Illinois, for example, recently signed a Uniform Disposition Reporting Law to require state law enforcement agencies to include the disposition of each case in their criminal records.[25]

In addition, there are questions that must be raised as to whether it is relevant for an officer in San Diego to know that an individual was arrested in Portland for public drunkenness 10 years ago. Since the vast majority of all crimes are misdemeanors, this is an important question, since the existence of any kind of previous record may dispose an officer to arrest where he otherwise would have not. In the words of David Burnham, "Do we want the police making arrests for *current* activities based partly on the basis of past behavior?"[26]

Of equal importance with the questions of how much information the government collects is how much information the government disseminates and what percentage of that information is accurate. In a 1982 study, the OTA found that about one-fifth of the FBI Identification Division and NCIC arrest records were inaccurate when compared with charging, disposition, and/or sentencing information in local records.[27] The 50 states alone handed out 10.1 million records in 1978, with 2 million going to private corporations and government agencies not part of the system itself. The OTA report noted that, as of mid-1981, 27 states authorized dissemination of criminal-justice records to private-sector organizations and individuals.[28] The same report noted that, as of 1979, an estimated 36 million living U.S. citizens had criminal history records held by federal, state, and/or local repositories.[29] With millions of employers seeking this type of information, much of which appears to be inaccurate, there is a very real possibility that we are creating a permanent class of unemployed or underemployed individuals with criminal records, given the obvious reluctance of employers to hire people with such records.

Despite these concerns, the FBI is continuing to test and refine the III system. Eventually, the system will be completely computerized and will consist of the NCIC along with the FBI Automated Identification Division (AIDS), which maintains fingerprint files, the National Law Enforcement Telecommunications System (NLETS, an interstate electronic switching system), participating state files, and state and local telecommunications networks.[30]

The NCIC, with all its inaccuracies and erroneous information, is tied into a much larger computer system, the El Paso Information Center (EPIC). EPIC originally began as a liaison system between the Drug Enforcement Administration (DEA) and the Immigration and Naturalization Service (INS). It grew rapidly and today includes data not only from the DEA and INS but also from the Coast Guard, the Customs Service, the Bureau of Alcohol, Tobacco, and Firearms, the Federal Aviation Administration, the U.S. Marshals Service, and the FBI. A recent Progress and Activity Report from EPIC reads like an advertisement for the Center, noting that "today EPIC is a full-service intelligence center, providing round-the-clock operational support and intelligence on smuggling of drugs, aliens, and weapons."[31] EPIC contains the names of millions of individuals, boats, and planes.

Another organization, the Internal Revenue Service, has also proposed making its data base easier to access. The IRS proposed in 1976 that it be given authority to create a new computer system entitled the Tax Administrative System (TAS), a $1 billion system that according to the Office of Technology Assessment would have allowed the IRS to decentralize IRS files, making them instantaneously available to those who share and use federal tax information. Most ominously of all, it would have allowed the IRS to significantly increase its intelligence-gathering capabilities by greatly increasing the amount of information the system could hold, thus allowing the IRS to begin keeping information of a non-tax type. The threat this poses for civil liberties and its potential for harassment of "deviate" subgroups was clear enough that the Carter administration scuttled the project in 1978.[32]

However, the IRS has continued to seek to expand its data base by gaining access to local governmental data banks. It has recently attempted to establish electronic links with the computers of 80 counties in Texas in an effort to gain access to information on voter registration, property taxes, and automobile ownership.[33] Though the IRS claimed that it would use such information only to track down individuals who had failed to pay their taxes, the move has been strongly opposed by local and state officials as well as by civil rights groups on the grounds that such information could be used to compile a huge centralized data base and that the Privacy Act provides that information collected by the government for one purpose will not be used for another without the individual's permission.

What is to prevent the government from taking the information gleaned from these data banks and applying it to other projects that lack specific legislative and even societal approval? Practically nothing, given the fact that the Privacy Act's many "external-disclosure" clauses, including the "routine use" provision,[34] have been so broadly interpreted that it allows dissemination for practically any reason; witness the recent debate over "computer matching" to detect fraud.[35] And since it is almost a principle of bureaucracy that organizations constantly seek to expand their power, we must assume that they will use it for other purposes.

Indeed, there is ample evidence already that the NCIC is being expanded far beyond its original purpose. The NCIC's Policy Board recently began discussing the expansion of the system to include information about people who are considered "suspicious" but are not wanted for crimes.[36] The new guidelines would allow information to be stored on whether an individual was *thought* to be involved in organized crime or terrorism, or was a "known associate" of someone who had been convicted of "possession for sale, sale, or traffic in narcotics." The path would thus be left open to monitor drug users and other "suspicious" people. This recommendation comes only six months after the Bureau agreed to work with the Secret Service to include the names of individuals whom the Service decides might represent a danger to the president or other people it guards.[37] Perhaps most importantly, the FBI does not consider that the expansion of the NCIC to include such "suspicious" persons would require Congressional approval.[38]

All of these government agencies claim, of course, that their machines are designed for a purely "neutral" purpose, i.e., to improve efficiency. Since efficiency is not in itself political, fears that an authoritarian government will develop as a result of these "improvements" is unfounded.

This argument merely serves to confuse the means with the end. In the words of James B. Rule: "Incremental developments over a long period are bound to bring about qualitative change. These changes will amount to new kinds of social relations between central investigations and 'private' citizens. The question is, What social interests are the new systems most apt to serve?"[39] Thus, a slavish, mindless devotion to efficiency as an end in itself serves only to obscure the more fundamental issues underlying the "efficiency criterion," to wit, at what point does efficiency become too much of a good thing? Does efficiency always serve a benevolent end? The answer to this question, of course, depends on who is doing the asking, but one look at the issue of government surveillance should cast reasonable doubt on the maxim of "efficiency at all cost."

Government Surveillance

The growing sophistication of governmental surveillance programs is of even greater concern than that of corporate and government data-base linkage. Surveillance itself, of course, is not a new development: Abraham Lincoln's administration successfully monitored telegraph communications during the early months of the Civil War.[40] The U.S. Army has kept information on potential dissidents for many years going back to WWI. By the late 1960s, it had an estimated 100,000 people under surveillance, most of them protesters against the war in Vietnam.[41]

During this time, the CIA also conducted Operation CHAOS and Project RESISTANCE. Though CHAOS was ostensibly designed to investigate foreign influences on domestic dissent, in practice that mandate was exceeded and much of the surveillance was purely domestic. Project RESISTANCE was a CIA study of dissident groups in the U.S. that developed an index of approximately 12,600-16,000 names.[42]

What is new is the technology that is now becoming available for surveillance and the growing power of the executive branch's intelligence agencies. President Reagan's Executive Order in December 1981 allowing the CIA to conduct covert operations in the U.S.A., despite his claim that these new powers would not include the right to investigate the domestic activities of U.S. citizens or corporations, provoked a howl of concern from many citizen organizations, including religious groups.

Even local police organizations got into the surveillance business in the 1960s. The Los Angeles Police Department, for example, established a Public Disorder Intelligence Division that kept track of thousands of individuals and organizations between 1971 and 1983. The extent of the surveillance has prompted an ACLU lawsuit against the LAPD.[43]

Despite the tremendous increase in the power of the CIA, its role in the surveillance business is dwarfed by that of the National

Security Agency (NSA). To this day, there is no statutory law defining the NSA or its work. It was created by President Truman in 1952 by an Executive Order whose contents remain a secret. As of 1975, the NSA had an estimated 25,000 employees and a budget of $1.2 billion.[44] It has two goals—offensive and defensive. First, it seeks out relevant foreign intelligence by intercepting electronic and written communication. Second, it seeks to protect information bearing on the national security of the United States. To accomplish this goal, the NSA employs sophisticated, state-of-the-art surveillance technology, including satellites, aircraft, sea vessels, and some 2,000 manned interception posts at fixed locations all over the world. All of this information is fed into NSA headquarters in Fort Meade, Maryland, where it is analyzed by computers.[45]

As part of its functions, the NSA monitors incoming and outgoing international electronic communications made from or to the United States. However, interception of international telephone and telegraph messages had been going on even before the NSA was created. In 1948, the U.S. Communications Intelligence Board issued a top-secret directive stating in part that: "Orders, directives, policies or recommendations of any authority of the Executive Branch relating to the collection. . . . of intelligence shall not be applicable to Communications Intelligence activities, unless specifically so stated. . . . "[46] The Communications Intelligence (COMINT) community thus exempted itself from any ban on electronic surveillance almost from the beginning, despite the existence of the Communications Act of 1934, which specifically forbade eavesdropping.

Since 1946, the NSA and its predecessors have conducted Operation Shamrock, whereby *all* the incoming and outgoing commercial and private cable traffic of Western Union, ITT, and RCA was read on a daily basis.[47] The NSA is also permitted to monitor international phone calls of U.S. citizens. Their computer system enables them to monitor 54,000 telephone calls and cable messages in the U.S. simultaneously.[48]

However, the NSA rarely initiates surveillance by itself, relying instead on requests from the CIA, the FBI, the Defense Department, and the Secret Service.[49] To accomplish this goal, the NSA creates "watchlists"—lists of words and phrases designed to identify communications of intelligence interest. Selected communication spectrums are then scanned by NSA computers in search of watchlists entries; any relevant information so obtained is selected for further analysis and then disseminated to the appropriate agencies.[50]

Despite the substantial Fourth Amendment and Privacy Act considerations inherent in the dissemination of such reports to other governmental agencies, the U.S. Court of Appeals for the Sixth District ruled in *Jabara v. Webster* that such agencies do not require a warrant in order to obtain information from the

NSA.[51]

The *Jabara* case is an instructive one that illustrates the fragility of the wiretapping laws. Abdeen Jabara, a Michigan lawyer who was active representing Arab-American citizens and alien residents, was targeted for surveillance by the FBI in 1967. At that time, the FBI asked the NSA to supply any information on Jabara, who traveled extensively in the Mideast. Jabara was never accused of a crime, and the government has admitted that they did not believe he was involved in any criminal activity. The NSA did supply information to the FBI, relating to phone conversations that Jabara had made, and then disseminated the information to 17 other law-enforcement agencies. The court, in ruling that the NSA may disseminate such information to law-enforcement agencies without a warrant, essentially left the NSA free to act as a clearinghouse for intelligence information for virtually all law-enforcement agencies. Law-enforcement agencies frustrated by legal constraints can now simply go to the NSA, and they are apparently free to use any information so obtained in court.

Nor is Jabara an isolated example; hearings held in the mid-1970s revealed that the FBI and Secret Service had both asked the NSA to supply information on 1,200 Americans whom they suspected were involved in civil and anti-war demonstrations.[52] In testimony before the Senate, former NSA Director General Lew Allen estimated that the Agency had issued about 3,900 reports to other domestic U.S. spy agencies concerning approximately 1,680 U.S. citizens who had engaged in international phone conversations.[53]

Even the ability to litigate a claim that one's Fourth Amendment rights have been violated by the NSA is in doubt. In *Halkin v. Helms,* the Court of Appeals for the District of Columbia circuit ruled that *the mere admission or denial of acquisition of information about individuals by the NSA was a state secret.*[54] The Vietnam protesters who filed the suit were thus denied the right even to know if they had been part of a watchlist. A dissenting judge in the case noted that upholding the state-secret privilege in the case "precludes all judicial scrutiny of the signals intelligence operations of the NSA, regardless of the degree to which such activity invades the protections of the Fourth Amendment."[55]

The "right" of the NSA to conduct warrantless surveillance of international communications was supposedly grounded in the Constitutional right of the president to control the conduct of foreign affairs.[56] Such surveillance generated intense criticism, however, and in response Congress passed the Foreign Intelligence Surveillance Act of 1978.[57] The Act limits electronic surveillance of U.S. citizens and resident aliens in the United States to situations where there is probable cause to believe that the target of the communications is a foreign power or an agent of a foreign power, and requires that such surveillance be conducted pursuant to a warrant issued by special judges appointed by the Chief Justice.

While attractive on the surface, the FISA statute does not offer as many reforms as would appear. What it does do is prevent the specific targeting by name of an American citizen without a warrant. However, the FISA court has never once denied a warrant to the government to conduct such surveillance.[58] Moreover, such requirements exist only so long as the American citizen is in the United States. Once the citizen is outside the U.S., the provisions of the FISA statute do not apply and the NSA is free to monitor U.S. citizens in any way it wishes. In addition, the FISA statute in no way prevents general monitoring by the NSA; it is free to monitor every telephone call and message entering or leaving the country on a random basis, so long as it is done by microwave interception.[59]

Additionally, concern has been expressed over the differences between the FISA and federal Title III wiretapping laws,[60] especially over disclosure of the surveillance application before the evidence may be used (required under Title III, discretionary under FISA), the probable cause standard required (less precise under FISA than under Title III), and the method by which the legality of the surveillance can be challenged (an adversary hearing is held under Title III, an *in camera, ex parte* determination is made under FISA when national security interests are declared in danger).[61] While Congress, in enacting FISA, clearly refused to recognize any inherent power of the Executive to conduct warrantless national security surveillance, a recent court decision, *United States v. Falvey,*[62] left open the possibility of legal warrantless national security surveillance outside of FISA.

Does the NSA monitor conversations between U.S. citizens in the United States? General Allen himself, when asked by Senator Richard Schweiker if the Agency had the capability to monitor domestic conversations of Americans, replied that "such a thing is technically possible."[63] Although this is "technically" forbidden under the Foreign Intelligence Surveillance Act, there is no prohibition preventing agents of other governments, such as the British Government Communications Headquarters (GCHQ), from intercepting and disseminating such information.[64]

By way of addendum, it should be noted that signals intelligence operations in the United States are not just limited to the U.S. and its allies; the Russians have been monitoring phone calls in this country, especially those in and around Washington, for many years.[65] In fact, the Russians have one of the prime spots in Washington for monitoring; their Embassy on Tunlaw Road in the Capital sits on one of the highest hills in the city and directly in the line of a number of important microwave beams.

Moreover, this type of monitoring will only become easier thanks to direct data-base linkage; in 1983, the NSA planned to put into operation an enormous worldwide computer network, code named Platform, that will tie together 52 separate computer systems around the world.[66] Among the participants will be GCHQ, making direct communication and information dissemination even easier.

What little is known about the NSA reveals a frightening methodology. Not only does it seek to gather any kind of information that even remotely can affect "national security interests" but it actively seeks to prevent Americans from disseminating new devices or techniques to protect their privacy or expand technical know-how. Nowhere is this more obvious than the NSA's involvement in encryption devices designed for "secure" (read: "surveillance-free") electronic communications.

As corporate awareness of the fragility of conventional means of communications such as phone lines has grown, there has been a corresponding increase in private research into encryption devices that could encode electronic data in a form that would be indecipherable to anyone who did not possess such devices.

The NSA views such developments with a suspicious eye, and has consistently sought to either stop such private research altogether or co-opt it by taking over the research itself. However, the scientific community has reacted suspiciously to attempts by the NSA to take over private research. One of the most outspoken critics of the NSA has been George Davida, a professor of electrical engineering and computer science at the University of Wisconsin, who developed an encryption device known as a "stream" cipher system. When he applied for a patent for the device in 1977, he was issued a secrecy order by the Commerce Department at the request of the NSA. The order was later rescinded only after Davida succeeded in focusing attention on the NSA's censorship of academic research. In the words of Carl Nicolai, an inventor who developed a new type of voice scrambler and who had similar problems with the NSA, "They've been bugging people's telephones for years and now someone comes along with a device that makes this a little harder to do and they oppose this under the guise of national security."[67]

Without the use of private encryption devices, it will only become easier for the government to monitor electronic activities such as phone conversations. The chances are good that within the next five years most of the voice communications in this country will be converted from analog technology, where sound is carried by waves of electricity, to digital technology, where sound is converted into electronic pulses.[68] This conversion process, known as the Integrated Services Digital Network (ISDN), will enable the intelligence agencies to have access to vast new amounts of information, since such signals can be run through a computer that can electronically "scan" the signals for key words. Due to the wording of the 1968 federal wiretapping law, the interception of such digital signals by computers is not illegal under current law.[69]

Given that the NSA now has a relatively free hand in gathering information for itself and other intelligence agencies, we can only assume that technical limitations are the last barriers preventing near total acquisition of information the NSA deems necessary to accomplish its job. For example, much speculation is currently under way as to whether the Agency has developed a computer that can automatically "scan" human voices and pick out key words and phrases it has been programmed to recognize. Such a computer would be a tremendous technological advance and would enable mass monitoring on a level undreamed of previously. According to author Ford Rowan, voiceprints can already be computerized so that the computer can spot key individuals.[70] When the computer recognizes the voice of a person on its watchlist, a copy of the message can be produced for analysis.

The potential that such devices can have for domestic law enforcement cannot be overlooked. Today, even the simplest wiretapping operations are highly labor-intensive, requiring hundreds of hours of monitoring. Even given such labor intensiveness, the number of surveillance orders issued by the Reagan administration increased nearly 280% between January 1981 and September 1982; an increase was also registered with regard to the Foreign Intelligence Surveillance Act (FISA) warrants.[71] In 1981, 589 wiretaps were authorized under state and federal laws, excluding FISA warrants. While this may not seem like an excessive number at first, it becomes a much larger one when we discover that *the voices of 50,000 persons were overheard by those 589 wiretaps.*[72] Moreover, even though most of those whose conversations were intercepted are not suspected of any criminal wrongdoing, the mere fact that they called a tapped line may be enough to land them in yet another of the FBI's computers, the Electronic Surveillance Index (ELSUR). ELSUR cross-references names of persons mentioned in wiretaps and keeps a running "record" of such persons, even if no criminal activity is suspected.[73]

The average citizen, when faced with such overwhelming technical material, may well throw up his hands in despair and forget about trying to understand what is happening. However, a way out of the intellectual quagmire is suggested by discarding such technical information and merely trying to discern the logical outcome of such surveillance efforts. Or, more to the point, the citizen should ask, "What is the ultimate goal of a modern intelligence agency such as the NSA?" Any answer to such a question must clearly be tentative, but we can speculate by offering a modernized theory of intelligence gathering. Under this theory, widespread social upheavals around the world have forced intelligence agencies to change the nature of their security collection apparatus, which prior to this time had concentrated on tracking a few individuals and trends on a macro level. Such an approach did not work well (witness the CIA's failure to forewarn of the collapse of the Shah's regime), and in response to the question "How can we best predict future political, social, and economic changes around the world in order to influence events and protect our interests?" a new approach evolves concentrating not just on information of obvious intelligence interest but also on hundreds of thousands of events on a micro level, such as newspaper articles, social and political gatherings, even private conversations—what might collectively be referred to as "microintelligence." Such intelligence may not have much value individually but when considered with millions of other pieces of information and in a synergistic fashion begins to make sense in terms of discerning trends, patterns, and modes of possible action on a macropolitical level.

What I am describing is not merely fanciful speculation; it has practical applications on many different levels. For example, James Danowski, a university-based communications researcher, has developed computer programs that analyze the telephone-traffic patterns inside an organization and can yield an accurate picture of who the leaders are and how they function—just from analyzing dialing information. Seemingly innocuous actions, such as misdialing calls, can reveal information about an individual's state of mind. Danowski told *InfoWorld* that his techniques can be applied to groups of phones in a ghetto or student community, thus making invisible social networks visible and identifying key members of a community.[74] Such methodologies can be employed on a much larger, i.e., societal, scale, though they would require correspondingly greater amounts of information.

If we accept the premise of the need for the collection of such "microintelligence," and that seemingly innocuous or disconnected pieces of information can attain great importance when considered as parts of the whole, then we must conclude that the goal of the modern intelligence agency is *total awareness of all events*. As such, the apparatus of the intelligence agencies must be directed toward the attainment of that goal. The means required to attain the goal are: 1) massive computer capabilities, and 2) unrelenting surveillance of individuals and organizations who may not themselves be specific targets but are necessary to understanding developments within the system as a whole. This goal has not yet been attained; however it is technologically within their grasp. Once the technology is firmly in place, the will to attain the goal is undeniably present.

We can assume that as more sophisticated technology is introduced and the ease with which electronic surveillance can be accomplished is increased, the surveillance of citizens, whether it be for "foreign intelligence," "national security," "law enforcement," or whatever, will greatly increase. If experience is our guide, the parameters under which such surveillance is conducted will be expanded (or, alternately, the definition of "national security" or "law enforcement" will be expanded) until virtually the entire population is under some form of surveillance.

While the use of such technology in a democratic society such as the United States is cause for concern, its use in a non-democratic or authoritarian society can be devastating. SAVAK, the Shah of Iran's secret police, used telephone technology developed by Stanford Technology Corporation to monitor thousands of telephone conversations and to keep track of dissidents within Iran.[75] The technology employed was primitive compared to what is available today. In the hands of an authoritarian leader without the constraints of a Bill of Rights, such surveillance could be used to keep track of the movements of the entire population, which would have no legal recourse to prevent such actions.

Deviance and Mass Monitoring

It seems clear that data-base linkage and the advances in the technology of surveillance will permit greatly increased monitoring of citizens by the government. While certain types of monitoring can be beneficial for the citizen when services are provided (e.g., education, health care, etc.), I am primarily concerned with the negative impact that monitoring can have on individuals or groups by whom the government feels threatened. Such groups can include anti-nuclear or anti-war activists, civil rights demonstrators, socialists, draft protesters, labor union organizers, marijuana users, homosexuals, women's rights groups, John Birchers, Hare Krishnas, Iranians, fundamentalist Christians, Scientologists, and others. Surveillance techniques are now becoming so efficient that such "deviant" groups are at a special risk of privacy invasion, and we should not doubt the will of the government in its desire to monitor such groups. As James Rule has written: "When a given form of deviant behavior offends particularly powerful interests, the efforts to seek out information on its possible correlates can become intense."[76]

Surveillance is also capable of influencing one's actions independently of anything done with the information itself. Judge Abner Mikva, a former member of the House of Representatives from Illinois and now a judge for the U.S. Court of Appeals for the District of Columbia Circuit, was himself one of the subjects of the Army's surveillance program in the 1960s. In testimony before the U.S. Senate in December 1971, he described how surveillance could corrupt the electoral process by tainting those under surveillance:

> The scenario might go like this. Those who speak out strongly in opposition to those in power are subjected to precautionary surveillance by the military. Constituents learn that their elected representative is under surveillance. The inference is made, either explicitly or implicitly, that he must be doing something wrong or at least questionable, and that suspicion will be evident in the next election results. After all, who wants to be represented by a man who is so disreputable

that the Army feels that the national security requires that his activities be monitored?[77]

Despite the enormous difficulty in monitoring the financial activity of every American, the IRS manages a remarkably high degree of conformity with the tax laws because it has managed to project an omnipresent image to the American public. *Fear* keeps us paying our taxes, fear that the IRS would somehow know if we cheated.

Imagine now if the same omnipresence that the IRS manages to project with regard to our finances was available to all the other branches of the federal bureaucracy with regard to our other activities. Imagine if every time we signed a petition, or joined an organization whose goals were antithetical to those of the government, or attended a rally, or ordered a subscription to a periodical, these acts were recorded and noted by the government. Imagine further if we were *aware* that the government was aware of all our actions. There is no doubt that many people would voice their opinions or participate in dissent only if they could assume a reasonable expectation of privacy. Absent such an expectation, many would simply choose not to participate.

Kent Greenawalt, a professor at Columbia University and a former member of the Privacy Protection Study Commission, discussed some of the possible effects that surveillance could have on "deviant" members of society:

> If there is increased surveillance and disclosure and it is not offset by greater tolerance, the casualties of modern society are likely to increase as fewer misfits and past wrongdoers are able to find jobs and fruitful associations. The knowledge that one cannot discard one's past, that advancement in society depends heavily on a good record, will create considerable pressure for conformist actions. Many people will try harder than they do now to keep their records clean, avoid controversy or "deviant" actions, whatever their private views or inclination. Diversity and social vitality is almost certain to suffer, and in the long run independent private thoughts will be reduced.[78]

Should large segments of the public ever come to widely believe that the government and corporations are storing information on them to be used to their detriment, this fact could have enormous implications for the manner in which the public deals with these bureaucracies. Increased distrust, coupled with a greater inclination to refuse requests for information, could become commonplace. Such distrust may, however, prove to be a blessing in disguise, as it would create a huge pool of disaffected consumers. Competitive market pressures would force the creation of new companies to cater to this disaffected group, perhaps with the promise that their privacy would be observed absolutely within the bounds of the law and that full disclosure would be made to their customers if they were required to divulge such information.

The public, however, would have less recourse with regard to government bureaucracies, which of necessity possess a monopoly on certain types of services. It can, of course, lobby for legislative change, but it is then faced with three difficulties: (1) Given the enormous increase in the ability of the government to handle constituent requests for services due to the computer, does the legislative branch possess the political will to mandate that less information should be demanded, that data-base linkages should be halted; (2) Is the public prepared to accept any possible reduction of services that this might entail; and (3) Can every problem concerning dissemination or collection of information be cured by legislative fiat? For example, what political and technical difficulties are presented by the difficulty in monitoring an enormous intelligence agency such as the NSA that is itself shrouded in secrecy?

While it is possible to concede that it is unlikely that we are headed toward the same kind of totalitarian system as practiced by Stalin, it is possible to make a plausible argument that subtler forms of tyranny, perhaps more properly labeled an "informational tyranny," revolving around the government's total access to the facts of an individual's life, may well be developing.

Under this thesis, the relevant question becomes, How much will the government and the corporations ultimately know about each of us, and to what use will they put this information? I believe that the technology now exists to enable the government to know as much as it wants to know about each and every one of us. I further believe that this knowledge will be used not only to "improve efficiency" but also to harass, intimidate, and force a certain type of behavior on each of us that we may not have engaged in otherwise.

Arguments that such an "informational tyranny" will not occur usually revolve around the thesis that a new set of checks and balances is developing to counter the government's growing power. Whenever this theory is advanced, it is usually explained by noting that everyone will have their own computers shortly and this will give individuals rough parity with the government and the corporations, i.e., we will all be able to spy on each other and everyone will enjoy equal surveillance under the law. However, my concerns over privacy will not be assuaged by allowing citizens access to government data banks. Secondly, it is obvious that we will not all enjoy equal access to the same data bases, even if we do have computers. Hardware is not software, and the recent publicity surrounding computer break-ins by technological whiz-kids should not deceive us into thinking that this represents a "check" to government excess. What is important is *power* (read: "access to information") and the motivations of those seeking to develop such systems.

Just what are the interests and motivations of the government and those developing these systems? Are there really hordes of deformed, dwarfish men and women locked in silicon dungeons who are eagerly at work on new ways to destroy our last ounce of privacy and freedom—technological Igors rubbing their hands and smacking their lips in delight at the thought of serving their corporate and governmental Frankensteins toward the ultimate goal of *total information, total power?*

I doubt it. While one should never be so naive as to dismiss the sinister intent of many at the top of the corporate and governmental hierarchy, most of those actively involved in the development of these systems are technocrats who are motivated by competitive desires and, in the case of government researchers, by a genuine desire to improve efficiency. However, this fact should not leave us any more complacent, for we are now in the paradoxical position where the lack of a stated desire to attain a goal does not mean that the goal will not be achieved. The difficulty is that technology is a hydra; it is a means to many ends. One can easily work toward an end of improved efficiency, while at the same time remaining unaware of another totalitarian "end" resulting from the same means. As James B. Rule has written:

> Orwell foresaw—and made unforgettable—a world in which ruthless political interests mobilized intrusive technologies for totalitarian ends. What he did not consider was the possibility that the development of the intrusive technologies *would occur on its own, without the spur of totalitarian intent.* This, in fact, is what is now happening.[79]

What Can Be Done

We are entering an era where wealth will no longer necessarily be physical; it will be electronic. Knowledge will be power. Modern bureaucracy is now following an "informational imperative" that seeks to gather all possible information on its constantly expanding objectives. These objectives have never been properly confronted or analyzed. Whatever their motives, it is a non sequitur to state that the government or the corporations will create new informational systems and not choose to use them. If the government is using these systems to keep track of "deviant" groups within the meaning of this paper, it is absurd to think that they will not act to protect their interests.

In days gone by, power was of a different sort. Who can forget the words of Stalin when he wondered aloud, "How many legions does the Pope have?" Today, as intelligence surpasses the physical accoutrements of war in importance, such a question is almost an anachronism. Instead, the civil libertarian must ask, "How many data bases does the government have, and what will it do with them?"

What, then, is the answer? What possible "solutions" can be advanced to stem the steady erosion of privacy? It may be instructive for us to turn the question on its head and ask, "Why is it so desirable to seek such a 'solution'? Since people are voluntarily surrendering information, why is this not viewed as an evolution of the concept of privacy that should be permitted to develop?"

This is a reasonable question to ask, and is in fact frequently brought forth by those who feel that rising concern over privacy is really much ado about nothing. According to this thesis, the concept of privacy as I have been attempting to define it stems from a very quaint colonial notion of the right to be left alone that has no place in a modern technological society governed by interdependence and ease of information flow. As such, I am essentially engaged in a debate over a non-issue.

The difficulty I have with this laissez-faire attitude is that the logical outcome of such a position involves such a heightened level of governmental and corporate intrusion in and awareness of the smallest details of one's life. The mere fact of such awareness is enough to cause concern, but when one realizes that both these groups will employ this knowledge for their own purposes (much of which, if not outright illegal, is certainly ethically questionable), the cost becomes intolerable.

Let us examine one possible scenario revolving around the "laissez-faire" approach to privacy. A very good one has already been advanced by science-fiction author John Brunner in his 1975 book, *The Shockwave Rider*.[80] In that book, Brunner depicted a not-too-distant future where detailed knowledge on the lives of all the inhabitants of the United States is stored in computers. In this society, money has practically disappeared in favor of electronic "debits" each individual must spend in order to use the communications system. Since using the system is practically indispensable, the government is capable of constantly monitoring the whereabouts of its citizens. Moreover, the society is almost totally information-open; that is, the average citizen has almost total access to any information via a phone booth. However, instead of spreading joy and happiness, the system creates considerable anxiety since everyone can learn virtually every detail of anyone's life merely by plugging into the computer.

In Brunner's scenario, all communications are monitored by the government to keep track of "deviants" and computer saboteurs. Those who are repulsed by such surveillance form small communities, known as "paid avoidance areas," where cash is accepted and monitoring by the government is very difficult. However, even the fact that one does not use the electronic debit system is noted by the government and you are consequently automatically labeled as a "deviant."

In order to alleviate much of the anxiety caused by technological oppression, many of the citizens use a computerized system known as Hearing Aid, which is operated entirely by the citizens in a particularly remote paid-avoidance town known as Precipice. What makes Hearing Aid such a godsend is that there is always someone listening, though never conversing, with the caller, and the system cannot be tapped by the government due to the existence of "worms" in the system that electronically "eat" the tracer. Much of the book revolves around the efforts of a single person as he attempts to outwit and harass the government's information monitors.

It should be noted that Brunner's scenario (which he created after speaking with Alvin Toffler about the privacy implications of the technology) involved a largely incremental evolution toward loss of privacy. However, an equally plausible scenario could be created revolving around a "shattering discontinuity" (to use Arthur Schlesinger's term), where privacy is suddenly "revoked" by government to deal with a real or perceived threat.

Author David Goodman described a very plausible scenario along these lines while writing for *The Futurist* several years ago.[81] Goodman described a situation in which the threat of nuclear blackmail by ideology-crazed students created a mass panic among both civilians and the government, leading to calls by some for a Constitutional Convention to amend or dissolve the Bill of Rights in order to deal with the extraordinary security needs presented by the problem. When the terrorists are suddenly captured and the crisis abates, the president abruptly goes on television, states that the problem is likely to occur again, and that in order to take as many precautions as possible the Constitutional Convention should be convened and the Bill of Rights should be suspended indefinitely. Though the story ends there, Goodman clearly implies that the populace would willingly give up civil rights for the "promise" of survival, hence creating the same conditions for a *1984*-type government without ever actually exploding a nuclear device.

Other scenarios have also been described revolving around nuclear blackmail, notably by authors Larry Collins and Dominique Lapierre in their 1980 book, *The Fifth Horseman*.[82]

Though not strictly laissez-faire in their approach to the privacy issue, the latter two scenarios lead to the same state as does Brunner's: a new, subtler form of tyranny bordering on totalitarianism. Because of this threat, I believe that a "laissez-faire" approach, or the failure to speak out against loss of privacy and other liberties should a "shattering discontinuity" occur, is unacceptable.

Another, far more rational approach to the issue involves the legislative approach: to simply prevent the government or corporations from linking data bases together. Such an approach has been going on for many years over the FBI III system, opposed by many in the executive and legislative branches. Taken to its logical extreme, such an approach would involve the partial or wholesale dismantling of data-base-linkage or surveillance systems.

This approach does have a certain appeal. Many previous attempts to deal with legislative means to protect privacy have resulted in legislation that merely improves the efficiency of data banks. Everyone has an interest in eliminating false information—the citizen, the buyer, and the seller of such information all want files as accurate as possible. It is therefore easier for corporations and government agencies to support "reforms" aimed at eliminating inaccuracies (such as the Fair Credit Reporting Act), which offer mild procedural reforms that are advantageous to the company or agency while at the same time legitimizing the activities they are engaging in, i.e., the collection and dissemination of information. By concentrating exclusively on efficiency we miss the point: do we want such systems *at all?*

This issue has troubled a number of authorities, most notably James Rule.[83] Rule concluded that the intrusive power of these technologies is so great that less information gathering, not improvements in the system, is the answer: "All of these considerations—the dangers of excessive concentrations of social power, the visceral revulsion at excessively intrusive monitoring, and the drawbacks of punishing people too severely for past misdeeds—may warrant curtailment of surveillance under some conditions."[84]

The Privacy Protection Study Commission acknowledged the dilemma posed by Rule without endorsing his (or anyone else's) conclusion: "Quite simply, there is no vehicle for answering the question: 'Should a particular record-keeping policy, practice, or system exist at all?' . . . To deal with this situation, the Congress and the Executive Branch will have to take action."[85]

One difficulty with dismantling systems is the perceived disruption that it would have on services and the threat to the ever-growing "informational imperative" that governs large information systems. If the public were actually presented with this option, many may choose lesser services once appraised of the effect on privacy that the continued growth of these systems entails. However, it may be a mistake for data-system operators to simply *assume* that there is a direct correlation between amount of information gathered and services provided. No one has yet attempted to demonstrate that similar services could be delivered employing less-intrusive information demands. Indeed, as postulated earlier, commercial alternatives could very well arise that promise less-intrusive data collection without loss of services and become commercially viable *as a result of offering such an option.*

The most plausible alternative at this point appears to be legislative and technological attempts to stem loss of privacy. Under this proposal, a mix of legislation to better protect the traditional concept of privacy, combined with technological innovations such as data encryption and other secure communications systems, could, if properly implemented, significantly retard erosion of privacy.

It should be noted that there are already a number of federal and state laws, as well as private regulations, in existence that directly address various aspects of the privacy issue. For example, the Right to Financial Privacy Act of 1978[86] was passed to provide a mechanism regulating government access to bank records. The Act requires a court order in order for a federal agency to gain access to bank records and prohibits a federal agency from disclosing an individual's financial records to another agency without informing the individual concerned and receiving assurances that the records are required for some legitimate law-enforcement purpose. The Act, however, only covers disclosure of records of financial institutions to federal agencies, not to state or local governments or private institutions.[87] At least nine states have laws modeled on the Act that regulates government access to financial records in possession of banks and other financial institutions.[88]

The Fair Credit Reporting Act of 1970[89] regulates the use by consumer reporting agencies of personal and financial data regarding individuals. Its stated purpose is to assure that information collected by the credit agencies is accurate, that it is relevant for the purposes for which it is used, and that the privacy of the consumer is respected. It forbids the collection of obsolete information, allows the consumer to find out the "nature and substance" of information about him or her in the file, requires the user of such information to notify the consumer if a credit agency report is responsible for the refusal to issue credit and provide the consumer with the name and address of the company, establishes a procedure for the consumer to correct inaccurate or erroneous information, and allows a plaintiff to sue for violations of the Act. Approximately 11 states have enacted similar consumer credit reporting statutes.[90]

A number of other federal laws touch upon the privacy issue at least in part. For example, the Electronic Funds Transfer Act[91] established consumer rights with respect to electronic funds transfer (EFT). The Act requires that banks inform consumers of the terms and conditions governing use of EFTs, including under what circumstances information will be disclosed to third parties. The Equal Credit Opportunity Act[92] imposed limits on the type of information that could be collected by a creditor, specifically forbidding inquiries into a person's sex, marital status, race, color, or religion, except for limited purposes. However, it permits such information to be retained when gathered from third-party sources such as credit agencies. It also requires the applicant to be notified if credit has been revoked and the reasons why. The Fair Credit Billing Act of 1974 [93] was enacted to protect consumers against unfair credit billing practices. It establishes procedures for the correction of billing errors, and forbids the agency from notifying a third party that the bill is outstanding until the agency complies with specific procedures. The Fair Debt Collection Practices Act[94] limits the communications that debt-collection agencies may make about debtors whose accounts they are attempting to collect.

Before more federal laws are proposed to prevent data-base

310

linkages, however, it may be instructive to see how little existing federal laws have prevented dissemination. The most important piece of federal legislation with regard to this issue is the Privacy Act. Its purpose was summarized in a recent report by the Office of Management and Budget to the Congress:

> The Privacy Act of 1974 (Public Law 93-579) was enacted to ensure an appropriate balance between the Federal Government's need for information about its citizens and the individual's right to privacy. The Act seeks to achieve this objective by establishing procedures to regulate the collection, maintenance, use and dissemination of personal information by federal agencies. The Act establishes a system of checks and balances to ensure the effective operation of these procedures. These checks and balances include provisions for the exercise of individual rights, public scrutiny of agency recordkeeping practices, Office of Management and Budget and congressional oversight of agency activities, and both civil and criminal sanctions.[95]

While the Act prohibits most exchanges of personal information among federal agencies, the "external disclosure" clauses of the Act, especially the "routine use" provision permitting dissemination of information to other agencies compatible with the use for which the information was originally gathered, has been so broadly interpreted that it is hardly an effective barrier to dissemination.[96] There are now 11 "external disclosure" clauses permitting an agency exemption from the terms of the Act, the most recent allowing disclosure to a consumer reporting agency by a federal agency to whom the consumer owes money.[97]

A recent congressional study of the Privacy Act concluded that the Office of Management and Budget, entrusted with developing guidelines for implementation of the Act, had little interest in overseeing the Act and that it "does not actively supervise, review, or monitor agency compliance with Privacy Act guidelines."[98] A 1977 study by the Commission on Federal Paperwork concluded that "implementation and compliance with the Act have been rather poor."[99] Moreover, several witnesses at the recent congressional hearings "agreed that the routine use provision was interpreted so flexibly that an agency could make virtually any disclosure of information that it wanted as long as the proper notice was published in the Federal Register."[100]

One of the most important legislative tasks is thus the strengthening of the Privacy Act. In recent testimony in front of the House of Representatives Committee on Government Operations, a number of groups and individuals urged that an independent agency be created to monitor compliance with the Act.[101] Such a Privacy Commission was part of the original legislation that became the Privacy Act, but was later omitted from the final bill.[102] Representative Glenn English, chairman of the subcommittee that held the most recent oversight hearings, noted that one of the main reasons to conduct oversight hearings on the Privacy Act was to "generate some discussion about the need for some type of privacy protection board."[103] Such a plan is similar to that of the Privacy Protection Study Commission, which proposed the creation of a "Federal Privacy Board" to monitor compliance with privacy legislation in general.[104] The agency should be given broad powers to set standards for the operation of every personal data bank in the country.

John Wicklein has suggested that the Board should require private and governmental agencies to register their computerized files with regional offices of the Board and to indicate what steps they have taken to insure compliance with regulations. The Board should have authority to inspect such files, and aggrieved citizens should have direct administrative redress by applying to the Board's regional offices. Those offices should have the power to order the expungement of improper or incorrect entries from a person's dossier.[105]

A similar system has been operating in Sweden since 1972. In that year, the Swedish Parliament created the Swedish Data Inspection Board, which was empowered to inspect data systems and to license operators to run such systems. An 11-member board oversees the operations, consisting of representatives from the major parties, labor unions, industry, and the public sector. A citizen has the right to see his files once every year, and to seek the assistance of the Board in correcting inaccuracies. The Board can take those who refuse to correct files to court, where they are liable to a fine or a year in prison. By 1982, Denmark, West Germany, Canada, Norway, Finland, and Austria had also set up data boards.[106] The West German law has been described as a particularly effective model.[107] Unlike in Sweden, the Federal Data Protection Commission in West Germany does not have legal power to order that something should or should not be done, but its access to the media as well as the yearly reports it is required to file have been persuasive enough.

Though President Carter rejected the concept of a Federal Privacy Board, he did propose several pieces of legislation, among them the Fair Financial Information Practices Act. The Act would have given consumers the right to see and copy credit and investigative reports about them. Under present law (the Fair Credit Reporting Act), credit agencies can merely supply a summary of the nature and substance of the records. The Act would also have required the credit grantor to allow the consumer to see the original of the report sent by the credit agency. Given the growing use of credit agencies, a law of this type should be enacted in some form.

Other parts of the Privacy Act also need to be reevaluated. It has often been noted that the Act has no effective enforcement mechanism; that the right of a person to see and copy records about himself is actually fairly restricted, especially with regard to criminal records; and that the "routine use" provisions are overly broad and effectively destroy the very purposes for which the Act was created.[108] Since the creation of the Privacy Act over a decade ago, it has not been amended to reflect the considerable changes that have occurred since its inception. If the Act is to have any meaning at all, it is time for it to be seriously evaluated and amended.

Another area that should be closely examined is computer matching, which is the comparison of unrelated computer files to identify suspected violators of the law. The use of this technique has been growing rapidly since the Department of Health, Education, and Welfare began its hunt for welfare cheats in 1977. The privacy implications of such matching are enormous. Aside from the problems with accuracy and presenting an incomplete picture of the person, there are substantial constitutional questions involving presumption of innocence, the right to due process, and the right to limit information voluntarily turned over to the government to the purpose for which it was collected. Finally, uncontrolled use of computer matching could easily cause the creation of a national data bank on all Americans. For this reason, the Privacy Act should be clarified to state that computer matches cannot automatically be considered "routine uses," and no further computer matching should be done without thorough study and authorization by Congress.

In addition, hearings should be held in Congress on the feasibility of revising the Communications Act of 1934[109] and Title III of the Omnibus Crime Control Act of 1968 (Wiretap Act).[110] The Wiretap Act in particular should be amended to prevent interception of digitized voice communications. Consideration should also be given to amending the 1968 Act in such a way as to prevent unauthorized interception in any form, thus negating the necessity of revising the Act constantly in order to keep up with new technological developments. The House of Representatives recently held hearings on "Civil Liberties and the National Security State" at which this issue was discussed.[111]

Another important, albeit far more difficult, legislative goal is to replace Truman's 1952 directive establishing the NSA with a legislative charter. In the words of David Kahn, one of the foremost civilian experts on cryptology and the NSA, "An institutionalized mechanism to seek out violations and punish the guilty can best deter the sort of intrusion that so many Americans fear—and that destroys the very freedom that the NSA was created to protect."[112] The Senate Committee that investigated the NSA found that "there is a compelling need for an NSA charter to spell out limitations which will protect individual constitutional rights without impairing NSA's necessary foreign intelligence mission."[113] The House intelligence committee, in its own report, came to the same conclusion.

In addition, private efforts to protect against surveillance can and should be pursued. The technology now exists to make it possible to install small scrambler devices on telephone and electronic communications that would make it nearly impossible for all but the most insistent organizations to eavesdrop. Indeed, cryptology has advanced to the point where it is now theoretically possible to develop an unbreakable code.[114] James Bamford, in the final pages of his book on the NSA, *The Puzzle Palace,* came to a similar conclusion:

> If there are defenses to such technotyranny, it would appear, at least from past experience, that they will not come from Congress. Rather, they will most likely come from academe and industry in the form of secure cryptographic application to private and commercial telecommunications equipment. The same technology that is used against free speech can be used to protect it, for without protection the future may be grim.[115]

Increased civilian use of cryptology will not come without opposition. As noted earlier, the NSA has been actively opposed to civilian involvement in cryptology, primarily because it fears that successful cryptological techniques developed here will be employed by other countries, thus severely reducing the amount of signals intelligence the NSA will be able to decipher. However, the NSA is already severely limited in the quantity of information it can collect by such means. In the words of David Kahn, "The NSA, in other words, cannot get the most desirable communications intelligence—the high-level messages of the Soviet Union and Communist China."[116] What it is limited to primarily are codes of Third World countries, and it is only a matter of time before they switch to more secure communications systems. The NSA's attempt to "buy time" should not require that civilian organizations halt cryptological research and development.

Technological efforts to protect privacy represents, in my view, the strongest tool available. Many aspects of the privacy issue, such as clandestine intelligence gathering by the government, are not as responsive to legislation. In addition, the difficulty in adequately monitoring government information is enormous, even assuming the existence of adequate legislation. Technological responses such as data-encryption systems assume the existence of monitoring and act to thwart its accomplishment.

So important are technological efforts to protect privacy that the government should actively assist private enterprise in the development of secure cryptographic systems. In the last several years, much of private industry has come to accept the 56-bit Data Encryption Standard (DES).[117] Despite some criticism that the standard promoted was just strong enough to protect from private codebreaking efforts but not strong enough to withstand the efforts of a determined NSA,[118] no other standard seems to have evolved. The DES is now accepted by the National Bureau of Standards, the American National Standards Institute, and the National Communication System. It is also recommended by the American Bankers Association and the International Organization for Standardization.[119]

David Chaum, a computer scientist at the University of California at Santa Barbara, has proposed an unusual method of protecting privacy based on a cryptographic system of identification by pseudonyms.[120] He proposes that individuals would provide each institution with which they have business with a different pseudonym, generated by cryptographic techniques. The pseudonym would be able to serve as identification because certain cryptologic techniques make third-party identification of the pseudonyms possible. However, these pseudonyms could not be connected. Under this system, an individual could not be traced against his will, but could use third-party identification to prove his identity. He would be able to pay his bills without identifying himself, and payment could be authenticated using a cryptographic process. Information about an individual could be passed from organization to organization, but the organizations would not be able to collaborate to derive which pseudonyms belong to which individuals. An individual would also be able to change pseudonyms periodically. This unusual proposal deserves further investigation.

In the long run, however, little real privacy protection will emerge without two of the pillars of modern society: an informed, aroused citizenry and a free press. The press needs to maintain an aggressive posture on the privacy issue, not only to expose the more blatant attempts at invasion of privacy, but also to focus on privacy as an issue in order to assemble the disparate pieces of its loss in an intelligible form. The public needs to recognize the existence of the incremental loss of privacy and to debate the degree to which it wishes to surrender such privacy. Before it can engage in such debates, however, it needs to be educated on the issue. In our society, this means the formation of a special-interest group dedicated to the privacy issue. Because privacy lacks a natural constituent "base," it has been unable to attract sufficient numbers of people to make it a true issue; it has been, in effect, a cause in search of a constituency. Therefore, one of the most essential first steps in raising public consciousness on the privacy issue is to form a special-interest group dedicated to the privacy issue. Ideally, such a group should be a coalition of many interests, from civil liberties and consumer groups to business associations to academic and university organizations.

A good example of building coalitions around the privacy issue was demonstrated recently in Canada. On May 18, 1983, the solicitor general of Canada, Bob Kaplan, introduced Bill C-157, a bill to establish the Canadian Security Intelligence Service (CSIS).[121] The bill would have removed responsibility for national security from the Royal Canadian Mounted Police and placed it in the hands of the civilian CSIS. It would have authorized formerly illegal practices such as opening mail and accessing confidential files. The Service would not have been subject to direct ministerial control or parliamentary review. The CSIS would have had almost unlimited power to investigate four threats to Canadian security: 1) espionage or sabotage; 2) clandestine attempts by foreigners to advance their interests to the detriment of Canada; 3) political violence or terrorism; and 4) attempts to undermine or destroy the constitutionally established system of government in Canada.[122] The bill was so vaguely worded, however, that the CSIS could have investigated almost any type of political activity, from supporters of the British in the Falklands war to church groups to Third World support groups to socialists.[123]

The implications that Bill C-157 held for privacy and other civil liberties in Canada, especially in light of the recently enacted Canadian Charter of Rights and Freedoms,[124] were apparent to the Canadian Rights and Liberties Federation, which immediately organized a national coalition to oppose the bill. One local coalition, the Ottawa-Hull Coalition Against Bill C-157, which consisted of a large number of labor, women's, and civil rights groups together with several district councils, was particularly effective. News stories were written on the implications of the bill for civil liberties, and public rallies and forums were held in Ottawa and Toronto.[125] Shortly thereafter, the solicitor general agreed to let the bill die. In November 1983, the Canadian Senate published a report on the bill prepared by a special committee that considered many of the concerns of the national coalition. The report concluded that, while there was a need for the CSIS, the bill needed to be tightened considerably to adequately protect the right to privacy and other civil liberties. Specifically, proposals were made to narrow the mandate of the CSIS, to increase ministerial responsibility, and to enhance the provisions for control and review. In January 1984, the solicitor general again introduced the bill, renamed C-9, this time incorporating most of the changes recommended by the Senate Committee.[126]

Since many of the concerns involved in the privacy issue, such as cable television, are in the province of local jurisdictions, small but vocal regional privacy organizations can have a significant impact. One good example is Citizens for Privacy in Cable TV, a Nashville, Tennessee-based organization that organized to educate local citizens on the privacy implications of cable TV and to write privacy protections into the ordinance establishing the system. They sought to require the cable company to tell subscribers what information the computer would be collecting on them, to forbid them to sell or transfer information obtained from the system to any third party without the express consent of each subscriber, and to require the erasure of most information on a subscriber upon the termination of service to that subscriber.[127] They are now seeking to pass a state law to require similar terms from any cable company seeking to operate in Tennessee.

The federal government has also been taking a look at interactive cable technologies. Two bills, S. 66 and H.R. 4103, are presently being considered that would address at least in part some of the privacy issues inherent in these systems. Both bills would limit a company's right to collect data on individual subscribers unless it is for billing purposes or consented to in writing. However, S. 66 has an override clause that would prohibit states from enacting stronger efforts to protect privacy. Because S. 66 is weaker than many of the state bills now being considered, many of those involved in the privacy issue have argued that this provision should be removed from the bill.[128]

A strong movement to enact state and local privacy ordinances will undoubtedly encourage those in the data-marketing business to enact industry standards of their own. The Videotex Industry Association (VIA), for example, recently announced the promulgation of its own set of privacy guidelines that would prohibit disclosure of information on individuals without either their permission or a court order.[129] It also provides that an individual will be promptly notified if a government agency without a court order seeks information about the individual in conjunction with an investigation.

The insurance business has also attempted to promote standards in the insurance industry. In 1979, the National Association of Insurance Commissioners approved a model privacy law known as the Insurance Information and Privacy Protection Model Act.[130] The law was designed to establish standards for the collection, use, and dissemination of information collected by the insurance industry. It requires insurance companies to notify policy holders of the nature and scope of information that may be collected about them, including from third parties, and to maintain accuracy of records and right of access to them by the policy holder; it also defines to whom insurance information may be disseminated, and provides a procedural review mechanism through the state insurance commissioners in the event of a dispute between the policy holder and the insurance company.

There is good evidence that enhanced media discussion of privacy issues is causing an increase in public sensitivity to the issue in the United States as well. In a recent Harris poll, two-thirds of the people contacted through a random telephone sample felt that records were being stored on them without their knowledge. Large majorities felt that it was "possible" or "likely" that the government would use confidential information to intimidate individuals and that this information would be used to take away privacy and personal liberties.[131]

Clearly, we need to be moving toward what John Wicklein has referred to as a "philosophy of privacy protection." Wicklein, a former reporter for the *New York Times,* noted that such a philosophy would need to address the following minimum concerns:

A person must have the right to see any file kept on him or her by a computer, make corrections in that file if it is in error, and have the corrections transmitted to all third parties to whom information from the files will be sent. Beyond that, the individual has less-precisely defined rights that will have to be negotiated. These include the right to minimum intrusion by computers and their attendant investigators; an expectation of confidentiality concerning medical records, family data, and legitimate financial transactions; and the right not to have information about the individual known and transmittable by One Big Computer, either governmental or commercial.[132]

These principles should not be looked on as some sort of utopian ideal, but rather as a reasonable response to a growing problem. Indeed, a "philosophy of privacy" seems to be evolving on an international level. The Organization for Economic Cooperation and Development (OECD) has implemented voluntary guidelines for its members on the protection of privacy and transborder data flows.[133] In 1980, The Council of Europe approved a Convention for the Protection of Individuals With Regard to Automatic Processing of Data.[134] More recently, the United Nations Sub-Commission on Prevention of Discrimination and Protection of Minorities presented a report to the Commission on Human Rights concerned with international guidelines on data protection.[135] All three of these documents adhere to the main principles of fairness, accuracy, public knowledge, individual access, and security in information collection.[136]

Regardless of whatever legislative or private "answers" are proposed to the problem, I cannot believe that we will ever go back to the relatively pristine state we existed in before; the computer revolution, with all its implications, seems to be inexorable. If we then assume that some form of increasingly sophisticated monitoring will occur, we must wonder if the public is ready for the radical alteration in privacy that such a change would entail. For many, such a change is seen as beneficial; in the Candide-like world thus envisioned, all information is for the best of all possible worlds. While not in any way denying the benefits of the information revolution, nor the need for legitimate intelligence-gathering activities on the part of the government, I am convinced that we are engaged in a headlong plunge into a Great Experiment of whose consequences we have precious little knowledge. I am concerned that, in the future, privacy may become a precious commodity, sought after by many but in the possession of few.

In addition, I am concerned that, should the public's gradual acquiescence to a loss of privacy continue unabated, little or no outcry will occur when the government attempts to utilize the new technologies to monitor "deviant" groups and to act against them based on such knowledge. By then, the public may be so inured to intrusive technologies that little demand will exist for stringent anti-surveillance laws. Even assuming the existence of such legislation, I have doubts that laws would be able to adequately protect such groups, given the sophistication of the systems and the adroitness of those employing them in avoiding detection.

Finally, the NSA's insistence on total control of data encryption technology for "national security" reasons can only be taken as a precursor for a much larger government involvement in science and everyday life. The Reagan administration's recent order requiring all government officials in sensitive positions to sign a statement indicating that they will submit any future writing for pre-publication review (a move only recently abandoned after intense adverse publicity[137]) is another example of how the government can gradually move into the private sphere and control not only actions but also thoughts and ideas.

Whether or not we possess the will to protect our traditional concept of privacy against these encroachments is subject to debate. Certainly, the concept of privacy as we understand it is not an immutable one. In the words of Anthony Oettinger, "At any moment in history it is a mix of politics, industrial organization and technology, among other factors, that determines how the privacy of individuals weighs in the balance with other values prized by both individuals and the society these individuals make up."[138]

In 1947, George Orwell wrote and published what was to be his most famous book, *1984*. In it, a continent named Oceania was perpetually at war with two other continents, Eurasia and Eastasia. Probably the two most outstanding features of Oceania were that the government knew everything about everyone and that the past was changed at will. One individual, Winston Smith, discovered the truth, and it was to change his life forever. The high point of the book came when Winston's tormenter, O'Brien, said to him, "If you want a picture of the future, imagine a boot stamping on a human face—forever."

Clearly, Orwell's vision has not materialized as he described it. It seems strange and alien to us because it depicts a world that seems antithetical to our concept of free will and privacy. However, our confidence that a brutal authoritarianism a la Orwell could not happen here should not leave us blind to the fact that subtler forms of tyranny may well be developing, nor should we lose sight of the fact that a slow, methodical trodding of the boot on the human face may well leave as indelible a mark on the human psyche as if that boot had come down on us with all the suddenness that Orwell himself had envisioned.

Notes

1. Brandeis, Louis, and Warren Samuel. "The Right to Privacy," 4 *Harvard Law Review* 193 (1890). For additional information on the history of privacy in the United States, see Flaherty, David H., *Privacy in Colonial New England,* Charlottesville, University Press of Virginia, 1972; and Seipp, David, *The Right to Privacy in American History,* Cambridge, Mass., Harvard University, Program on Information Resources Policy, 1978.

2. Commerce Department, National Bureau of Standards, *Computer Security Publications,* Glossary, p. 17.

3. Federal Data Banks, "Computers and the Bill of Rights," Hearings Before the Subcommittee on Constitutional Rights of the Committee on the Judiciary, United States Senate, 92nd Congress, 1st Session, 1971—Part II, Relating to Departments of Army, Defense, and Justice, p. 1665.

4. Rule, James. B., et al. *The Politics of Privacy.* New York, Elsevier Press, 1980, p. 29.

5. Burnham, David. *The Rise of the Computer State.* New York, Random House, 1983, p. 42.

6. Wicklein, John. *Electronic Nightmare: The Home Communication Set and Your Freedom.* Boston, Beacon Press, 1981, p. 191.

7. Office of Technology Assessment, "Selected Electronic Funds Transfer Issues: Privacy, Security and Equity," OTA-BP-CIT-12, Washington, D.C., March 1982, p. 29. Hereafter referred to as "OTA Electronic Funds Report."

8. Burnham, op. cit., p. 42.

9. *Privacy Journal,* Washington, D.C., January 1983, p. 3.

10. Burnham, op. cit., p. 161.

11. Burnham, op. cit., p. 32.

12. *Time,* November 21, 1983, p. 85.

13. "Big firms team up on videotex project," *Infoworld,* March 12, 1983, p. 13.

14. Wicklein, *Electronic Nightmare,* op. cit., pp. 11, 18.

15. *Privacy Journal,* September 1983, p. 6.

16. Burnham, David. "IRS Starts Hunt for Tax Evaders Using Mail-Order Concerns List," *New York Times,* December 25, 1983, p. 1.

17. The two companies recently formed a single venture, Warner-Amex, to own and operate the Columbus, Ohio, based Qube interactive cable system. Warner owns Warner Brothers, Warner Publishing, D.C. Comics, Franklin Mint Corporation, Atari, Panavision, and Warner Records. American Express owns American Express International Banking, American Express Publishing, Fireman's Fund Insurance, and Showtime. *Privacy Journal,* February 1983, p. 4-5.

18. *Privacy Journal,* February 1983, p. 6.

19. *Privacy Journal, 1982-83 Supplement to Compilation of State and Federal Privacy Laws, 1981.* A similar bill was recently introduced in New York; see *Privacy Journal,* February 1984, p. 6.

20. *U.S. v. Miller,* 425 U.S. 435 (1976); see also *Personal Privacy in An Information Society: Report of the Privacy Protection Study Commission.* U.S. GPO, Washington, D.C., July 1977, pp. 20, 27, 34, 101, 106, 350, 351, 361.

21. Rule, op. cit., p. 39; Burnham, *Rise of the Computer State,* p. 66.

22. Burnham, *The Rise of the Computer State,* p. 54.

23. Office of Technology Assessment, "An Assessment of Alternatives for a National Computerized Criminal History System," Summary Report, OTA-CIT-162, Washington, D.C., October, 1982, pp. 15-16, 21-22. Hereafter referred to as "OTA Crime Report."

24. Ibid., p. 7.

25. P.A. 83-752; reported in *Privacy Journal,* January 1984, p. 4.

26. Burnham, *Rise of the Computer State,* p. 72. OTA Crime Report, p. 14.

27. OTA Crime Report, p. 14.

28. Ibid., p. 15.

29. Ibid., p. 22.

30. "Interstate Identification Index: Operational Summary"; also see "Re-

port, National Crime Information Center, Interstate Identification Index Subcommittee of the Advisory Policy Board," Alexandria, Virginia, September 20, 1983.

31. El Paso Information Center, *1981 Annual Progress and Activity Report,* Washington, D.C.

32. Burnham, *The Rise of the Computer State,* p. 108.

33. Burnham, David. "IRS Seeks Links to County Computers in Texas to Find Debtors," *New York Times,* March 13, 1984, p. A23.

34. 5 U.S.C. 552a(b)(3).

35. *Privacy Journal,* December 1982, p. 1. See also *Oversight of Computer Matching To Detect Fraud and Mismanagement Programs,* Hearings Before the Subcommittee on Oversight of Government Affairs, U.S. Senate, December 15-16, 1982. Washington, D.C., U.S. GPO, pp. 79, 80-81, 84, 104, 120, 156-57.

36. Burnham, David. "FBI Panel Weighing a Plan on Expanded Access to Files," *New York Times,* January 1, 1984, p. 1.

37. For notification of modification of the NCIC records system, see *Federal Register,* Vol. 47, No. 236, December 8, 1983, pp. 55343 ff.

38. Burnham, op. cit., note infra at 26.

39. Rule, James B. "1984—The Ingredients of Totalitarianism." In Howe, Irving (editor), *1984 Revisited—Totalitarianism in Our Century,* New York, Perennial Library, 1983, p. 173. Emphasis in the original.

40. Rule, *The Politics of Privacy,* p. 16.

41. Burnham, *The Rise of the Computer State,* p. 36.

42. Center for National Security Studies, "Operation Chaos: Comparison of Documents Released in *Halkin v. Helms* with the Final Report of the Church Committee," CNSS Report No. 104, Washington, D.C., October 1979, p. 9.

43. "ACLU Lawsuit Questions Spying by L.A. Police Unit," *Philadelphia Inquirer,* January 29, 1984.

44. "NSA: Inside the Puzzle Palace," *Time,* November 10, 1975, p. 14.

45. The most detailed source on the workings of the NSA is found in 5 *Intelligence Activities: Hearings Before the Senate Select Committee to Study Governmental Operations With Respect to Intelligence Activities,* 94th Congress, 1st Session (1975), and the *Final Report* of the Select Committee, S. Report No. 755, 94th Congress, 2nd Session, 1976.

46. Bamford, James. *The Puzzle Palace.* New York, Penguin Books, 1983, p. 69.

47. Bamford op. cit., pp. 304-8; Burnham, *The Rise of the Computer State,* p. 130; *Halkin v. Helms,* 598 F.2d at 4 (1978).

48. Krajick, Kevin. "Electronic Surveillance Makes a Comeback," *Police Magazine,* March 1983, p. 95.

49. Gruner, Richard. "Government Monitoring of International Electronic Communications: NSA Watchlist Surveillance and the Fourth Amendment," 51 S. Cal. Law Rev. 429 (1978).

50. *Halkin v. Helms,* 598 F.2d at 4; Gruner, op. cit., pp. 429-31.

51. *Jabara v. Webster,* 691 F.2d 272, *cert. denied,* case 82-1682, October term 1983.

52. *Halkin v. Helms,* 598 F.2d at 4.

53. Bamford, op. cit., p. 381.

54. *Halkin v. Helms,* 598 F.2d at 5.

55. Ibid., at 12.

56. Bamford, op. cit., p. 462.

57. Public Law 95-511, 92 Stat. 1783, 50 USC 1801 et seq.

58. Bamford, op. cit., p. 466.
59. Ibid., p. 468.
60. 18 USC 2510-20.
61. For a discussion of these issues, see Anderson, Judith B., "The Constitutionality of the Foreign Intelligence Surveillance Act," 16 *Vanderbilt Journal of International Law* 231 (1983).
62. *United States v. Falvey,* 540 F. Supp. 1306 (1982). See also Anderson, op. cit., p. 251.
63. Quoted in Bamford, p. 382.
64. Ibid., p. 468.
65. Kahn, David. *Kahn on Codes.* New York, Macmillan Publishing Company, 1983, p. 190-91.
66. Bamford, op. cit., p. 138.
67. Ibid., p. 449; also see Davida's testimony at "1984: Civil Liberties and the National Security State," Hearings in the House Judiciary Committee, Subcommittee on Courts, Civil Liberties, and the Administration of Justice, Washington, D.C., November 3, 1983. Hereafter referred to as "House Civil Liberties Hearings."
68. Schaffer, Richard. "Global Data System Is Seen As Telephones Use More Digital Gear," *The Wall Street Journal,* December 23, 1983, p.1.
69. Burnham, David. "Loophole in Law Raises Concern About Privacy in Computer Age," *The New York Times,* December 19, 1983, p.1.
70. "Electronic Surveillance Menaces Personal Privacy," *InfoWorld,* Vol. 5, No. 15, August 1983, p.16.
71. Krajick, op. cit., p. 98.
72. Ibid., p. 94.
73. Ibid.
74. "Technology and Privacy: Reach Out and Tap Someone." *InfoWorld,* Vol. 5, No. 14, August 1983, p. 10.
75. Ibid.
76. Rule et al. *The Politics of Privacy,* op. cit., p. 133.
77. Burnham, *The Rise of the Computer State,* p. 38.
78. Ibid., p. 47.
79. Rule, "1984—The Ingredients of Totalitarianism," op.cit., p. 179.
80 Brunner, John, *The Shockwave Rider,* New York, Ballantine Books, 1975.
81. Goodman, David. "Countdown to 1984," *The Futurist,* December 1978, p. 345. Goodman found that over 100 of 137 predictions made by Orwell in *1984* had come true by 1978.
82. Collins, Larry, and Dominique Lapierre. *The Fifth Horseman.* New York, Avon Books, 1980.
83. *The Politics of Privacy,* pp. 7, 8, 69-72, 116-17.
84. Ibid., p. 151.
85. *Report of the Privacy Protection Study Commission,* op. cit., p. 536.
86. Right to Financial Privacy Act, P.L. 95-630, 12 USC 3401 et seq.
87. OTA Electronic Funds Report, op. cit., p. 36. Specifically, the federal government is allowed access to financial records only under a court order for purposes related to law enforcement.
88. See Aldrich, Michael, "Privacy Act of 1974: Hearings Before a Subcommittee on Government Operations," 98th Congress, 1st Session, 1983, p. 507. Hereafter referred to as "Privacy Act Hearings."
89. Fair Credit Reporting Act, P.L. 90-321, 84 Stat. 1128, 15 USC 1681 et seq.
90. Aldrich, Privacy Act Hearings, p. 506.

91. Electronic Funds Transfer Act, P.L. 95-630, 92 Stat. 3728, 15 USC 1693 et seq.

92. Equal Credit Opportunity Act, P.L. 94-321; 15 USC 1591 et seq.

93. Fair Credit Billing Act, P.L. 90-321, as added Oct. 28, 1974, P.L. 93-495, 15 USC 1666 et seq.

94. Fair Debt Collection Practices Act, P.L. 90-321, as added Sept. 20, 1977, P.L. 95-109, 91 Stat. 874, 15 USC 1692 et seq.

95. "Administration of the Privacy Act of 1974," OMB, January 4, 1980, reprinted in Privacy Act Hearings, p. 605.

96. The routine-use provision has generated considerable controversy. See Privacy Act Hearings, pp. 46-47, 50-53, 90-93, 252-53, 261-62, 276-79.

97. Debt Collection Act of 1982, Public Law No. 97-3652, 96 Stat. 1749 (1982), 5 USC 552a(b)12.

98. "Who Cares About Privacy? Oversight of the Privacy Act of 1974 by the Office of Management and Budget and by the Congress," Eighth Report by the Committee on Government Operations, House Report No. 98-455, Washington, D.C., U.S. GPO, 1983, p. 2. Hereafter referred to as "Oversight Report."

99. Quoted in Oversight Report, p. 8.

100. Ibid., p. 22.

101. See, e.g., Statement of David Flaherty, Privacy Act Hearings, p. 188-222; Statement of Ronald Plesser, p. 249; Statement of John Shattuck, p. 261.

102. *Legislative History of the Privacy Act of 1974,* U.S. Senate Committee on Government Operations and U.S. House Committee on Government Operations, Subcommittee on Government Information and Individual Rights, Washington, D.C., U.S. GPO, p. 15.

103. Opening Statement of Congressman Glenn English, Privacy Act Hearings, p. 6.

104. *Report of the Privacy Protection Study Commission,* p. 36.

105. Wicklein, *Electronic Nightmare,* op. cit., p. 257.

106. For a summary of the Swedish Data Inspection Board, see Wicklein, *Electronic Nightmare,* op. cit., pp. 198-211.

107. See Privacy Act Hearings, Statement of David Flaherty, pp. 212-13.

108. See Privacy Act Hearings, Statement of Ronald Plesser, p. 231; Statement of John Landau, pp. 260-61, 281.

109. P.L. 19-416, 48 Stat. 1064.

110. P.L. 90-351, 82 Stat. 212, 18 USC 2510 et seq.

111. See esp. testimony of Willis Ware, Rand Corporation, House Civil Liberties Hearings, January 24, 1984.

112. Kahn, op. cit., p. 185.

113. Quoted in Kahn, op. cit., p. 185.

114. For an introduction to this subject, see Rapoport, Roger, "Unbreakable Code," in *The Omni Book of Computers and Robots,* New York, Zebra Books, 1983, pp. 359-70. Kahn has also commented on the general difficulty of breaking codes when the complexity level is raised. He quantifies this problem by advancing a rough rule of thumb: "If you double the capacity of a code, you square the work that the codebreaker has to do." Op. cit., p. 295.

115. Bamford, op. cit., pp. 476-77.

116. Kahn, op. cit., p. 182.

117. For a summary of recent developments in this field, see Branstead, Dennis K, and Smid, Miles E., "Integrity and Security Standards Based on Cryptography,," *Computers and Security,* Vol. I, No. 3, November 1982, p. 255.

118. Kahn, op. cit., p. 170; see also Rapoport, op. cit., note at 114.

119. Oral communication to the author by Miles E. Smid, senior mathematician, U.S. Bureau of Standards, March 14, 1984.

120. "Taking a pseudonym can prevent 'dossier society,' " *InfoWorld,* September 12, 1983, p. 19.

121. Solicitor General of Canada, News Release: "The Hon. Bob Kaplan, P.C., M.P., Solicitor General of Canada, Introduces Legislation to Establish the Canadian Security Intelligence Service (CSIS)," May 18, 1983.

122. Ibid., p. 3.

123. Gandall, Marvin. "Bill C-157: The Real Threat to Security," *Labour-Focus, Bulletin of the Ottawa Committee for Labour Action,* Vol. 6, No. 4, October 1983, pp. 7-10.

124. The Canadian Constitution, 1981, a resolution adopted by the Canadian Parliament, December 1981.

125. Rapoch, Andy. "A Dry Run for 1984," *Rights and Freedoms,* Canadian Rights and Liberties Federation, No. 49, November-December 1983, p. 13.

126. Solicitor General of Canada, News Release: "The Hon. Bob Kaplan, P.C., Q.C., M.P., Solicitor General of Canada, Proposes Major Changes to the Canadian Security Intelligence Service (CSIS) Legislation," January 1984.

127. Oral communication to the author by Harry Lewis, attorney for Citizens for Privacy in Cable TV, March 13, 1984.

128. Personal communication, Harry Lewis, March 13, 1984. Also see American Civil Liberties Union, *Civil Liberties Alert,* Vol. 7, No. 3, March 1983, p. 3.

129. "Videotex association members set privacy guidelines," *InfoWorld,* Vol. 5, No. 31, August 1983, p. 14.

130. For a copy of the guidelines, see National Association of Insurance Commissioners, 633 West Wisconsin Avenue, Suite 1015, Milwaukee, Wisconsin 53203.

131. *Privacy Journal,* December 1983, p. 1.

132. Wicklein, *Electronic Nightmare,* op. cit., p. 217.

133. OECD, "Recommendation of the Council Concerning Guidelines Governing the Protection of Privacy and Transborder Data Flows of Personal Data," adopted by the Council in Paris, 23rd September 1980, Document C(80)58(Final).

134. Council of Europe Convention for the Protection of Individuals with Regard to Automatic Processing of Personal Data, approved by the Council of Ministers in Strasbourg, September, 1980.

135. *Privacy Journal,* February 1984, p.2.

136. The general concept of "fair information practices" is also embedded in the U.S. Privacy Act. For a comparison of the Privacy Act, the OECD Standards, and the Council of Europe Convention, see Privacy Act Hearings, op. cit., p. 655.

137. "Reagan to Relent on Secrecy Pledge," *New York Times,* February 15, 1984, p. 1.

138. Testimony of Anthony Oettinger, Professor of Applied Mathematics, Harvard University, at the House Civil Liberties Hearings, op. cit., January 24, 1984.

Down with Little Brother!
Orwell and the Human Prospect

by

W. Warren Wagar

On February 2, 1984, the Chinese of the world ushered in their New Year. According to the sexagenary cycle of the Chinese lunar calendar, 1984 is the Year of the Rat. In world literature, it is also the Year of the Rat—the horror lurking for Winston Smith in Room 101 in George Orwell's *1984*. By exploiting Smith's mortal fear of rats, the Thought Police are able to break his mind and spirit, converting him into a zombie who truly loves Big Brother.

Orwell's message to posterity is clear: unless the freedom-loving peoples of the Western world take care, they will someday fall victims to a superstate just as ruthless and just as dehumanizing as the Oceania of his novel. Like virtually all dystopian tales, *1984* is an urgent warning of danger ahead, a tocsin ringing in the night. It issues no predictions of things to come, but it does make plain what can happen if the political disease of totalitarianism spreads westward. As Orwell explained in an autobiographical essay near the end of his life, "Every line of serious work that I have written since 1936 has been written, directly or indirectly, against totalitarianism and for democratic Socialism."

Yet, inescapably, Orwell has been tagged as a futurist. Much of the attention paid in both journalism and scholarship to *1984* dwells on its effectiveness in anticipating the real world of 1984. And why not? Surely the setting of the novel in a future imagined with fierce realism helps explain its success as a work of fiction. In its own oblique way, *1984* has made a contribution to serious futures inquiry.

It is also one of the authentic marvels in the history of letters. It has terrifying strength. From time to time, Orwell's prose jumps off the page and punches the reader in the mouth. Today, 35 years after it was published, the book is just as fresh, just as cogent, just as lethal as when it first arrived on the scene.

W. Warren Wagar is professor of history at the State University of New York, Binghamton, New York. He is the author of Terminal Visions *(Indiana University Press, 1982).*

Apart from its sheer virtuosity, what accounts for the continuing influence of *1984?*

The commonest answer to this question is the simplest. Orwell—so his admirers often claim—not only looked into the future: he got it substantially right. Throughout the world in the 1980s, the power of government grows, public and private surveillance of citizens intensifies, language is more and more systematically debased, the arms race fuels a permanent war economy, and demagogues and dictators rule in the name of "democracy."

Argued in these terms, the case for Orwell as a prescient futurist may seem strong. It may seem even stronger if one conveniently neglects to read or re-read the novel, which many of us have not touched since that high school English class back in '59 or '71.

For one particularly sad example, whoever wrote the copy for the Olivetti advertisement that began appearing in magazines late in 1983 clearly relied too much on memory. The advertisement shows a little girl cuddling a pink-eared lamb, followed by the stern admonition in heavy black capitals: "1984: ORWELL WAS WRONG." Reading on, we discover that "according to Orwell, in 1984 man and computer would have become enemies. But his pessimistic outlook was wrong." Olivetti's product proves that computers are actually man's best friends, by implication just as fuzzy and lovable as a pink-eared lamb.

The problem with the ad, of course, is that Orwell never said a word about computers and knew nothing about them. The legend of Orwell's prowess as a prophet of high technology has grown from a single forecast, the two-way "telescreen" that enables the Thought Police to watch people in their homes. But Orwell did not anticipate computers.

In any event, the use of high technology by government is not really the point in *1984.* Orwell had little interest in technology of any kind. He was a student of politics, and *1984* is one of the greatest political novels of all time.

But the political realities it analyzes, for the most part, are those of the first half of the twentieth century, not the second. Orwell did not foresee the flow of events from 1949 to the present day. His fictional Oceania resembles the United Kingdom or the United States of the 1980s only superficially, when it resembles them at all; it misses what was coming in the Soviet Union by a margin almost as wide.

Consider the world depicted in *1984.* Instead of looking high and low for analogies with life in Reagan's America or Thatcher's Britain, ponder what is actually there. For example, the controlled scarcity of consumer goods, including everyday necessities like razor blades, or buttons, or shoelaces. The nasty food, the synthetic coffee and gin. The shabby clothing. The cold, cramped living quarters.

Or what about the pleasures of Eros? None at all, except for the degraded Proles. The Junior Anti-Sex League campaigns vigorously against sexuality itself. Even Winston's mistress, Julia, is an active member of the League, although on the sly she makes love with angry abandon. When Julia shows no real concern for revolutionary theory, Winston accuses her of being a rebel only from the waist down. But most people in the Party are hopelessly frigid, like Winston's wife, Katherine. Anything that might subvert the member's absolute commitment to the apparatus is necessarily taboo.

It follows that another distinctive feature of life in Oceania is the disappearance of privacy and private time. Each day is meticulously planned, leaving almost nothing to chance or preference. Party members work 60 hours a week or more, eat in government canteens, and spend their evenings at the Community Center, where they hear lectures on Party doctrine and take part in carefully staged discussion groups.

The Party, after all, dominates every aspect of life. At its apex is Big Brother, whose picture is everywhere, a rugged man with a heavy black moustache. All people in responsible positions belong to the Party, whose ideology is a corruption of socialism. The economy is in the hands of the bureaucrats, now well into their ninth consecutive Three-Year Plan. Industrial statistics fill the unspeakably dreary television news programs. History is constantly rewritten to make the Party look infallible. No art, no literature, no journalism, no culture of any kind exists outside the Party.

Worse still, telescreens, hidden microphones, and fiendishly clever secret policemen monitor every move you make and every word you say. What they do not catch, your own children will. When the little daughter of Smith's neighbors overhears her father muttering "Down with Big Brother!" in his sleep, she turns him over to the authorities for thoughtcrime.

Such errant Party members are invariably arrested, jailed, tortured, interrogated, broken, brainwashed, and forced to confess everything, even crimes they never committed. The Thought Police scrub their minds clean. Their will to resist is shattered, and they can be shot or released: it no longer makes any difference which. Those who do leave prison are guaranteed to be loyal. They will love Big Brother dearly. They will hate the enemies of Big Brother with a passion, from the foreign country that happens to be fighting Oceania at any given time to the supreme traitor Goldstein, whose face is prominently displayed at every public Hate session.

There is much more, including the forced-labor camps for lesser criminals, the elimination of laws and lawyers, the routine opening of private mail, the Party purges of the 1960s, and the stripped-down jargon of Newspeak.

The point is that every one of these unpleasant features of life in Oceania is based directly on something that was already happening in Orwell's own day, although not (except for the war-time shortage of consumables) in Orwell's own country. His model for Oceania, beyond the slightest question, was the Soviet Russia of Joseph Stalin in the 1930s and 1940s.

As a rule, Orwell distorts or exaggerates conditions in the U.S.S.R., but seldom by much. The managed scarcity, the sexual puritanism, the Party discipline, the control of language and history and culture, the hypocritical ideology, the planned economy, the television news, the techniques of forcing confessions, the brainwashing, the labor camps—it was all there. The rugged face with the heavy black moustache was not only Big Brother's— it was Stalin's. The "primal traitor," the loathsome Jewish renegade with a small goatee, Emmanuel Goldstein, was not only Goldstein—it was that goateed Jewish arch-rival of Stalin's, Leon Trotsky. The purges of Oceania's 1960s corresponded to the real-life purges in Soviet Russia in the 1930s, when Stalin eliminated his chief confederates. The change of enemies from Eurasia to Eastasia and back to Eurasia mirrors the on-again, off-again history of Soviet relations with Nazi Germany between 1933 and 1941, when Germany was billed first as a deadly enemy, then a bosom friend, and finally a deadly enemy once more.

For Orwell in *1984* (and also in *Animal Farm* and many lesser works), the threat to freedom in our time was not something vague and impersonal. It was the drift to a totalitarian politics patterned after Soviet communism, and abetted at every turn by the Soviet Union itself. None of the other horrors of the 1940s remotely compared to it, in Orwell's political imagination. Not the Holocaust, not World War II, not the atom bomb, not the growing power of giant multinational corporations, not the arms race and the danger of a third and final world conflict. Not even fascism, for which Orwell harbored a sneaking half-admiration, in spite of his many formal denunciations of totalitarianism in all its colors—red, black, and brown. What really gnawed at his vitals was the totalitarianism of the Left, summed up in the life and work of Joseph Stalin.

If this interpretation of *1984* is correct, then its success as a work of prophecy must hinge on the extent to which Soviet-style communism has spread westward and has strengthened its hold on minds and hearts both in Russia and in the West. Obviously, measured by such a criterion, the novel fails.

Anyone who looks at the real world of 1984 cannot deny that, although it may be just as ugly in its own way, it bears scant resemblance to Orwell's nightmare vision. The trend that Orwell extrapolated into the future proves to have been a blind alley.

In the Western bourgeois democracies, even in the throes of a worldwide business recession that has been going on since at least 1970, the majority of people live pretty well. Consumer goods are not scarce. Just the opposite. Most of us are deluged with more products than we can ever use. We live in a society of skillfully contrived abundance, where everyday existence is so comfortable that rebellion and revolution are unthinkable. There is plenty of injustice abroad in the land, even authentic poverty, but it is not massive enough to destabilize the society—thus far. Government and business in the Western countries long ago learned that the best way to head off dissent is to keep the majority of the population stuffed with consumables. As in the operant conditioning of laboratory animals, rewards motivate more effectively than punishments. The carrot turns out to be mightier than the stick.

All the same, it cannot honestly be reported that citizens in the bourgeois democracies are less free in 1984 than they were in 1949, or 1849. Increasingly sophisticated means of surveillance and intimidation have become available to those in power, but they are rarely used to full advantage, thanks to the restraints imposed by the legal system, the mass media, the electoral process, the rivalry of scores of semi-autonomous pressure groups, the watchdogging of civil libertarians, and the stubborn drag of public opinion.

As Harvey Cox points out in *The Secular City,* modernity brings another qualified blessing, the blessing of anonymity. For the very reason that so much of modern industrial and commercial life is impersonal, that to cope with all its dry complexities so much of it has been commodified and reduced to rows of numbers, wily individuals can often thread their way through its gears largely undetected, like mice in a mansion. Standardization in the workplace has not been infallibly translated into control of private life. The typical city-dweller of 1984 in the Western countries has many more chances to dodge authority and deflect suggestion than the typical villager of the pre-electronic era, when everybody knew everybody else, good and evil were defined down to the last detail, and squires, clergymen, schoolmasters, and gossips kept everybody in line.

Nor do the Western bourgeois democracies groan under one-party dictatorships, as in *1984.* They have no prescribed ideology, the press is not enslaved, and there is not the least indication of any falling-off in the number of laws or lawyers. Better still—or is it worse?—the hideous stability supplied to mankind by the superstate system of world order described in *1984,* which may have looked quite plausible in the bipolar days of the late 1940s, has no echo in the real world of 1984. Wherever one looks, as Amnion Rubinstein argued recently on the op ed page of the New York Times ("Too Much Foolish '1984'ing," December 4, 1983), tribalism endangers the integrity of nations and "ethnic and religious loyalties have erupted all over the globe with a ferocity unforeseen and unforeseeable in 1948." It is difficult to imagine Big Brother co-existing with Shiite truck-bombers, Sicilian mafiosi, Afghan hill fighters, Sikh separatists, and the guerrillas of the IRA, ETA, and PLO. He would have smashed them all flat years ago. More to the point, the unspoken agreement among the superpowers of Orwell's novel not to fight a total war involving nuclear weapons does not protect us. In some ways our world is far more dangerous than Orwell's, precisely because it is more free.

As for the Soviet Union, only a relic from the McCarthy era could seriously claim that it has evolved further in the direction charted by Orwell. True, there are now almost 20 Soviet-style "people's democracies" in the world, instead of one. True, most of the institutions and structures of the Soviet political system that Orwell deplored are still in place, in one form or another. But the Stalinist mode of rule has softened with time, just like the Maoist mode in China. More consumer goods are available than before, there is more opportunity for dissent, less torture and imprisonment, more private initiative, and—above all— less love of Big Brother.

In *1984,* Orwell's direst fear was that totalitarian societies would be able in due course to transform all subjects of the state into loyal, mindless public servants without individuality or conscience. So far it has not happened, even in the worst of them. Soviet citizens may be patriotic, but few of them stand in awe of their rulers. They are tepid communists. And they believe only bits and pieces of what they read in the state-controlled press.

The best currently visible evidence of the failure of thought control is communist Poland. Independent polls conducted by French journalists reveal that only one voter in fifty in Poland would choose a communist candidate in a free election. Yet this comes after a third of a century of relentless indoctrination by a tough regime in nominally full control of the economy, the media, and the apparatus of government.

If Big Brotherism has gained any ground at all since Orwell wrote his novel, it is in the Third World, where astonishing personages like the Ayatollah Khomeini and Pol Pot have demonstrated a gift for absolutism that even Orwell's grand inquisitor, O'Brien, might have felt compelled to admire. But Orwell did not see the Third World in such terms. For him, it was simply a convenient battleground for the limited wars of the superpowers.

All of which brings us back to the original question. Why has Orwell's *1984* been such a hit, year after year, since its publication in 1949? If not because it explains our own time to us, if not because of its uncannily correct forecasts, then why?

I can offer two reasons why *1984* has worked so well for so many readers—and a third reason why it may still have some residual value as a book of prophecy.

It is important to recall, at this juncture, Orwell's motives in writing his novel. As noted earlier, he did not intend it in any formal sense as a prediction of future time. He meant it to stand as a warning of what could and might well happen if free societies, embarked on a long and difficult journey to true social democracy, chose the disastrous shortcut of totalitarianism.

You will rarely find anywhere in literature, not even in Koestler's *Darkness at Noon* or Solzhenitsyn's *The Gulag Archipelago,* a more persuasive brief for freedom, conscience, and privacy against the claims of state power than Orwell's *1984.* The images are sharp, the argument is lucid, the terror is graphic.

And his warnings have struck a responsive chord in millions of readers, not only because he knew how to write, and how to sublimate effectively the tell-tale streak of sadomasochism in his own personality, but also because his mission, the defense of liberty, has acquired the status of a religion in modern Western secular culture. For many of us, God is indeed dead. With God the traditional sense of good and evil has evaporated as well—and sometimes the capacity for patriotism.

But almost everyone, Right or Left, believer or atheist, can agree on one thing. The individual's right to do and say and think what he pleases is sacred. Nobody has the right to strip a man or woman of selfhood. Most of the other great novels of the future in our time, like *Brave New World, We,* and *A Clockwork Orange,* make the same point that Orwell does. Nothing, they tell us, justifies the suspension of the basic civil liberties of a free society. The same theme permeates our best political films, many of our novels of contemporary life, and the rhetoric of our politicians. Television dramas are awash with it. The little guy who fights the big slick faceless forces at work behind the facades of democracy is the eternal hero of our secular culture. Orwell milked this grand political myth for all it was worth.

There is a second reason for Orwell's triumphs. *1984* was also the first major novel of the Cold War. It feeds on Western fears of totalitarianism, but not just of totalitarianism in the abstract: its real target, as we have shown, is the system of politics and government invented by Lenin and Stalin. There are no specifically Nazi or fascist touches in the novel. The whole scenario is taken directly from Stalin's Russia.

The novel tells us that anything would be preferable to ingestion by such a Russia, or by the agents and fellow travelers of Stalinism in the Western world. Better dead, even in a nuclear war, than Red. Orwell virtually says so. As we learn in the novel, a war fought with hundreds of atom bombs occurred in the 1950s. The new stabilized global order of Oceania and Eurasia came into existence after the war, in part to make the world safe for despotism. Yet Orwell leaves us no doubt that such despotism is a fate literally worse than death.

Confirming evidence comes from an article published in *The Partisan Review* in 1947, where Orwell surveyed the political consequences of the atomic bomb. The "worst possibility of all," he wrote, was the chance that the bombs would never be used but would instead inspire the division of the world into hierarchic superstates that "might remain static for thousands of years."

Did Orwell intend his novel to serve as a weapon in the Cold War on the side of the United States and its NATO allies? Perhaps not. During his lifetime, which ended in January 1950, he refused to associate himself with right-wing anti-communist groups. But that he saw *1984* as another salvo in his own personal war against Stalinism is unquestionable. Had he lived through the 1950s and 1960s, to witness the invasion of South Korea, the full absorption of Eastern Europe into the Soviet sphere, the Maoization of China, the smashed resistance in Hungary in 1956 and Czechoslovakia in 1968, the Berlin Wall, and the Cuba missile crisis, who can say what line he would have taken? Norman Podhoretz's argument that he would have joined the neo-conservative camp, like so many other former leftists of his generation, is far from implausible.

At all odds, *1984* has become a force in the Cold War on the side of the United States and its NATO allies since Orwell's death. For every left-wing liberal who has read the novel and viewed it as a cogent plea for freedom against big government of almost any kind, there is a right-wing liberal or a conservative who has read it and been inspired to wage the Cold War against "world communism" with redoubled zeal. Trotsky's biographer Isaac Deutscher rightly called it an "ideological superweapon" in that struggle. Along with *Animal Farm,* it helps explain the dogmatic anti-communism of American policies in the Carribean, Central America, Indochina, the Middle East, and throughout the planet. The crusades of the Kennedy, Johnson, and Reagan administrations to prevent the Stalinization of the Third World have an "Orwellian" cast—not just in the usual sense of the adjective but in the sense that they bear the imprint of the influence of George Orwell's political philosophy. At the same time, the continuing savagery of the Cold War adds to the appeal of *1984.* Each serves the other.

There is a third reason for the success of *1984,* beyond its resonance with civil libertarianism and with Cold War anti-communism. This is not a reason that, up to now, counts for much, but it may help Orwell's novel in the future and it may do wonders for his reputation as a prophet.

I refer now to the analysis of the ruling class in *1984,* derived by Orwell in good measure from James Burnham's 1941 classic, *The Managerial Revolution.* Although the Western world has not been Stalinized, and the Soviet Union has been at least partially de-Stalinized, Orwell may turn out to be right concerning the long-term trend in all advanced industrial societies toward the replacement of self-government by centralized systems of control in the hands of managerial and technical experts—or, as one might call them, the technocrats.

In the novel, the real power in Oceania and the other superstates is wielded not so much by Big Brother as by a small elite of men and women who constitute the Inner Party. This elite is composed, writes Orwell, of "bureaucrats, scientists, technicians, trade-union organizers, publicity experts, sociologists, teachers, journalists, and professional politicians," a new aristocracy of people with expertise in technology, communcations, and management. These are the real masters in Oceania. They live modestly, by the standards of the very rich of the old days; they are largely unknown to the general public; they comprise a small army of Little Brothers, quite different from the virile Big Brother who serves as the nominal leader of the Party—and who may no longer even exist.

Obviously, Orwell's sociological analysis of the governing circle of Oceania does not really gibe with the rest of his novel. The logic of technocratic domination would prescribe policies far less crude than those employed by the Thought Police.

Nor can it be said that the Western countries today are wholly at the mercy of anonymous technocrats. The technocrats thrive and they pull more than their share of strings, but the time is still distant when they might wield absolute power, as in *1984*. Even what Milovan Djilas calls the "New Class" of party hacks in the Soviet sphere falls short of absolute power in our time.

Nevertheless, in a century or so—say, by the year 2084—the whole world may have slipped under the rule of the Little Brothers. If the multinational corporations keep spreading their tentacles everywhere, if the now emerging worldwide system of division of labor is consolidated, if every country (including the nominally socialist or communist nations) is fully incorporated into the capitalist world economy, if the nuclear powers finally learn to work together and use their collective muscle to crush unruly elements anywhere on the globe, a technocratic cosmopolis might arise in all its glory, with centralized planetary control systems run by experts who could keep the peace—at the price of liberty and justice—forever.

They will not be power-mad tyrants, these Little Brothers. They will seldom need to resort to torture and brainwashing. For the most part, they will control the world's peoples by using technology and the sciences of management to ensure a tolerably high level of material life for the majority of mankind. The apparatus of domination will be so vast and so complex that few ordinary citizens will understand it, much less have a chance of bringing it under democratic rule.

I see this as the deeper truth hiding in Orwell's novel. He may not have been entirely aware of the significance of his analysis of the Oceanian governing class. He was so obsessed with Stalinism and other problems of his own day that he failed to develop his analysis in much detail. For that matter, the same case is argued more authoritatively in Aldous Huxley's *Brave New World,* and even in Yevgeny Zamyatin's *We*. But Orwell did come to grips with the issue of technocracy, and many careful readers of *1984* have had their eyes opened.

So in the long run this may be the greatest of Orwell's gifts to us, unless the Cold War in which he also played his part begets a Hot War that ends the human experiment prematurely. Going beyond the terrors of the immediate future, we can readily imagine with his help a regime of technocrats in business suits who govern all our affairs through the "friendly fascism" of behavioral engineering. These Little Brothers are even more frightening, perhaps, than the rats in Room 101 of the Ministry of Love. But George Orwell gave us fair warning, and for this, whatever else may be said, we must thank him.

Can the coming reign of the Little Brothers be thwarted? Orwell furnished the beginnings of an answer to that question, too, by showing how the manipulation of truth by an omnipotent state and its denial of a liberal education to the masses negates the possibility of movements of liberation from below. Without a vigilant, critical, informed citizenry, the technocrat is just as invincible as the jackbooted bully.

The struggle will be exhausting. The odds are against us. But if we fight successfully to preserve and enlarge our civic autonomy, if we outsmart the Little Brothers, if we make Orwell as poor a prophet of life in 2084 as he was of life in 1984, his shade in the Great Beyond will surely thank us.

Heaven knows, he never wanted to be right.

A Common
Global Project

Senate Joint Resolution 236

On February 22, 1984, Senators Spark M. Matsunaga, Claiborne Pell, and Charles McC. Mathias, Jr., sent a letter to their Senate colleagues in which they set forth their reasons for offering their Senate Joint Resolution 236, "a joint resolution relating to cooperative East-West ventures in space as an alternative to a space arms race."

> We have introduced this resolution because of our conviction that Congress would be derelict in its duty if we allowed space to become yet another arena of conflict without exerting every effort to achieve cooperation in activities of mutual interest and advantage. Such important initiatives can be taken without impinging in any way upon present or future use of space for such military-related activities as communications, surveillance and national technical means of inspection for control purposes. S. J. Res. 236 declares that the President should:
>
> 1. Renew the 1977 agreement between the United States and the Soviet Union on space cooperation for peaceful purposes, which expired in 1982;
>
> 2. Initiate talks with the governments interested in space activities to explore the opportunities for cooperative East-West ventures in space as an alternative to an arms race in space, including cooperative ventures in such areas as space medicine and space biology, space rescue, planetary science, manned and unmanned space exploration; and
>
> 3. Submit to the Congress at the earliest possible date, but not later than October 1, 1984, a report detailing the steps taken in carrying out paragraphs (1) and (2).
>
> Our resolution has been endorsed by many of the nation's leading space scientists on the pragmatic grounds that the United States has obtained impressive technical and scientific benefits from space cooperation with the Soviets.

In their letter, the senators cite Thomas Donahue, president of the Space Science Board of the National Academy of Sciences;

The U.S. senators who introduced Senate Joint Resolution 236 are: Spark M. Matsunaga (D-Hawaii), Claiborne Pell (D-Rhode Island), and Charles McC. Mathias, Jr. (R-Maryland).

David Morrison, director of the Solar System Exploration Commission established by NASA; and Donald "Deke" Slayton, a former astronaut and participant in the 1975 U.S.-Soviet Apollo-Soyuz project and currently a leader in the commercialization of space, as strong supporters for such an undertaking.

Senate Joint Resolution 236 and its key supporting documents are as follows:

Senate Joint Resolution 236

Whereas the United States and the Soviet Union are on a course leading toward an arms race in space which is in the interest of no one;

Whereas the prospect of an arms race in space between the United States and the Soviet Union has aroused worldwide concern expressed publicly by the governments of many countries, including most of the allies of the United States, such as Australia, Canada, France, the Federal Republic of Germany, India, Japan, and the United Kingdom of Great Britain.

Whereas an arms race in space would open the door to a range of new weapons systems that would seriously threaten global stability, undermine the prospects for successful arms control agreements, and create pressures for new defense expenditures unprecedented in scope even for these times;

Whereas the 1972-75 Apollo-Soyuz project involving the United States and the Soviet Union and culminating with a joint docking in space was a significant success, thus proving the practicability of a joint space effort;

Whereas shortly after the completion of the Apollo-Soyuz project, and intended as a follow-up to it, the United States and the Soviet Union signed a formal agreement to examine the feasibility of a Shuttle-Salyut Program and an International Space Platform Program, but that initiative was allowed to lapse;

Whereas the United States signed a five-year space cooperation agreement with the Soviet Union in 1972, renewed it in 1977, then chose not to renew it in 1982, despite numerous scientific benefits accruing to the United States as a result of joint activities initiated under that agreement;

Whereas the opportunities offered by space for prodigious achievements in virtually every field of human endeavor, leading ultimately to the colonization of space in the cause of advancing human civilization, would probably be lost irretrievably were space to be made into yet another East-West battlefront; and

Whereas allowing space to become an arena of conflict without first exerting every effort to make it into an arena of cooperation would amount to an abdication of governmental responsibility that would never be forgotten: Now, therefore, be it

Resolved, By the Senate and House of Representatives of the United States of America in Congress assembled that the President should—

(1) Renew the 1972-1977 agreement between the United States and the Soviet Union on space cooperation for peaceful purposes;

(2) Initiate talks with the Government of the Soviet Union, and with other governments interested in space activities, to explore the opportunities for cooperative East-West ventures in space as an alternative to an arms race in space, including cooperative ventures in such areas as space medicine and space biology, space rescue, planetary science, manned and unmanned space exploration; and

(3) Submit to the Congress at the earliest possible date, but not later than October 1, 1984, a report detailing the steps taken in carrying out paragraphs (1) and (2).

1977 United States-Soviet Space Cooperation Agreements

AGREEMENT BETWEEN THE UNITED STATES OF AMERICA AND THE UNION OF SOVIET SOCIALIST REPUBLICS CONCERNING COOPERATION IN THE EXPLORATION AND USE OF OUTER SPACE FOR PEACEFUL PURPOSES

The United States of America and the Union of Soviet Socialist Republics;

Considering the role which the U.S.A. and the U.S.S.R. play in the exploration and use of outer space for peaceful purposes;

Striving for a further expansion of cooperation between the U.S.A. and the U.S.S.R. in the exploration and use of outer space for peaceful purposes;

Noting the positive cooperation which the parties have already experienced in this area;

Desiring to make the results of scientific research gained from the exploration and use of outer space for peaceful purposes available for the benefit of the peoples of the two countries and of all peoples of the world;

Taking into consideration the provisions of the treaty on Principles Governing the Activities of States in the Exploration and Use of Outer Space, including the Moon and other Celestial Bodies, as well as the Agreement on the Rescue of Astronauts, the Return of Astronauts, and the Return of Objects Launched into Outer Space;

Encouraged by the progress made in the course of mutually agreed activities pursued under the Agreement Between the United States of America and the Union of Soviet Socialist Republics Concerning Cooperation in the Exploration and Use of Outer Space for Peaceful Purposes, signed May 24, 1972;

In accordance with the General Agreement between the United States of America and the Union of Soviet Socialist Republics on Contacts, Exchanges and Cooperation in Scientific, Technical, Educational, Cultural and Other Fields, signed June 19, 1973, and in order to develop further the principles of mutually beneficial cooperation between the two countries;

Have agreed as follows:

ARTICLE 1

The Parties will continue to develop cooperation in such fields of space science and applications as space meteorology; study of the natural environment; exploration of near earth space, the moon and the planets; and rescue systems; and, in particular, will cooperate to take all appropriate measures to encourage and achieve the fulfillment of the Summary of Results of Discussion on Space Cooperation Between the U.S. National Aeronautics and Space Administration and the Academy of Sciences of the U.S.S.R. dated January 21, 1971, periodically renewed.

ARTICLE 2

The Parties will carry out such cooperation through their appropriate national agencies by means of mutual exchanges of scientific information and delegations, and meetings of scientists and specialists of both countries, and also in such other ways as may be mutually agreed. Joint Working Groups may be created for the development and implementation of appropriate programs of cooperation.

ARTICLE 3

The Parties will take all necessary measures for the further development of cooperation in the area of manned space flight for scientific and practical objectives, including the use in joint flights of compatible docking and rendezvous systems derived from those developed during the experimental flight of Apollo and Soyuz spacecraft in July 1975. Joint work in this direction will be carried out in accordance with the Agreement Between the U.S. National Aeronautics and Space Administration and the Academy of Sciences of the U.S.S.R. on Cooperation in the Area of Manned Space Flight dated May 11, 1977.

ARTICLE 4

The Parties will encourage international efforts to resolve problems of international law in the exploration and use of outer space for peaceful purposes with the aim of strengthening the legal order in space and further developing international space law and will cooperate in this field.

ARTICLE 5

The Parties may by mutual agreement determine other areas of cooperation in the exploration and use of outer space for peaceful purposes.

ARTICLE 6

This Agreement shall enter into force May 24, 1977 and shall remain in force for five years. It may be modified or extended by mutual agreement of the Parties.

Done at Geneva this 18th day of May 1977 in duplicate in the English and Russian languages; both equally authentic.

For the United States of America
CYRUS R. VANCE.
For the Union of Soviet Socialist Republics
A. GROMYKO.

REPORT TO CONGRESS: SCIENTIFIC EXCHANGE ACTIVITIES WITH THE SOVIET UNION, FISCAL YEAR 1981 AND FISCAL YEAR 1982, DEPARTMENT OF STATE AUTHORIZATION ACT, SECTION 126. (A) AND (B)

EXECUTIVE SUMMARY
OVERVIEW

This summary section will provide a brief overview of the history and current status of the U.S.-Soviet cooperative science and technology exchange agreements, followed by a statement on "the risk of the transfer to the Soviet Union of militarily significant technology through research, exchanges, and other activities conducted pursuant to those agreements," as requested in Section 126. (a) (1).

The balance of the report will contain the individual agency submissions, which will address the information requested in Section 126. (a) (2).

The list of Soviet nationals participating during the upcoming academic year in the U.S. and the Soviet Union under the graduate student/young faculty exchange or senior scholar exchange, their topics of study and where they are to study shall be provided not later than July 1 as specified in Section 126. (c).

Background

Since 1958, agreements between the United States and the Soviet Union have provided for science and technology exchanges with the Soviet Union, as well as those in the fields of education, culture and information. Science and technology exchange activities were conducted under specialized cooperative agreements which were signed by the U.S. and USSR during summits in Moscow (1972 and 1974) and Washington (1973). This framework led to a significant increase in science and technology activities, which remained at a high level throughout much of the 1970s.

FISCAL YEARS 1981 AND 1982:
U.S.-USSR COOPERATION IN SPACE RESEARCH

Under the 1972 intergovernmental U.S.-USSR Agreement on Space Cooperation (renewed in 1977), NASA carried out specific joint activities and projects with Soviet counterparts during 1981 and 1982 within the framework of four Joint Working Groups (JWGs): Space Biology and Medicine; Near-Earth Space, the Moon and Planets; Study of the Natural Environment; and Space Meteorology. A fifth area of cooperation envisioned in the 1977 Space Agreement renewal—satellite search and rescue systems—continued to be developed during this period but moved beyond

341

the bilateral framework under a 1980 multilateral agreement involving participation by Canada and France, the U.S. and the USSR. During 1981, bilateral exchanges under the Space Agreement continued to be curtailed significantly as part of the U.S. response to the Soviet invasion of Afghanistan, and were reduced even further by the U.S. during 1982 in response to Soviet actions in Poland. Among the sanctions announced by the Administration in December, 1981, was the decision that the U.S.-USSR Space Agreement would not be renewed when it came up for renewal. The agreement thus expired on May 24, 1982.

1981 activities

The majority of joint U.S.-USSR space activities during 1981 took place in the areas of space biology and medicine and planetary research. Highlights of projects and activities which occurred in 1981 are given below:

Space Biology and Medicine. During 1981, NASA continued to participate in preparations for a Soviet biosatellite mission scheduled for launch in 1982 (the launch has since slipped to the fall of 1983). This "Cosmos" biosatellite mission will fly primates for the first time in the Soviet program, and the U.S. will provide technical support for planned cardiovascular and biorhythm measurements on two small rhesus monkeys. In addition, U.S. scientists are participating in investigations using rats to study calcium metabolism and embryology. In return for its assistance, the U.S. will receive the unique biomedical data obtained during the mission for subsequent analysis and interpretation.

In May, agreement was reached on a new cooperative project to measure human vertebral bone mineral changes resulting from long-duration manned spaceflight. Through a series of computer-assisted tomograph (CAT) scans taken of cosmonaut vertebra, the effects of extended periods of weightlessness on overall bone development processes may be observed and analyzed. Under this cooperative project, Soviet scientists are responsible for taking the prescribed pre-flight and post-flight CAT scans of cosmonauts using U.S.-provided magnetic tapes, and then shipping these tapes with the raw data to the U.S. for subsequent analysis and interpretation. The final result of the U.S. study is then to be shared with the Soviets. This type of study, using the most modern medical techniques, should result in a greater understanding of the physiological changes occurring both during space missions and following return to the normal gravity environment on Earth.

In November, 1981, the twelfth meeting of the Space Biology and Medicine JWG was held in Washington. A special feature of the meeting was a two-and-a-half-day Cardiovascular Symposium, which brought together U.S. and Soviet specialists to exchange information and data from ground-based simulations of weightlessness and actual space missions. U.S. scientists learned firsthand the biomedical results from the Soviet 185-day Salyut manned mission, as well as the results of a later 75-day Salyut mission. The agreed work in bone mineral measurements using CAT scanning techniques was broadened in scope to include studies of bone mineral mass and muscle density. In addition, U.S. participation in the USSR "Cosmos" biosatellite mission was further defined. Finally, the participants agreed to publish the final results of their Joint Bedrest Study (completed in 1979) independently during 1982.

Near-Earth Space, the Moon and Planets. During 1981, a number of scientist-to-scientist exchanges took place in the areas of planetary geology, planetary atmospheres and space plasma physics. The Soviets also contributed a large body of written material on the results of their past Venera missions to Venus for incorporation in future NASA publications on Venus.

In August, the Soviet Academy of Sciences complied with a NASA request to reduce the potential for radio-frequency interference (RFI) during the Voyager 2 spacecraft's nine-day encounter period with the planet Saturn. Similar Soviet cooperation had been extended to NASA in connection with previous U.S. planetary encounters in 1978 (Pioneer-Venus), 1979 (Pioneer 11-Saturn), and 1980 (Voyager 1-Saturn).

A highly-successful meeting of the U.S.-U.S.S.R. JWG on Near-Earth Space, the Moon and Planets was held in San Francisco in October, 1981. During this meeting, scientific results were presented from the 1978 U.S. and Soviet missions to Venus (Pioneer Venus and Venera 11 and 12, respectively). Reports were given on the state of current research in the following topic areas: the solar wind interaction with non-magnetized or weakly magnetized solar system bodies; geological interpretation of Mars data; lunar sample analyses; and Antarctic meteorite and cosmic dust studies. The participants also exchanged detailed information on plans for future planetary missions, and reached agreement on a joint program of collaboration in the analysis and interpretation of X-ray and gamma-ray remote sensing data for planetary exploration using ground-based and balloon flight studies.

During the October planetary discussion, the two sides agreed to consider as a primary objective for their next JWG meeting the establishment of several kinds of coordinated efforts which could enlarge the scope of current bilateral activities. That meeting was to have taken place in the Soviet Union in May, 1982, but was not held due to the non-renewal of the U.S.-U.S.S.R. Space Agreement.

Space Meteorology. In the rocket meteorology area, cooperation has focused on the exchange and analysis of data from the Eastern and Western Hemispheric meridional network. During 1981, these joint efforts continued but at a reduced level due to the closing of several U.S. rocket ranges in 1979 and 1980, and changes in NASA's budget priorities. In the satellite meteorology area, laboratory and field data were exchanged during 1981 to establish common data processing procedures for atmospheric temperature sounding with the objective of making international sources of meteorological data more compatible.

Short-term and long-term exchanges during 1981

A statistical summary of the total mandays spent in short-term and long-term exchanges during 1981 under U.S.-U.S.S.R. Space Agreement is given below:

Type	U.S. mandays spent in U.S.S.R.	U.S.S.R. mandays spent in U.S.
Short term (less than 60 days)	88	406*
Long term (over 60 days)	0	0

*Due largely to two Joint Working Group (JWG) meetings held in the U.S. during the year. Other exchanges were approximately in balance.

Value of information exchanged during 1981

The overall value of the scientific and technical information exchanged during 1981 would appear to be approximately balanced. It should be noted, however, that certain data (particularly biomedical data related to long-duration manned spaceflight) is available only from the U.S.S.R.

1982 activities

Following the decision on non-renewal of the Space Agreement, NASA received interagency authorization to complete its participation in the Soviet "Cosmos" biosatellite mission (discussed in an earlier section) on the basis of agency-to-agency agreements with the Institute of Biomedical Problems in Moscow dating from 1978-81. These agreements continue in force independent of the Space Agreement. Continuation of other agency-level activities was and is subject to case-by-case interagency review, as would be any proposals for NASA involvement in future Soviet biosatellite missions.

During 1982, several U.S. specialists in planetary geological and atmospheric research visited space research institutes in the Soviet Union as guests of the U.S.S.R. Academy of Sciences. The specialists were NASA contractors and grantees from universities and private industry. These scientist-to-scientist discussions were particularly fruitful since they occurred during and after the successful landings of the U.S.S.R.'s. Venera 13 and 14 spacecraft on the Venusian surface in March, 1982.

Other bilateral activities envisioned by or dependent upon the existence of the U.S.-U.S.S.R. Space Agreement essentially ceased with its lapse in May, 1982. No meetings of the JWGs established under the Agreement took place during 1982. No new joint space activities or projects were initiated during 1982.

Short-term and long-term exchanges during 1982

A statistical summary of the total mandays spent in short-term and long-term exchanges in 1982 under the U.S.-U.S.S.R. Space Agreement prior to its expiration on May 24 is given below:

Type	U.S. mandays spent in U.S.S.R.	U.S.S.R. mandays spent in U.S.
Short term (less than 60 days)	55	0
Long term (over 60 days)	0	0

Value of information exchanged during 1982

For the five months of 1982 in which U.S.-U.S.S.R. exchange activities took place under Space Agreement auspices, the overall value of the scientific and technical information clearly favored the U.S. For example, visits to the Soviet Union clearly benefited the U.S. scientific community involved with planetary exploration, especially since these visits coincided with receipt of data and results during and after the March Soviet Venus lander missions. No comparable U.S. information flow to the Soviets was possible during 1982, since the U.S. had no Venus mission of its own to Venus during this period. In fact, at present there are no plans to launch another U.S. spacecraft to Earth's sister planet before 1988.

In the biomedical area, the U.S. continued to receive the raw data from Soviet CAT scans of cosmonaut crews involved in long-duration manned spaceflight for subsequent processing and reduction. Such data are unique in light of the current short-duration focus of the U.S. manned spaceflight programs using the Space Shuttle. Since human physiological changes become more pronounced with the increase in staytime in the weightless environment of space, U.S. biomedical information provided to the Soviets during 1982 was of relatively limited research value.

Level of U.S. and U.S.S.R. funding during 1981 and 1982

Since the entry into force of the U.S.-U.S.S.R. Space Agreement, NASA has conducted its cooperative activities and projects with Soviet counterparts on the basis of mutual interest and reciprocity. During 1981 and 1982, as in previous years, funding for approved joint projects has been provided within the budgetary constraints of existing programs. No specific R&D line items for U.S.-U.S.S.R. activities are included in NASA budgets.

Conclusion

The reduction of the nuclear peril to humanity on the one hand, and the emergence of a sense of global cooperation on the other, offer a bright vision of the future.